CW00351363

Mediation Law and C Practice

Tony Allen
Solicitor

Mediator and Senior Consultant to CEDR

Bloomsbury Professional

Bloomsbury Professional Ltd, Maxwelton House, 41–43 Boltro Road, Haywards Heath, West Sussex, RH16 1BJ

© Bloomsbury Professional Ltd 2013

Bloomsbury Professional, an imprint of Bloomsbury Publishing plc

A CIP Catalogue record for this book is available from the British Library.

ISBN: 978 1 78043 213 7

Typeset by Phoenix Photosetting, Chatham, Kent

Printed in Great Britain by Hobbs the Printers Ltd, Totton, Hampshire.

Mediation Law and Civil Practice

Foreword

Eighteen years in the Court of Appeal convinced me, if I had needed convincing, that there is no certainty in litigation. Time without number we have gone into court with the firm view (always, of course, a preliminary view!) that that appeal was bound to succeed or was bound to fail, only to find that our views shifted this way and that during the course of argument, oral argument being the great strength of our appellate procedure, and that in the end, we, or one of our number, had changed sides. If no case is an obvious winner, are those who refuse to consider mediation at the earliest possible stage not blinded by their arrogance and by their misguided belief that they know best, that they can be confident every witness will come up to proof and even that the judge is not going to have a particularly dyspeptic day? The realisation that mediation is at least worth a try may have been, and, alas, still is slow to dawn. Nevertheless, even the sceptics have to concede that mediation is now firmly established as an acceptable alternative to litigation. Mediation has a proper place in the administration of civil justice as a parallel track towards the goal of achieving finality in the resolution of disputes at proportionate cost. I fundamentally disagree with Professor Dame Hazel Genn QC's catchy sound-bite that, 'The outcome of mediation is not about *just* settlement – it is *just about* settlement' (her emphasis). Where is the injustice in parties, invariably with the help of their legal advisers, compromising their differences? Parties are not compelled to settle: they do so voluntarily, aware of the benefits of doing so and aware of the risks of continuing, usually at disproportionate expense, down the gambler's litigation track. As I have been reported as saying with characteristic understatement, to turn one's back on mediation is 'simply potty'.

The process involved in mediation is, however, not yet well understood, not only by the judiciary, not only by die-hard litigators. This book will enlighten them. Given the growing tide in favour of mediation, Tony Allen's ground-breaking treatise should find its place on the desk (and not just the bookshelf) of every self-respecting litigator. It should be compulsory reading for every trainee solicitor and every pupil barrister for its invaluable insights into the practice of civil litigation. There are hidden gems in every chapter. The litigation department should make the book available to the commercial department and the transactional lawyers with an exhortation to read and the to embrace the wisdom of Chapter 8 on Contracting to Mediate so that mediation clauses become as common as arbitration clauses in commercial contracts. Above all others, the judiciary would benefit from having this as much a part of their training as *Jackson's ADR Handbook*.

I am, of course, fatally biased. As the author has noted, a bit of schmoozing is a good way to get a foreword written: 'Ward LJ has repeatedly bemoaned disproportionate litigation costs in an honourable track record of exhorting use of mediation'. In addition, Tony and I learnt our law from the much-loved Director of Studies at Pembroke College Cambridge, the late James Campbell. That said, it would be difficult to deny Tony's great achievement in the mediation world. Having been accredited by CEDR back in 1996, he forsook private practice as a solicitor to become a director of CEDR in 2000. With the other doyens of this emerging profession, Karl Mackie, Bill Marsh and David Miles, he wrote *The ADR Practice Guide: Commercial Dispute Resolution*. He is published widely in the legal journals. He has vast practical experience and is himself a highly-rated mediator, especially in the fields of personal injury and clinical negligence. He has been awarded the Lord Slynn Memorial Prize for his contribution to the development of mediation in the UK. His expertise is, therefore, beyond question. That vast accumulation of practical experience has been deployed to our advantage in his gathering together in an eminently readable yet erudite volume the hitherto arcane law and practice of mediation. Here you have all you need to know and more. As mediation grows in importance – and it will – this textbook will become the ADR bible. I unreservedly commend it.

The Rt Hon Sir Alan Ward
Chairman of the Civil Mediation Council

August 2013

Preface

The purpose of this book can probably be defined as much by what it is not as by what it is. This paradox starts with its very title, as in England and Wales there is virtually no enacted law relating to mediation, and very few procedural rules, though as the Table of Cases to this book suggests, there are an increasing number of relevant judicial decisions. Mediation is not a creature of statute here. It is a process which has developed alongside the mainstream of civil justice system as a way of seeing whether parties to any dispute, whether or not yet the subject of court proceedings, might agree to settle it, rather than initiating or continuing litigation to, or at least towards, a binding judicial or arbitral decision. By its very nature it operates free of procedural rules, and one of its most significant features (giving rise to scope for controversy of itself) is its asserted right, broadly accepted by the judiciary, to operate behind a curtain of privacy. However, in the last 20 years or so, the courts have nevertheless been invited to rule on matters of considerable importance relating to the use and status of mediation. The primary purpose of this book is to gather together what English law and procedure has had to say about mediation so as to render it conveniently accessible in one place, while also reflecting on its uncertainties and silences, and perhaps tentatively commenting on some apparent mistakes and misconceptions.

One such topic is the degree to which the privacy of what passes at a mediation is right, whether by virtue of some concept of inherent evidential privilege or contractually created by some consensus of the parties. The nature and purpose of this privacy needs to be carefully considered and understood so far as possible by all who discuss and operate the mediation process: mediators, lawyers, parties and judges too. This is especially required when it comes to discussing any future reforms to the legal framework for mediation. We need to know what the relevant law is before it can safely be stated or amended.

So although this book will indeed attempt reasonably authoritative statements about the law and civil procedure of England and Wales in relation to mediation, it will also attempt to stimulate discussion about the areas where there is doubt or controversy. Much of the thinking behind this book is based upon my work as a Director of the Centre for Effective Dispute Resolution (referred to as 'CEDR' from now on) for 12 years, where my first task in 2000 was to update and edit the second edition of *The ADR Practice Guide: Commercial Dispute Resolution,* then authored by my great friends and colleagues Karl Mackie, David Miles and Bill Marsh. That second edition was eventually published in 2000 and had to take account of the dramatic changes wrought by the Civil Procedure Rules 1998 introduced in April 1999, which I had tried to assimilate and operate as a solicitor in my law firm. The same authors have since worked together to produce its third edition in 2007. The Civil Procedure Rules 1998 needed (we felt) interpretation in relation to alternative dispute resolution (ADR) in general, and mediation in particular. It is striking that even the second edition in 2000 had no list of decided cases at the front, despite the inclusion of three chapters in a new section entitled 'The Legal Framework of ADR'. By the time we produced the third edition in 2007, we had added a five-page list of relevant decisions, including the very important cases of *Dunnett v Railtrack* and *Halsey v Milton Keynes General NHS Trust*. This book has even more cases to cite.

Re-reading the third edition today, the other main framework sections of *The ADR Practice Guide*—dealing with ADR concepts and mediation practice, written essentially by my three co-authors—are unsurprisingly just as relevant today as when last revised in 2007, and I commend them strongly to readers and students of ADR. But its greatly enlarged Legal Framework section, of which I admit to being the lead author, has quickly got out of date. So rather than revising the whole book for the sake of one section, it seemed to us better to reconstitute the law and practice section as a separate publication.

So this book is not about the practicalities and skills of being a mediator or of representing or being a party at a mediation. That job remains well done by *The ADR Practice Guide* and other books and training course publications. Nor will it discuss comparative concepts between other types of ADR, again a task undertaken by *The ADR Practice Guide* and other books such as the third edition of *ADR Principles and Practice* by Henry Brown and Arthur Marriott and *Mediation: Principles, Process, Practice* by Laurence Boulle and the sadly missed Miryana Nesic. There is only passing reference here to arbitration. My aim is to concentrate on how the substantive law and the rules governing civil practice in England and Wales impinge on mediation as a particular process, with discussion essentially limited to the relationship between the courts and mediation as developed over the last few decades, illustrated by reference in text or footnotes to all the significant court judgments related to mediation over the last 20 years. This has meant a somewhat historical emphasis in tracing the development of case-law and law reform which is less often found in a purely legal text.

My early involvement with *The ADR Practice Guide* led CEDR to encourage me to continue wider reflections on this area, as a result of which I have had the opportunity to write many articles for CEDR's excellent website and the legal press on new developments in mediation. I have reviewed each important decision and procedural development as it has emerged and spoken on many platforms about them. This book is the natural development of that thinking, hence the fact that, besides discussing law and procedure relevant to mediation, it also comments on, evaluates and looks for areas for reform and improvement. To that extent it may feel as if it belongs more to journalism than academe, though I am neither journalist nor academic. Reform is a proper topic, as with such an unregulated professional activity as mediation with such a vaguely defined place in English civil justice, there will always be calls for review and even regulation. One of the aims of this book is to contribute to the thinking which might go into such a review, especially bearing in mind the rather modest quantity of substantive procedural law which implementation of the EU Mediation Directive has necessitated. With discussions about widening the Directive-driven legislation, currently limited to cross-border application, so as to embrace domestic mediation, we need to be ready with clear thinking and argument on such matters, as there will almost certainly be only one opportunity to legislate about mediation, and possibly not even one. So it is vital that any statutory reform is appropriate, proportionate and accurately focused. Doing harm to the efficacy of mediation through under-informed or under-understood Parliamentary intervention would be all too easy. Hence there is also some discussion of comparative mediation-related civil procedure from other jurisdictions.

A perceptive reviewer of the third edition of *The ADR Practice Guide* commented that there was little reference to academic articles in it, wryly remarking that perhaps it was none the worse for that. This book does not seek to encapsulate the huge US and Commonwealth literature on mediation. There are some parallel references to mediation law in the US and Australia, and some limited references to English academic opinion. On the whole, English academia has interested itself in the socio-legal and anthropological aspects of mediation, and it has also featured as a side interest in the work of some academic proceduralists. This book leaves the anthropological approach to the excellent work by Simon Roberts and others. It does engage in some discussion of the socio-legal approach, as represented by the work of Professors Dame Hazel Genn of UCL and Linda Mulcahy of LSE.

The only conceptual debate in which I could not resist dabbling occupies the first chapter, which discusses the question of whether it is right and proper for civil justice systems such as ours actually to give any formal consideration to facilitating or requiring parties to consider settlement. Provocation for my entering such a debate stemmed from the enthusiastic onslaught on mediation's proper place in civil justice in Professor Dame

Hazel Genn QC's 2008 Hamlyn Lectures. This is an important question which comes up again in other parts of the book when dealing with ADR orders and costs sanctions, as there is no doubt but that her views have been influential among at least some of the judiciary since they were published. Hazel Genn was good enough to invite me to contribute to the impressive seminar at University College London and some of what that chapter contains is based on what I said there. I am very grateful for her openness to my critiques, and we have remained firm friends despite our areas of disagreement. But perhaps this book relates more closely to the proceduralist work of Professor Neil Andrews of the Cambridge Law Faculty, to whose civil procedure students I have given seminars on ADR for a number of years. He has given me great encouragement, though I do not remotely aspire to his level of authority.

This book also does not seek to deal with family mediation, as I am no expert on that. There are other substantial texts which discuss that longer-established cousin of my own area of interest. Mine can be clumsily styled 'civil non-family mediation' or more often, but slightly less accurately, 'commercial mediation'. It is the latter that is the subject of this book, so long as the 'commercial' aspect of this sector is seen as embracing such sectors as personal injury, clinical negligence, public sector law, inheritance and family provision, education, workplace and employment, all areas which have occupied my mediation practice as well as more mainstream commercial disputes, and which combine to show that 'commercial mediation' is an inadequate umbrella term.

Quite apart from the developments already discussed above, civil justice is still working its way through yet another upheaval in relation to costs and funding, brought about by implementing the recommendations in the reports of Sir Rupert Jackson. Costs are a frequent topic for fierce debate at mediations, where difficulties over agreeing legal costs at stake often dominate the settlement of substantive claims, with costs discussions usually taking up a matching proportion to the comparative amounts of damages (modest) and costs (huge) at stake. As one of the main reasons for considering settlement through mediation is to minimise future feared costs, and one of the main ways in which the courts have influenced the use of mediation has been by threatening or imposing costs sanctions, a review of the costs reforms through the prism of mediation is timely, even if early in the life of the April 2013 reforms. Mediators are all too often involved in party discussions about the likely impact of pre-mediation or post-mediation Part 36 offers under the CPR, so this too is a legitimate area for debate, comment and understanding by those who attend mediations in any capacity. The Jackson reforms are very new, and a degree of guesswork will be needed to discern how they will work out, perhaps stimulated by some challenges such as this book seeks to make.

I should also position this book in relation to *The Jackson ADR Handbook,* written by three academics under the guidance of a distinguished editorial board, and published while I was in the process of completing the text of this book. I write this book as a lawyer turned mediator and the views expressed are mine alone, right or wrong. *The Jackson ADR Handbook* clearly seeks to be an authoritative text on this area for the guidance primarily of judges, but also, like its cousin *The JSB Guide to Personal Injury Damages*, available also to practitioners whose reading of that text allows them to know what judges can be presumed to know, enabling them to frame submissions accordingly both at procedural hearings and trials. *The Jackson ADR Handbook* should do its job as a textbook and a sourcebook, so long as it is actually read by judges. Its length and detail will be challenging to them, when taken with all the other new demands that costs budgeting and management will make on them with ever-decreasing resources, even if the content will undoubtedly be useful. It is written as if the law is largely settled by the authorities it cites, but very few of these authorities are Court of Appeal decisions, and from my viewpoint as a lawyer turned mediator turned commentator the law feels to me very much less settled and very much less perfect and right than *The Jackson ADR Handbook* seems to suggest. This book will be more discursive and reflective of how the current (albeit uncertain) state of the law was reached. It may therefore be liberated from the strait-jacket of having to be a source of judicial authority. It is intentionally more opinionated and argumentative than a pure legal textbook usually is, and I have decided to run the risk that readers may disagree with my views or regard them as unsound or even wrong. However, I hope that some judges may be interested to explore some of the debates that underlie past decisions in order to inform future ones.

I also fear that *The Jackson ADR Handbook* will not seem easily accessible to non-lawyer mediators, for whom I have been running a course for the last ten years in an endeavour to equip them with sufficient understanding about civil law and practice to enable them to work effectively as mediators. This book will, I hope, be helpful and interesting for them. I hope too to have highlighted some areas where a mediator (whether a lawyer or not) might seek to test out asserted positions by parties and their lawyers in the light of what the courts might do if the case proceeded unsettled by mediation to a trial.

Perhaps the greatest challenge in writing this book has been to hit upon a logical order to the topics covered. There are so many links and assonances in the somewhat haphazard way that the law and practice relating to mediation has developed. For instance, while Europhiles might carp at the location of the chapter on the impact of Europe on mediation, discussion of that topic really has to be postponed until after consideration of English

Preface

law on privilege and confidentiality to understand the impact that the EU Mediation Directive makes, or perhaps ought not to make. The discussion of privilege and confidentiality is later in the book than its real significance in under-pinning the success of the mediation process might suggest. So there are numerous cross-references to be made between mediator compellability, privilege and confidentiality. And looming over most topics (whether it is wholly right or partly wrong in what it decides) is the leading Court of Appeal case of *Halsey v Milton Keynes General NHS Trust*, still the premier source of senior judicial opinion about mediation, even though two members of the court have expressed subsequent doubts about some aspects of what they decided there. So I hope the reader will feel more helped than irritated by such cross-referencing.

I have adopted neutral case citations unless there appears not to be one. I hope that any judge reading this book will forgive my simply using one or other of their proper styles, usually as at the date that they gave a particular judgment or speech, rather than either promoting them before their time or constantly using '(as he then was)'. Sir Rupert Jackson, Lord Dyson MR and Sir Alan Ward come in for repeated quotation so I apologise to them particularly. It is a mark of their contributions to this whole area that they feature so often.

The law and procedural rules quoted in this book are (it is hoped) up to date as at 31 July 2013.

Tony Allen
August 2013

Contents

Contents

Table of Statutes

All references are to page numbers.

Table of Statutory Instruments

All references are to page numbers.

Table of European Legislation

All references are to page numbers.

Table of Cases

All references are to page numbers.

Table of Cases

Chapter 1

Mediation and civil justice: the politics of encouraging settlement

Settlement is undoubtedly the primary way in which civil disputes are concluded worldwide. So a book dealing with how one of the primary settlement processes fits into the civil justice system needs to discuss how settlement generally is perceived by that system in order to understand that fit. There is a potential for tension between government (fixed with budgetary responsibility for the infrastructure of civil justice) and the judiciary (responsible for delivery of civil justice) over such matters, hence the political and the academic approaches to these issues. This chapter looks in particular at whether civil court process should or should not function as if settlement is the way in which most cases referred to the courts are resolved. This may then assist in deciding the extent to which courts should take an interest in whether and, if so, what settlement processes should be encouraged by the judiciary.

1.1   Settlement as a proper concern for civil justice

Has the civil justice system in England and Wales ever regarded settlement as part of its proper concerns? In a controversial book called *Saving Justice*, self-published just before the Civil Procedure Rules 1998 (CPR) came into effect in April 1999, Rowland Williams, an experienced litigation solicitor, wrote:

> 'Practically everything written about the law is expressed in trip to trial terms. The trip to settlement is practically never discussed. There is no literature on it and practically no data'.

He included civil court rules in these strictures. He argued that even the CPR were little improvement on the Rules of the Supreme Court 1965 (RSC) and County Court Rules 1981 (CCR) which they supplanted, asserting that they too were written as if civil justice was a trip to trial and not a trip to settlement. Identifying it as one honourable exception to this approach among the manifold reviews and reports which had looked at these issues in the second half of the twentieth century, he quoted from the 1979 Report of the Personal Injuries Working Party[1] chaired by Mr Justice Cantley:

---

1 (Cmnd 7476).

'The practice and procedure of the Queen's Bench Division [which was then the main forum for all significant personal injuries trials, rather than, as now, the county courts] might more properly be regarded as the procedure for the settlement of actions rather than a procedure for trial and at all times should be considered primarily in that context'.

With the vast majority of cases settling, Williams suggested that civil procedure needed to be drafted so as to encourage, indeed require, parties to discuss settlement as early as possible. His radical solution was to propose a continuing statutory duty to attempt settlement arising before the issue of proceedings and effective until final disposal by trial or otherwise. He proposed giving a right to either party to seek sanctions because their opponent had failed to observe that duty, with evidential privilege being withdrawn for the purpose of assessing the extent of any breach. Either party would be able to serve notice of their wish to go for trial instead, provided they demonstrated that they were good for any costs liability if they lost at trial. Needless to say, his proposal has never been taken up.

While his might have been a slightly unkind judgment on the thrust of the Woolf reforms, made shortly before those reforms were implemented and without the benefit of practical experience of their workings, nevertheless the procedural rules governing the conduct of civil justice in this jurisdiction seem not to have been greatly concerned with promulgating or encouraging settlement. This was certainly true under the RSC and CCR. A supervisory role was maintained (as now) over settlements which affected the rights of minors, patients and potential beneficiaries without legal capacity or with contingent interests, to ensure that such vulnerable parties were not sold short. But the only positive procedural tool which encouraged attempts to settle was the payment into court, before 1999 only available to defendants. The consequences were broadly mechanical. Beat a payment into court by 1p and the claimant wins: merely match the payment into court or lose by 1p and the claimant bore the costs of both sides from the date that the offer should have been accepted. As noted by Waller LJ in *Straker v Tudor Rose (a firm)*[2], a 2007 appeal where a judge penalised a claimant in costs even though he had beaten the defendant's offer:

'... in the pre-CPR world one would have had no hesitation is saying the judge must have gone wrong. A payment into court was the touchstone in relation to costs – if it was beaten by a plaintiff, the plaintiff got their costs; if the plaintiff failed to beat it the

---

2 [2007] EWCA Civ 368, 151 Sol Jo LB 571.

defendant got their costs. There was hardly an exception to that rule'.

So the civil courts incentivised settlement only by generating a threat of an adverse costs outcome for plaintiffs who got their risk assessment wrong in the light of a payment into court, while defendants were allowed (though not particularly encouraged) to value their risk and protect themselves from liability for both sides' costs by paying into court their best guess of the plaintiff's worst case. Information about any payment into court was (and still is) kept from the judge, so as to prevent the judge from being influenced by any settlement offer when setting damages. Judges have thus traditionally conducted trials as if there had been no question of settlement discussions, even if they have privately suspected that attempts to settle must have been made. They only find out whether and how settlement has been attempted when the substantive decision has been made and the question of costs liability arises. This limited interest in settlement flew in the face of the fact that settlements have always outnumbered trials by a huge majority. Civil justice was conducted on the basis of its being the prime, if not the only proper, dispute resolution process. If parties chose to settle cases that was a matter for them and not the courts. Anything outside the mainstream was to be regarded as alternative and not necessarily to be acknowledged, let alone encouraged; hence the development of the concept of the *alternativeness* of Alternative Dispute Resolution (ADR).

As emerges in **Chapter 4**, the CPR have modified this cultural attitude somewhat, though in terms of procedural machinery, the Part 36 offer is still not far removed from the RSC/CCR payment into court. The main differences now are that defendants no longer have to pay what they offer into court; claimants too can now make a formal offer to settle, with adverse costs consequences for defendants if they do not persuade the court to award less; and offers remain open for acceptance indefinitely unless formally withdrawn, albeit with modified costs consequences. But the continuing question is to consider what stance to settlement is appropriate for a civil justice system, perhaps especially one which seeks to take responsibility for case management, another of the major changes wrought by the CPR. Should it loftily ignore settlement altogether? Should it to some extent acknowledge the significance of settlement, or, going further, encourage settlement indirectly by exhortation coupled with penalties for unreasonably declining to engage with the settlement processes? Or should it actually encourage it directly by incorporating settlement processes into its procedural fabric? All these approaches have been tried in civil jurisdictions around the world in varying degrees. Which approach is right, and which would be best to adopt in England and Wales?

1.2 The relationship between civil courts and settlement in the US

The beginnings of mediation as a potential settlement process within the ambit of civil justice can readily be traced to the famous multi-door court-house speech of Professor Frank Sander to the Pound Conference in 1976. It was not long after he made it before a backlash to court-encouraged settlement was articulated. Professor Owen Fiss's paper *Against Settlement*[3] appeared in 1984, arguing that settlement of civil claims enervated any civil justice system which is dependent on new law by way of prec-edent, and that adjudication served as a bulwark against power imbalance between litigants. He noted the newly-emerged concept and acronym of 'ADR' and commented:

> 'The [ADR] movement promises to reduce the amount of litiga-tion initiated and accordingly the bulk of its proposals are devoted to negotiation and mediation prior to suit. But the interest in the so-called "gentle arts" has not been so confined. It extends to on-going litigation as well, and the advocates of ADR have sought new ways to facilitate and perhaps even pressure parties into settling pending cases'.

He also noted proposals to import the facilitation of settlement into pre-trial conferences as an explicit agenda item, and even (with evident dis-taste) to amend the rules to provide that a party who rejects a settlement offer and receives a less favourable judgment can be made liable for the other party's legal costs. The horror which this apparently engendered in an academic writing about a civil justice system where parties almost always pay for their own lawyer, win or lose, looks odd to us in a jurisdic-tion in which outcome-based costs shifting is the norm and payments into court are long established.

Fiss went on:

> 'I do not believe that settlement as a generic practice is preferable to judgment or should be institutionalised on a wholesale and indis-criminate basis. It should be treated instead as a highly problem-atic technique for streamlining dockets [ie relieving overcrowded lists]. Settlement is for me the civil analogue of plea bargaining. Consent is often coerced; the bargain may be struck by someone without authority; the absence of a trial and judgment renders sub-sequent judicial involvement troublesome; and although dockets are trimmed, justice may not be done. Like plea bargaining, settle-

---

3 [1984] 93 Yale LJ 1073.

ment is a capitulation to the conditions of mass society and should be neither encouraged nor praised'.

His analogy between civil settlement and criminal plea-bargaining is striking, especially in a jurisdiction such as England and Wales, where explicit plea-bargaining in criminal cases has generally been regarded as wrong and unacceptable. With civil settlement processes burgeoning and criminal plea-bargaining rampant in the US, Professor Fiss must have felt seriously depressed about justice there.

Are his views merely rather old-fashioned, understandable in 1984 but no longer in the twenty-first century? Despite winning some academic support, they certainly appear not to have stemmed the tide of mediation growth in the US or indeed across the world. This debate highlights the clash between the purist approach and the realist approach. For no civil claimant can be compelled to bring proceedings in the first place or to conclude them once started. The enforcement of private rights by a claimant is elective. Only the defendant is compelled to participate by the authority of originating process, in this country up to 1999 actually by a Royal Command contained in a writ. What has happened in practice has been a huge reduction in the volume of English civil litigation. It follows that claimants are free to compromise or drop their claim as they choose, facing of course whatever procedural consequences may be visited on such decisions. Settlement is undoubtedly the dominant way in which disputes are concluded worldwide. The debate now centres largely around what is the best process to achieve it, and to what extent the courts should promote or facilitate settlement.

Meanwhile formal civil justice (in the shape of full-scale civil trials) appears to shrink, in some jurisdictions at least. The consequence of growing settlement practices was famously noted by US Professor Marc Galanter in his much-quoted 1994 article 'The Vanishing Trial'[4]. His primary finding was that in federal courts, issued cases between 1962 and 2002 which reached a conclusion (what he calls 'dispositions') actually **increased** by a factor of five, from 50,000 to 258,000 cases. But the number of civil **trials** in 2002 was more than 20% lower than the number in 1962, down to 4,569 in 2002 from 5,802 in 1962. So the proportion of dispositions by trial was less than one-sixth of what it was in 1962, or down to 1.8% by then, as opposed to 11.5% in 1962. He traced a steep decline from 1985 onwards, when trial numbers peaked at 12,529. From then until 2002, the number of trials in federal court dropped by more than 60%, with the proportion of cases disposed of by trial falling from 4.7% to 1.8%.

---

4 The Vanishing Trial: An Examination of Trials and Related Matters in Federal and State Courts (2004) 1(3) Jnl Empirical Legal Studies, November (American Bar Association).

1.3   Civil courts and settlement in England and Wales

The most striking feature of the US statistics is the huge growth in issued actions when set against the huge drop in trials. Are there comparable statistics for England and Wales? Looking at the Annual Judicial Statistics to assess trends from 1990 to date (and not treating them as fully reliable data, as cautioned by Sir Henry Brooke in his report on amalgamating the civil courts[5]), the peak year for commencing civil litigation in the last three decades was 1990, when total non-specialist High Court actions issued were, in round figures, 19,000 in the Chancery Division, 374,000 in the Queen's Bench Division and 3.31 million in the county court. In 1998, just before the CPR came into effect, the comparable figures were 9,800 Chancery, 91,000 Queen's Bench and 2.24 million county court actions issued. This would be explained partly by the shift in cases from the High Court to the county court, except that the county court total of issued proceedings itself reduced by a third. In 2011, the comparable figures were 7,500 Chancery, 14,000 Queen's Bench and 1.17 million county court actions.

It is extremely difficult to extract persuasive statistics about the number of trials from the annual statistical reports. Looking broadly at the trial statistics, it would appear that in 2004, for instance, trials in the London Chancery Division list totalled 371, with 310 trials in the Queen's Bench Division London list, a total of 681. In 2011, the comparable figures appear to have been 183 London Chancery Division trials and 193 Queen's Bench London trials, a total of 376 and a drop of nearly 45%. The English statistics do look a little surprising in a jurisdiction in which it is said that a compensation culture exists, with people said to be more ready than ever before to initiate claims against others perceived to be to blame for wrongs. But the trend in terms of proceedings generally (unlike Galanter's US figures) has been firmly downward, and there is no real basis for suggesting that the correlation between issued actions and trials will be as disparate as Galanter suggests was the case in the US. For instance in Queen's Bench Division cases, issued proceedings will take between one and three years or more to reach trial, with a corresponding delay in correlation between proceedings issued and trials. If a compensation culture really is being acted out, then there are huge numbers of cases being settled before proceedings. The alternative explanation is that there are huge numbers of claims not being brought, perhaps through fear of litigation or the law (or of course that the compensation culture is a myth).

Has judicial business decreased correspondingly? It would appear not. The table below shows the comparative numbers of judges in the main

---

5 *Should the civil courts be unified?* by Sir Henry Brooke, published by the Judicial Office in August 2008.

Senior Courts over the last 35 years or so, being the main courts which set precedents:

Year	Court of Appeal	Chancery	Queen's Bench	Total
1979	21	12	48	81
1989	32	13	53	98
1999	41	18	67	126
2009	45	18	73	136

The Court of Appeal and Chancery figures are probably of most significance, as Queen's Bench Division judges hear a lot of criminal cases, but there is little sign of savings on the judicial salary budget through increased rates of settlement or the reduction in issued cases. Add to these figures the statistics quoted by Professor Dame Hazel Genn QC in her 2008 Hamlyn Lectures[6], published under the overall title *Judging Civil Justice,* showing that between 1999 and 2009 Circuit Judge numbers have gone up from 553 to 653, Recorders and Assistant Recorders from 1,353 to 1,405[7], District Judges from 383 to 438, with a further 773 Deputy District Judges in 2008. Thus there appears to be no shortage of decision-makers, even where the Ministry of Justice presumably can control the flow of temporary appointments of Deputies and Assistants.

Galanter's diagnosis of the causes of reduction in trials is: litigation aversion arising from the trade-off between risk and certainty; court list crowding; possibly some diversion into ADR; the sheer cost of trials in a jurisdiction where parties bear their own legal and witness expenses, subject to very limited exceptions; and what he calls 'managerial judging' (comparable to judicial case management introduced fully in England and Wales by the CPR in 1999), which is highly discretionary, and thus free from review, with judges directing parties towards settlement in a way unlikely to commend itself to Professor Fiss. Galanter views the consequences as including the loss of precedent and a shift towards inquisitorial judging with multiple shorter hearings, both thus shrinking the shadow of the law in which settlement needs to operate.

What is the academic and judicial view in England and Wales of the parallel phenomenon here? The strongest expression of similar concerns was set out in Professor Hazel Genn's 2008 Hamlyn Lectures, where her fundamental premise was that it is the hallmark of a civilised society to have a strong civil justice system for the resolution of private disputes and dis-

---

6 *Judging Civil Justice (The Hamlyn Lectures)* (CUP, 2009), 'Judges in civil justice', fn 85.
7 This is presumably the right figure, having been misprinted in the published lecture footnote as 1,305.

putes between citizens and state institutions. However, she was concerned about signs of decline in civil justice in England and Wales, caused externally by poor government funding for court facilities and staffing and legal aid, with civil justice in competition with needs of the criminal courts, and with a Treasury requirement that civil justice should be effectively self-funded by greatly increased court fees.

Her second lecture then articulated the concept of 'an **internal** threat to civil justice emanating from sections of the judiciary and the emerging ADR profession in search of a market for their services'. She continues:

> 'In the process of seeking necessary and laudable improvements to the administration of civil justice, voluble reformers have attacked its principles and purpose in a "post-modernist" rhetoric which undermines the value of legal determination, suggests that adjudication is always unpleasant and unnecessary, and finally promotes the conviction that there are no rights that cannot be compromised, and that every conflict represents merely a clash of morally equivalent interests'.

She too noted and lamented the reduction in trials and appears to suggest that cases worth a public decision should somehow get before judges to enable them to declare and enhance the common law, and thus (it would seem) be barred from settling.

Among her concerns, she asserted that:

> 'the case for mediation has routinely been made not so much on the strength of its own benefits, but by setting it up in opposition to adjudication and promoting it through anti-adjudication and anti-law discourse'.

In terms of her approach to settlement of civil disputes, Professor Genn asserted that ADR processes are:

> 'called "alternative" because they are ways of resolving disputes that theoretically do not require the involvement of any aspect of the legal system and because the approach to achieving settlement will not depend on reference to legal rights of or the legal merits of the dispute, but will approach the dispute as a problem capable of solution'.

Later she said, even more forcefully:

'mediation specifically requires that parties relinquish ideas of legal rights during mediation, and focus instead on problem-solving. Are mediators concerned about substantive justice? Absolutely not. That is the wrong question to ask. Mediation is about searching for a solution to a problem. There is no reference to the hypothesised outcome at trial. The mediator's role is to assist the parties to reach a settlement of their dispute. The mediator does not make a judgement about the quality of the settlement. Success in mediation is a settlement that the parties can live with. **The outcome of mediation is not about just settlement – it is just about settlement.**' [emphasis supplied]

There is too much controversial material in these views to be able to deal with all of them in this book[8]. Her lectures were a remarkable outburst to English eyes and ears, especially to those of people reasonably versed in ADR in this country. To suggest that 'sections of the judiciary' and other reformers driven by financial self-interest have been undermining the value of adjudicated decisions in the courts is a startling accusation.

To assuage the most potentially alarming aspects of her views by checking whether there is indeed any reduction in the quantity and standard of justice, even a simplistic approach suggests that there is no obvious shortage of precedental output. As a crude measure of this, in 1990 the normal output of the All England Law Reports was three annual volumes. This output has since increased to four annual volumes, each with over 1000 pages. Since 1999, these have been augmented by two similar-sized volumes of commercial cases and a volume of cases on European law. There is no measurable reduction in the numbers of judges either, as noted above.

Further, there is in truth little evidence of anti-adjudication discourse in the UK, whatever the enthusiasms displayed by academics and practitioners in the US might be. Anti-adjudication attacks by proponents of ADR would be a poor basis indeed for encouraging judges to order it or to encourage its use or sanction failure to use it, and it is a measure of the symbiotic nature of mediation's relationship with civil justice that it needs the support of the judiciary and judicial decisions for it to flourish. Those who contemplate settlement sometimes recruit the powers of the courts to prepare the ground for well-informed settlement discussions. A claimant may need to persuade a defendant of serious intent and commitment to a claim by actually issuing tribunal or court proceedings, thus requiring a defendant to respond to originating process or by compelling disclosure of evidence. Certainly there are some over-enthusiastic views among the

---

8 See the author's article *'Judging Judging civil justice: A critique of the 2008 Hamlyn Lectures'*, on the CEDR website at www.cedr.com/Library.

bevy of academics in the US who have written copiously about the 'magic' of mediation in civil justice as a better way to resolve disputes and differences, but this vast output of US academic analysis has not been imported into, or embraced by, the perhaps more pragmatic world in the UK, and some of the diagnoses made by US academics do not cross the Atlantic well. US writers postulate theories which simply have rarely, if ever, been deployed in the UK to justify settlement within civil justice in general, and mediation in particular.

There is one very active area of dispute resolution which is authorised by statute, conducted in private and which leads not just (if at all) to settlement, but to binding determinations of law and fact without contributing any precedental value to the common law at all when such cases very well could, and subject to very limited oversight by the public courts. This, of course, is arbitration, from which no generally binding decisions emerge, and in which, in theory at least, arbitrators and lawyers can be paid time and again to produce the same decision on the same facts, opinions and law (which is one reason why arbitration is generally not regarded as a true ADR process in the UK, unlike the US). Engagement in arbitration is consensual, either having been selected in advance in a dispute resolution clause in a contract, or by mutual agreement when a dispute arises. This amounts therefore to a private choice to avoid the jurisdiction of the civil courts. So decisions which theoretically might have contributed to the common law do not get published for the common good. Logically, arbitration should be an especial target for those asserting the primacy of publicly-conducted civil law. But their fire seems to be kept for mediation, which perhaps represents a softer target. Dare one make a link with the occasional ambitions of retiring judges to sit as arbitrators? Such a link might be seen as a parallel with the fact that good numbers of judges in the US choose to become mediators as well as arbitrators when they retire, often early, and presumably for financial reasons. Mediation gives rise to no such financial incentive in the UK as yet.

Research on ADR in the UK has been largely empirical socio-legal commentary of the kind valuably undertaken by Professors Hazel Genn, Linda Mulcahy and others, or of what might be termed the anthropological approach typified by Professor Simon Roberts of the London School of Economics. The philosophical schools of mediation theory, propounded by Baruch Bush and Folger and quoted by Hazel Genn, do not underpin mediation theory or practice in the UK, where no academics have written in such terms. Of course mediation facilitates collaborative problem-solving, but although 'the touchstone is always trial' it does not follow that trial 'is always set up as damaging and negative' by those who urge the use of mediation here. It is highly unlikely that any UK judge has been persuaded (or ever would be) to order mediation or any party or lawyer to

participate in it on the basis that participation has 'transformative potential'. While 'transformation' can happen for parties through engagement in
the mediation process, by achieving closure and moving on from problem
to solution, and by generating benefits and outcomes which would not
be in the gift of a judge, few in the UK would seek to persuade others
into mediation because of its potential for personal transformation. Parties
and their lawyers are usually far too wedded to conflict and remedy for
their rights as they see them to be impressed by the possibility of personal
change. Trial too is doubtless capable of transforming at least one party's
life, although since win for one party and loss for the other is the norm,
one party at least will emerge defeated from litigation, and possibly (in
financial terms) both. It is certainly true that community mediation can
help to achieve social justice and a wider vision. Perhaps nuisance abate-
ment laws based on criminal and civil sanctions can do the same, but such
processes are rather less likely to achieve positively chosen harmony.

On the whole, UK mediation writers have argued for a strong civil justice
system in which ADR operates as an adjunct, always in the shadow of the
law. *ADR Principles and Practice*, written by two distinguished litigation
solicitors and mediators, Henry Brown and Arthur Marriott QC, the first
edition of which was published in 1993 and the third in 2011. It discusses
the philosophy of ADR and cautionary views about it, citing among others
Professor Owen Fiss. Brown and Marriott capture their views of the
essence of ADR as follows:

'ADR complements litigation and other adjudicatory forms, providing processes which can either stand in their own right or be used
as an adjunct to adjudication. This enables practitioners to select
procedures (adjudicatory or consensual) appropriate to individual
disputes. ADR gives parties more power and greater control over
resolving the issues between them, encourages problem-solving
approaches, and provides for more effective settlements covering substance and nuance. It also tends to enhance co-operation
and to be conducive to the preservation of relationships. Effective impartial third party intercession can help to overcome blocks
to settlement, and by expediting and facilitating resolution it can
save costs and avoid the delays and risks of litigation. Sometimes,
but not necessarily, it can help to heal or provide the conditions
for healing underlying conflicts between parties. ADR processes,
like adjudicatory procedures, have advantages and disadvantages
which make them suitable for some cases but not for others'[9].

9 *ADR Principles and Practice* (3rd edn, 2012), para 3-079.

An Australian perspective on the UK situation is embodied in *Mediation: Principles, Process, Practice*[10], by Laurence Boulle and Miryana Nesic. They review much of the academic thinking from the US and Australia and widen the debate to discuss many of the topics of concern to Professor Genn. They remind us that litigated trial has always represented a tiny proportion of the widely varying processes for resolving society's disputes.

But they go on to comment:

> 'Although mediation is presented as an "alternative" to law and litigation, it also operates within "the shadow of the law". This expression signifies that parties in mediation operate with a perception of how the legal system would resolve the matter, and with a sense of the time, costs and implications of a litigated outcome'.

They also note that mediation thinking operates to influence the law too, as has happened particularly in family mediation. They also note the extent to which mediation is subject to policing by the courts, as to reviewing whether settlements have been agreed and enforcing them.

These views are not evidence of anti-adjudication bias, but of a process which needs to live alongside a strong civil justice system, against which the right level of settlement is to be measured and either accepted or rejected. Critiques of mediation, whether academic or judicial, sometimes appear to overlook two very crucial features of non-family commercial mediation. First, mediators are not decision-makers and parties are free to disengage from any mediation if they believe that their interests are best served by continuing to trial, without any damage being done to their rights and arguments at trial through what has happened at the mediation. It is both true and right that a proportion of mediations do not settle, probably for this reason alone. Second, in the vast majority of such mediations, each party is legally represented by a lawyer with a professional duty to protect their clients' interests and advise on the very question of whether to settle or not at the mediation. ADR is not a self-contained civil justice system in competition with the courts and tribunals. It lies alongside the courts and there is always a route back from mediation into the mainstream. There is no obligation or compulsion to settle, and decisions as to whether to settle or not are made by each party with the benefit of their own privately tendered legal advice, with plenty of time to consider options and risks. This is why mediation and other settlement processes must be essentially voluntary as to continued participation in the process. This does not mean that initial participation in mediation needs to be voluntary.

---

10 (Bloomsbury Professional, 2001).

1.4   Settlement as an inevitable concern for civil justice

Returning to the general propriety of settlement as a feature of civil justice systems, it must be right that criticisms aimed specifically at mediation can and should be tested out as being strictures against settlement generally. Is a civil justice system with a high level of settlement inherently or necessarily to be regarded as weak? It seems just as arguable that a civil justice system with a high settlement rate is strong, in that declaration of the law (by statute and judicial decision) has been achieved well, enabling parties to know what their rights and obligations are and to be able to settle disputes by reference to them. Judges are essentially there to clarify what remains unclear. Judicial decisions are about what is still unclear, and as has been seen, there are still plenty of decisions made by plenty of judges. There is no sign of any diminution in need for such a service, and judges in England and Wales do this job well when required by determined litigants. The greater threat to judicial decision-making in the UK may well be the funding and provision of courts within which to make such decisions, and the costs charged by those who assist parties to obtain decisions.

It is worth testing this proposition out against experience in systems where the settlement rate is low and the trial rate is high. Settlement rates in India, Pakistan and Nigeria are closer to 10% than 90%, so that the vast majority of cases are only concluded by trial. Furthermore, these jurisdictions all have virtually unfettered rights of appeal against any trial decision. Despite relatively inexpensive legal costs and court fees (thus superficially affording litigants easy 'access to justice') judges are swamped with work and have little time to devote to each case. Cases can take up to ten or more years to conclude. A culture of adjournment as a purportedly useful step in litigation is pervasive, and whole systems are undermined in accordance with the maxim 'justice delayed is justice denied'. Mediation in those systems (as was the case in the early years of its development in the US) is seen as a way of bringing principled outcomes sooner to avoid delay, and some of the best multi-door courthouse schemes are to be found in Lagos (Nigeria) and Karachi (Pakistan). The access to justice problems in the UK now revolve around high legal costs and court fees, and not around pressure on court lists and delay.

So settlement generally appears to be an inevitable component of the civil justice system in England and Wales, and this was the case long before mediation developed into a readily available settlement process. Settlement reduces and caps the risk of high expense, enabling parties to buy up such identified risks and uncertainties as may exist in any given case, if they so choose. The sad truth is that civil justice is itself not without its challenges for litigants. Every law report describes a case in which, broadly, one party won and another or others lost, and the consequences of loss in the expensive English costs environment can be severe, especially as even a defendant who pays out for liability can win back huge advantages on legal costs by making a well-judged and well-timed offer to settle. The party who wins will have a different opinion about the nature and quality of their encounter with justice and the civil justice system from the one who loses. It is hardly ever possible for both parties to win, though perfectly possible for both parties to lose in practical terms. The element of chance as to which cases are driven to trial will remain just that: a chance which is dependent not so much on the inherent value of the decision to be made as on such peripheral matters as capacity to fund the litigation, stubbornness, errors in risk analysis, absence of a sense of proportion and, just occasionally, a determination to see one's own concept of justice done, coupled with the power and freedom to see it through. Freedom to see a case through to trial, however, requires a party to be acting in person, or possessed of substantial funds or (rarely) a Legal Aid certificate, or some other kind of funding arrangement, preferably insurance-backed and represented by a lawyer willing to take on the client's risks on a given case.

There are hazards about trials which it is sensible to assess coolly. It is not merely rubbishing civil justice to comment that advocates, witnesses, experts and judges are all fallible, as are the existence and interpretation of documents and the meaning and effect of the law[11]. An unexpected failure by one of these to deliver what had been hoped for can lead to surprising and painful results. Mediation may not be a panacea, in the sense of a universal cure for all the ills engendered by legal and other disputes, but a party who loses at trial will be unlikely to regard the civil justice system as a panacea either at a personal level. Nor will a loser at trial feel the merits of having achieved certainty and finality. A settlement to which both parties contribute concessions must surely be a respectable alternative at least worth discussing.

It is not merely that settlements are an inevitable feature of litigation. There is simply no mechanism available to compel someone with a civil claim to commence litigation or to take it to trial, and parties and their advisers will unsurprisingly act or desist from action through self-interest. They may suffer costs consequences if they discontinue an action, but no one will continue an interesting case unless they are indemnified as to the cost of doing so, something that may only have happened when the Revenue have agreed to finance both parties' representation on tax appeals to the House of Lords. Given this, is there any proper reason why a civil justice system should not ensure that settlement is considered at appropriate times and by means of a suitable process, both to save parties unnecessary expense and the court

---

11 See the analysis by Sir Gavin Lightman in his lecture: *Mediation the first and not the last resort*. Speech to AvMA Conference July 2003 available at www.cedr.com/news/news/archive/LightmanJ_speech_to_AVMA_Conf.pdf.

system unnecessary demands? There are those who litigate unwisely and hazard loss through unrealistic attitudes. If settlement is so likely (which is unarguable) it is surely proper for the courts to assist actual and potential litigants to check their intentions and ensure that the estrangement between parties which inevitably occurs when litigation is initiated does not wastefully break channels of communication and lead to deeper disputes than necessary. The quality of the settlement process proposed is also important, where it is recommended by a court. Should this simply be left to the parties and their advisers to choose? What mediation offers is a guaranteed quality of process, involving the privilege of freedom from judicial scrutiny while discussions continue (except where obvious wrongdoing or serious doubts as to what was agreed is involved), and giving parties an open choice to proceed with litigation without having damaged anyone's litigation case.

The next three chapters examine the nature of mediation, the status in law of mediators and how the CPR have sought to approach the location of settlement in the civil justice system in England and Wales, with some first thoughts on the ways in which the Jackson reforms, introduced on 1 April 2013, have advanced or modified that approach (the Jackson reforms are considered in detail in **Chapter 13**). Of course there may be continuing debate about which is the best way to achieve settlement and the most appropriate time to try, and whether the courts can or should assist in such decisions, and more able to be done to help judges decide about such matters. There is still a considerable degree of ignorance about what mediation is and can achieve, as was acknowledged by Sir Rupert Jackson in Chapter 36 of his *Review of Civil Litigation Costs: Final Report* of December 2009 where he suggested the need for more education of lawyers (including judges) about ADR. Indeed, his own learning process is vividly illustrated by contrasting his attitudes to ADR as expressed in his preliminary and his final reports. His preliminary report made no mention at all of ADR in its index and had no chapter on it, devoting a few cautiously positive paragraphs to mediation. Indeed, he described ADR (wrongly, in my view) as 'by definition the antithesis of the administration of justice by the courts', and accepted Professor Hazel Genn's criticism of a culture which 'wishes to drive all litigants away from the courts and into mediation, regardless of their wishes and regardless of the circumstances of individual cases'. In his final report, he devoted a chapter to ADR, and recognises it as efficacious in many kinds of dispute, including personal injury and clinical negligence claims, as a means of settlement and of cost saving, and while not supporting compulsion for its use, he regarded it as under-appreciated and under-used. His recommended ADR Handbook has now been published[12] to make information about ADR readily available to the judiciary as it exercises its case management role.

---

12 *The Jackson ADR Handbook* (OUP, 2013).

The limited knowledge and experience of mediation among senior judges who were not in practice while mediation has been a generally available process, particularly in commercial work, is unsurprising for the very reason that mediation itself operates confidentially. This places severe restrictions on what can be published about its successes and strengths. This will undoubtedly change as a new generation of judges are appointed who have practised as mediators and advocates at mediations. The difference in judicial expectation of what mediation can achieve is vividly illustrated, for instance, by comparing the 2012 judgments in *Swain Mason v Mills & Reeve (a firm)*[13] and *PGF II SA v OFMS Co*[14]. In the former, the Court of Appeal doubted that a mediation could have closed a gap of £750,000. In the latter, the deputy High Court judge, an experienced mediator and mediation advocate, dismissed a number of arguments against imposing a costs sanction on a refusing party, clearly basing his view on experience of what mediation can actually deliver.

What other important ways are there to embody settlement organically into civil justice systems? It should be remembered that in many common law jurisdictions, particularly in the US and Australia, mediation is a mandatory step before trial, even sometimes in jurisdictions where there is also a pre-trial settlement conference in which the trial judge or another colleague effectively give firm, if provisional, indications as to where they think a given case might go in order to generate settlement pressure. Its use is growing in Singapore and Hong Kong. Its use is growing in jurisdictions across the EU, stimulated in part by the EU Mediation Directive, which has made it plain that mandatory use of mediation is permissible. Mediation is (at least in theory) mandatory in Italy, a civil law country, and it is thought-provoking on the question of where self-interest might truly lie in relation to mobilising mediation that the immediate response to that proposal when introduced into Italian law was a strike by lawyers. Civil justice systems exist to deliver outcomes to those who need and want them. This is not necessarily by judgement, though this is always needs to be available, nor will parties always feel that the best outcome to their dispute is to win in court, if another possible outcome is to lose. Court orders are limited in what they can deliver: as Brooke LJ said in *Dunnett v Railtrack plc (in railway administration)*[15]:

> 'Skilled mediators are now able to achieve results satisfactory to both parties in many cases which are quite beyond the power of lawyers and courts to achieve'.

---

13 [2012] EWCA Civ 498, [2012] STC 1760.
14 [2012] EWHC 83 (TCC).
15 [2002] EWCA Civ 303 at para 14 of the costs judgment.

As to the Jackson reforms, there is frankly no sign of any material change in judicial approach to the respectability of encouraging settlement in the 2013 amendments to the CPR triggered by the Jackson proposals. A formidable structure of cost budgeting and management, with costs capping available to limit costs, a tighter definition of proportionality, and warnings of firmer sanctioning of failure to observe procedural obligations, is erected. The fear of adverse consequences is the main tool used to prevent unreasonably conducted litigation, which echoes the same fears felt in the preparation for the CPR in 1999. The actual levers available for judges to encourage and facilitate the use of mediation remain precisely the same as were introduced in 1999 when the CPR came into effect. Interestingly, the use of mediation shot up in 2000 for a time, a trend reinforced by the decision in *Dunnett v Railtrack* in 2002, at least until judges were found after all not to be imposing tough sanctions for non-compliance. However, the 2013 amendments do not directly promote settlement, except by giving claimants who obtain more by way of judgment than their previous Part 36 settlement an extra reward. The fierceness of the costs regime, the introduction of damage-based agreements (contingency fee funding) and the irrecoverability of success fees and insurance premiums from defendants may all act as indirect financial incentives to settle. With threats of firmer enforcement of orders and directions, in cases where an ADR Order is made and ignored, the recalcitrant party may feel that it is more likely that a sanction will be imposed. But nothing in the actual amendments makes it any likelier that an ADR Order will be made in the first place, and certainly not where one or both lawyers argue that a case is inappropriate for ADR or that their clients want their day in court (usually asserted in the absence of those clients).

There is, however, a climate of opinion expressed openly by some judges that civil litigation is ludicrously expensive and that settlement should always be attempted. These views have been buttressed in some cases by sanctions being imposed on parties who unreasonably declined even to enter into negotiations, let alone mediation, though not so much by ordering mediation to be tried. These issues will be examined in more detail in later chapters. But in general, the CPR have tried to create a system in which judges can respectably recommend and even facilitate settlement processes, and some judges have responded positively to this permission. By no means all judges have done so. This is unsurprising if those judges regard settlement and ADR processes as in competition with the services they offer, supplied in a largely unregulated way and without the imprimatur of constitutional status attached.

The remainder of this book looks at how the judiciary and Parliament have approached some of the questions raised in this chapter as to whether and how they should accommodate mediation into the scheme of civil justice and where they might go in the future, with mediation operating firmly in the shadow of the law promulgated by a strong civil justice system, with a discussion in **Chapter 13** as to how things might be changed further[16].

---

16 For a fascinating account of the impact on the shape and thinking of the legal profession made by the growth in importance of settlement practices in the US and Canada, see Julie Macfarlane, *The New Lawyer: How Settlement is Transforming the Practice of Law* (University of British Columbia Press, 2008).

Chapter 2

The status of mediation in terms of the law

2.1 Defining mediation

A book about mediation, especially one which seeks to concentrate on mediation as distinct from other alternative dispute resolution (ADR) processes, of necessity needs to tackle first what mediation actually is. While this might seem a straightforward task, there is less agreement about it than might be expected. As has been observed by Spencer and Brogan[1], 'there is some debate as to what mediation really is, or should be', which presents problems to those who either seek to draft a definition or define what it is (two subtly different activities). The very flexibility of mediation, arguably one of its greatest advantages, makes it hard to pin down. Yet it seems inappropriate in a legal context to rely entirely on the time-honoured answer to the problem of defining a camel: 'I can't define it but I know one when I see one'. As will be seen, the areas of controversy about how to define mediation run in parallel with several of the significant legal controversies over the nature and place of mediation within civil justice. What is discussed in outline now is discussed in greater detail in later chapters.

The EU Mediation Directive defines mediation as:

> 'a structured process, however named or referred to, whereby two or more parties to a dispute attempt by themselves, on a voluntary basis, to reach an agreement on the settlement of their dispute with the assistance of a mediator. This process may be initiated by the parties or suggested or ordered by a court or prescribed by the law of a member state[2]'.

Furthermore, it defines a mediator as:

> 'any third person who is asked to conduct a mediation in an effective, impartial and competent way, regardless of the denomination or profession of that third person in the member state concerned

---

1 In *Mediation Law and Practice* (Cambridge, 2006), ch 1.
2 Article 3(a) and (b).

and of the way in which the third person has been appointed or requested to conduct the mediation'.

By implication, however, judges are excluded from being such a 'third person', in that the Directive specifically excludes from its ambit:

'attempts made by the court or the judge seized to settle a dispute in the course of judicial proceedings concerning the dispute in question'.

The Civil Procedure Rules 1998 (the CPR) do not define mediation or ADR anywhere. The glossary to the CPR describes ADR as 'a collective description of methods of resolving disputes otherwise than through the normal trial process'. CPR 2.2 underlines that terms in the glossary are not definitions but a 'guide to the *meaning*' of such terms, although judges have occasionally adopted this gloss as a definition[3]. But the gloss in the CPR certainly goes far wider than just mediation. It encompasses all forms of non-adjudicative dispute resolution, even including mere negotiation, as well as adjudicative processes such as expert determination and arbitration. Arguably it might even include resolution through any litigation process short of trial, such as discontinuance or acceptance of an offer made under CPR 36. For the CPR to gloss ADR as anything and everything other than judgment makes the term ADR hugely unspecific and cumbersome, in effect ensuring that civil trial – presumably regarded by the CPR as mainstream dispute resolution – is in practice an even tinier part of civil justice, bearing in mind the minuscule proportion of issued cases which ever reach trial, ignoring also the myriad disputes which are either settled or discontinued before proceedings are ever issued.

Indeed the word 'mediation' itself scarcely appears in the CPR themselves, just in the rules dealing with the implementation of the EU Mediation Directive, where CPR 78.23(2) adopts the Mediation Directive's definition. The word does appear frequently in most of the various Pre-action Protocols, with a rough indication of what it means. Judges have often been prepared to use the word 'mediation' specifically in judgments, assuming mediation to be the lead non-adjudicative ADR process, or because the decision sought of them was based specifically on the use or effect of a mediation or refusal by a party to enter into the mediation process. Cases have dealt far less often with other types of ADR. But many judges have resorted to the unspecific term ADR (or even, in one instance, 'an ADR', whatever that may be[4]). There is thus a marked lack of consistency of

---

3 Eg Dyson LJ in *Halsey v Milton Keynes General NHS Trust; Steel v Joy* [2004] EWCA Civ 576, [2004] 4 All ER 920, at para 5.
4 Dyson LJ in *Halsey*.

approach to the specifying of mediation and other ADR processes when it comes to court rulings over using or failing to use ADR, which is unnecessary and at times unhelpful for litigants. It may be evidence of general judicial discomfort over making rulings about processes of which they themselves never had any experience in private practice. The impact of the promotion to judgeships of those who have experience of mediation and other forms of ADR is just beginning to emerge.

The *Jackson ADR Handbook*[5], published in May 2013, does not really attempt a precise definition of mediation or ADR. It even opens by saying that ADR generally 'has no agreed definition', and satisfies itself with noting its broad identifying features. It is said to cover any option where there is a dispute between two or more parties which relates to civil rights and/or duties, and which could go to court for resolution. 'Option' presumably means 'process used', and 'court' must include 'tribunal'. The process may or may not, it is said, involve a third party neutral, and the parties have a degree of control over the process and the decision taken (presumably meaning the outcome of the dispute) through agreeing the form the process should take and 'in some circumstances the final outcome'. As well as the vagueness of this last sentence, there feels like a degree of stretch about these characteristics, seeking to include the huge range from purely adjudicative arbitration to mere negotiation and joint settlement meetings within this portrait, even if inclusion of discontinuance and Part 36 settlements has implicitly fallen out of its scope. The Handbook's chapter dealing specifically with mediation is again descriptive, its essence being that a mediator facilitates discussions and negotiations between disputing parties within a relatively structured but flexible process, in a formal setting, during a defined period of time, 'all of which' creates an impetus for settlement. It notes that the parties remain in control of the issues and the outcome, which can be broader than just legal rights and remedies and tailored to the parties' needs.

The implication of this approach is to buttress the concept that all dispute resolution processes are alternative except civil court trial. The irony of this is that trial is, in numerical terms, probably the rarest form of dispute resolution used in England and Wales. Of course trial has both the kudos of state provision (at least so long as the courts are not privatised) and also the imprimatur of the ECHR, Article 6. But maybe this exclusivity of approach in the judiciary has had something to do with its slow and cautious recognition of the value and position of mediation. In truth there is a wide spectrum of choice available for dispute resolution now, and it could actually be professionally inappropriate for a lawyer to advise a client that a civil trial is their best option.

---

5 *The Jackson ADR Handbook* (OUP, 2013).

Looking at some more definitions, Spencer and Brogan cite[6] a definition produced by the US National Alternative Dispute Resolution Advisory Council and much used by its members, as being:

> 'a process in which the parties to a dispute, with the assistance of a dispute resolution professional (the mediator), identify the issues, develop options, consider alternatives and endeavour to reach agreement. The mediator has no advisory or determinative role in regard to the content of the dispute, but may advise on or determine the process of mediation whereby resolution is attempted. Mediation may be undertaken voluntarily, under a court order, or subject to an existing contractual agreement'.

They also offer a briefer form, as being:

> 'a process in which the parties to a dispute, with the assistance of a dispute resolution professional (the mediator), negotiate in an endeavour to resolve their dispute'.

CEDR's definition, now embodied in its Model Procedure[7], and one which has been widely adopted in the UK and Europe, is:

> 'A flexible process conducted confidentially in which a neutral person actively assists the parties in working towards a negotiated agreement of a dispute or difference, with the parties in ultimate control of the decision to settle and the terms of resolution'.

The US Uniform Mediation Act is discussed fully in **Chapter 9**. The Act[8] defines mediation as:

> 'a process in which a mediator facilitates communication and negotiation between parties to assist them in reaching a voluntary agreement regarding their dispute',

and a mediator is defined simply as 'an individual who conducts a mediation', though 'conducts' is not defined.

Ignoring certain infelicities and circularities in these various definitions, it is comforting to note several common features:

---

6 In *Mediation Law and Practice* (CUP Australia, 2007).
7 (10th edn).
8 Uniform Mediation Act, § 2(1) and (3).

- that mediation is a process expressly or implicitly managed by the mediator;

- that a third party (the mediator) assists the disputants, implying a degree of positive intervention by the mediator;

- that the disputants, not the mediator, determine their own outcome, and either or both may choose **not** to settle the dispute, but revert to an adjudicated outcome, implicitly with no adverse consequence either from conduct during the mediation or their decision not to settle, by commencing or continuing an adjudicative process.

Most of the definitions are apt to cover commercial, community and family mediation, all being mediation sectors with similar overarching principles but whose processes are very different.

But there are also some important differences and omissions in each. For instance only the CEDR definition includes the words 'confidentially' and 'neutral'. In fact, there are those who practise 'non-neutral' and 'non-private' mediation, which embody at least two different types of activity – international diplomacy and workplace disputes – where the independent third person clearly has a partisan status and even responsibility, and where there are real challenges to the concept of having confidential conversations as part of the process. Diplomats who intervene as third party peacemakers in international situations inevitably do so in the public eye, and their interventions are based on varying degrees of discernible national self-interest, coupled with underlying willingness to deploy national power as a way of influencing outcomes. Perhaps the most telling illustration of that fact was the remark, made only partly in jest, to a mediation conference in New York by the late Richard Holbrooke, the US diplomat who masterminded the Dayton Accords in the Balkans, when he said 'If they don't agree to what we say, we bomb them!' Perhaps this attitude unfairly undermines the reputation of generations of UN peacekeepers or such apparently disinterested and selfless interventions as the Norwegian initiative that led to the Camp David agreement in Palestine, but self-interest and national agendas are never far below the surface when a nation intervenes on the world stage, even purporting to take the role of a neutral 'honest broker'.

Workplace mediators employed by a company to mediate with employees in dispute owe their own overall duty to their employers, and this complicates the neutrality of their interventions. There will also be doubt about the extent to which their work can truly be treated as 'confidential', either by the parties or by their superiors. It is often desirable and certainly possible to contract for confidentiality during the mediation process in order to encourage frank disclosure of each party's private positions. But if both parties and the mediator are fellow employees of the same employer, the disputing parties may well feel discomfort about disclosure of what they say to someone who either may feel under an overriding obligation to report it higher, or be required to do so in the company's interest. Furthermore, environmental and community mediators, however neutral, usually operate in the public eye and can never ensure confidentiality, but theirs is undoubtedly a recognisable mediation process. CEDR, which included confidentiality and neutrality in its definition, is primarily a commercial mediation provider, so its narrower definition to some extent reflects its narrower approach.

It is interesting that the word 'voluntary' appears in some but not all the definitions of mediation. 'Voluntary' participation in the context of mediation requires careful appreciation and interpretation. Not even in the *Jackson ADR Handbook* does any sense of voluntary participation emerge as a necessary characteristic, despite its sponsor's opposition to any degree of mandatory ADR. The EU Mediation Directive's definition talks of parties attempting by themselves (presumably, that is, without court intervention) 'on a voluntary basis' to reach settlement with the help of a neutral. The Uniform Mediation Act talks of the parties 'reaching a voluntary agreement'. 'Voluntary' used to appear in an earlier CEDR definition, which then read 'a voluntary, non-binding, private dispute resolution process, in which a neutral person helps the parties to try to reach a negotiated settlement', but the word 'voluntary' has now been deleted. The key to understanding the real significance of voluntariness in relation to mediation is explained by Spencer and Brogan when they say 'mediation may be undertaken voluntarily, under a court order, or subject to an existing contractual agreement'[9]. The EU Mediation Directive makes the same distinction clear in its Preamble. It is an important one when considering the continuing controversy in England and Wales as to whether judges can or should order parties to mediate, discussed in greater detail in **Chapter 13**. There is a distinction between compelling parties into a process, and ensuring that they are entirely free to withdraw from the process without penalty once under way. Their continued participation in any mediation is thus entirely 'voluntary'. It should go without saying (though some judicial comments might perhaps suggest that this may be misunderstood) that there is never any compulsion to settle during a mediation. It is an essential characteristic of mediation that there is at all times an open choice for every party over whether or not to accept terms which emerge in mediated discussion, or to revert to litigation or arbitration.

---

9 Spencer and Brogan *Mediation Law and Practice* (CUP, 2006) p 9.

No one (including the judiciary in England and Wales) appears to argue with the need for freedom for parties to leave a mediation without penalty if acceptable terms do not emerge, whereas there is a spectrum of views about whether parties can and should be compelled into initiating a settlement process. Certainly there has been considerable reluctance among the judiciary in England and Wales to support compulsion to mediate, despite the fact that it is normal in many common law jurisdictions in the US, Canada and Australia, and a number of civil law jurisdictions in Europe, such as Italy. Views vary as to whether a degree of compulsion adversely affects the outcome, but so long as continued participation is voluntary, many experienced mediators would argue from experience that a degree of compulsion over entering the process does not damage its prospects of success.

There has been some empirical research where compulsion to mediate has been piloted. In Ontario a major experiment was tried in the civil courts of Toronto and Ottawa, and reported on by Professor Julie Macfarlane[10]. The difference in attitude of the legal profession in each of the two cities points to the significance of cultural attitudes about compulsory imposition of mediation, with far less opposition to it found in Ottawa than in Toronto.

The Ontario project led to a parallel experiment in England at the Central London County Court, where a court-annexed scheme was then in place, in which a number of cases were referred automatically to mediation, with the right to apply for opt-out. This was reviewed by Professor Hazel Genn in her report *Twisting Arms* ('ARMS' standing for 'automatic referral to mediation')[11]. By an unfortunate piece of timing, the launch of the scheme coincided almost exactly with a judicial pronouncement in the Court of Appeal in *Halsey v Milton Keynes General NHS Trust; Steel v Joy* that courts could not in law order parties to use ADR. This inevitably led to a very high number of applications to opt out of the automatic referral to mediation, and did much to undermine the value of the experiment, which was not extended, and was soon followed by the general demise of almost all court-annexed mediation schemes throughout England and Wales.

By contrast, there had been an earlier pilot scheme in England to investigate the usefulness of mediation for dealing with clinical negligence claims which was established on the fundamental principle of purely voluntary participation by both parties, which was reviewed by Professor Linda

---

10 See the evaluation of the Ontario Project by Hann and Baar (2001), published by the A-G for Ontario, and 'Culture Change? A tale of two cities and mandatory court-connected mediation' (2002) 2 Jnl of Dispute Resolution University of Missouri-Columbia 242.
11 *Twisting Arms: Court referred and court-linked mediation under judicial pressure*: Genn Ministry of Justice Research Series 1.07.

Mulcahy[12]. Only 12 cases went through the scheme in 18 months, but all settled, one on the basis of withdrawal of the claim in the light of freshly-disclosed information greatly valued by the claimant and regarded as a sufficient result, and the rest with payments at varying levels to claimants. The voluntary nature of the pilot was seen as greatly diminishing take-up, which was also hampered by doubts as to whether Legal Aid was available and lack of support for participation sought from the newly-formed NHS Litigation Authority.

From all of this, it follows that any general definition of mediation which does not restrict mediation's 'voluntary' nature to continued participation in the process once started means that it may be conceptually inaccurate on a global basis, even if accurate in relation to a specific jurisdiction. Professor Hazel Genn's definition in her 2008 Hamlyn lectures[13] was of 'a voluntary process in which a neutral third party assists disputing parties to reach a consensual solution to their dispute'. Her definition is imprecise, bordering on inaccurate, in general terms, as voluntary is used in its overall sense. Perhaps it is merely an expression of her personal viewpoint of what **ought** to be the case, as she has long been a vocal advocate of non-mandatory mediation. Her definition even seems to hint that mediation involves compulsion to settle, with settlement being the only possible outcome, and without acknowledging that the parties are free **not** to settle, facing no adverse consequences if they decline to do so. Contrast the CEDR definition on this point. If definitions are drafted and adopted without care, there is a risk that they can be used as a way to criticise the mediation process by attacking what was never true or phrased accurately in the first place.

The concept of the mandating of mediation by judges is considered further in **Chapter 5** on ADR orders, and revisited in **Chapter 13**. But before leaving this outline of the controversy over voluntariness, it is worth mentioning that many commercial mediations in England and Wales now take place by virtue of a contractual obligation to undertake the process which was written into their original deal by businesses. For many years, commercial parties opted to refer disputes to arbitration, as this provided a private forum for potentially embarrassing matters to be authoritatively decided (albeit on a case-by-case basis with little precedental force), regardless of the considerable cost of hiring the decision-makers as well as the legal teams to argue the respective cases. Since the latter years of the twentieth century, dispute resolution clauses have become increasingly sophisticated. Multi-layered or 'stepped' or escalating resolution

---

12 Mulcahy *Mediating medical negligence claims: an option for the future?* (The Stationery Office, 2000).
13 *Judging Civil Justice: the Hamlyn Lectures 2008* (CUP).

clauses are now commonplace, in which the parties to a commercial contract agree that when a dispute emerges there shall first be a negotiation stage, often between defined levels of executive, followed by formal mediation and only then by some method of adjudication, whether by judge or arbitrator. Arbitration clauses have for a long time been held to oust the court's jurisdiction, but there was initial doubt as to whether courts would accept their jurisdiction being ousted in the face of escalation clauses. As can be seen in **Chapter 8** on contracting to use mediation, the trend has been for the courts to say, in effect, that parties have voluntarily nominated and defined a dispute resolution process, and they must fulfil their contractual obligation before being able to come to court. This doubtless leads to mediations where at least one party comes unwillingly, yet nevertheless has to submit to the process, having once agreed in advance to do so. Arbitrators have been somewhat less inclined to refuse to hear disputes where parties have not exhausted their contractual dispute resolution obligations, as was noted in the report of the CEDR Commission on Settlement of International Arbitrations[14].

Reverting briefly to the various definitions set out above, this book makes no choice between them. The general principles inherent in all the above definitions should suffice, and the tensions and differences between them are what will stimulate debate about mediation's place in civil justice. Any future legislation dealing with the place of mediation (and ADR) in civil justice would doubtless have to settle upon a form of words, which will not be easy in view of the flexibility of the mediation process which is at the heart of its attractiveness and strength. Summarising its essential characteristics, these are:

- a process managed by a third-party mediator who is neutral as between the disputants;
- the mediator actively engages with the parties during the mediation;
- what transpires during a mediation is privileged from adjudicative review and remains confidential, except as specifically agreed by the parties in advance or in retrospect;
- any agreed outcomes are chosen by the parties and are not limited to what an adjudicative process may award or decide; and may or may not be binding and enforceable at law and are not decided by the mediator: any party may choose to revert to an adjudicative process without adverse consequence to their case.

---

14 *CEDR Commission on Settlement in International Arbitrations: Final report* Nov 2009: to be found at www.cedr.com/about_us/arbitration_commission/Arbitration_Commission_Doc_Final.pdf.

2.2   Mediation contrasted with other ADR processes

There can be little doubt that so far as formal ADR procedures are concerned, and using the CPR gloss as the basis for saying what ADR comprises, the main adjudicative form of ADR is arbitration, though mention should be also made of adjudication under the Housing Grants Construction and Regeneration Act 1996[15], which has had a major impact on construction claims by offering a summary form of decision about problems to enable building projects to continue unimpeded by dispute, but which are subject to formal arbitration later if a party wishes to challenge it. Expert determination, outside the ambit of the Arbitration Acts, is certainly used quite frequently to determine land and share valuation disputes in particular by a formal and binding adjudication of rights.

The leading non-adjudicative format is mediation, and judges often specify mediation as the process they expect parties to use or to have used when the topic comes up. When they refer to ADR, they may well mean mediation. Other processes which are not infrequently used in other jurisdictions, especially the US, such as early neutral evaluation and mini-trial or executive tribunal have not caught on here. What has developed in this jurisdiction, building on the co-operative spirit engendered by the Woolf reforms, has been the use of round-table meetings (RTMs), also called joint settlement meetings (JSMs) or 'without prejudice' meetings (WP meetings). These might be described as mediations without a mediator, as their broad format involves the assembly of fairly complete negotiating teams on both sides, sometimes with and sometimes without lay clients, but with legal teams for each party, in order to discuss settlement off the record. In effect these are without prejudice negotiations, protected only by the explicit or implicit label of 'without prejudice' and without a formal agreement in writing to govern the process which characterises almost all mediations. Some might argue that such meetings are not properly described as ADR, as bilateral negotiation is nothing new, and has always been a feature of civil claims. But JSMs/RTMs have certainly increased in number as a result of the drive to settlement initiated by the CPR and have come to be treated as a type of ADR almost by default. Their advantages and drawbacks are reviewed in **Chapter 9** when considering the nature and scope of mediation confidentiality. It is true that many mediations take place after the failure of such a meeting to achieve settlement. But many do lead to settlement, and certainly judges are referred to them when asked to consider what costs orders to make.

---

15 As amended in 2009 and 2011.

2.3 The formalities associated with the mediation process

The legal framework for mediation in the UK is essentially created by
the mediation agreement which is signed at the beginning of the process
by both parties and mediator. There is not yet any legislative framework
in the UK to govern the status of mediation, its parties or the mediator,
as there is in many US States. The rights and obligations of all participants in a mediation are therefore a matter of private contract law, though
underpinned by some important general legal principles, which are usually extended by specific contractual terms included in such agreements.
Some of those contractual terms have begun to receive comment and
open support from the courts on the basis of public policy. The boundaries of such principles and commentaries need to be understood, however,
so that ADR agreements can be drafted and amended sensibly, and areas
where uncertainty still exists are identified and understood.

The rest of this chapter looks at the principal terms typical of mediation agreements and their status in law. **Chapter 9** looks separately and more broadly
at the significance of evidential privilege and confidentiality in relation to
the conduct of mediations, a topic which arises partly by operation of law
and partly by the provisions of mediation agreements. The CEDR Mediation
Agreement and Model Procedure are in **Appendices 1** and **2** respectively.

2.4 The content and status of a mediation agreement

A typical mediation agreement provides:

- for the appointment of the mediator;
- that the parties will 'attempt in good faith to settle the dispute by
  means of a mediation';
- a definition of the dispute about which the mediation is to take
  place;
- for a representative of each party to attend with authority to
  settle;
- for confidentiality of the process and documents produced in
  relation to it, being both general confidentiality agreed by all
  and also by the mediator in respect of private meetings and conversations with each party during the mediation;
- for the mediator to observe a given code of conduct, covering
  such matters as conflicts of interest and exceptions to confidentiality, in relation to possible criminality or danger;
- that the parties will not call the mediator to give evidence in
  later or continuing litigation;

- that the terms of any settlement must be in writing and signed by the parties for them to be binding and enforceable;
- that parties can withdraw at any time, and the mediator can withdraw for defined reasons;
- for the proper law of the mediation contract and the forum for later dispute resolution;
- for limitations on the mediator's liability for fault: these may vary from an absolute bar on liability to excluding liability except for fraud or wilful default;
- for the basis on which the costs and fees associated with the mediation will be borne.

Usually a draft is circulated between the mediator and the parties in preparation for the mediation. Once finalised it may be signed in advance or, more usually, it will be signed by the parties and the mediator at the beginning of the formal mediation meeting, when all are together for the first time. The mediator may arrange for several copies of the agreement to be signed as originals, or retain the original and circulate copies as signed.

The first question to ask is whether a mediation agreement is itself a binding and enforceable contract. There is certainly a theoretical basis for challenging this, on the same basis as challenges to the validity of ADR contract clauses, namely that they represent at their heart a mere agreement to negotiate. The validity of ADR contract clauses is discussed in **Chapter 8**, and the debate will not be repeated here. It would be of considerable concern if a mediation were conducted on the basis of a mediation agreement with the provisions listed above, only for one party to argue that the agreement was void for uncertainty or as being an agreement to agree, rendering all the purported obligations in the agreement (such as confidentiality) of no effect.

Does a mediation agreement with the sort of terms set out above meet the requirements of a valid contract in English law? It is certainly intended to create legal relations (though whether it actually does makes this point rather circular). It is clear in terms. It need not comply with any special formalities. What of valid consideration? The mediator certainly agrees to provide mediation services to the parties for an agreed fee. But what consideration binds the parties as between each other? Arguably they do so by agreeing a temporary forbearance from suing by entering into good faith negotiations, or perhaps by agreeing to attend represented by someone with authority to settle, and agreeing mutually to treat mediation discussions as confidential. It has to be accepted that these are all tenuous as valid valuable consideration.

However, no attempt has so far been made in the UK to set aside the effect of a mediation agreement or any of its clauses, and there are a number of cases where the courts have operated on the assumption that mediation agreements are valid and contain enforceable provisions, especially as to the confidentiality of the process[16], and that settlement terms must be in writing signed by the parties[17] to be binding. It is highly likely that the courts would treat mediation agreements as fully enforceable as a matter of public policy, if for no other reason.

2.5   Formalities relating to mediation agreements

The main distinction between mediation and other types of settlement meeting is the formality with which it is framed, by means of a signed mediation agreement which sets out rights and obligations of those engaged in it, as opposed to leaving the legal framework largely or entirely a matter of implication under the general law. The purpose and effect of the mediation agreement thus needs careful examination.

There is no requirement in England and Wales or indeed imposed by the EU Mediation Directive that any mediation must be conducted under the aegis of a written and signed mediation agreement. By contrast, many US jurisdictions have enacted all the basic requirements and protections usually incorporated in an effective mediation agreement. Because these arise by implication of law, signature of a formal mediation agreement is unnecessary, depending on the applicable State or Federal law. In the UK such obligations, rights and protections only arise, in anything other than a very basic way, if they are embodied each time in a mediation agreement.

As noted above, the mediation agreement is signed at the beginning of the formal mediation meeting itself. However, providers and mediators frequently have pre-mediation contact with parties to set up the arrangements, even to debate the wording of the mediation agreement, but also discern the issues and prepare parties and their teams for the main event. The question thus arises as to when the contracted obligations start. Pre-mediation discussions before the agreement is signed with each party might well involve dealing with confidential issues which one party would want the mediator not to reveal to the other party. Mediators often (and should as a matter of practice) indicate that they are treating such pre-agreement contact as subject to the same terms as to confidentiality as

---

16 Eg *Instance v Denny Bros Printing Ltd* [2000] FSR 869 and *Venture Investment Placement v Hall* [2005] EWHC 1227 (Ch), [2005] All ER (D) 224 (May). The certainty of the procedure commended itself to Colman J in *Cable & Wireless plc v IBM United Kingdom Ltd* [2002] EWHC 2059 (Comm), [2002] 2 All ER (Comm) 1041 sufficiently to allow him to enforce an ADR contract clause in that case.
17 See *Brown v Rice* [2007] EWHC 625 (Ch), [2008] FSR 61.

if a mediation agreement had been signed, and at the very least 'without prejudice' protection would automatically apply to negotiations about setting up a mediation. However, statutory provision is needed to clarify this grey area. Lloyd J in *Instance v Denny Bros Printing Ltd*[18] suggested that privilege does indeed apply to negotiations leading up to a mediation. But if this is so, and the formal mediation does not take place, does a court later have the right to enquire into the reasonableness of conduct demonstrated by each party in deciding whether to impose a costs sanction or not? *Reed Executive plc v Reed Business Information Ltd*[19] suggests not, in the absence of an express classification of such material as 'without prejudice save as to costs'. This anomaly may need clarification[20]. If clear definition of the moment at which a mediation starts becomes necessary for suspending limitation defences, this might have benefits in this respect also.

The Cross-Border Mediation (EU Directive) Regulations 2011[21], dealing with the suspension of limitation periods in cross-border disputes by the commencement of mediation until its conclusion, define the start of a mediation as being *'the date of the agreement to mediate that is entered into by the parties and the mediator'*. This definition gives rise to several questions, which are discussed in **Chapter 10** dealing with the EU Mediation Directive, and is fortunately not yet generally applicable in English law.

2.6 A 'good faith' commitment by the parties to seek settlement

This language is reminiscent of some of the provisions of the Commercial ADR Order[22] commended by the Court of Appeal in *Halsey v Milton Keynes General NHS Trust*[23]. This form of order has been in existence since the mid-1990s, and despite its soft wording has been extremely successful as a way of persuading parties into mediation without the need to threaten costs sanctions. Requirements that parties 'shall in good faith endeavour to agree a neutral' and to 'take such serious steps as they may be advised to resolve their disputes by ADR' hardly smack of the cut and thrust of adversarial litigation. Nor does failure to comply with such directions sound particularly capable of enforcement or sanction. Yet they have worked well.

---

18 (2000) Times, 28 February.
19 [2004] EWCA Civ 887, [2004] 4 All ER 942.
20 See also on this *Qualifying Insurers Subscribing to the Assigned Risks Pool v Ross and Co (a firm)* [2004] EWHC 1181 (Ch).
21 SI 2011/1133.
22 To be found in Appendix 7 to the Admiralty and Commercial Court Guide.
23 [2004] EWCA Civ 576, [2004] 4 All ER 920.

There has been considerable litigation in the US and Australia seeking to demonstrate that a party approached or behaved at a mediation in bad faith. Quite how to prove damage in such a situation is unclear, but such attempts have not been reported in the UK to date. With considerable costs penalties awaiting a litigant who is found to have acted unreasonably during litigation, it is hard to imagine an irredeemably unreasonable party succeeding in limiting his unreasonableness only to when privilege protects that party's conduct from scrutiny. An ill-judged Part 36 offer made shortly after a mediation by an unreasonable party which does not settle a case may well, when weighed with the judge's finding of facts or law, justify a swingeing adverse costs order.

One theoretical basis for revealing unreasonable conduct behind the veil of 'without prejudice' privilege would be to enlist the 'unambiguous impropriety' exception to privilege. The serious problem with that is that recent cases demand a high level of impropriety, and with a wide spectrum of possible outcomes in most disputes, few judges would be prepared to be bold enough to admit evidence as to alleged bad faith involvement on the basis of a finding of unambiguous impropriety. This is fully examined later in **Chapter 9**.

2.7 Authority to settle

Most mediation agreements provide that someone should attend for each party who possesses full authority to settle the dispute to be mediated. This is sometimes done by requiring the nomination of an identified 'Lead Negotiator', who must attend with such authority.

Such a term in the agreement reduces to a minimum any risk that the person who attends the mediation does not have actual and ostensible authority in law to bind the party represented as his or its authorised agent. Making this an express term of the mediation agreement helps to emphasise the importance of this principle to those representing each party.

But while it is highly desirable that each party should be represented at the mediation by someone with full authority to settle the dispute, this does not always happen. Possessing authority does not, of course, mean that a settlement will be agreed. This may be because of a perfectly proper disagreement in good faith over an acceptable outcome. Sometimes, however, for a variety of reasons, a party may send a negotiator with limited or fettered authority who is not authorised to deal at the level proposed, however much that level looks sensible. A company might send a manager or director; a partnership might send one or more partners. Either might send simply a lawyer, whether in-house or external, with a degree of authority to settle. The authority may extend up or down to a certain financial limit, or may require the representative to discuss the matter with others before concluding a settlement. This situation is by no means ideal. If a deal is struck after 12 hours of mediation, and final agreement is subject to a phone call to someone who has not been present, the latter may object to certain proposals. Not having been present to hear all the debate and watch the deal slowly emerge, the absentee is not well placed to judge the wisdom of accepting or rejecting those terms, not having been able to assess how they emerged within the mediation.

If this happens, then the parties and the mediator simply have to work within that constraint. The question is whether there is any remedy in the hands of the aggrieved party for the fact that their opponent has actually breached the terms of the mediation agreement, by not disclosing any limitation on authority before signing the agreement and in effect warranting full authority to settle, or by disabling themselves from being able 'in good faith to settle the dispute' by means of the mediation. While there has been considerable litigation to seek remedies for such matters in the USA and Australia, no such litigation has yet been determined in the UK. As any allegation of want of authority or bad faith engagement has to emerge from the confidential confines of the process itself, there will be difficulty in initially adducing evidence of it. As noted above, it is unlikely to fall into the 'unambiguous impropriety' exception to the 'without prejudice' rule, even if a way around any specific confidentiality clause can be found. Furthermore, even if liability can be established, there may be problems over proof of damage. But where the US and Australia go first, the UK often follows, so points of this nature may well come to be litigated in the future.

Four further situations relating to authority to settle are worth bearing in mind.

Insured parties

Where the liability of one or more parties is to any extent covered by insurance, the insurer's consent will be required to any settlement, perhaps depending on the level of self-insurance or excess on the policy. If insurers carry the whole or the majority of the risk themselves, they will attend the mediation and control it as they would any litigation, having been subrogated to the rights of their insured. This is obviously the optimum solution. If the insurers are unable or unwilling to attend, the lines of settlement authority should be clearly set up in advance, but it is less than ideal not to have the decision-maker present in person.

If there is a dispute between insurer and party as to indemnity, the insurer ought to attend the mediation as an additional party, enabling the subsidiary dispute between insured and insurer to be settled at the same time.

At least the presence of the insurer will allow the insured to settle the main dispute with the insurer's authority, leaving the indemnity problem between them to be sorted out later. Similar considerations apply to reinsurance contracts. In whichever capacity they attend, they should be bound into the other contractual provisions relating to 'without prejudice' status, confidentiality and mediator immunity.

With legal costs insurance so prevalent, and likely to remain so even after the 2013 amendments to the CPR, it may well be necessary to have a channel of communication open to the costs insurers (or even have them present, hitherto unheard of) as their interests can readily become significant over negotiating legal costs liabilities towards the end of a mediation.

Groups of companies and partnerships

Where a party is one of a group of companies, care should be taken to ensure that authority to settle is present on behalf of all those companies in the group who are likely to be involved in the settlement. This may well be a wider group than those who are party to the dispute. The same principle applies to appropriate channels of authority and consent in respect of a partnership. Again, with both companies and partnerships it is unlikely that the whole main board or all the partners will attend, giving rise to the need for care to be taken over authority to settle.

Public bodies

Complications may well arise with public bodies. Given the decision-making structures of national or local government, it is unlikely that any individuals will be able to attend a mediation with completely unfettered authority to settle. It is more likely that those who attend will be authorised to agree settlement terms subject to obtaining final approval from the relevant minister or an appropriate committee, typically a finance committee. Although not ideal for the reasons given above, mediation can and does still operate effectively in these circumstances. It may be helpful, however, to obtain a commitment in advance that the appropriate committee will meet within a specified and short time period following the mediation, so that the matter is not left unresolved for too long. Further, it may be relevant to ascertain the track record of the person attending the mediation as Lead Negotiator in securing approval of recommended settlements.

Parties under legal incapacity

It is clearly impossible for a binding agreement to be made at a mediation which affects the rights of a party to a dispute who does not possess legal capacity to contract. This may well arise in mediations relating to personal injury and clinical negligence claims, where there may be claimants who are infants or who have suffered serious brain damage. This is not to say that such cases cannot be effectively dealt with by mediation. Terms that are agreeable are worked out and agreed, conditional upon court approval. Application is then made to the court for approval by the judge.

For this reason, it is wise for counsel who is to advise on the reasonableness of any provisional settlement for this purpose, to be actually present at the mediation, so as to play a full part in the debate which leads to the terms to be referred to the court. Counsel can then give due explanation to the judge from direct knowledge of any appreciable discount for litigation risk.

2.8 Imposing formalities on settlement terms

No formality would normally be required for most settlements negotiated at a mediation. Contracts for the sale of land must be evidenced in writing, but money settlements have no such requirement. However, standard mediation agreements almost always require that for any settlement terms to be binding, it is necessary for such terms to be in writing signed by the parties. This was a security measure imported into mediations in a further effort to ensure clarity as to whether agreement has been reached and a high level of certainty as to the terms of such an outcome. Mediators will tell parties that 'no deal will be reached unwittingly or by mistake' because even a partial agreement needs written signed confirmation. So if, for instance, the parties agree to leave offers open for an agreed period of time, such an agreement, even on a matter of process, should be put in writing and signed.

This is vividly illustrated by in *Brown v Rice*[24]. An offer was left open after an otherwise inconclusive mediation until noon the following day, but this was not put in writing. Before that time the other party purported to accept the offer. While the judge found ultimately that the absence of written signed terms was conclusive, and ruled that the offer was not open for acceptance, he still admitted evidence to see whether an oral waiver or estoppel or collateral contract might have arisen, despite opposition on the part of both the other party and the mediation provider on behalf of the mediator. Counsel intervening for the mediation provider drew to the judge's attention the fact that the parties had specifically agreed there could be no binding agreement unless it was recorded in writing and signed, which had not happened. Despite this, the judge heard evidence about what would normally be regarded as 'without prejudice' material at the instance of one party and in the absence of any waiver. He did so

---

24 *Brown v Rice* [2007] EWHC 625 (Ch), [2008] FSR 61.

relying on the fact that one of the established exceptions to the 'without prejudice' rule is the admission of evidence to see if an agreement had been reached. He further argued that, despite the terms of the mediation agreement requiring signed writing, it was still possible for parties to make a binding collateral agreement orally which could be enforceable despite the requirement for written settlement terms, or to have waived or be estopped from that requirement. However, after reviewing substantial amounts of otherwise privileged evidence, he found that none of these things had happened and that, as the requirement for writing had not been satisfied, no binding agreement had been made on the facts. By that time, the damage had been done to the security of the mediation process.

Two subsequent first instance decisions[25] have raised the possibility that contractual confidentiality might of itself prevent a judge from hearing such evidence, so whether the court would decide the facts of *Brown v Rice* similarly in future is unclear. This illustrates the frustratingly piecemeal development of the law relating to mediation, mainly through first instance decisions of issues which emerge by happenstance for trial and in no controlled or logical order, and which turn out to need modification and re-interpretation in the light of later decisions.

Confidentiality and evidential privilege in relation to mediation are discussed fully in **Chapter 9** and also touched on in **Chapter 10** relating to implementation of the EU Mediation Directive. The totality of these discussions suggest firmly that this whole area needs attention from the Court of Appeal or Parliament at some time.

2.9   The status of mediated settlements

In many, if not most, mediations, the aim is to achieve an agreed suite of settlement terms enforceable in law in the event of default by any party. In effect a new contract is agreed which either replaces or modifies an earlier contract over which the initial dispute arose, or which settles a prior tortious liability, for instance agreeing compensation for an accident claim of some kind. Quite apart from the requirements for a written and signed agreement which the mediation agreement may have imposed on the parties, or which may arise if a sale of land is involved, such a contract must conform to the basic rules of the law of contract. Thus the parties must have legal capacity, the terms must be reasonably certain, there must be an intention to create legal relations, and there must be valuable consid-

---

25 Eg *Cumbria Waste Management Ltd v Baines Wilson (a firm)* [2008] EWHC 786 (QB), [2008] BLR 330 and *Farm Assist Ltd (in liquidation) v Secretary of State for the Environment, Food and Rural Affairs (No 2)* [2009] EWHC 1102 (TCC), [2009] BLR 399: see **Chapter 9** for a full discussion.

eration for the obligations which arise under the contract. Very often at a mediation the consideration will be acceptance by one party of a sum of money in consideration of the other's forbearance from initiating or continuing to pursue the original claim.

The precise way in which the agreement is formulated into a binding set of obligations depends on the stage of the dispute reached. If the mediation has taken place *before* the issue of any civil proceedings, then the settlement agreement forms a simple contract enforceable as such in the event of default. To do so would require proceedings to be issued based on the settlement agreement, and there may be reasonable prospects of securing summary judgment swiftly after issue. In the case of cross-border disputes (those which involve at least two EU member states), but not domestic or non-EU international disputes, CPR Part 78.25 sets out a procedure for recording agreed settlement terms, crisply called a Mediation Enforcement Settlement Order, with a view to swift enforcement in the event of default. This was introduced in May 2011 as a result of the EU Mediation Directive, and is discussed in detail in **Chapter 10**.

If the mediation occurs *after* the issue of proceedings, then it is necessary not only to deal with the agreed settlement terms but also with the proceedings, including provision for responsibility of the costs of those proceedings. In default of any specific agreement as to who bears the costs of a claim, no default liability arises and no one can recover their costs from another party. The normal method of dealing with these matters at one stroke is to agree a consent order named after its inventor, Tomlin J, which provides for a stay (ie suspension without dismissal) of proceedings on the agreed terms, which are usually set out in a schedule to the order and need not be made public, with the right to apply to the court only for the purpose of enforcing the settlement terms. The agreement as to costs appears on the face of the order, as the court may be involved in assessing these if agreement is not reached as to how much any paying party's costs liability should be. Thus, in the event of default, the party seeking enforcement does not have to initiate new proceedings: rather, an application can be made to the court to lift the stay and seek enforcement of the mediated settlement under the terms of the consent order in the existing compromised proceedings.

It should be noted that the court can and will enforce obligations under the settlement even if they go beyond what the court itself could have ordered in the event of a trial, so long as the terms do not infringe the overarching requirement of legality. An illustration of circumstances in which illegality was raised but which did not ultimately result in overturning the settlement is in the related cases of *Thakrar v Thakrar*[26] and *Re*

---

26 [2002] EWCA Civ 1304.

Ciro Citterio Menswear plc[27]. In a complex company action a mediation led to settlement terms which were embodied in a draft consent order staying proceedings except for any need to enforce implementation of the agreed terms (a Tomlin Order). The Court of Appeal initially held that the consent order should not be upheld, as it might compromise the position of unsecured creditors by being a fraudulent preference. In later proceedings to enforce the settlement agreement, the Vice-Chancellor decided that the settlement agreement was binding, it being unconditional and enforceable, within the power of the liquidator to agree and not in fact illegal in any way.

The settlement agreement can provide that any dispute arising from the settlement terms should itself be mediated before resorting to the courts. Such an agreement to oust the jurisdiction of the courts until an agreed resolution process has been exhausted is very similar to contracting to use mediation in the event of dispute contained in any commercial contract. Courts are very likely to enforce such a provision, for the same reasons as are discussed fully in **Chapter 8**.

If settlement agreements are contracts, then they are of course subject to the same remedies as all contracts. So if one party misrepresents a material fact to the other, who relies upon it in entering the settlement, the representee may have a remedy, subject only to being able to get evidence of it admitted. There may be problems about this if the alleged misrepresentation occurs during the mediation and is theoretically subject to the evidential privilege and contractual confidentiality created by the mediation agreement. The nature and extent of such confidentiality is discussed fully in **Chapter 9**. To avoid such a problem, if there is a material fact upon the truth of which the parties rely in agreeing settlement terms, it needs to be recited in the preamble to the settlement agreement.

Mistake, frustration and duress may also come into play. For instance, an allegation of economic duress generated during a mediation was allowed to be raised in *Farm Assist Ltd (in liquidation) v Secretary of State for Environment, Food and Rural Affairs*[28], though it was never ruled upon, as the claim was withdrawn before trial.

Not all settlement agreements are intended to create legal relations. For instance, in workplace mediations the outcome may be about how two employees treat each other in very practical terms in the workplace. Breach of an agreement to smile or greet each other every morning is not going to be enforced by a court or tribunal. Sometimes parties can only

---

27 [2002] EWHC 1975 (Ch).
28 [2008] EWHC 3079 (TCC), [2009] BLR 80 and see also *(No 2)* at [2009] EWHC 1102 (TCC): discussed fully in **Chapters 3** and **9**.

agree heads of terms by the end of a mediation day, recognising that a full agreement needs time and further consideration before being completed.

So where the parties choose clearly to bind themselves contractually to the terms that emerge at a mediation, they can do so, whether mediating before or after the issue of proceedings in ways that could lead to prompt enforcement in the event of default. In practice, mediated settlements rarely fail, probably because the parties feel they own the terms and very often accept that, even if they have had to make concessions to achieve certainty, the other parties to the dispute have similarly conceded important matters. The terms agreed can, of course, take account of much wider considerations and outcomes than a court could impose. A business relationship which has been fractured by dispute can, with consent and goodwill, be repaired, re-crafted and restored, through a shift away from the past and from outcomes decided by legal precedent to the future. Attending to present needs not available through the courts can also enhance and encourage settlement. For instance in clinical negligence and professional indemnity claims, the professional under scrutiny can deliver apologies and explanations and indications of changed practice. Even just giving a person or a company with a sense of grievance the opportunity to air concerns freely in a private environment, giving the hearer a chance to respond respectfully and appropriately, can be inherently beneficial. Sadly, such an opportunity is rarely available in a modern trial, with evidence largely given in writing. It is the combination of these associated benefits that can make a settlement negotiated at a mediation stick and confer a sense of satisfaction on parties. Trial almost always means win/lose (or possibly lose/lose). While mediation rarely delivers the fantasy of win/win, it can and often does deliver a sense of equality about the outcome, even where the parties entered a dispute with a significant power imbalance between them[29].

---

29 A vivid illustration of how one party mistakenly thought that the head of terms agreed at a mediation had produced a binding agreement can be found in *Frost v Wake and Tofields* [2013] EWCA Civ 1960.

Chapter 3
Mediators and the law

Having looked at the legal status of mediation as a process, this chapter looks at the legal status of mediators themselves, and how they fit into the England and Wales civil justice system.

3.1 The legal status of mediators

Courts in England and Wales have had few opportunities to consider the legal status of mediators, unlike other jurisdictions. But there are some important matters to consider nevertheless. A mediator is held out as being neutral and impartial, working with and between the parties engaged in trying to settle their dispute. The mediator usually contracts to observe a published Code of Conduct and to observe confidentiality of what transpires during a mediation. Are there limits to any of these self-imposed responsibilities, and what remedies exist if a mediator breaches any of them?

The proper starting-point for this discussion is to emphasise that mediators have absolutely no implied authority by virtue of their role. Their status and power is derived solely from what the parties choose to confer upon them. Nor does a mediation agreement do anything other than impose obligations and responsibilities on them: it confers no powers upon them. A mediator cannot make directions or orders, or make rulings. All has to be done by consent, trust and co-operation, and this paradoxically may be what generates the true strength of the mediator within the mediation process.

It is also important to remember that mediators are not neutrals in the same way as adjudicative neutrals such as judges and arbitrators, to whom the rules of natural justice always apply. While both mediators and adjudicative neutrals are bound to observe the rule against bias, at all times acting as neutrally as possible, judges and arbitrators must additionally ensure that each party has the opportunity to hear any evidence of significance which either party adduces to influence the outcome in order to deal with it with in the relevant process. The practical manifestation of this is that judges and arbitrators may not have separate private meetings with each party. However, mediators frequently meet parties separately and privately, undertaking not to disclose any of what is said during such meetings without the permission and authority of the party with whom they met. They are not subject to that aspect of the rules of natural justice because they are not decision-makers. This places considerable responsibility on them to act neutrally and fairly as between parties, as they cannot be under scrutiny by one party when meeting privately with another. But the opportunities that private meetings give to mediators to assist parties to make progress are an important reason for the success of the mediation process as practised in the UK.

Also, mediation is not an officially regulated profession. Providers and individual mediators hold themselves out as observing certain standards, which depend on the terms of each mediation contract and the Code of Conduct imported into it. If a mediator has been accredited by a specific provider and fails to deliver what has been promised, there will be a complaints process offered by the provider, and either a formal disciplining and even removal of accreditation, or an informal decision by that provider not to nominate that mediator again. The Civil Mediation Council[1] offers an umbrella oversight and may be prepared to intervene in the event of a complaint. If the mediator is a barrister, solicitor, surveyor, accountant or a member of another regulated profession, there may be recourse to professional discipline in the event of default. Otherwise the remedies are those of the common law – breach of contract or negligence or other tortious breach. The other available control is the market-place. Providers take feedback on mediators and are unlikely to nominate one who seriously or consistently attracts complaints. Many law firms have databases of mediators and, again, at least give themselves the freedom to break away from familiar mediators if they cease to provide the expected service. Clearly it is part of any lawyer's best practice responsibilities to each client to make sensible and informed suggestions as to who might be best to instruct as a mediator in a given dispute.

A brief comparison of the main species of neutral highlights the differences in legal status accorded to each.

Judges

High Court judges clearly possess the authority of their constitutional position by custom and statute, and are immune from action for anything done or said in their judicial capacity. County court judges possess statutory authority and probably have similar immunity from suit.

---

1 www.civilmediation.org.

Magistrates

Magistrates may have somewhat more limited immunity from suit, where in particular they are protected by legislation for acts done within their jurisdiction and also for acts outside their jurisdiction, unless shown to have acted in bad faith[2].

Arbitrators

Arbitrators possess statutory authority by virtue of the Arbitration Act 1996, and enjoy general immunity from suit (ie not limited to the parties to the arbitration) for acts and omissions except where bad faith is shown[3]. This does not affect any liability incurred by an arbitrator by reason of his resigning[4].

Adjudicators of building and allied disputes

These individuals make provisional decisions (subject to later challenge) and are appointed either by contract or by contractual terms compulsorily required in building contracts since 1 May 1998 by the Housing Grants Construction and Regeneration Act 1996[5]. The Act provides that adjudicators are not liable to anyone (not just parties) for any acts or omissions in the discharge of their functions unless shown to have acted in bad faith. They are not protected from claims by anyone who is not a party to the contract under which the adjudicator operated, and will require indemnity insurance to cover claims.

Evaluators in early neutral evaluation

They derive their authority simply from the parties. They probably have no immunity because they are never decision-makers. They produce opinions or evaluations which parties are free to accept or reject.

Experts giving a determinative view

They derive their authority from a contract between the parties, and specifically are not arbitrators subject to the Arbitration Act 1996, nor do they derive any statutory authority from it. Their authority is usually absolute in the sense that the standard contract provides that no party to the dispute may challenge their decisions. Expert determiners also depend on the terms of their appointing contract to afford them such immunity from suit

---

2 Courts Act 2003, ss 31–32.
3 Arbitration Act 1996, s 29.
4 Arbitration Act 1996, s 29(3) and see s 25.
5 Section 108(4).

as the parties are prepared to confer (usually again expressed as absolute, though it is hard to see how an expert could resist scrutiny for alleged bad faith in his decision-making).

Mediators

As already observed, the mediator's authority derives entirely from the parties, and endures only so long as all parties continue to confer it. Withdrawal by one party unilaterally ends it. The mediator has no immunity from suit and must insure against legal liability (perhaps most likely to be established by a party's claiming for breach of confidence, negligence or defamation), though there is no recorded claim against mediators in the UK, and their professional indemnity premiums remain low. It is hard to see how a claimant could prove both breach of duty and damage caused by a mediator, certainly when operating in a broadly facilitative mode. This is another good reason for mediators not to evaluate too much.

3.2   Mediator Codes of Conduct

The principal published Codes of Conduct for mediators used in England and Wales are the European Code and the CEDR Code. The latter applies to all forms of ADR provided by CEDR, whereas the European Code is specifically for mediators. The CEDR Code is set out in **Appendix 5**. In most standard mediation agreements, the mediator contracts to observe one or other of these in consideration of their fee, undoubtedly a binding contractual obligation. Provisions typical to both Codes are undertakings by the mediator to:

–   act impartially and independently, declaring any actual or possible perceived conflict of interest;

–   be competent and with proper time available to deal with a given mediation;

–   be transparent as to fees charged;

–   observe agreed procedures and give equal opportunity for the parties to participate in the process;

–   observe confidentiality (in the CEDR agreement by importing the confidentiality provisions in its Model Mediation Procedure);

–   withdraw where asked or where in breach or asked to act in breach of the Code.

Under the CEDR Code, mediators undertake additionally that they will not prolong any mediation unnecessarily; that they have taken out adequate professional indemnity insurance, and that they will co-operate with CEDR's complaints system. The Code also provides for a mediator being able to withdraw if a party acts unconscionably or illegally or if settlement looks impossible, or the mediator is accused of not acting neutrally by one party. The European Code additionally provides that the mediator will ensure informed consent to any settlement, and may (if qualified) give some guidance as to the settlement terms and how they can be made enforceable. These latter provisions are not regular features of mediations in England and Wales.

3.3   Breach of a mediator's obligations

Mediators who breach confidentiality clearly breach their contractual obligations, whether this be by wrongly disclosing what has been imparted confidentially by one party in a private meeting to another party, or by disclosing to the world outside the mediation suite details of what went on at a mediation. They may or may not be protected by an exemption clause excluding liability which falls short of fraud or wilful misconduct. The usual rules as to exemption clauses, as set out in the Unfair Contract Terms Act 1977 and allied consumer legislation, will apply, and any ambiguity in the clause will be construed against the mediator. However, even if there is a breach of contractual or tortious duty (such as making disclosure negligently), it is by no means easy for any party to prove that such a breach caused damage.

3.4   Compelling a mediator to give evidence

Mediator compellability is inextricably entangled with the concept of privilege and confidentiality. The question as to whether some kind of mediation privilege arises by operation of law, by virtue of the mediator's position in relation to information received, is controversial, and the position is not clear. Several decisions have raised the possibility of the existence of such a privilege, without stating firmly that it exists. The decision which comes closest to this is *Re D (minors)*[6], a family case in which the Court of Appeal found that statements made to a conciliator could not be introduced by a party as evidence in proceedings under the Children Act 1989, except where future harm might be threatened. Sir Thomas Bingham MR talked of the law '... recognising the general inviolability of the privilege protecting statements made in the course of conciliation', and leant towards identifying an independent head of privilege. In *Brown v Rice*[7], the judge pondered whether such a privilege might exist. In neither of these cases

---

6 [1993] Fam 231, [1993] 2 All ER 693.
7 [2007] EWHC 625 (Ch), [2008] FSR 61.

was there apparently any question of calling the mediator or conciliator. The general current view is that no such general mediation or mediator privilege currently exists so as to make a mediator immune from being called as a witness as to what happened at a mediation. However, this is one of the areas in which the EU Mediation Directive has intervened in a way limited in England and Wales to cross-border disputes. The detail of that provision, how it fits with current English law, and discussion of these related matters, is to be found in **Chapters 9** and **10**.

So in the absence of any clearly implied protection for mediators, well-drawn mediation agreements normally provide that the parties will not call the mediator or any mediation provider involved in setting up the process to give evidence as to what happened at the mediation. Although no mediator or provider has so far been called to give evidence in an English court of this kind, *Farm Assist v DEFRA (No 2)*[8] shows that in certain circumstances a judge might contemplate allowing this to happen. It is on first flush clearly undesirable for a mediator to be called as a witness for the parties' purposes. A mediator has almost certainly become the repository of confidential information and attitudes to settlement during the mediation process from each party, and to be compelled to disclose details of these in open court would frankly undermine the essence of the mediation process, as well as compromising the mediator's neutrality in the eyes of at least one and possibly all parties. *Farm Assist* suggests that this will be a rare event in any case. As Lord Wilberforce said in the House of Lords in *British Steel Corpn v Granada Television Ltd*[9], a civil case in which a television company was compelled to disclose its confidential source of information to the claimants:

> 'As to information obtained in confidence and the legal duty which may arise to disclose it to a court of justice, the position is clear. Courts have an inherent wish to respect this confidence whether it arises between doctor and patient, priest and penitent, banker and customer, between persons giving testimonials to employees, or in other relationships ... But in all these cases the courts may have to decide that the interests in preserving this confidence are outweighed by other interests to which the law attaches importance'.

The extent of the agreed immunity from evidence-giving varies in the standard mediation agreements currently in use. The term used in the Farm Assist/DEFRA mediation agreement signed in 2003 provided that:

---

8 *Farm Assist Ltd (in liquidation) v Secretary of State for the Environment, Food and Rural Affairs (No 2)* [2009] EWHC 1102 (TCC).
9 [1981] 1 All ER 417 at 455.

'none of the parties to the Mediation Agreement will call the Mediator as a witness, consultant, arbitrator or expert in any litigation or arbitration in relation to the Dispute and the Mediator will not voluntarily act in any such capacity without the written agreement of all the Parties',

(the latter qualification presumably meaning evidence in a dispute between different parties). Since 2003 (though well before the *Farm Assist* decision highlighted the need to do so) such clauses have been drafted on the basis of an absolute bar on calling the mediator. CEDR's standard clause reads:

'The Parties will not call the Mediator or any employee or consultant of CEDR Solve as a witness, nor require them to produce in evidence any records or notes relating to the Mediation, in any litigation, arbitration or other formal process arising from or in connection with the Dispute and the Mediation; nor will the Mediator nor any CEDR Solve employee or consultant act or agree to act as a witness, expert, arbitrator or consultant in any such process'.

This also extends the bar to evidence about not just the dispute but also the mediation itself, far-sightedly trumping the distinction of which Ramsey J in *Farm Assist (No 2)* availed himself by saying that the mediator there would not be giving evidence about the *dispute* but about the *mediation*. This absolute bar on a mediator being required to give evidence was the earlier position under the draft EU Mediation Directive[10], but even that provision was softened in its final form, so that the parties can agree that the mediator is called and the mediator cannot prevent it, in effect making the mediator compellable if all the parties other than the mediator agree. The EU Directive's provision specifically authorises jurisdictions in member states to set a higher standard of protection for mediators. So the question arises as to what the standard in English law actually is and, frankly, this is not clear.

In an unreported case in the Bristol County Court in 1997, *Bezant v Ushers Brewers*, District Judge Gillian Stuart Brown refused to hear evidence from a mediator who had been subpoenaed to give evidence about what had happened at a mediation; and upheld the binding force of the agreement negotiated at the mediation. Several other attempts have been made to call mediators as witnesses, but none has succeeded so far. In *Brown v Rice*[11], it appears that a District Judge summoned the mediator to attend to give evidence, but it was conceded at trial by both sides, and not chal-

---

10 This topic and the change in wording is discussed more fully in **3.3**.
11 [2007] EWHC 625 (Ch).

lenged by the judge, that the mediator should not (and possibly could not) be called as a witness.

Returning to *Farm Assist v DEFRA (No 2)*, this was a decision which pre-dated the implementation of the EU Mediation Directive by CPR 78.24 and which in any event was not a cross-border dispute, to which those provisions would have applied. DEFRA issued a witness summons to call the mediator to give evidence (presumably) to support their case that no economic duress had been applied to Farm Assist at the mediation which had settled Farm Assist's claim for payment in respect of their disposal services work during a foot-and-mouth disease epidemic. Ramsey J found that the mediator could rely on the agreed contractual confidentiality created by the mediation agreement even in the face of willingness by the parties to have her evidence admitted. However, the judge also found that he could overrule even that objection by the mediator if it was 'in the interests of justice' to do so. Herein lies the inconsistency between what appears to be English law and what the EU Mediation Directive requires as a minimum standard relating to the compellability of mediators as witness to what happened at a mediation, albeit only in force in England so far in respect of cross-border disputes. The default position under the Directive is that mediators and providers should not be called to give evidence about a mediation, but both or all parties can overrule this if unanimously agreed to the calling of the mediator. If there is no such unanimity between the parties on this, the mediator may still be called:

–   where this is necessary for overriding considerations of public policy of the member state concerned, in particular when required to ensure the protection of the best interests of children or to prevent harm to the physical or psychological integrity of a person; or

–   where disclosure of the content of the agreement resulting from the mediation is necessary in order to implement or enforce that agreement.

There is a world of difference between 'overriding considerations of public policy' of the type envisaged by the Directive and 'the interests of justice' utilised by Ramsey J to justify allowing the witness summons against the mediator to stand. Pending a decision as to whether the EU provisions should apply to English domestic law and procedure, ordinary domestic mediations must work on (or seek to challenge) the ruling in *Farm Assist*. Court of Appeal guidance on this issue will be welcome. The *Farm Assist* decision is considered further when dealing with confidentiality and also the EU Mediation Directive in **Chapters 9** and **10**.

The exemption set out in mediation agreements from being called as a witness is merely contractual. It is not at present reinforced by any statutory provision or rule of court in relation to domestic mediations, and only modified very slightly by CPR Part 78 in respect of cross-border disputes. The CPR give the judge the right to exclude evidence, and it would be a robust judge with understanding of the requirements of the mediation process who would regard it as appropriate for a mediator to give evidence merely as a tie-breaker between the parties. If there were an allegation of mediator wrong-doing, however, a judge might feel that the need to investigate the allegation outweighed the need to protect the mediation process. Clarity is still required about this, and even the limited final provisions of the EU Mediation Directive call for protective legislation to establish the parameters of protection for mediators in circumstances which will undoubtedly undermine their neutrality in the eyes of one party to whom the mediator has undertaken to act neutrally.

An illustration of what might give rise to difficulty arose in the case of *Nicholson v Knox Ukiwa & Co (a firm)*[12], where a claimant sued his third set of solicitors for negligently allowing him to settle at an undervalue in a mediation. Both the claimant and his solicitors wanted the judge to hear what happened at the mediation to prove their separate cases on the facts. Insofar as the original mediation agreement went, they were both on the same side, so would have needed agreement from the other party to the mediation agreement to waive privilege (which was obtained). They would also probably want the mediator to give tie-breaking evidence, though from the report it seems as if this did not happen. But it is easily seen that pressure might build up for a mediator to be called in these circumstances.

Alleged perception of economic duress by one party was accepted as the basis for the court allowing the mediator to be called in *Farm Assist v DEFRA (No 2)*. It will be of concern if mediator compellability might be open to challenge simply on the basis of a doubtful allegation of duress, fraud, misrepresentation or similar behaviour, especially if the decision is made on the strength of a mere assertion, rather than after testing out whether there is any reasonable prospect of success in such an argument. This raises the question as to the type of forum in which such issues should be tried – perhaps an initial confidential hearing with the outcome reported later. Such a confidential hearing was used in *Re D* to assess the merits of the evidence of the counsellor before it was openly admitted.

Can judges instigate the calling of a mediator to give evidence on their own initiative, even if the parties choose not to do so? It would seem that

---

12 [2008] EWHC 2430 (QB), [2007] All ER (D) 456 (Jul).

no such power exists in CPR Part 32, so long as the words of that Part are read restrictively:

> '32.1 (1) The court may control the evidence by giving directions as to—
>
> (a) the issues on which it requires evidence;
>
> (b) the nature of the evidence which it requires to decide those issues; and
>
> (c) the way in which the evidence is to be placed before the court.
>
> (2) The court may use its power under this rule to exclude evidence that would otherwise be admissible.
>
> (3) The court may limit cross-examination'.

Despite the changes wrought by the CPR, evidence still appears to respond to the adversarial nature of litigation, and trial judges have no inquisitorial rights over evidence, despite the possible ambiguity of CPR 32.1(1)(a) and (b). Again, perhaps it would be wise to remove any such doubt. This is one area where even the mild provisions of the EU Mediation Directive required legislation, and it would seem sensible to give statutory weight to something which is otherwise merely the subject of a private contract, and which might be subverted in effect by a determined party motivated to try calling a mediator as a witness. In *Farm Assist v DEFRA (No 2)*, the judge did not seek of his own initiative to call the mediator; DEFRA sought it by issuing the witness summons, and the judge effectively decided that the mediator should be called by declining to strike it out.

It is unlikely that there will be any great desire among mediators to alter their status as to liability. Their very absence of authority empowers them in a way that makes it difficult for judges in office to mediate in anything like the same way. Because suing a mediator is rare and difficult, modifying immunity from suit is probably unnecessary. But compellability remains a significant issue.

3.5 Mediator compellability by external legal authority

There are a number of circumstances in which a mediator might be compelled by law or feel compelled by moral considerations to break confidentiality. In the unlikely event that a party disclosed to a mediator information or intentions which might lead to injury or death of others or to the future commission of a crime, then most Codes of Conduct and mediation agreements relieve the mediator of their normal obligations to keep confidential what they are told. Standard agreements often provide specifically that the duty of confidentiality may be removed if:

- the mediator is required under the general law to make disclosure;

- the mediator reasonably considers that there is a serious impending risk of significant harm to the life or safety of any person if the information relating to that risk is not disclosed;

- the mediator reasonably considers that there is a serious risk of being made personally subject to criminal proceedings unless the information sought is disclosed.

A number of official investigators have considerable powers under the 'general law' to compel co-operation besides the police: HM Revenue and Customs; the Security Services; liquidators; administrators and trustees in bankruptcy under the Insolvency Act 1986 and related legislation.

There is also the whole question of possible disclosure required by the Proceeds of Crime Act 2002 (POCA 2002), and allied provisions under the anti-terrorism and drug trafficking legislation. The main risk under POCA 2002 relates to the offence under s 328 of 'arranging' (entering into or becoming concerned in an arrangement), or aiding, abetting, counselling or procuring such an arrangement, which the mediator knows or suspects facilitates the acquisition, retention, use or control of criminal property by or on behalf of another person. 'Criminal property' is defined widely as proceeds or benefits, whether direct or indirect, of any conduct which constitutes a criminal offence in the UK. It will include tax evasion, benefits obtained through an illegal cartel, bribes paid and even saved costs from failing to comply with a regulatory requirement, failure to observe which is a criminal offence.

It is probably easy to avoid acquiring actual knowledge as a mediator, but suspicion is a subjective and somewhat slippery concept. A mediator must consider all factors in deciding how to secure protection in the circumstances of any given case. To defend a charge of arranging, the mediator must make an authorised disclosure to the National Criminal Intelligence Service (or any successor organisation), who have seven days within which to confirm that a transaction is untainted and may proceed. This is hardly of much practical use in a mediation. At the same time, the mediator must not 'tip off' a suspected party, or an offence may be committed under POCA 2002, s 333. The mediator may thus have to adjourn the mediation without explanation so as to fulfil the duties imposed by the legislation.

Some guidance, but no apparent general protection for mediators as such, emerged from the Court of Appeal in *Bowman v Fels*[13], where a solicitor acquired information in the course of litigation which he felt suggested that criminal conduct over VAT avoidance might be involved. The court held that such disclosure of information during litigation was not intended to be covered by POCA 2002. The proper interpretation of s 328 was that it was not intended to cover or affect the ordinary conduct of litigation by legal professionals. That included any step taken by them in litigation from the issue of proceedings and the securing of injunctive relief or a freezing order up to its final disposal by judgment and included agreement to dispose of the whole or any aspect of legal proceedings on a consensual basis. The originating EU Directive and POCA 2002 did not envisage that any of those ordinary activities fell within the concept of 'becoming concerned in an arrangement which … facilitates the acquisition, retention, use or control of criminal property'. The court disapproved the decision to the contrary by Dame Elizabeth Butler-Sloss in *P v P (ancillary relief: proceeds of crime)*[14]. They went on to say that even if s 328 did apply to the ordinary conduct of legal proceedings, it did not override legal professional privilege or a solicitor's implied duty to the court not to disclose information gained from documents disclosed by another party to adversarial litigation and not read in open court.

Whether this decision affords any protection to a mediator is open to doubt. Perhaps the only comfort to mediators, whether they are solicitors themselves or not, is that there will almost certainly be someone else under precisely the same duty of disclosure in a mediation as they are themselves. This is a topic which can only be dealt with superficially here, and in view of its huge importance to mediators in terms of potentially disastrous outcomes, they must be advised to acquaint themselves with their responsibilities under this legislation and ensure that they err on the side of caution in discharging them. Very useful guidance on this topic has been issued by the Civil Mediation Council in a paper entitled *Guidance on the obligations of mediators under the Proceeds of Crime Act 2002*[15], issued in June 2010. Even if a mediator feels up to asking an awkward question on such matters, they might be well advised not to insist on hearing the answer.

---

13 [2005] EWCA Civ 226, [2005] 4 All ER 609.
14 [2003] EWHC 2260 (Fam), [2004] Fam 1.
15 Guidance Note No 2 on the Civil Mediation Council website www.civilmediation.org in the Reference section.

3.6 Mediator immunity in the US and Australia

The US Uniform Mediation Act, an advisory model mediation statute adopted by a number, though not all, of US States, which draws upon wide sources of practical and academic thought, confers absolute protection on a mediator from disclosing information given to the mediator by a party, while not giving mediators any power to restrict disclosure by parties. Further, there are restrictions on mediators: they are not allowed to give evidence in proceedings brought to set aside a settlement or to allege misconduct by a party. They can be compelled to give evidence in proceedings alleging misconduct by the mediator or where there is risk to life or limb or a threat of danger to children.

In Australia, as to the compellability of mediators, Australian courts have apparently been much readier to admit evidence from mediators than has so far happened in the UK, and in some cases considerable weight has been placed on the evidence of the mediator.

As to liability of mediators and its converse, immunity from suit, Australia is the home of the leading case of *Tapoohi v Leuwenberg*[16], decision of the Victoria Supreme Court, which opened a theoretical door to suing a mediator who over-evaluates the outcome and thereby causes loss. The decision is only on a preliminary point of law, so that all facts were assumed adversely to the mediator, whose counsel made it clear that his eminent client contested many of the factual allegations strongly. However, where the mediator had (allegedly on each point) insisted on a written settlement without allowing time for tax advice to be obtained, and proposed a share valuation figure which turned out to create a capital gains tax liability, it was held that liability in negligence could *theoretically* arise. No contractual, common law or statutory immunity was found to exist to protect the mediator. The case was settled on an undisclosed basis, coincident, it is said, with a sharp rise in mediators' indemnity policy premiums.

There are statutory immunities in Australia for mediators in certain types of process. Again, mediation compulsion may have affected this. In some cases the immunity is equivalent to a judge (see above as to Western Australia), in others to a magistrate, and in yet others qualified by a requirement for having acted in good faith. In the New Zealand decision of *McCosh v Williams*[17], the mediator was given power under a mediated settlement agreement to make decisions about implementation. He was asked to make decisions which amounted to rectification of the contract, to which one party objected. That dispute was settled, but the mediator was then sued for exceeding his role negligently. He sought to defend

---

16 [2003] VSC 210.
17 [2003] NZCA 192.

the claim by an exclusion clause which purported to exclude liability even for negligence. The Court of Appeal held that he had not been negligent, although they did find that he had indeed exceeded his brief. The difficulty of proving attributable loss was also pointed out.

Issues arise from cultural differences in approach between mediators in the UK and in Australia. As in the US, Australian mediators are often called upon to operate at the evaluative end of the facilitative/evaluative spectrum. On the whole (though there is not much objective evidence to substantiate this one way or the other) the impression given in the UK is that mediators tend to be less evaluative. If litigation is all about seeking to shift the consequences of decision-making onto another, then so long as well-insured professionals with skill and experience in a certain sector are used as evaluative mediators, such a tendency to hire mediators with evaluative authority will continue. Mediators with no underlying professional indemnity cover from their first profession to act as evaluative mediators need to be very careful as to how far they can go.

Chapter 4

Mediation and the Civil Procedure Rules 1998

This chapter discusses the impact of the CPR as amended, particularly in 2013, on civil justice and on settlement in general and specifically on the relationship between the CPR and the parallel development of mediation.

4.1 The path to the CPR

The number of lawyers in England and Wales with experience of practice before the CPR, which came into effect on 26 April 1999, is rapidly decreasing, though maybe a higher proportion of judges of middle and senior rank practised then. Few newly-qualified lawyers will have troubled to read the seminal reports compiled by Lord Woolf in the mid-1990s which led to the CPR or appreciated the reasons why it was then felt that the procedural regime under the Rules of the Supreme Court 1965 and the County Court Rules 1981 needed reform. So a rapidly diminishing number of practising lawyers will recall the old highly adversarial litigation culture which was said to have been the spur for reform. They may even perceive the current system to be unduly adversarial. Viewed in retrospect, the Woolf reforms have not escaped criticism, especially as to their having done little to save costs. Indeed, the commissioning of the report on costs reform by Jackson LJ in 2009 was predicated on the fact that there are still serious problems over the cost of litigation, albeit seen by him to be derived from the vagaries of litigation funding as much as, if not more than, simply from the CPR.

This fading of collective memory makes a brief survey of the historical journey into the CPR useful. Lord Woolf's historic interim and final *Access to Justice* reports of 1995 and 1996[1] identified expense, slowness and complexity as the problems still besetting the civil justice system, despite numerous previous proposals for reform. He took the view that the basic principles that should underpin an accessible civil justice system were that it should be:

---

1 *Access to Justice:* Interim and Final Reports by Lord Woolf to the Lord Chancellor published then by the Department for Constitutional Affairs (now the Ministry of Justice).

- **just** in the results delivered;
- **fair** and seen to be so, by ensuring equal opportunity to assert or defend rights, giving adequate opportunity for each to state or answer a case, and treating like cases alike;
- **proportionate,** in relation to the issues involved, in both procedure and cost;
- **speedy** so far as reasonable;
- **understandable** to users;
- **responsive** to the needs of users;
- **certain** in outcome as far as possible;
- **effective** through adequate resources and organisation.

His aim was to change the whole approach to civil litigation from a wasteful adversarial mind-set to one of co-operative problem-solving by encouraging settlement rather than trial of disputes.

Encouraging the development of ADR was one of the ways in which Lord Woolf felt these aims could be achieved. In Chapter 18 of his 1995 Interim Report, he decided not to recommend that ADR should be compulsory, resisting the urge to import US approaches into the courts wholesale, noting that there were appreciable practical differences between each jurisdiction, such as jury trial of civil actions and easily accessed appeals. Treating arbitration, mediation and the work of ombudsmen as the primary forms of ADR process then, he advocated court encouragement of the use of ADR rather than developing court-annexed schemes. He was also clear that, in deciding 'on the future conduct of a case' (ie in considering case management directions), a judge should be able to take into account a litigant's unreasonable *refusal to attempt* ADR. He placed initial reliance on case management which incorporated encouragement and facilitation of ADR rather than contemplating retrospective costs sanctions for past unreasonable litigation conduct, upon which he said he would consult further.

However, in his Final Report of 1996, he recommended[2] that courts *should* take into account unreasonable refusal of a court's proposal that ADR should be attempted when considering costs orders. He even suggested sanctioning unreasonable behaviour *in the course of* ADR. Whether he meant in terms of co-operating with involvement in setting up or continuing the process or actually by adopting unreasonable attitudes on the merits within the process is not explained. If the latter, fortunately this

---

2 Final Report recommendations 40 (interim report recommendation 71) and 41.

proposal was not implemented, as it could have threatened the confidentiality of the mediation process that underpins its usefulness and success. By that time too he was expressing less certainty about not providing for compulsory referral to ADR. The debate which he initiated on these two topics continues. He also specifically recommended that ADR should be kept in mind at all stages of clinical negligence claims; that the topic of ADR should be considered as a matter of course at case management conferences; and that the courts and the Lord Chancellor's Department (as it then was) should raise the profile of ADR.

The new approach to litigation advocated by Lord Woolf, with its profound implications for the whole of the civil justice system, had actually started to emerge just before the *Access to Justice* interim report was published. In a January 1995 Practice Direction issued by the Lord Chief Justice and the Vice-Chancellor, introducing what was said to be the first of a wide range of procedural reforms and improvements, Lord Bingham LCJ said:

> 'the aim is to try and change the whole culture, the ethos applying to the field of civil litigation'.

As part of this change, the courts in England and Wales had begun to devise an express duty on lawyers to consider using ADR. A consistent source of encouragement since the early 1990s was the Commercial Court, which issued its *Practice Note: Commercial Court; Alternative Dispute Resolution* in 1994[3], requiring lawyers to bring ADR to their client's attention. That Practice Note required legal advisers in all cases to:

> '(a) consider with their clients and the other parties concerned the possibility of attempting to resolve the particular dispute or particular issues by mediation, conciliation or otherwise; and
>
> (b) ensure that parties are fully informed as to the most cost-effective means of resolving the particular dispute'.

Whilst this stopped short of making engagement in 'mediation or conciliation' (two concepts which remain legally indistinguishable in English practice) a mandatory step in the court process, it did make it virtually mandatory for lawyers to *consider* ADR with both client and other parties. The Commercial Court's subsequent track record shows that parties have taken this judicial encouragement very seriously, making the Commercial Court the forum in which gentle but firm judicial persuasion to try ADR has operated most effectively. From the start, its judges have required a

---

3 [1994] 1 All ER 34.

high level of understanding among commercial practitioners about ADR and its practical application to commercial cases. Take-up in this sector has consequently grown, as satisfaction levels too have increased with experience. The judges have developed various types of order as their contribution to this area. These are discussed in more detail in **Chapter 5**.

The Commercial Court's approach was subsumed in general terms across the High Court by the 1995 *Practice Note (Civil Litigation: Case Management)*[4] issued by the Lord Chief Justice and Vice-Chancellor (touched upon above), introducing a case management role for judges in all civil cases for the first time. A slightly different approach was adopted. Legal advisers conducting cases were required to lodge a checklist at least two months before trial. This included questions as to whether the advisers had discussed the possibility of using ADR, both with their client and with the other side, and whether they considered that some form of ADR might assist in resolving or narrowing the issues.

In response to Lord Woolf's particular concerns in his Interim Report about clinical negligence claims, *Queen's Bench Practice Direction 49* was issued on 16 November 1996, dealing with cases in the specialist Clinical Negligence list in the Queen's Bench Division. This required the parties to state at the first summons for directions:

> 'whether ADR has been considered and if not why not and if ADR has been rejected why this is so'.

This lacked the specific requirement for mutuality of approach characterised by the Commercial Court. The ADR enquiry by the court was arguably a little too early in the process of exchange of expert opinions. ADR was not made mandatory.

There can be no doubt that what has followed, culminating in the CPR and the Access to Justice Act 1999, has radically and irrevocably changed the face of civil litigation and the culture in which it operates. As a result, ADR has been brought firmly into the mainstream of dispute resolution in England and Wales, and has become a significant topic for debate in the Court of Appeal, as the rest of this book shows. There are signs of parallel reform in the closely related jurisdictions of Scotland, Northern Ireland and the Irish Republic, especially the last of these. The EU Mediation Directive has consolidated the position of mediation as a proper component of European civil justice systems, even if its implementation in the UK has been minimalist, as becomes clear in **Chapter 10**.

---

4 [1995] 1 All ER 385.

4.2 The Civil Procedure Rules 1998 (the CPR)

The CPR came into effect on 26 April 1999. They represented the most extensive overhaul of the civil justice system since the Judicature Acts 1873–75, and embodied throughout the aspirations for change articulated by Lord Woolf (then Master of the Rolls and later Lord Chief Justice) and Lord Bingham (then Lord Chief Justice).

The significance of the CPR goes far beyond a mere rationalisation of High Court and county court procedure into one coherent and reasonably readable set of procedural rules for most types of claim, convenient though this may have been. It has been the change of culture in litigation to a higher level of inter-party co-operation, as clearly demanded and intended by Lord Woolf, that the CPR were designed to deliver and which has been substantially achieved. Such a change was and remains entirely congruent with the culture in which ADR can flourish. Co-operative problem-solving was welcomed, and arid confrontation, ambush, procedural warfare and aggressive positioning all face the risk of being penalised by costs sanctions. It is perhaps this fundamental culture change that is the greatest surprise and the greatest achievement of the Woolf civil justice reforms. The results of the revolution in relation to costs and funding remain less clearly positive.

An illustration of how a relatively simple recommendation proposed by Lord Woolf dramatically altered the face of civil practice emerges from the impact made by a Practice Direction shortly before the CPR came into force, which required that judges should assess costs summarily for any hearing lasting no more than a day, and order that they be paid forthwith, rather than being lost in the normal cost adjustments that used to be made when a case settled or was tried. Lawyers were obliged to inform their clients of any adverse costs award of this kind. At a stroke the huge numbers of tactical interlocutory applications which were the normal diet of High Court Masters and District Judges vanished.

The following sections set out some of the specific ways in which the CPR have sought to achieve this culture change, commenting on the inter-relationship between the CPR and mediation.

4.3 The overriding objective and active case management

For the first time in this (and maybe in any) jurisdiction[5], the court set itself an overriding objective, to be found at the very head of the CPR in

---

5 Rather amusingly, the comparable provision in Hong Kong, introduced some years after the Woolf reforms but influenced by them, has been called 'the *underlying* objective'.

Part 1. It is intended as a guide for all court users – lawyers, judges and the public as a whole – as to the essential purpose of the civil litigation process, against which to test any issue or procedural decision or direction that may arise. The overriding objective has remained an important reference-point since its introduction, especially in relation to the place of ADR within the new order introduced by the CPR, though judicial reference to it has perhaps been relatively infrequent. The overriding objective as defined in 1999 remained unchanged until the amendments to the CPR consequent upon the Jackson reforms introduced in April 2013. Its headline provision is as follows, with the 2013 amendments in bold type:

'CPR 1.1 (1) These Rules are a new procedural code with the overriding objective of enabling the court to deal with cases justly **and at proportionate cost.**

(2) Dealing with a case justly **and at proportionate cost** includes, so far as practicable:

(a) ensuring that the parties are on an equal footing;

(b) saving expense;

(c) dealing with cases in ways which are proportionate to the amount of money involved, the importance of the case, the complexity of the issues and to the parties' financial position;

(d) ensuring that it is dealt with expeditiously and fairly;

(e) allotting to it an appropriate share of the court's resources;

(f) **enforcing compliance with rules, practice directions and orders'.**

It can be seen that proportionality to what was at stake, complexity and affordability for parties was only one of a number of defined features of handling a case 'justly' until 2013. But at that point the Civil Procedure Rules Committee (not based on any specific recommendation from the Jackson report as to CPR Part 1) added the words 'and at proportionate cost' to the overall objective, promoting the concept of proportionality to equality with whatever 'dealing ... justly' might otherwise mean. Proportionality receives further attention and amendment in CPR 44.3 as amended in 2013, which requires, when assessing costs to be paid between parties, a reasonable relationship between the sums in issue, the value of non-monetary relief, complexity, reputation and wasted work generated by the party liable to pay costs at the conclusion of the litigation.

Besides proportionality, the list of illustrations as to what this now double objective means include attention to equality of arms, economy of cost and of demands on limited court resources, speed and fairness. To this list is now added an extra element as a result of the 2013 amendments, namely a warning that enforcement of compliance with the court's rules, directions and orders is promoted in importance, giving a distinctively disciplinary flavour to the CPR. This lurked beneath the surface of its 1999 unamended version but it perhaps did not emerge with the same rigour as the 2013 amendments seem to threaten. Whether this rigour will apply to judicial requirements as to observing ADR Orders and other obligations to consider settlement and mediation, for instance in the Pre-action Protocols, is yet to emerge.

Further emphasis on the tougher disciplinary approach to non-compliance recommended by Sir Rupert Jackson and accepted into the CPR is found at the new CPR Part 3.9(1), which now provides (as from April 2013) that when a party seeks relief from a court-imposed sanction, the court will consider all the circumstances of the case to enable it to deal justly with the application, including the need for litigation to be conducted efficiently and at proportionate cost, and to enforce compliance with rules, practice directions and orders. There is some concern among human rights lawyers that striking out a claim or defence may breach a litigant's Article 6 rights to a fair trial under the European Convention on Human Rights[6]. Striking out for want of prosecution disappeared as a procedure frequently used by defendants in stale claims as a result of the CPR, largely for this reason, and reversion to vigorous striking out may give rise to controversy. This is undoubtedly an area to watch.

The court is placed under an obligation to further the overriding objective by actively managing cases, a phrase defined in CPR 1.4(2) and which has remained unamended to date. Illustrations of active case management are then are set out below, with some key phrases italicised for emphasis in relation to mediation:

'CPR 1.4(2)

(a) encouraging the parties to *co-operate* with each other in the conduct of the proceedings[7];

(b) identifying the issues at an early stage;

(c) deciding promptly which issues need full investigation and trial and accordingly disposing summarily of the others;

(d) deciding the order in which issues are to be resolved;

---

6 See Shirley Shipman: *Compulsory mediation: the elephant in the room* 30(2) CJQ 163.

7 Tellingly, this was a new illustration which headed the list in the final version of the CPR but which did not appear in the first draft.

(e) *encouraging the parties to use an alternative dispute resolution procedure if the court considers that to be appropriate and facilitating the use of such procedure;*

(f) *helping the parties to settle the whole or part of a case;*

(g) fixing timetables or otherwise controlling the progress of the case;

(h) considering whether the likely benefits of taking a particular step will justify the cost of taking it;

(i) dealing with as many aspects of the case as it can on the same occasion;

(j) dealing with the case without the parties needing to attend court;

(k) making appropriate use of technology; and

(l) giving directions to ensure that the trial of a case proceeds quickly and efficiently'.

Part of the change in culture produced by CPR Part 1 was achieved simply by transferring control over the pace and conduct of litigation from the legal profession to judicial case management, as recommended by Lord Woolf. There was much professional and academic[8] scepticism about the effectiveness of doing this, much of which remains. Certainly, the illustrations of active case management set out above and in CPR 1.4(2) generate a picture of a co-operative partnership between legal profession and judiciary in pushing litigation through efficiently and to the benefit of litigants. The fact that a need for greater discipline seems to pervade the 2013 amendments suggests that the rule-makers perceive a need to change the balance, with a major risk of mixed attitudinal messages underpinning the CPR. Paradoxically, it is a short step from mixing these two discordant activities to imposing sanctions on one party or even both parties for not trying mediation under some duty to do so, or for ignoring a court's recommendation to try it, as embodied in an ADR Order.

It is a highly significant demonstration of the culture change which the Woolf reforms aimed to achieve that the delineation of active case management in CPR 1.4(2) set out above is fully congruent with the aims and objectives of ADR. Indeed, the case management obligations laid on the court might themselves (with minor modifications) describe what a mediator seeks to do. The specific mention of ADR at para 1.4(2)(e) was the first official recognition of ADR in the court rules in England and Wales, and is perhaps the best indication of its arrival in the mainstream of civil

---

8 For instance as articulated by Professor Michael Zander in a number of articles in New Law Journal in 1999 and 2009 (10 years on).

justice. Commenting retrospectively in 2005 on mediation's place in civil justice in the appeal case of *Burchell v Bullard*[9], Ward LJ spoke of:

> 'not only the high rate of a successful outcome being achieved by mediation but also its importance as a track to a just result running parallel with that of the court system. Both have a proper part to play in the administration of justice. The court has given its stamp of approval to mediation and it is now the legal profession which must become fully aware of and acknowledge its value'.

The CPR have been amended more than 60 times since they were implemented in 1999, with many amendments and additions contained in each edition. The most fundamental changes have been made by the Civil Procedure (Amendment) Rules 2013[10], through which the reforms proposed by Jackson LJ were introduced. It is hard to say how much positive impact the overriding objective still has on the conduct of civil litigation after the passage of time. It remains there as a beacon, and has certainly been referred to by judges in decisions, But whether the judiciary or legal professionals regard it as directly modifying what directions they make or how they conduct cases on a regular basis is perhaps open to question.

4.4 Pre-action conduct and the protocols

The CPR introduced three other related concepts which have revolutionised thinking and practice over strategy, timing and tactics among litigators.

Pre-action conduct

Under CPR 44.5, when determining what costs orders to make in any case, the court became entitled to take into account the reasonableness of *pre-action* conduct as well as what it has always examined, namely post-issue conduct of each party. This most fundamental change enshrined in the CPR was prefigured by Lord Woolf's remark in Chapter 7 of his *Final Report*, where he said that his recommendations were intended, among other objectives, to:

> 'make the court's powers to make orders for costs a more effective incentive for responsible behaviour and a more compelling deterrent against unreasonable behaviour'.

---

9 [2005] EWCA Civ 358 at para 43.
10 SI 2013/262.

If proceedings are, in a court's opinion, unjustifiably or prematurely issued, or oppressively or aggressively conducted, or based on exaggerated claims, even an apparently 'successful' party may be penalised in costs. Until the CPR, judges were extremely reluctant to penalise perceived pre-action misconduct, or indeed post-action 'misconduct' by a party who broadly won the litigation. Judicial assessment of how parties behaved prior to issue of proceedings was both permitted and encouraged by the CPR, with the further novel tool of Pre-action Protocols to define and measure the reasonableness of pre-issue conduct. This principle remains untouched by the 2013 amendments to the CPR.

The Pre-action Protocols

The CPR append Pre-action Protocols which give guidance as to what best practice is before proceedings are issued. The protocols, initially drafted by sector practitioners rather than either the executive or judiciary, in effect define in broad terms what constitutes reasonable pre-action conduct, providing a yardstick against which the judge can later, if necessary, assess the reasonableness of a party's approach to pre-action behaviour. The first set to be published covered the specialist sectors of personal injury and clinical negligence, and have been followed by protocols relating to construction and engineering, defamation, professional negligence, judicial review, disease and illness, housing disrepair and possession actions over rent arrears. Later protocols deal with low-value personal injury claims (the so-called RTA portal procedure) and dilapidations claims. Until 2006, each took a slightly different approach to pre-action disclosure of positions and evidence, and also to pre-action negotiation. Then a further Practice Direction to the protocols made it clear that actions of all kinds should be conducted in the spirit which informs these protocols and, since April 2009, have provided that the letter of claim should:

> 'state (if this is so) that the claimant wishes to enter into mediation or another alternative method of dispute resolution, and draw attention to the court's powers to impose sanctions for failure to comply with this practice direction',

with a reciprocal requirement required in the letter of response.

The 41st amendment to the CPR introduced a standardised approach to ADR for each of the protocols and their Practice Direction, largely (it is believed) at the initiative of the judiciary. All of them now embody a common requirement:

> 'The parties should consider whether some form of alternative dispute resolution procedure would be more suitable than litiga-

tion, and if so, endeavour to agree which form to adopt. Both the Claimant and Defendant may be required by the Court to provide evidence that alternative means of resolving their dispute were considered. The Courts take the view that litigation should be a last resort, and that claims should not be issued prematurely when a settlement is still being actively explored. Parties are warned that if the protocol is not followed (including this paragraph) then the Court must have regard to such conduct when determining costs'.

Each protocol goes on to summarise methods appropriate for each sector which might be adopted. Common to each sector are the following:

– discussion and negotiation;
– early neutral evaluation by an independent third party;
– mediation – a form of facilitated negotiation assisted by an independent neutral party.

Each protocol and the former Practice Direction (but not the Practice Direction: Pre-action Conduct mentioned below which replaced it) concludes with the statement, still oddly printed in italics:

'It is expressly recognised that no party can or should be forced to mediate or enter into any form of ADR'.

This bald statement is perhaps not quite as clear or as absolute as it might seem to be, and may yet be both a source of controversy and subject to amendment (see **Chapters 5, 6** and **7**).

The *Practice Direction: Pre-action Conduct* was issued in April 2009, confirming the court's expectations that parties should observe any relevant protocol, and warning that possible penalties can include stay of proceedings and costs and interest sanctions. There is a reminder applicable to all cases, whether governed by a protocol or not, that issue of proceedings should be a last resort. It says:

'although ADR is not compulsory, the parties should consider whether some form of ADR procedure might enable them to settle the matter without starting proceedings',

warning that the court may enquire as to whether this has been done.

Again it lists options (in a slightly different order, promoting mediation somewhat) as being:

- discussion and negotiation;
- mediation;
- early neutral evaluation;
- arbitration,

and emphasises that giving consideration to settlement is a continuing duty once proceedings are issued, and up to and during trial. As noted above, though, the express proviso that no party can be forced to mediate or enter ADR is not repeated.

Sir Rupert Jackson reported that a number of consultees in sectors not covered by the existing list of Pre-action Protocols objected to the terms of the *Practice Direction: Pre-action Conduct*, persuading him that this should be abrogated. This formed one of the recommendations in his report, but so far nothing has been implemented, nor have any amendments to the existing protocols been promulgated, though changes have been discussed by a variety of interest groups.

Pre-action offers to settle

Formal offers to settle, which can deal with both monetary and non-monetary proposals, can now be made before issue of proceedings by any party which, if not accepted, can have adverse costs and interest consequences for the offeree. The details are more fully set out in **4.9**, which deals with Part 36 offers. So-called *Calderbank* offers[11] and other offers specifically not made within the Part 36 regime (mostly so as to avoid the normal costs consequences of making a Part 36 offer) are also capable of consideration by the court[12]. Pre-action offers to mediate may also, if ignored, give rise to costs sanctions against a refusing party[13].

For the reasons set out in the three previous sub-sections, there has since 1999 been appreciable pressure placed on parties to consider settlement through ADR or otherwise before proceedings are issued. The pressure derives from the aims of the protocols, which (as the April 2009 *Practice Direction: Pre-action Conduct*[14] sets out) are:

'1.1   The aims of this Practice Direction are to:

---

11 Derived from the important family case of *Calderbank v Calderbank* [1975] 3 All ER 333.
12 *Trustees of Stokes Pension Fund v Western Power Distribution (South West) plc* [2005] EWCA Civ 854, [2005] 3 All ER 775.
13 *Burchell v Bullard* [2005] EWCA Civ 358.
14 At the head of Section 1.

(1) to enable parties to settle the issue between them without the need to start court proceedings (that is, a court claim); and

(2) support the efficient management by the court and the parties of proceedings that cannot be avoided.

1.2 These aims are to be achieved by encouraging the parties to:

(1) exchange information about the issue; and

(2) consider using a form of Alternative Dispute Resolution'.

They are intended to generate sufficient exchange of information before issue to improve the chances of settlement without the need for proceedings, and thus to maximise costs savings. However, compliance is seen inevitably to lead to the 'front-loading' of work and thus additional costs. While it is true that the number of issued cases has reduced markedly since the CPR came into effect[15], costs overall seem not to have reduced much (if at all), and this may be one period in the life of disputes where the cost-saving dividend from front-loading still remains to be secured.

In fact there is little evidence of enforcement of protocol obligations by any court once proceedings have been started, in particular as regards duty to consider and deploy mediation or ADR. In *Paul Thomas Construction Ltd v Hyland*[16], the court punished premature and unnecessarily aggressive issue of proceedings by ordering the claimant to lay indemnity costs. However, in *Straker v Tudor Rose (a firm)*[17], a claim against solicitors, the trial judge awarded the claimant damages of more than a pre-trial Part 36 offer, but awarded costs only up to that pre-trial date and made no order as to costs thereafter. He appears to have felt that the defendants did not engage in pre-action negotiations adequately and had not observed the protocol. The Court of Appeal found this to be too severe a sanction because broadly the claimant had won, though they only gave him 60% of his costs. But in *Higginson Securities Developments Ltd v Hodson*[18] the court refused a stay to the defendant because there had been no pre-action meeting set up by the claimant, despite the protocol providing that the parties 'should normally meet'[19]: the defendant had not asked for a meeting and had himself made unreasonable demands as to his costs.

---

15 For instance, from roughly 9,800 Chancery and 107,000 Queen's Bench proceedings in 1998 to 7,500 Chancery and 14,000 Queen's Bench proceedings in 2011, and from 2.24 million county court money claims in 1998 to 1.55 million in 2011.

16 [2002] 18 Constr LJ 345.

17 [2007] EWCA Civ 368.

18 [2012] EWHC 1052 (TCC).

19 In para 5.1.

Of course sanctions for not mediating before issue will normally be dealt with during directions by the procedural judge and may never surface in a court whose judgments are reported. But, anecdotally at least, there is very little other evidence of cases where failure to use ADR before issue have resulted in a sanction.

4.5 Stays for ADR and settlement at directions stage: the multi-track and fast-track

The one moment when the CPR specifically raise the possibility of ADR is at the directions stage (before April 2013 called the 'allocation' stage), when the court decides, assisted by the comments of the parties, into which track the claim should be allocated. This process is triggered by filing and serving a defence to the claim, at which point the parties must file a directions questionnaire, the claimant normally either paying a court fee at this point or being struck out in default of doing so. CPR 26.4 provides that:

'(1) A party may when filing the completed questionnaire make a written request for the proceedings to be stayed while the parties try to settle the case by alternative dispute resolution or other means.

(2) Where—

(a) all parties request a stay under paragraph (1); or

(b) the court, of its own initiative, considers that such a stay would be appropriate, the court will direct that the proceedings be stayed for one month.

The court may extend the stay until such date or for such period as it considers appropriate'.

Though this has been the first reference in the CPR to a time when the courts might order ADR after inter-party discussion, experience suggests that this happens less at this stage than at case management conferences and pre-trial reviews. The directions questionnaire sent out by the court, as considerably revised and strengthened in 2013, says in Section A, at the top of the form:

'Under the Civil Procedure Rules parties should make every effort to settle their case before the hearing. This could be by discussion or negotiation (such as a roundtable meeting or settlement conference) or by a more formal process such as mediation. The court will want to know what steps have been taken. Settling the case early can save costs, including court hearing fees'.

There then follows a certificate for completion by legal representatives only stating:

'I confirm that I have explained to my client the need to try to settle; the options available; and the possibility of costs sanctions if they refuse to try to settle'.

The form continues:

'1. Given that the rules require you to try to settle the claim before the hearing, do you want to attempt to settle at this stage?

2. If Yes, do you want a one month stay?

3. If you answered 'No' to question 1, please state below the reasons why you consider it inappropriate to try to settle the claim at this stage'.

Section A then concludes:

'**For all:** Your answers to these questions may be considered by the court when it deals with the questions of costs: see Civil Procedure Rules Part 44.3(4)'.

This is a great improvement on its predecessors and it remains to be seen whether the questions and warning will have an impact on the way Masters and District Judges deal with settlement at this stage in the future.

A rare reference specifically to mediation in the CPR is to be found in the 2013 amendment, where the relevant time for considering stays under CPR Part 26 is defined (in 26.2A(6)) as being when:

'(a) all parties have filed their directions questionnaires;
(b) any stay ordered by the court or period to attempt *settlement by mediation* has expired'.

One of the contentious issues over mediating is as to the best time to do so. No obligation to disclose documentary or other evidence has arisen by directions stage under CPR post-issue procedure, nor of course does any arise simply by virtue of agreeing to participate in a mediation, though in practice parties are often very frank and open about what they disclose to each other prior to and at a mediation. Pre-issue disclosure may derive either from proper compliance with any relevant Pre-action Protocol, or a formal application can be made before issue under CPR 31.16 for pre-action disclosure of documents. So while it is best to mediate when each party has sufficient information available (or can gain access to it by voluntary disclosure at the mediation) to be able to advise and consider settlement safely and responsibly, the directions stage is relatively soon after issue of proceedings. Little more will have emerged by the allocation stage apart from the formal definition of issues in the Statements of Case, though this may be the time that a party keen to mediate has the first opportunity to seek an ADR Order against a party reluctant to engage in mediation. If a case is not ready for mediation by directions stage, then mediation can and should be left until later. In fast-track cases, normally from £10,000 up to £25,000 in value[20], there will not be a directions hearing. In multi-track cases, there will usually be at least one case management conference and a pre-trial review, both of which would almost certainly be good occasions to see whether mediation has anything to offer in that case.

It should be noted that Part 26.4 provides for the court *of its own motion* to be able to order a stay where it thinks it appropriate, regardless of the wishes of either party. This provision was slightly amended by the Civil Procedure (Amendment) Rules 2013 and now reads as follows:

'(2) If all parties request a stay the proceedings will be stayed for one month and the court will notify the parties accordingly.

(2A) If the court otherwise considers that such a stay would be appropriate, the court will direct that the proceedings, either in whole or in part, be stayed for one month, or for such other period as it considers appropriate'.

An instance of judicial intervention at the earliest moment is to be found in the case of *C v RHL*[21], in which Colman J was asked to grant an anti-suit injunction to stop international proceedings in relation to a share sale dispute. Instead, he suggested that the overall interests of all parties would be served by referral to mediation, commenting that:

'That procedure provides scope for the kind of commercial solution to these disputes which it is beyond the power of the court or of the ICC arbitrators to engender'.

He consequently made an ADR in Commercial Court form. These are discussed more fully in **Chapter 5**.

---

20 CPR 26.6(4): the upper limit was increased to £25,000 from £15,000 for claims issued on or after 6 April 2009.
21 [2005] EWHC 873 (Comm).

There is no essential need for existing proceedings to be stayed for mediation. If a party or the court believes that a request for mediation is another party's ploy to gain time by delay, the timetable for the case can, if desired, continue unabated, with costs continuing to be incurred meanwhile. It is only where all parties agree to engage in mediation in good faith that there is little point in expending more time and cost on forwarding litigation when there is a good chance that mediation or some other form of ADR will settle it.

4.6   Case management and mediation

A provision was introduced into the CPR by the 41st amendment in October 2005 which reflects the options for the court to make directions about ADR at allocation where there is no allocation or case management hearing. Paragraph 4.10 of the Practice Direction made in relation to CPR Part 29 provides that:

> 'Where the court is to give directions on its own initiative without holding a case management conference and it is not aware of any steps taken by the parties other than the exchange of statements of case, its general approach will be:
>
> (1)   to give directions for the filing and service of any further information required to clarify either party's case,
>
> (2)   to direct standard disclosure between the parties,
>
> (3)   to direct the disclosure of witness statements by way of simultaneous exchange,
>
> (4)   to give directions for a single joint expert on any appropriate issue unless there is a good reason not to do so,
>
> (5)   unless paragraph 4.11 (below) applies, to direct disclosure of experts' reports by way of simultaneous exchange on those issues where a single joint expert is not directed,
>
> (6)   if experts' reports are not agreed, to direct a discussion between experts for the purpose set out in rule 35.12(1) and the preparation of a statement under rule 35.12(3),
>
> (7)   to list a case management conference to take place after the date for compliance with those directions,
>
> (8)   to specify a trial period; and
>
> (9)   in such cases as the court thinks appropriate, the court may give directions requiring the parties to consider ADR. Such directions may be, for example, in the following terms:

'The parties shall by [date] consider whether the case is capable of resolution by ADR. If any party considers that the case is unsuitable for resolution by ADR, that party shall be prepared to justify that decision at the conclusion of the trial, should the judge consider that such means of resolution were appropriate, when he is considering the appropriate costs order to make.

The party considering the case unsuitable for ADR shall, not less than 28 days before the commencement of the trial, file with the court a witness statement without prejudice save as to costs, giving reasons upon which they rely for saying that the case was unsuitable.'

This makes it possible for a procedural judge to make such an order in fast-track cases where there is normally no case management conference. Implicitly, such a direction can be also be made at a case management conference where the parties actually attend, as is the norm in clinical negligence cases for which Master Ungley developed the wording of this Order. Its wider use was approved by the Court of Appeal in *Halsey v Milton Keynes General NHS Trust*[22]. The Order does not define what type of ADR is to be used.

4.7 The specialist jurisdictions and Court Guides

The CPR are not the sole source of procedural wisdom for court users. Several specialist jurisdictions have published their own guides, sometimes establishing procedures appreciably different from the mainstream provisions of the CPR, the Admiralty and Commercial Court Guide being the prime example. This disapplies CPR Part 26.4 (which provides for a stay of proceedings while settlement by ADR or otherwise is explored), but reproduces and extends much of what was in the Commercial Court Practice Direction about ADR. Part G of the Guide deals with the topic of ADR. Adjournment for ADR is preserved; the Commercial Court judges will in appropriate cases invite the parties to consider ADR and may make orders to encourage its deployment, setting out a draft order in Appendix 7. Paragraph G1.4 provides that:

'G1.4 Legal representatives should in all cases consider with their clients and the other parties concerned the possibility of attempting to resolve the dispute or particular issues by ADR',

---

22 [2004] 4 All ER 920 at para 32: see **Chapter 5** for a full discussion of its significance.

and later:

> 'G.1.6   At the case management conference, if it should appear to the judge that the case before him or any of the issues arising in it are particularly appropriate for an attempt at settlement by means of ADR but that the parties have not previously attempted settlement by such means, he may invite the parties to use ADR'.

The Practice Guides issued by the Chancery Division[23], the Queen's Bench Division[24], the Technology and Construction[25] and Mercantile Courts[26] all specifically raise such a possibility in various ways and at various stages to suit such specialist types of case.

4.8   Small claims track cases

The small claims track developed from the most successful innovation in the civil justice system in the late 20th century, namely the county court small claims procedure. With legal costs virtually never being awarded whoever wins, it has been kept as a simple and accessible forum for low-value disputes for which mediation used to be regarded as hardly necessary and unlikely to be cost-effective. The current jurisdiction is up to £10,000 for money claims, except personal injury and housing repair claims, where the ceiling is £1,000. Claims higher than that level will normally be fast-track and will attract a costs award, albeit for fixed costs for the successful party in addition to damages. Road traffic claims up to £10,000 (until 31 July 2013) or (on or after 31 July 2013) up to £25,000 (joined also as from that date by public and employer's liability claims of up to £25,000) are to be handled through the RTA Portal, largely on-line[27]. The procedure is governed by special Pre-Action Protocols[28].

Some mediation of small claims track cases was offered through court schemes, but the initial flush of court schemes has now ended. However, one of the Ministry of Justice's most successful innovations, the Small Claims Mediation Service now flourishes in its place. Each county court region has at least one trained small claims mediator, usually but not necessarily former court staff, paid from the court's budget, who is available free of charge to litigants as a mediator in small claims cases. Most of their

---

23 Chapter 17.
24 Chapter 6.6.
25 Section 7.
26 Annex A questions 30–33 and Annex C question 10.
27 See the revised Practice Direction 8B introduced by the 65th amendment to the CPR, with details of fixed costs set out in CPR Part 45 and its PD.
28 PD 8B made under the 65th amendment to the CPR effective from 31 July 2013.

work is done by telephone, but they have achieved striking settlement rates and satisfaction levels since the service was introduced in 2007. The only continuing court scheme is the Court of Appeal Mediation Scheme, where a single Lord Justice may, when granting permission to appeal, indicate that a case may be suitable for referral to mediation through the court's scheme: alternatively, the scheme can be invoked voluntarily by parties to any appeal.

4.9 Part 36 offers and settlement

Like their predecessors the RSC and CCR, the only settlement procedure is a much-extended version of the long-standing right of a defendant to seek to transfer a potential costs liability from defendant to claimant by making a payment into court, in effect 'without prejudice except as to costs'. This is contained in Part 36 of the CPR, probably the most significant part of the CPR for mediators, as it is often mobilised before a mediation and threatened to be mobilised afterwards if settlement does not occur. When initially introduced in 1999, CPR Part 36 empowered both claimants and defendants to make a formal offer to settle either before or after proceedings are issued, indicating what they would be prepared to pay or accept, and also specifying any acceptable non-monetary terms for a settlement agreement. Defendants then still had to pay into court what they had offered.

However, Part 36 has undergone further important changes since 1999. Defendants no longer have to pay the amount offered into court to await judgment. If the offer is accepted, the defendant has 14 days to pay the amount, and in default the claimant can enter judgment for the amount of the offer[29]. Claimants who do better at trial than a defendant's Part 36 offer will normally be awarded their standard costs in addition to their remedy, and (if the defendant has behaved particularly unreasonably) possibly indemnity costs. Claimants who do less well than a defendant's Part 36 offer will normally (but not always) have to pay both sides' costs from the date of the Part 36 offer. Defendants who reject a claimant's Part 36 offer and do worse at trial can expect penal interest at anything up to 10% above current base rate awarded on damages and costs, the latter probably being awarded on a indemnity basis. A further potential penalty for a defendant's failure to beat a claimant's Part 36 offer has been added by the Jackson reforms[30]. The defendant is liable to pay an additional sum not exceeding £75,000 calculated as 10% of the damages awarded, or in a

---

29 See CPR 44th amendment, effective from 6 April 2007.
30 Embodied in the Offers to Settle in Civil Proceedings Order 2013, SI 2013/93 and CPR 36.14(3).

non-damages case 10% of the costs awarded on the first £500,000, and 5% on the balance up to £1 million.

It is now clear that Part 36 offers remain open for acceptance at any time, unless they are specifically withdrawn. If accepted after the prescribed initial 21 days, the costs incurred subsequent to that period will normally be the responsibility of the party who accepts the offer late, unless an alternative basis is agreed between the parties, or the court orders otherwise. Thus more than one Part 36 offer can remain open by the time a mediation or trial take place, with potential costs consequences. So if a defendant made un-withdrawn Part 36 offers two years ago of £10,000 and another of £20,000 a month ago, with trial expected in another month's time, even if the claimant beats the earlier one and gets his costs up to date, he may still lose against the later one and have to bear both sides' costs of trial.

These are the normal consequences to Part 36 offers. However, there have been a number of cases in which the courts have departed from these normal expectations, giving rise to uncertainty for advisers in being able to predict accurately what costs orders a judge might make[31]. These are considered in more detail in **Chapter 11**, in the context of costs and funding issues.

Part 36 procedure has almost certainly led already to more settlements, both before and after issue of proceedings. Mediations are often preceded by such offers and very often followed by them if a case does not settle. The mediation throws up more information upon which to assess the right level for such a proposal to be made. Nothing obliges a Part 36 offer to match what was offered at a mediation, and this adds an extra dimension to negotiations at a mediation.

4.10   Costs and the CPR

Lord Woolf regarded the problem of costs as 'the most serious problem besetting our litigation system'. As has been seen in relation to the Pre-action Protocols, the CPR give permission for judges to take unreasonable pre-action conduct into account in determining costs orders even against otherwise successful parties. The same range of tools is available to deal with post-issue unreasonableness. These include summary orders for costs on interim hearings, payable immediately; full information about costs expended and anticipated to be prepared and exchanged at every case management occasion; and orders for costs to be based on unrea-

---

31 See for instance *Ford v GKR Construction Ltd* [2000] 1 All ER 802 and *Painting v University of Oxford* [2005] EWCA Civ 161 for cases on either side, and *par excellence, Dunnett v Railtrack* [2002] EWCA Civ 303, [2002] 2 All ER 850.

sonable litigation conduct, which is specifically said (in CPR 44.3(5)) to include:

'(a) conduct before as well as during the proceedings and in particular the extent to which the parties followed any relevant pre-action protocol;

(b) whether it was reasonable for a party to raise, pursue or contest a particular allegation or issue;

(c) the manner in which a party has pursued or defended his case or a particular allegation or issue;

(d) whether a claimant who has succeeded in his claim, in whole or in part, exaggerated his claim'.

The other key feature to the new costs regime was the requirement of **proportionality** between the costs incurred and claimed by the receiving party and the subject-matter of the litigation. Costs payable on the (usual) standard basis which are disproportionate to the amount or importance of the litigation will be disallowed. CPR 44.5(1) provides that, in deciding how much should be allowed for costs, the court must have regard to all the circumstances in deciding (when applying the standard basis for assessment) whether costs were proportionately and reasonably incurred and were proportionate and reasonable in amount. It is only when costs are to be assessed on an indemnity basis that proportionality is ignored. This emphasis picks up on the provisions of CPR 1.1(2)(c) and the overriding objective. Dealing with cases justly is said to include adopting ways which

'are proportionate to the amount involved in the case, to the importance of the case, to the complexity of the issues and to the financial position of each party'.

The net effect of these linked provisions, put bluntly, is that a party can 'succeed' in litigation, but because of either unreasonable or disproportionate conduct of the claim may not 'win' in terms of recovering all or most of the legal costs of winning. In an extreme case, the court even has jurisdiction to order the 'winning' party to pay costs to a 'losing' party[32]. This has had profound implications for disciplining those who refuse to mediate, as it has been clearly established that an unreasonable refusal to mediate may be treated by the courts as unreasonable conduct within the meaning of CPR 44.2(5) (formerly 44.3(5)) and attract a costs sanction[33].

---

32 As happened over costs prior to a Part 36 offer in *P4 Ltd v Unite Integrated Solutions plc* [2006] EWHC 2924 (TCC), in a case where, had the successful defendant not refused mediation, Ramsey J would have awarded all costs against the unsuccessful claimant.

33 First memorably decided in *Dunnett v Railtrack* [2002] EWCA Civ 303.

The courts have already demonstrated their willingness to make tougher costs orders, sometimes much to the surprise of the party which might have thought it had 'won', especially under the pre-CPR regime. The net result for mediators will be to provide ample grounds for testing whether success at trial might not be of doubtful worth. The attractions of settling a case on a party's own terms will increase in proportion to the uncertainty of the litigated outcome, and uncertainty over the exercise of wide judicial discretion is found in the costs aspect of the CPR more than any other.

A new and tougher definition of proportionality has been introduced in to the CPR by the Civil Procedure (Amendment) Rules 2013. This, together with the wider implications of the court's costs jurisdiction for mediation practice, is considered in more detail in **Chapter 11**.

4.11 The Jackson reports and the Civil Procedure (Amendment) Rules 2013

The amendments to the CPR brought about by the Civil Procedure (Amendment) Rules 2013 as from 1 April 2013 have little to say directly about the use of mediation. They signal tighter supervision and control on the costs expended on litigation, with costs management, budgeting and capping; greater use of fixed costs; a tighter definition of proportionality; and an apparent determination to enforce obligations under the CPR, practice directions and court orders. Unsurprisingly, the provisions as to potential costs sanctions for unreasonable litigation conduct remain in place, and although there is no sign of increased determination to order mediation, this remains an option for judges in giving directions at any stage of a case, and costs sanctions for unreasonable refusal to mediate are still permitted. Whether the challenges and demands posed to litigating in such a forbidding regime will indirectly encourage wider use of mediation will only be seen over time.

The overall effect of the Jackson reforms is considered fully in the context of future developments in mediation law and civil practice in **Chapter 13**.

4.12 An ADR jurisprudence

Two main questions have occupied the courts in thinking about judicial intervention in relation to ADR since the CPR, and they remain as significant as ever after the 2013 amendments to the CPR. These are:

– Can and should the courts *order* parties to undertake ADR?
– Can and should the courts *impose costs or other sanctions* on parties who unreasonably refuse to engage in ADR?

The first option, if legitimate, makes it possible for judges to try to ensure that parties use ADR before proceedings are concluded by judgment. If settlement is achieved through that course, appreciable costs, time and pressure are likely to be saved for the benefit of the parties. If settlement is not achieved, then issues may well have been clarified and narrowed, albeit at some cost, and the courts can proceed on the expectation that after being tested out in the crucible of mediation, a case will stand up for trial and not collapse late. The second option, if legitimate, is too late to influence conduct of that particular case before trial, but might be seen as having the force of precedent to advisers generally in warning them of what might happen to them if they act unreasonably in subsequent litigation. Part of the problem behind these questions is the same: how should courts take steps to achieve the overriding objective by use of this particular tool of active case management, especially in the light of the view that ADR is normally regarded as a purely voluntary process? Ordering a party into ADR might seem to offend the concept of voluntary choice, whereas penalising someone for not voluntarily choosing to engage in ADR sounds like a contradiction. There is also the question of a litigant's right to access to the courts. Each of these questions are discussed in detail in the following chapters.

Chapter 5

The courts and ADR orders

The European Convention on Human Rights (the ECHR) was embodied into English law by the Human Rights Act 1998, but has in effect always been observed by the UK since it was promulgated by the Council of Europe (and with the strong support of the UK) in 1950. Article 6 of the ECHR provides that:

> 'in the determination of his civil rights and obligations ... everyone is entitled to a fair and public hearing within a reasonable time by an independent and impartial tribunal established by law'.

It was submitted to the Court of Appeal in *Halsey v Milton Keynes General NHS Trust*[1], the leading English court decision on the place of mediation in this civil justice system, which is referred to repeatedly in this book, that to order parties to enter mediation compulsorily constituted a breach of their right to a public trial under Article 6. The court accepted that view. Were they right to do so? And whether or not they were right, what orders can the courts of England and Wales make, if any, as to the deployment of mediation?

5.1 Mediation as a *necessarily* voluntary process?

Perhaps the greatest irony related to the development of mediation has been the fact that what is asserted to be an essentially voluntary process should have become entangled with the question of compulsory use within civil justice systems. As noted in **Chapter 2**, definitions of mediation have often contained the word 'voluntary' as being an essential feature. Some used to do so and have removed it. Yet in many common law and civil law justice systems, the use of mediation is effectively a compulsory stage in the normal public civil justice procedure[2]. But what does 'voluntariness' really mean? There is an important distinction to be made between voluntary *initial engagement* in mediation and voluntarily *continued engagement* once the process is under way. No proponent of mediation would ever

---

1 [2004] EWCA Civ 576.
2 Eg many States jurisdictions in the USA and Australia, and in Italy.

argue that a party to a mediation is not free to walk away from the process and back to adjudicative determination, whether by judge or arbitrator. In the sense of continued participation, mediation is emphatically voluntary. Furthermore, participation in the process must be on the basis that nothing said during the mediation can be used against a party on returning to an adjudicative process, and that even unreasonable disengagement from a mediation is not open to criticism or penalty in later proceedings[3]. The confidentiality of the mediation process is considered in detail in **Chapter 9**. What has been diluted over the years in many jurisdictions has been the need for *initial engagement* in mediation to be necessarily free from constraint. Each civil and common law will have its own special characteristics which will impact on the extent to which settlement processes are made compulsory. However, there is a real practical difficulty for jurisdictions such as England and Wales where litigation costs form part of what the court can award in determining the parties' rights but can dwarf the damages at stake. Especially where there is an inevitable contractual nexus between the parties in dispute there may be an overriding need to compel use of mediation against their wishes but objectively in their own interests.

It ought to be unnecessary to emphasise that there is never any compulsion to *settle* during a mediation. It is all too easy for judges to regard the concept of ADR as signifying a self-contained sealed competitor process to which parties in dispute, disgruntled with the mainstream civil justice system, can turn for independent relief. While this might be broadly true of arbitration, which is a private adjudicative process supported by statute, it is certainly not true of mediation. As has been seen, mediation in commercial disputes operates firmly within the shadow of the law, since the alternative to the entirely free option of **not** settling during a mediation is a return to the courts (or indeed arbitration). However, occasional judicial remarks do raise questions as to whether this is universally understood. For instance, in a speech to a mediation symposium[4] in 2010, in which Lord Dyson accepted that insofar as he had said in *Halsey* that ordering mediation necessarily breached Article 6, this was wrong, he still felt it right to say that:

> 'forcing individuals who truly do not wish to mediate does raise a moral question: can it be right that a person who has exercised his constitutional right to go to court should be forced to sit down with the individual he believes to have wronged him to try and find a compromise which will probably leave him worse off than he would have been if he had had his day in court?'

---

3 An attempt to admit evidence of unreasonable mediation conduct was most recently rejected in *PGF II v OFMS Co* [2012] EWHC 83 (TCC).
4 To the Chartered Institute of Arbitrators' 3rd Mediation Symposium: October 2010.

Leaving aside the highly questionable assertion that an early mediation would be more expensive than going through to the end of a trial (a trial itself being highly unlikely with the prevalence of settlement), Lord Dyson concludes this section by saying:

> 'It doesn't seem to me that it is the role of a court of law to force compromise upon people who do not want to compromise'.

No one is **forced** to compromise at a mediation. And why should a compromise 'probably' leave someone worse off if there is no guarantee of winning in court? Mediation offers parties the opportunity, if they wish to take it, to compromise, coupled with the freedom to resume litigation or arbitration if they prefer. The mediation will have created a safe environment managed by a skilled neutral for inter-party discussion, in which the opportunity will arise for conversations to take place between people who believe that the other has wronged them (surely a sensible adult approach to reviewing disputes). The neutral mediator will have tested each party's strengths and weaknesses, set against the desirability of settling or not when viewed against the alternative, ensuring so far as possible that each party can make a fully informed sensible choice as to whether to settle or not. The debate as to whether courts should help people who may be under-informed or under-advised about such matters can (and will in this book) be conducted both at the level of principle (Lord Dyson's understandable instinctive approach) or at the level of practical reality, which may throw up a different answer to these questions. For the purposes of the rest of this book, however, reliance can perhaps be placed on what Lord Dyson MR said in his 2010 speech, to the effect that where mediation:

> 'is merely a preliminary step which the parties are required to go through which, if unsuccessful, would leave them free to litigate',

it would not breach Article 6. This in no way derogates from his view that compelling mediation is unwise or even perhaps morally wrong. But that at least delineates the discussion to be had, and this book does not argue for any greater status than that for mediation in the English civil justice system. However, while mediating before litigation has started is certainly underused and desirable, if pre-issue mediation has not taken place then courts should contemplate ordering or at least suggesting it at any stage of the life of a dispute before trial is actually fixed.

English courts and rule-makers have so far shied away from truly mandatory ADR. The judgment in *Halsey* quotes the 2003 *White Book* as follows:

'The hallmark of ADR procedures, and perhaps the key to their effectiveness in individual cases, is that they are processes voluntarily entered into by the parties in dispute, with outcomes, if the parties so wish, which are non-binding. Consequently the court cannot direct that such methods be used but may merely facilitate and encourage'[5].

No distinction is drawn in that passage between voluntary entry and voluntarily continuing to participate in ADR, and the reference to non-binding outcomes as a justification is a little opaque, as almost all mediation parties normally seek agreed outcomes that bind all participants. The fact that parties can opt for a non-binding outcome does not of itself seem to justify refusal to compel participation. Whether this passage is based on detailed research and understanding of the field is open to question.

However, judges in the Commercial Court have been making self-styled ADR orders since the mid-1990s which put considerable pressure on parties to engage in ADR. Implicit in such orders was that the Commercial Court might view failure to mediate with displeasure, which they might then mark in some way, perhaps by a costs penalty. The orders did not spell out such risks. The wording is firm and persuasive, but the orders remain tactfully silent over the consequences of refusal. Some judges were prepared to be more assertive where parties have been shown to dally in co-operating over administrative arrangements for a mediation for ulterior reasons, for instance by not agreeing a mediator. But anecdotally parties normally obeyed such advice and mediated unless they had a very cogent reason not to do so, and there is no reported case of any sanction being required to discipline reluctant commercial parties before the CPR were introduced.

5.2 The Commercial Court ADR order

Any review of ADR orders in the English courts must inevitably start with the draft order contained in Appendix 7 of the Admiralty and Commercial Court Guide, which has been used by the Commercial Court since 1995, well before the CPR. This is still acknowledged as the classic template for such orders.

This takes the following shape:

1   On or before [Day 1] the parties shall exchange lists of three neutrals or identifying one or more panels of individuals who are available to conduct ADR procedures in the case prior to [Day 4].

---

5 *Civil Procedure 2003*, para 1.4.11, quoted at para 9 of Dyson LJ's judgment in *Halsey* [2004] EWCA Civ 576.

2   On or before [Day 2] the parties 'shall in good faith endeav-
    our to agree a neutral individual or panel from the lists so
    exchanged or provided'.

3   Failing such agreement [by Day 3], the Case Management
    Conference will be restored to enable the court to facilitate
    agreement on a neutral individual or panel.

4   The parties 'shall take such serious steps as they may be
    advised to resolve their disputes by ADR procedures before
    the individual or panel so chosen by no later than [Day 4]

5   If the case is not finally settled, the parties shall inform the
    court by letter by [Day 5] [a specified stage of the proceed-
    ings] what steps towards ADR have been taken and (without
    prejudice to matters of privilege) why such steps have failed.
    If the parties have failed to initiate ADR procedures the Case
    Management Conference is to be restored for further consid-
    eration of the case.

6   [Costs].

It should be noted that the order uses the term 'ADR' throughout. It was
devised during the early importation of ADR processes to this jurisdiction from the US, when there were several possible processes that might
be used in commercial disputes, such as early neutral evaluation, expert
determination, or executive tribunal, as well as mediation. However, as
Dyson LJ pointed out in *Halsey:*

'In practice, however, references to ADR are usually understood
as being references to some form of mediation by a third party'.

Some of the main components of Commercial Court ADR orders are now
examined in more detail.

'Good faith'

There is a good deal of unfamiliar language in this form of order, such as
'shall in good faith endeavour' and 'take such serious steps as they may be
advised', with even the court offering to 'facilitate agreement' if the parties
cannot agree on a neutral. In fact no one seems to have found much difficulty in understanding what these concepts might mean, however difficult
they might be to enforce.

In the Central London County Court, where an inexpensive court mediation scheme used to run, a typical order made at a case management conference commences:

'The parties and legal representatives do now give serious consideration to using the mediation scheme at the court with a view to early settlement'.

In another county court, the wording used has been that 'there be a stay of proceedings to attempt a mediated settlement until' a specified date.

There has been some reluctance among judges to accept that there can be an enforceable duty to do things 'in good faith', as opposed to enforcing an obligation 'to use best endeavours'. Some of this debate is discussed in **Chapter 8** relating to the enforceability of ADR contract clauses. With a wide costs discretion, what is strictly enforceable as a matter of law may become less significant when sanctions can be imposed for unreasonable conduct. A dramatic illustration of this approach is to be found in *Rowallan Group Ltd v Edgehill Portfolio No 1 Ltd*[6], a decision of Lightman J, when he imposed indemnity costs on a claimant in summarily dismissing his claim under CPR Part 24 for, among other things, arranging for issue of proceedings **during** the mediation day itself with no prior letter before action, so as to 'get in first', and then asking the mediator to enquire at the mediation whether the defendant's solicitor would accept service.

Stay of proceedings

It should be noted that the normal form of this order does not specifically provide for a stay of the proceedings. What happens in practice very often is that the ADR form of words is embedded within the main timetable for an action, to minimise any delay if ADR does not settle a claim. This will sometimes provide for the completion of certain stages (such as amendment of statements of case, disclosure, exchange of statements of witnesses of fact or some or all expert evidence) before the mediation window is opened. It may then perhaps provide for a stay at that stage (though by no means in every case) of between a month and three months, and then for further directions in default of settlement, going so far as to fix a trial date or a trial window. Some orders are simply made on the basis of a stay for a fixed period to try mediation and adjournment of all other directions. Much depends upon the stage reached in the proceedings. It would appear that as many, if not more, orders are made at case management conference or on specific directions as are made at directions stage under CPR 26.4.

In one Queen's Bench claim in which the judge ordered a defendant to pay into court £10,000 as a condition of setting aside judgment in default of defence, the judge additionally ordered that the action be stayed for 28 days

---

6 [2007] EWHC 32 (Ch).

from the payment into court 'for the parties to explore ADR'. Exchange of witness statements of fact was ordered to take place thereafter.

Typically a stay is ordered until a specified date, but occasionally a court will order a stay 'until the conclusion of the mediation', perhaps a rather difficult moment to define precisely.

One Technology and Construction Court order made by the assigned judge at his first consideration of the case observed that:

> 'Mediation is not an alternative trial. Resolution of the differences between the parties seems to be a reasonable prospect by mediation without enlarging on the numbers participating and it should be attempted after close of pleadings'.

The judge ordered that, following service of the reply, there would be a stay for eight weeks, which was not to affect later dates already set in agreed directions. In the same order the judge, as is the practice in the TCC, set the trial date.

A stay may not actually be specified, but if a period is embedded in a timetable when only ADR is required of the parties (as sometimes happens), that really is as good as ordering a stay, since there are no other procedural deadlines during that period.

Liberty to apply in respect of the stay is often specifically ordered, though the CPR probably preserve an implied right to apply anyway.

Choice of mediator and mediation machinery

The standard order appears to mandate 'good faith' choice of a neutral by the parties, with the court facilitating any difficulty in reaching a decision. Some courts have been prepared to adopt a more robust approach, ordering that in default of agreement an ADR provider should have power to nominate a mediator. This happened in *Kinstreet Ltd v Balmargo Corpn Ltd*[7], an unreported decision of Mrs Justice Arden in July 1999, in which she also made an ADR order in the teeth of opposition from at least one of the parties. In one multi-party Commercial Court case in which the standard order was made, the parties failed to agree and on reference back to the court for 'facilitation', the same judge ordered that the mediator with the support of the majority of parties from a slate of three mediators was to act.

---

7 Also under the name *Guinle v Kirreh*.

In one unreported Chancery claim, the judge ordered 'the parties to try to settle this case by mediation' specifying a date by which this was to have occurred and for a report back to the court. It provided that CEDR was to administer the mediation and was to be 'responsible for the appointment of the mediator after consultation with the parties'.

In a major multi-party claim between a company in liquidation and its former employees, an interesting representative order was made 'in order that a process of mediation may be undertaken as soon as practicable in respect of actions ... suitable for mediation' between employer and employees. The lead solicitors for each side were ordered to make contact with CEDR to instruct them to administer the mediation, and apply jointly for the appointment of a mediator from CEDR's panel. A list of ten actions in which the liquidator and employees were willing to submit to mediation was to be exchanged and four actions identified for mediation. In an interesting postscript to the order, it was provided that:

> 'whereas any ensuing mediations can only continue on a voluntary basis and subject to the terms of such mediation agreements as may be entered into the Lead Solicitors ... in consultation with the mediator as appropriate shall in good faith attempt to agree a timetable, venue and procedures for mediation...'.

It went on to make it clear that the mediation order was not to affect the operation of existing orders or the progress of the court action, thus not staying the action pending ADR.

Some county courts have made orders that 'the parties try to settle this case by mediation' and identified a provider who was required to produce a list of potential mediators to facilitate agreement of a nominee by the parties. In default of agreement of a mediator by a specified time and date, the provider was to appoint a mediator, with the parties being bound by that appointment. In one such court a powerful extra paragraph was added which provided:

> 'Pursuant to the overriding objective and their duty to the court, both parties shall co-operate to implement the terms of this Order expeditiously and purposefully and without pre-conditions or qualifications. In the event of a party's default, the other party may apply forthwith for the defaulting party's Statement of Case to be struck out for judgment to be entered on that party's claim and for costs'.

In another unreported District Registry Queen's Bench case, an order stayed a claim involving a building dispute for six weeks 'in order for a formal ADR to take place', providing further that 'the expertise of the mediator should be preferably that of an engineer/surveyor' with a knowledge of the particular technical field 'rather than a lawyer'. The order continued:

'Any proposals in the mediation shall be without prejudice, but if as a consequence of one party's failure to co-operate and thereby sabotage the ADR, then either party can make an application to the judge with a view to lift the stay'.

The sanction visualised in that order for non-co-operation over setting up a mediation ordered by the court were thus to be able to get on with the proceedings without further delay, perhaps even being able to obtain an early termination through striking out, though courts have been very slow to do this since the CPR. Fortunately the temptation to threaten a penalty for unreasonable behaviour at the mediation was resisted. However, a party who is shown at trial to have failed to co-operate over participating in a mediation will, as can be seen in **Chapters 6** and **7**, face serious risks of a costs sanction even if he wins the case on the merits.

The main point to make about the appointment provisions of the standard order is that, in this respect at least, they sound mandatory. Parties 'shall' find a mediator and set a date within a determined period.

Costs of seeking an ADR order

The costs order made when parties have applied for an ADR order have normally been for costs to be in the case and thus to follow the final outcome of the case, though there is no reason why a party who has obstructed the other's proposal for ADR should not be penalised if an ADR order is made, either by an immediate costs sanction, or perhaps by having costs reserved to the trial judge.

Non-compliance with an ADR order

If a party fails to co-operate over setting up a mediation despite an ADR order in Commercial Court form, the ADR order requires the parties to report what steps towards ADR have been taken and (without prejudice to matters of privilege) why such steps have failed. If the parties have failed to initiate ADR procedures the Case Management Conference is to be restored for further consideration of the case.

This is an enquiry as to why parties did not enter into mediation, and, as shown in **Chapter 6**, may now give rise to costs sanctions, even against a successful litigant. However, the ADR order provision certainly falls well short of an enquiry as to why the mediation failed to settle the case, and whether a party failed to act reasonably at the mediation. The Commercial Court ADR order thus underlines the important distinction between court persuasion to mediate (buttressed by sanctions), and the general restraint shown by courts from seeking to peer behind the veil of confidentiality governing a mediation, which makes the content of mediation debate and reasons for terminating it confidential even from the judge at any later stage of the same litigation.

However, the Commercial Court has apparently not found it necessary to sanction failure to comply with ADR orders made by them. Colman J, the prime originator of Commercial Court ADR orders, has commented that the court finds that parties simply do not ignore such orders, whatever their true status as 'orders of the court' might be. He was unable to recollect any instance of a case where a party ignored the procedural judge's order to mediate and returned to explain why. There have been cases where mediation was tried and did not produce a settlement, but the court will not go behind such a report. Parties have ignored judicial recommendations in other courts, however, so the true status of the order and the court's response to it has become significant.

Dyson LJ in *Halsey*[8] makes it clear that:

> 'a party who, despite such an order, simply refuses to embark on the ADR process at all would run the risk that for that reason alone his refusal to agree to ADR would be held to have been unreasonable, and that he should therefore be penalised in costs. It is to be assumed that the court would not make such an order unless it was of the opinion that the dispute was suitable for ADR'.

5.3   The effect of the CPR on Commercial Court ADR orders

When ADR orders were devised by the Commercial Court judges, there was no defined overriding objective for civil justice, as there has been since 1999. CPR Part 1 has now identified ADR as one of the court's tools of active case management available to achieve that objective. The Commercial Court was never slow to encourage its use, and has continued to do so in largely unaltered form. But the new status of ADR as being of significance for the whole civil justice system has led to the judges discussing what this meant in terms of ordering ADR.

---

8 [2004] EWCA Civ 576 at para 31.

Matching the profession's general response to the CPR, there was a marked increase in the take-up of mediation immediately after their introduction, with a marked drop in the number of cases issued in the courts. Practitioners doubtless feared that they might indeed be criticised, and possibly face costs sanctions, if they did not try ADR. Courts began to assume that mediation would save costs and order it accordingly in various ways. In *Muman v Nagasena*[9], a dispute over control of a Buddhist temple, the court imposed a stay until mediation had been tried. In *Guinle v Kirreh* and *Kinstreet v Balmargo*[10], the judge dealt with three complex inter-related disputes. Several parties sought an ADR order: several opposed mediation. Mrs Justice Arden formed the view that mediation would save huge costs. She rejected criticism that the obligation 'to take such steps as the parties might seriously be advised' to settle was meaningless, agreed that there was no need for a stay of the hearing for ADR to take place, claimed jurisdiction to make such an Order and 'directed' ADR in the terms of the Commercial Court Appendix 7 form. She cited CPR Part 1 and noted that dealing justly included proportionality of cost, bearing in mind that one party (if unsuccessful) would not be able to afford the costs of trial. Whether there is any material difference between a direction and an order in this context is debatable.

Courts also began to give warnings and issue advice at the conclusion of cases that parties should seriously consider ADR or run the risk of costs consequences, though such advice fell short of an order. Lord Woolf was a member of the Court of Appeal in *Dyson & Field v Leeds City Council*[11], in which, citing CPR 1.4 (2) (e) for the first time in a reported appeal, Ward LJ said that the court:

'should encourage the parties to use an alternative dispute resolution procedure to bring this unhappy matter to the conclusion which it now deserves sooner rather than later'.

A claimant had successfully appealed against a judge's unexplained preference for the defendant's expert, but a retrial was required. The Court of Appeal made it clear that they would look very unfavourably on a repeat appearance before them if the insurer rejected their recommendation to mediate, in effect requiring future mediation of the remaining issues to avoid a retrial. Lord Woolf himself gave the lead judgment in *Cowl v Plymouth City Council*[12], delivering powerful strictures on both parties'

---

9 (1 July 1999, unreported): the court specified use of the CEDR Scheme for the National Council for Voluntary Organisations.
10 (3 August 1999, unreported), ChD.
11 (22 November 1999, unreported) CCRTF 1998/1490/B2.
12 [2001] EWCA 734 (Admin).

failure to use an available ADR process rather than the delay and cost of fiercely-contested judicial review proceedings. He produced the first general warning to practitioners when he said:

'Today sufficient should be known about ADR to make the failure to adopt it, in particular where public money is involved, indefensible'.

Lord Woolf was both openly trying to influence advisers in later cases as to what the courts would expect of them, and perhaps implicitly giving guidance to procedural judges as to what they should expect of parties in terms of knowledge about ADR, and their willingness to engage in it effectively.

As will be seen in **Chapters 6** and **7** dealing with costs sanctions, if one case can be said to have changed the course of ADR development more than any other in England and Wales, it is *Dunnett v Railtrack*[13]. No actual ADR order was made, simply a recommendation by the single Appeal Court judge (who allowed Mrs Dunnett to appeal after losing her claim against Railtrack) that the parties should mediate through the Court of Appeal Mediation Scheme, then available free of charge. That recommendation took on something close to the status of an order in its effect, and the Court of Appeal responded by depriving Railtrack of its costs.

Blackburne J followed the effect of *Guinle* and *Kinstreet* closely in *Shirayama v Danovo*[14] in making an ADR Order against the implacable opposition of the claimant in a dispute between the owners of County Hall and the Saatchi Gallery, a tenant of part. He decided in a later judgment in the same case that he could not order the attendance of a specified person at such a mediation against his will.

Halsey v Milton Keynes NHS Trust and the status of ADR Orders

It was not until the conjoined appeals in *Halsey v Milton Keynes General NHS Trust* and *Steel v Jones and Halliday*[15] that the Court of Appeal took the opportunity (rightly or wrongly) to review the status of ADR orders generally and the proper approach to judicial compulsion in relation to ADR. The actual facts of the appeals themselves concern whether costs sanctions should be imposed for ignoring an inter-party request to mediate, and as such are considered in the next chapter. But the court took the opportunity to express views about ADR orders too, which, while strictly obiter, were intended to give guidance and establish the working frame-

---

13 [2002] 2 All ER 850.
14 [2003] EWHC 3006 (Ch).
15 [2004] 4 All ER 920.

work within which decisions about ADR could and should be made. The court invited interested bodies to intervene with submissions, and these were received from CEDR, ADR Group, the Chair of the Civil Mediation Council and, at a late stage, the Law Society.

As noted above, the court considered that to oblige truly unwilling parties to mediate would impose an unacceptable obstruction on their right of access to the court, in violation of Article 6 of the European Convention on Human Rights. It is not clear whether this was fully argued. It was certainly a last-minute submission made in the name of the Law Society, and the only case cited – *Deweer v Belgium*[16] – dealt with waiver of court access through an agreement to arbitrate. The human rights argument is reviewed more fully in **Chapter 10**, but it seems rather strange to argue that ordering a party to try a settlement process which is emphatically **not** adjudicative, from which he can withdraw without penalty once started, might necessarily infringe Article 6 rights. Lord Dyson MR has informally accepted[17] that this interpretation does not stand up, accepting (albeit only in a speech) that mandating mediation does not *in principle* infringe European law, so long as it is set up in a way that does not obstruct free access to the courts.

Even supposing that this view was wrong, the Court of Appeal in *Halsey* took the view that mediation is best engaged in voluntarily:

> 'If the court were to compel parties to enter into a mediation to which they objected, that would achieve nothing except to add to the costs to be borne by the parties, possibly postpone the time when the court determines the dispute and damage the perceived effectiveness of the ADR process'[18].

Hitherto the judgment talks of parties in the plural, suggesting that it would be wrong for the court to direct ADR when every party to litigation wants to litigate. But after saying that judges should test out expressions of opposition to ADR and not take it at face value, para 10 of the judgment ends:

> 'But if the parties (or at least one of them) remain intransigently opposed to ADR, it would be wrong for the court to compel them to embrace it'.

---

16 [1980] EHRR 439.
17 In his speech to the Chartered Institute of Arbitrators Symposium on Mediation in October 2010.
18 In para 10.

What the court does have (the judgment continues) is power to *encourage* parties into ADR, and not to compel them. It goes on to approve the Commercial Court form of ADR order, and interprets it as 'the strongest form of encouragement', though falling short of actually compelling them to 'undertake an [sic] ADR'[19]. If such an ADR 'order' (or robust encouragement, as it should perhaps correctly be called) were to be ignored, a judge for that reason alone could impose a costs sanction on the party refusing.

Where does this leave the Commercial Court ADR order and the earlier cases decided in the light of it? Those who had opposed ADR in *Guinle/ Kinstreet* and in *Shirayama* certainly must have left court feeling that they had no alternative but to engage in mediation in accordance with the Commercial Court ADR 'order' made 'against' them. Railtrack ignored a recommendation to mediate in *Dunnett* and were penalised. *Dunnett* remains untouched by *Halsey,* as do any cases in which a proper ADR order was made. Indeed, the advice to mediate in *Dunnett* emanated from a single Lord Justice when giving permission to appeal, and never purported to be an ADR order at all. In practical terms, therefore, the true status of such ADR orders becomes academic. They are ignored at the costs peril of the refusing party, be they a true order of the court or a mere robust encouragement. Certainly no one has ever sought to commit a refusing party for contempt, or to have their statement of case struck out for contumely. However, since April 2013, even in the atmosphere of strict enforcement of court orders and directions encouraged by the Jackson reports as introduced by the Civil Procedure (Amendment) Rules 2013, there must be a risk that striking out a claim or defence for procedural irregularity or committal for contempt of court might be open to challenge in the European Court as infringing Article 6 of the European Convention on Human Rights if applied to what might otherwise be a valid claim[20].

When the CPR were first introduced, there was judicial reluctance to use CPR Part 3 to strike out claims for this very reason. Whether the draconian sanctions threatened to buttress the 2013 rule amendments will be found to offend Article 6 of the ECHR, especially if claims or defences are struck out for disciplinary reasons, remains unclear. Certainly there seems no way that breach of an ADR 'order' could lead to such an outcome. A costs sanction (which must presumably be proportionate) may be the only penalty possible.

Is there a fair distinction between cases where all parties oppose mediation or only one of two or more? Reverting to the overriding objective in CPR Part 1, the answer should be no. If mediation is a proper means of reducing

---

19 In para 30.
20 See Shipman: *Compulsory mediation: the elephant in the room.* 32(2) CJQ 163.

court time and party expense, then the fact that *both* parties oppose its use might well be criticised as in breach of the requirements to save expense, deal with matters expeditiously and allotting an appropriate share of the court's resources. This is so especially as the 2013 amendments have been introduced to ensure proportionality as between all court users. Where one party objects and others agree, why should the opposing party have a veto? It is certainly right that a costs sanction should be reserved for ill-judged refusals of that kind, but meanwhile the case has had to grind on to a conclusion despite the wishes of other parties. What is wrong with a judge intervening to make an ADR 'order' even if one party objects? Even where a mediation does not settle a case, issues are tested and narrowed, reality checked, determination to litigate reviewed and refined, and any unsettled case can be assumed to be worth trying by the judge, who can then be sure that the parties require a decision. Yet in *Nokia v Interdigital Technology*[21], in which the parties expressed interest in mediation but one wished to limit its scope to UK intellectual property issues while the other would only mediate if worldwide issues were included, Pumfrey J declined to make an ADR order, suggesting that the only sanction left to the court was to penalise unreasonable refusal to mediate at the end of the trial. This is surely a surprising position, especially where parties had at least agreed in principle to mediate, but disagreed as to the scope of the dispute to be discussed. The overriding objective requires active case management and facilitation of settlement attempts in order to avoid trial where possible, not simply to be resigned to a trial and a costs argument at its conclusion. Not to require use of a process which can start out on a narrow basis and easily be enlarged to embrace wider issues was surely an opportunity missed.

To summarise the fate of the ADR order, it appears to be alive and well, despite the ambiguity of its status. Its future deployment depends on whether procedural judges have the will to use it at the right time and in the right circumstances. Many senior judges have never been to a mediation because it was simply not available as a process when they were in practice. Time is changing this. But the need for judicial training over such matters remains paramount, especially while assertions made to judges by lawyers about mediation and its suitability are not necessarily based upon sound experience or training. As Dyson LJ said in *Halsey:*

> 'The value and importance of ADR have been established within a remarkably short time. All members of the legal profession who conduct litigation should now routinely consider with their clients whether their disputes are suitable for ADR'[22].

---

21 [2005] EWHC 2134 (Pat).
22 In para 11.

Treating parties as a judge's clients for the purposes of that statement, it holds true for them as well as lawyers representing parties, just as the overriding objective governs and guides what all professionals do when engaged in civil justice. The underlying problem is that the pace of ADR development still depends upon professional people with little personal experience of its value.

5.4 Other ADR orders and forms of judicial encouragement

Besides the Commercial Court Order, the court in *Halsey* noted with approval the encouragement given by the Queen's Bench, Chancery, Commercial Court and Technology & Construction Court Guides, characterising these as 'a less strong form of encouragement'.

The other form of order specifically considered in *Halsey* was the order used in clinical negligence cases, devised by Master Ungley and his colleagues dealing with such work. This provides that:

> 'The parties shall by [Day 1] consider whether the case is capable of resolution by ADR. If any party considers that the case is unsuitable for ADR, that party shall be prepared to justify that decision at the conclusion of the trial, should the judge consider that such means of resolution were appropriate, when he is considering the appropriate costs order to make. The party considering the case unsuitable for ADR shall, not less than 28 days before the commencement of the trial, file with the court a witness statement without prejudice save as to costs, giving reasons upon which they rely for saying that the case was unsuitable'.

The court in *Halsey* commended the fact that:

- – it recognises the importance of encouraging the parties to consider whether the case is suitable for ADR, and
- – it is calculated to bring home to them that, if they refuse even to consider that question, they may be at risk on costs even if they are ultimately held by the court to be the successful party.

The court suggested that it might be used more widely, especially in personal injury cases. Indeed, this wording has now found its way into the CPR Part 29 Practice Direction.

What this form of order does (rightly or wrongly) is to relieve the procedural judge from any responsibility for asserting the suitability of a given case for ADR, leaving it to the parties to assess that on the merits and taking the risk (if they refuse) that the trial judge will take a contrary view if the case proceeds to judgment. However, it is very hard to define what makes a case unsuitable for mediation. Even in *Halsey,* mediation was regarded as not inherently unsuitable. Many, if not most, cases will at some point in their life cycle be suitable for mediation. The better questions are whether it is ready for mediation and whether the cost benefit of mediating makes sense. It is, of course, open to a party to ask the procedural judge to specify in the order or direction the type of ADR process to be used, this almost always being mediation.

There are many other instances of courts encouraging parties to engage in mediation where they have not done so before. The Court of Appeal has issued such advice repeatedly when they have themselves driven to order a retrial because the trial judge erred. An early example is *Dyson & Field v Leeds City Council*[23], where Ward LJ warned the parties that if they did not engage in mediation before they returned to court (presumably a lower court) they might face sanctions under CPR 44.3. There are plenty of subsequent such decisions, either where future use of mediation is strongly urged in a particular case or class of cases, or where failure to use mediation is bemoaned or regretted[24]. A striking example of the latter is found in *Fitzroy Robinson v Mentmore Towers*[25]. In a dispute over a prestige development, it was alleged that the architects who initiated the litigation by suing for fees had deliberately concealed the fact that a key partner was going to leave their firm and cease to deal with the development. The judge had to assess the credibility of a senior member of the firm and found against him, saying that it was a great pity that mediation had not been used to avoid the risk of such an adverse finding as to credibility.

History (and precedent) do not report what happened as a result of these informal recommendations. It is unlikely that if one party refused to mediate after such a recommendation, the other would not use such a refusal to influence the lower court over what to order as to costs. If both ignored it, the judge would have to have discovered about the recommendation from the appeal judgment. Perhaps they all settled through mediation anyway.

Halsey was cited in *MD v Secretary of State for the Home Department*[26], a public law appeal relating to compensation claims for mishandled asylum

---

23 [2000] CP Rep 42.
24 Such as *Bates v Microstar Ltd* (4 July 2000, unreported), CA; *Couwenbergh v Valkova* [2004] EWCA Civ 676; *A v Burne* [2006] EWCA Civ 24; *Egan v Motor Services (Bath) Ltd* [2007] EWCA Civ 1002; *Dibble v Pfluger* [2010] EWCA Civ 1005; *Uren v Corporate Leisure (UK) Ltd* [2011] EWCA Civ 66; *Brewer v Mann* [2012] EWCA Civ 246.
25 [2010] EWHC 98 (TCC).
26 [2011] EWCA Civ 453.

applications. A complaints procedure had not been used by the applicants, who argued that *Halsey* established that courts cannot oblige unwilling parties to refer disputes to an alternative resolution process. The Court of Appeal rejected this argument, on the basis that *Halsey* was about civil litigation (oddly reciting the facts of *Steel v Joy* rather than *Halsey*), and where litigating a judicial review was pointless and a waste of time and money, the court could properly refuse to hear the case and refer the parties to the alternative procedure. Sadly the opportunity was not taken to decide whether *Halsey* was actually right on what it was said to have decided in relation to civil litigation.

5.5 The effect of encouraging ADR in the Pre-action Protocols

The remaining question is to consider what effect judges may feel that the consolidated provisions in the Pre-action Protocols relating to ADR might have. Will ignoring the recommendation to try ADR there be treated similarly to ignoring an ADR order or judicial recommendation? There is no guidance on this as yet, but some initial comments are worthwhile.

The general approach taken in the protocols is very similar to the Ungley Order, in that it is provided that:

> 'the parties should consider whether some form of alternative dispute resolution procedure would be more suitable than litigation, and if so, endeavour to agree which form to adopt. Both the Claimant and Defendant may be required by the Court to provide evidence that alternative means of resolving their dispute were considered'.

In such situations, the duty to consider ADR clearly lies on both parties equally, and it is also made clear that costs sanctions await parties who ignore the protocol requirements. It goes on to provide that 'claims should not be issued prematurely when a settlement is still being actively explored'.

This is slightly strange. Surely what is intended is that claims should not be issued if parties ought still to be exploring settlement. A bilateral contracting-out from settlement discussions ought not to be an excuse to prevent sanctions.

The concluding comment that 'it is expressly recognised that no party can or should be forced to mediate or enter into any form of ADR' reflects the court's traditional reluctance to compel parties into mediation. There is, of course, no such power to compel mediation before an action is commenced. It is arguable that someone keen to mediate before issue should have the right to seek a pre-issue ADR Order against a refusing party, comparable to pre-action disclosure. The only current remedy is to issue proceedings, paying the substantial court fee on issue, and seek an ADR order at directions stage. A recommendation by Sir Rupert Jackson that parties might be able to seek compliance with Pre-action Protocol requirements before issue of proceedings has not yet been implemented[27].

The main problem over enforcement of these protocol duties may lie in the breadth of the definition of what constitutes ADR at that stage. Besides any methods particular to that sector, every protocol and the Practice Direction lists the following:

- discussion and negotiation;
- early neutral evaluation by an independent third party;
- mediation – a form of facilitated negotiation assisted by an independent neutral party.

This revisits the very nature of ADR. As was said in *Halsey*:

'The term "alternative dispute resolution" is defined in the Glossary to the CPR as a "collective description of methods of resolving disputes otherwise that through the normal trial process". In practice, however, references to ADR are usually understood as being references to some form of mediation by a third party … The cases in which the question of displacing this rule have been discussed have usually been concerned with refusal of mediation by the successful party. The two appeals before this court fall into this category. In what follows we shall concentrate on the cost consequences of a refusal by the successful party to agree to mediation'[28].

Mediation then remains the focus of the case, with ADR being used synonymously with mediation, except that when considering whether use of other settlement methods might excuse refusal of mediation he says:

'But it is also right to point out that mediation often succeeds where previous attempts to settle have failed'.

---

27 Discussed in Chapters 35 and 39 of his Final Report, but during his implementation discussions, it was made clear that this revolutionary idea would be shelved for the time being, though remaining a possibility for the future.
28 [2004] EWCA Civ 576 at para 5.

Will judges accept that the protocol requirements to try to avoid litigation will be met by parties who say that they have had a quick but fruitless discussion or negotiation? Of course unassisted bilateral negotiation resolves the vast majority of cases settled before issue, but will judges expect another ADR process prior to the issue of proceedings to be tried first when discussions have failed?

There is an unarguable qualitative difference between discussion and negotiation on the one hand (including round-table conferences) and a more formal but less adversarial process such as mediation. The whole concept of having the added value of a third party neutral to engage actively with the parties so as to assist them to resolve their dispute, allowing them to determine whether terms are acceptable, is far beyond discussion or negotiation. A quick chat on the telephone or between solicitors without clients present could easily satisfy an incurious or uncritical judge in deciding whether the protocol requirements have been met. All such discussions are 'without prejudice', so how will a judge satisfy himself over the adequacy of compliance if discussion or negotiation are claimed to satisfy the protocol requirement? Will it be sufficient for parties to say 'we had a discussion' or 'we negotiated' for the litigation to be allowed to continue, or might a judge legitimately say, 'but you should also have used mediation'? Answers to these questions will doubtless emerge in time. Certainly there has been little evidence of robust enforcement of protocol requirements by procedural judges hitherto since their introduction along with the CPR.

5.6   Compelling use of mediation: the real litigation world

When it came to the making of ADR orders, *Halsey* had a profound, specific and immediate effect. Lord Dyson (then Head of Civil Justice) had just signed the Order in Council which set up the ARMS (the acronym for an 'automatic referral to mediation scheme') opt-out pilot mediation scheme at Central London County Court to explore what effect making ADR orders would have on take-up of mediation. At a stroke *Halsey* undermined this experiment by giving recalcitrant solicitors a perfect authority for refusing to accept compulsion. There were also reports that District Judges around the country who had been utilising ADR orders up to then overlooked *Halsey*'s explicit approval of ADR orders in Commercial Court form and ceased to make such orders at all. As noted above, in *Nokia v Interdigital Technology,* Pumfrey J's view was that *Halsey* meant that the court could not order mediation on a given basis against the wishes of one party, although it can stay an action for reconsideration and can later sanction unreasonable refusal. As this decision coincided almost exactly with

Hickman v Blake Lapthorn[29], where the judge declined to impose a costs sanction on a defendant who had refused to mediate in circumstances where mediation looked absolutely apposite, this did not feel a good time for any joined-up relationship between mediation and civil justice.

Meanwhile the Commercial Court remained unmoved by the purist view articulated in *Halsey*. In *C v RHL*[30], when C sought an anti-suit injunction to stop D from proceeding in the Moscow Arbitration Court, based on an ICC Arbitration clause choosing London for dispute resolution, Colman J demonstrated characteristic robustness in deciding that all these disputes should be referred to mediation. He made an ADR order with a strict time-table. There is no evidence in his judgment that either party asked him to do this.

Here matters stayed until 2010. Some judges made ADR orders, but many did not. Some Appeal Court judges recommended their Court of Appeal Scheme to those who sought permission to appeal, but many did not. Commercial mediations continued steadily, and the process spread vigorously into the employment sector, but the largest sector in civil justice, namely personal injury, remained largely mediation-free, with no sense of compulsion being permissible or acceptable to change that. Professor Dame Hazel Genn QC's Hamlyn Lectures in 2008 appeared to give succour to those who felt that mediation should not be imposed on unwilling parties by any kind of court order. Whether she misread or disbelieved Dyson LJ's judgment given on behalf of the full court when he said 'there are many disputes which are suitable for mediation'; and 'the value and importance of ADR has been established within a remarkably short time. All members of the legal profession who conduct litigation should now routinely consider with their clients whether their disputes are suitable for ADR'; and 'we recognise that mediation has a number of advantages over the court process' has never emerged, but her characterisation of him as 'a judicial non-believer or at least a judicial sceptic' was one that he felt constrained to deny in his 2010 lecture, saying that 'far from indulging in ADR atheism, I am a strong believer in its merits, though I do not think that it is necessarily appropriate for every dispute'. Perhaps with the benefit of hindsight and commentary, her mistake over this can be treated in the same way as other surprising assertions in those lectures, such as 'the proponents of mediation are anti-adjudication and anti-litigation and the proponents of adjudication are anti-settlement'; and 'the outcome of mediation is not about just settlement: it is just about settlement'[31], based as they seem to be on painful misunderstandings of the true nature of mediation.

---

29 [2006] EWHC 12 (QB), a decision later criticised by Lord Dyson in his October 2010 speech.
30 [2005] EWHC 873 (Comm).
31 See the discussion of these views in **Chapter 1**.

Her thesis was mainly directed towards asserting the purity and value of efficient civil courts as the proper source of law, which mediation tended to undermine and deflect, and hence that it was irrational for judges or the civil justice system to compel parties to mediate as a matter of principle. There were certainly signs that her views had some general influence on the judiciary. For example, both Lord Neuberger (then MR, now President of the Supreme Court) and Sir Rupert Jackson's costs review quoted her lectures approvingly in speeches and reports. The Jackson report largely endorsed the views of the court in *Halsey* by saying that mediation has a greater role to play in the system than was currently recognised. But Sir Rupert said, while judges should encourage its use and indeed direct parties to meet and discuss mediation (permitting the court to hear why it was rejected at the conclusion of any trial when considering what costs order to make), 'I do not believe that parties should ever be compelled to mediate', limited his recommendations to support of the court's power to impose costs sanctions for unreasonable refusal to mediate[32]. The 2013 amendments to the CPR add no direct encouragement to simple judicial recommendation of mediation.

The main trigger for a review of thinking about the applicability of Article 6 to ordering mediation was three-fold and came out of Europe. The first was the EU Mediation Directive and its predecessor draft, the preamble and text of which made it clear that compulsory mediation existed in Europe and was not inconsistent with voluntary continued engagement in the mediation process. This was followed and indeed relied upon in a speech by Sir Anthony Clarke MR (now Lord Clarke) to the Civil Mediation Council Conference in 2008, where he said mildly 'we can safely say that there may be grounds for suggesting that *Halsey* was wrong on the Article 6 point', giving a second impetus to this re-thinking.

The third strand was the decision of the European Court in *Alassani v Telecom Italia*[33] in 2010. Four Italian cases were referred to the European Court for a preliminary ruling. Italian national legislation mandated an attempt at out-of-court settlement during a 30-day window in certain consumer disputes about alleged breach of contract by telecoms providers before court proceedings could be started. The European Court considered Article 6 of the ECHR, Article 47 of the Charter of Fundamental Human Rights of the EU, and the encouragement given to simple dispute resolution provisions in the Universal Service Directive as to the benefits of out-of-court settlement procedures in consumer disputes. The applicants had started proceedings before invoking the settlement procedure

---

32 In Chapter 36 of the Jackson Final Report, para 3.4.
33 C-137/08.

and the respondents objected. The court applied the principles of equivalence and effectiveness so beloved of European jurists. They noted that:

- the outcome of the settlement procedure was not binding and did not prejudice the bringing of court proceedings;
- the 30-day limit did not impose a substantial delay;
- the limitation period was suspended during the required process; and
- no significant costs were involved in using the procedure.

They decided that the claimants should have used the procedure, and (as argued by the Italian government) it was not disproportionate to the objectives of quick resolution to have required them to do so, as it helped to reduce burdens on the Italian court system.

In his 2010 speech to the Chartered Institute of Arbitrators Symposium on Mediation, Dyson LJ undertook a very fair analysis both of the impact of those above events on the thinking in *Halsey* and the extent to which they have modified his own views as expressed in the judgment of the Court of Appeal in *Halsey*. Understandably he adhered to many of the views that he and his fellow judges expressed in *Halsey*: that mediation is important and should be used in many cases, while not being a universal panacea; that parties should not be compelled to mediate if truly unwilling; but that adverse costs orders are a proper way to encourage use of mediation. As noted above, he specifically conceded that European (and thus English) law does not actually prohibit compulsory mediation and that this is not a breach of Article 6. This does amount to a concession from the views expressed in the *Halsey* judgment, but a properly cautious one. He rightly pointed out that *Alassani* is limited in scope as an English-type precedent. It does not deal with mediation but another type of compulsory ADR process. It was given approval, among other reasons, because it was easily accessible, affordable and had no impact on limitation rights. His response to Lord Clarke's points was that the terms of the order requiring ADR are crucial in determining whether Article 6 is infringed. However, his main point was not that there is no power to order ADR: it was to doubt the wisdom of exercising such a power on wholly unwilling parties.

It is at this point, however, that the argument needs to be brought into the real world. Let us take as an illustration two building disputes considered in recent years by the Court of Appeal, namely *Burchell v Bullard*[34] and *Rolf v De Guerin*[35], and see what impact these cases have had

---

34 [2005] EWCA Civ 358.
35 [2011] EWCA Civ 78.

on judicial thinking in another more recent case, *Newman v Framewood Manor Management Co Ltd*[36]. The two earlier cases were relatively small disputes involving lawyers outside London. Both of them reached the Court of Appeal from county courts where inordinate sums of money had already been incurred in costs. In *Burchell,* the claimant proposed mediation before issue of proceedings, only to have the proposal turned down by a quantity surveyor on the client's behalf because the dispute was too complex, a reason described by Ward LJ as 'plain nonsense'. From then on mediation was apparently ignored both by the parties (as were the obligations imposed by the Construction and Engineering Pre-action Protocol) and the judges in the county court and the Court of Appeal. Despite the dire warnings given by Ward LJ to future generations of lawyers that 'a small building dispute is par excellence the kind of dispute which, as the Recorder found, lends itself to ADR'; and that 'defendants in a like position in the future can expect little sympathy if they blithely battle on regardless of alternatives', the defendant in *Rolf* ignored all invitations to mediate and settle until shortly before trial when huge costs had been run up and the defendant had run out of money, both of which made settlement virtually unaffordable. Nor is there any evidence that the county court or single judge in the Court of Appeal recommended it. The question is: did the civil justice system let these parties down? Surely the answer is 'Yes'. By far the best account of the devastating impact that involvement in litigation can have on the parties is the documentary article which appeared in The Guardian reporting interviews with both Mr Burchell and Mr and Mrs Bullard. There were no winners and the damage to private life and their finances was enormous[37].

Did these decisions make any difference to the court's thinking in *Newman v Framewood?* The answer is no, because they were not even referred to in the judgment. Mrs Newman and her husband were long lessees in a prestigious residential development. They sought specific performance and damages because the defendants had stopped up an internal access door giving them easy access to the complex swimming pool, and had replaced a jacuzzi with a sauna. They broadly lost at trial at which tricky legal issues were argued to deal with these claims, and won on appeal. There had been no proper settlement discussions and some desultory offers made. The costs at stake are unspecified, but there must have been substantial after a long trial and an appeal. The total damages at stake proved to be £6,000. These, together with costs, must presumably be paid out of the defen-

---

36 [2012] EWCA Civ 159.
37 In *Tarajan Overseas Ltd v Kaye* [2001] EWCA Civ 1859, a low-value construction claim, the court held that a person with authority for a party could be ordered to attend court personally at a case management conference to discuss the possibility of an ADR Order being made.

dants' maintenance fund, to which all the lessees (including presumably the Newmans) contribute, hardly a recipe for happy communal living. And yet there is no sign that the court endeavoured to encourage or 'order' the parties to use a mediator to try to instil some perspective and common sense into this dispute, especially as a consensual solution to the door emerged during the litigation. All they could do was in effect to wring their hands in impotence at having to supervise a wholly disproportionate piece of litigation, saying:

> 'This is a very sad and unfortunate case, in which the costs of successful litigation far, far exceed the amounts recovered by the claimant. Sadly, it is a situation, particularly where people are living in close quarters with others, that we see too frequently in these courts'.

Surely a civil justice system should do better than that for its users[38]. It is fine in legal theory for the court in *Halsey,* or Sir Rupert Jackson or Lord Dyson to say that no one should be compelled to mediate if they are truly unwilling to do so. But such an approach raises several important questions. Whose view is to be consulted about this? Is it each party, or each party's solicitor, or barrister or expert witness (as in *Burchell*)? If the party, is the party fully alive to what mediation is and can achieve? If the lawyer's view, does this represent advice based on proper training and experience? Is there any possible conflict of interest, actual or underlying, between client and adviser, which might mean that early settlement is something that the client might welcome but the legal adviser would not? Is the client being realistic and is the legal team actually concerned to enlist the help of a neutral who can sit beside their client and add weight to the possibility that litigation involves an unwise risk? Is mobilising subtle and obscure legal argument the best way to solve what was, in *Newman v Framewood*, a highly practical and easily soluble problem for people bound to live in close proximity for years?

There is surely a duty on the court to look behind assertions made by parties and their advisers in an open forum in front of an opponent as to the strength or weakness of each other's cases, and their willingness to admit the possibility of engaging in a process which offers the real chance of swift settlement before too much time, cost and pain are hazarded. A civil justice system is surely able to protect its users from themselves and

---

38 As early as 2000, Brooke LJ in *Walsh v Misseldine* [2000] All ER (D) 261, CA, a personal injury claim, commented 'it was a classic case for mediation by a mediator with experience in this field. If the dispute had been referred to mediation with the defendant's insurers present, it would almost certainly have been settled six years ago'.

to try to make sure that whatever is litigated in front of the courts justifies that level of judicial input. Moreover, it should only do so if party resolve to litigate despite examining every alternative is unshakeable.

Chapters 6 and **7** now look at the related issue of imposing costs sanctions for refusing to mediate.

Chapter 6

Costs sanctions for refusing to mediate 1: the journey towards *Halsey v Milton Keynes NHS Trust*

The previous chapter discussed whether, how and when the courts should order or otherwise encourage parties to enter into mediation. This and the next chapter examine whether and when a court should impose costs sanctions on a party who refuses to mediate. It is already clear that to ignore an ADR order or other similar encouragement given by a judge might of itself justify a sanction against even a successful party who refuses mediation, and **Chapters 6** and **7** look at how this works in practice, taking the decision in *Halsey v Milton Keynes General NHS Trust* as the watershed between the two chapters, but bearing in mind that many of the cases decided before *Halsey* are still good law. The additional issue considered in this chapter is what happens if one party spurns an invitation to mediate made by another party, when there has been neither an ADR order nor judicial recommendation to mediate. The issue comes into closest focus when considering this in relation to refusal by a successful litigant, who would otherwise normally expect to be awarded costs, but it may also affect what happens to an intransigent loser of litigation. The situation has been further complicated by the 2013 amendments to the CPR related to actions involving claims for personal injury or death (including therefore clinical negligence claims), in which the general rules over expectations for costs awards have been radically altered. These are all discussed.

6.1 The basis for sanctioning unreasonable conduct

As a reminder, CPR Part 44 provides as follows:

'44.2(1) The court has discretion as to:

(a) whether costs are payable by one party to another;
(b) the amount of those costs; and
(c) when they are to be paid.

(2) If the court decides to make an order about costs:

(a) the general rule is that the unsuccessful party will be ordered to pay the costs of the successful party; but
(b) the court may make a different order'.

The most important words here are *'the court has discretion'*. While the pre-CPR presumption that costs follow the event is noted, the court's power to depart from it is accorded similar prominence. Indeed, perhaps the main feature of litigation under the CPR has been judicial willingness to depart from costs orders that would have been regarded as normal before the CPR, both generally and in relation to Part 36 offers, and by no means only in relation to refusal of ADR. With the weaponry of unreasonable conduct, exaggeration and disproportionality available upon which to justify a non-standard costs award, plus willingness to apportion costs according to each party's success or failure to 'win' on different issues tried by the court, costs outcomes have, if anything, become harder to predict than before the CPR. The net effect of this issue-responsive approach to costs awards has been to generate a much greater chance that unsuccessful parties who might have been condemned to pay all the costs before the CPR can now aspire to rescue some of that costs exposure. In effect, success has become a relative matter, and quite frequently neither party can really claim to have won completely at trial.

This is perhaps most vividly illustrated in *Painting v University of Oxford*[1], in which the apparent winner was the claimant, she having comfortably beaten a Part 36 offer of £10,000 by a damages award of £25,330. However, she had declined a Part 36 offer of £185,000 after which earlier film showing her to be far less disabled than she alleged was disclosed, and with permission the sum in court was reduced to £10,000. The Court of Appeal found that she had grossly exaggerated her claim and had made no attempt to negotiate. As the trial had almost entirely concerned the exaggeration allegation, an issue on which she had lost, she was awarded her costs up to the date of the final Part 36 offer, but ordered to pay the defendant's costs thereafter, including the costs of the appeal, some on an indemnity basis. This costs liability will almost certainly have wiped out her damages.

As soon as those rules in CPR Part 44 were promulgated (and they remain largely unchanged despite the 65 or so later amendments to the CPR in the last 11 years and indeed untouched by the Jackson reforms of 2013) mediation commentators pointed out that to refuse mediation, whether before or after issue of proceedings, might well be regarded as constituting unreasonable conduct and thus giving rise to a possible costs sanction. A few judicial threats were uttered to this effect in such cases as *Cowl v Plymouth City Council*[2] and *Dyson and Field v Leeds City Council*[3]. In the former, Lord Woolf remarked:

---

1 [2005] EWCA Civ 161.
2 [2001] EWCA Civ 1935.
3 [2000] CP Rep 42.

'Today sufficient should be known about ADR to make the failure to adopt it, in particular when public money is involved, indefensible';

and in the latter Ward LJ, in ordering a retrial on appeal to correct a judicial error specifically recommended the parties to mediate before a new trial was fixed, reminding them that CPR 44 would allow sanction 'for unreasonable failure to do so'.

With the CPR requiring encouragement of ADR as a tool of active case management for the purposes of fulfilling the overriding objective, then it must be arguable that refusal to mediate by a successful party might indeed constitute unreasonable litigation conduct. The rest of this chapter sets out the ways in which the courts have developed their thinking in this area, and seeks to draw principles from what has happened to both wholly and partly successful parties when mediation has been proposed and refused.

The impact of costs and funding issues is examined in greater detail in **Chapters 11** and **12** respectively.

6.2 Early developments in post-CPR case law

Before the CPR came into force in April 1999, there was simply no basis for threatening costs sanctions for failure to mediate. The earliest relevant decisions, as seen in the last chapter, represent attempts by the court to order that ADR should take place, usually relying upon CPR Part 1. In *Dyson and Field v Leeds City Council*, the Court of Appeal gave the first indication that a court might consider depriving a party of a costs award which they might otherwise have expected. They firmly indicated that the parties should try ADR before the expense of the retrial which they had reluctantly ordered was incurred. Even back in 1999, Ward LJ was identifying the delicate balance between carrot and stick which has dominated judicial thinking on this topic:

'I would add that the court has powers to take a strong view about the rejection of the encouraging noises we are making, if necessary by imposing orders for indemnity costs or indeed ordering that a higher rate of interest be paid on any damages which might at the end of the day be recoverable. With that warning of dire consequences but essentially with a note of encouragement, I would allow this appeal and remit the matter back to the County Court'[4].

---

4 *Dyson and Field v Leeds City Council* ibid, paras 18–19. For a similar more recent encouragement to use ADR by the Court of Appeal on ordering a retrial, see *A v Burne* [2006] EWCA Civ 24.

A hint of what might develop emerged in the Technology and Construction Court case of *Paul Thomas Construction Ltd v Hyland and Power*[5], where Judge Wilcox found that the conduct of the claimant in both declining to co-operate without payment of a substantial sum, and then issuing High Court proceedings and seeking summary judgment and an interim payment under CPR Parts 24 and 25 was unreasonable and not in the spirit either of the CPR or of the Pre-action Protocol Practice Direction. The judge awarded the defendant indemnity costs, thus adding to the pain of a procedural defeat for a claimant who was indeed probably owed something. Recalcitrance over refusing to enter discussion was certainly part of the reason for the sanction, even if not strictly for refusing ADR.

Lord Woolf's judgment in *Cowl v Plymouth City Council*[6] was more of a discussion as to the duty of parties to try ADR and to regard litigation as the last resort. No costs sanctions were threatened, merely a reminder given, in this case to both parties, that to waste costs on proceedings was unacceptable.

6.3 The landmark case of *Dunnett v Railtrack*

The generality of Lord Woolf's warnings in November 2001 in *Cowl* moved with startling speed to a very specific penalty imposed in February 2002 in *Dunnett v Railtrack*[7] on a successful litigant for refusing to mediate. The facts and framework of this case need explanation. Mrs Dunnett had been told by contractors for Railtrack that they could not padlock a gate in the fence between her paddock and a railway line. When the newly installed gate was left open by strangers and her horses were killed by an express train, she sued for the loss of her horses and her psychiatric injury. She lost in the county court, partly perhaps because her lawyers wrongly framed the case. She appealed in person and in giving her permission to appeal, Schiemann LJ suggested that mediation be attempted. Railtrack rejected this out of hand, despite the fact that the Court of Appeal then offered a free mediation scheme, and they also (unsuccessfully) opposed an extension of time sought by Mrs Dunnett.

The Court of Appeal expressed regret that mediation had not been attempted before trial, noting that this had not been suggested by the Cardiff County Court. They then considered Railtrack's rejection of Schiemann LJ's suggestion, and whether the fact that Railtrack had made Part 36 offers – firstly of £2,500 after permission to appeal had been given, and later to bear their own costs if the appeal were withdrawn – made any dif-

---

5 (8 March 2000, unreported), TCC.
6 [2001] EWCA Civ 1935.
7 *Dunnett v Railtrack plc (in railway administration)* [2002] EWCA Civ 303.

ference to their position. Brooke LJ, giving the only judgment, decided that the offers were irrelevant and on the facts declined to make any order as to costs. In doing so, he made the following important observations[8]:

> 'Skilled mediators are now able to achieve results satisfactory to both parties in many cases which are quite beyond the power of lawyers and courts to achieve. This court has knowledge of cases where intense feelings have arisen, for instance in relation to clinical negligence claims. But when the parties are brought together on neutral soil with a skilled mediator to help them resolve their differences, it may very well be that the mediator is able to achieve a result by which the parties shake hands at the end and feel that they have gone away having settled the dispute on terms with which they are happy to live. A mediator may be able to provide solutions which are beyond the power of the court to provide'.

He went on:

> 'It is to be hoped that any publicity given to this part of the judgment of the court will draw attention of lawyers to their duties to further the overriding objective in the way that is set out in Part 1 of the Rules and to the possibility that, if they turn down out of hand the chance of ADR, when suggested by the court, as happened on this occasion, they may have to face uncomfortable costs consequences'.

Railtrack undoubtedly won both below and on appeal. They even protected any risk to their firm denial of liability by a modest Part 36 offer. No ADR order had been made, nor did any protocol require use of ADR as best practice. They rejected mediation because they felt that engagement would necessarily have meant that they had to offer more, a view firmly rejected by the court as a 'misunderstanding' of the purpose of ADR as they pointed to the fact that mediation could deliver outcomes impossible to obtain from a court. Was it right for them to be sanctioned? There have been many who have criticised the decision since.

The court was surely right in taking this approach, and that criticism of the decision is misplaced. Changing the perspective slightly, all that Railtrack had to do was to attend a free Court of Appeal Scheme mediation, perhaps without an external lawyer, to meet with Mrs Dunnett, listen to the concerns and emotions she chose to air, express regrets without admitting legal liability, and see if there was any other way in which their future relationship as neighbouring landowners with conflicting interests might

---

8 In paras 14 and 15.

be improved. They could then have decided whether anything they heard within the confidentiality of the mediation process justified improving on any previous offer within a confidential settlement and, if no consensus emerged through the good offices of the mediator, continuing with the appeal with nothing changed by the mediation. What was to be lost in not doing that? They discovered all too quickly that by not making a modest investment in a mediation, they lost their costs of the appeal.

Dunnett v Railtrack actually had a disproportionate effect on legal thinking about mediation, best demonstrated by CEDR's published case numbers statistics. In the year following the CPR, CEDR's caseload increased by 140%. In the following two years the numbers first plateaued and then reduced by about 20%. In each of the two years after *Dunnett*, the annual upward trend was just over 25%. One cogent interpretation of these figures is that with judges having shown little sign of ordering ADR or sanctioning failure to use it after the CPR, it took the shock of *Dunnett* to compel advisers to realise that to ignore recommendations and invitations to mediate might be risky. *Dunnett* was probably the first and certainly the most notorious decision to show that even a successful litigant who correctly called their legal risk might face a costs sanction if perceived by a judge to have acted unreasonably in relation to the process choices made.

There are several points to note about the case, though. First, Mrs Dunnett was undoubtedly the weaker party, represented for free by the Bar Pro Bono Unit against a major corporation well able to afford the consequence visited on them as an example to others. Second, the reason for the decision was based firmly on ignoring a judge's recommendation to mediate, and not on a mere offer on Mrs Dunnett's own initiative. Though believed to be so at the time (many unwilling parties cited *Dunnett* as the reason for mediating in the months that followed, often merely when the other party had proposed it), it is not an authority for saying that there may be costs consequences for ignoring another party's proposal to mediate rather than a judge's order. Third, the order simply deprived the successful party of their costs, and did not completely reverse the normal costs expectation: Railtrack was not ordered to pay Mrs Dunnett's costs, such as they were.

However, *Dunnett* revolutionised thinking overnight about the general place of mediation in civil justice, besides simply confirming the proposition that refusal to mediate *could* indeed be regarded as an instance of unreasonable litigation conduct, so as to deprive even a successful party of their normal costs expectations. Although apparently overtaken by *Halsey* as the lead case, it is clear that nothing said in *Halsey* overrules *Dunnett*, which remains good law, if for no other reason than that *Halsey* strictly concerned *inter-party offers* to mediate and *Dunnett* involved ignoring a *judicial recommendation* to mediate, each being different triggers to the decision-making process about whether to mediate. Indeed, *Halsey* suggests specifically that ignoring a judicial recommendation might well *of itself* constitute unreasonable litigation conduct. *Rolf v De Guerin*[9] confirms the validity of the *Dunnett* view.

6.4   Other cases where sanctions were imposed

The Court of Appeal thereafter adopted the *Dunnett* line in several subsequent cases. An insurer which broadly won its appeal in a personal injury case, reducing a damages award of £260,000 by just over £60,000, had its costs reduced by £5,000 for failing to accept judicial advice to mediate[10]. In *Leicester Circuits Ltd v Coates Brothers plc*[11], the defendants in a commercial dispute withdrew from a mutually agreed mediation the day before it was due to be held. At the trial a month later, the claimants won, but the defendants successfully appealed and sought their costs of the appeal and in the court below. The Court of Appeal accepted the claimants' criticism of the defendants' withdrawal from mediation, and only awarded the defendants their costs below up to eight days before the mediation date and then costs of the appeal, requiring them to bear their own costs for the remainder of the time before trial and the three-week trial itself.

The defendants sought to justify withdrawal from mediation as being merely akin to a negotiation that failed. Judge LJ responded:

> 'The whole point of having mediation, and once you have agreed to it, proceeding with it, is that the most difficult of problems can sometimes, indeed often are, resolved'.

The Court of Appeal regarded the issue as being whether there had been a realistic prospect of successful resolution through mediation. This test had particular significance in one of the major first instance decisions on this topic, *Hurst v Leeming*, which is discussed below, and which promulgated a similar test. Judge LJ took a firm view in *Leicester Circuits* in commenting:

> 'It hardly lies in the mouths of those who agree to it to assert that there was no realistic prospect of success'.

Dunnett was (perhaps for the first time) cited to the Court of Appeal. Judge LJ quoted from Brooke LJ's judgment, particularly his assertion that the

---

9   [2011] EWCA Civ 78.
10 *Neal v Jones Motors* [2002] EWCA Civ 1757.
11 [2003] EWCA Civ 333.

parties themselves have a duty to further the overriding objective. The key passage in Judge LJ's judgment on costs reads:

> 'It seems to us that the unexplained withdrawal from an agreed mediation process was of significance to the continuation of this litigation. We do not for one moment assume that the mediation process would have succeeded, but certainly there is a prospect that it would have done if it had been allowed to proceed. That therefore bears on the issue of costs'.

In a decision obverse to *Paul Thomas Construction v Hyland*[12], the Court of Appeal in *Virani Ltd v Manuel Revert y Cia SA*[13] ordered that an unsuccessful defendant who had refused to mediate or negotiate before losing at trial and again on his appeal (despite advice from the single Lord Justice) should pay the successful claimants' costs on an indemnity basis.

In *Royal Bank of Canada Trust Corpn Ltd v Secretary of State for Defence*[14], the defendant won on most but not all issues in a dispute over the validity of notices served under the break clause of a lease, but they had declined several invitations to mediate. The claimant drew attention to the government's public pledge of March 2001 to use mediation in suitable cases wherever an opponent agreed to it. Lewison J found that the case was suitable for ADR, criticised the MoD's failure to abide by the pledge, and declined to award costs to the defendant[15].

In *Malkins Nominees Ltd v Societe Financiere Mirelis SA*[16], the claimant won but had costs reduced by 25% for failing to mediate, the judge having observed that the case had been 'eminently suitable for ADR'. Even after the costs award was reviewed, the court still deducted 15%.

Apart from the mutually agreed mediation in *Leicester Circuits,* and the government pledge factor in the *Royal Bank of Canada* case, the other cases cited above all involved ignoring a judge's recommendation to use ADR. The decisions in which mediation was proposed by one party and ignored by others, without any judicial pressure, are the ones where controversy has been heightened. These were almost all first instance decisions, until the whole topic was reviewed in the second leading case of *Halsey v Milton Keynes General NHS Trust* in 2004.

---

12 See **6.2** above.
13 [2003] EWCA Civ 1651: the costs award is only reported in the Lawtel report and not in the full transcript of the judgment on the merits.
14 [2003] EWHC 1479 (Ch).
15 The pledge aspect of this case is criticised in *Halsey v Milton Keynes NHS Trust*, para 35: the real issue is one of suitability.
16 [2002] EWHC 1221 (Ch).

6.5 Cases where sanctions were not imposed on a refusing party

One of the early decisions where a sanction was **not** imposed has been claimed as theirs by both proponents and opponents of sanctions to mediate. In *Hurst v Leeming*[17], Lightman J established a demanding test for those who refused to mediate to avoid a sanction, but decided that the defendant had met it. The case involved a last-ditch claim against a barrister by a bankrupt solicitor acting in person over a partnership dispute, after he had unsuccessfully sued most other available parties. Lightman J persuaded the claimant that his case was hopeless and had to be discontinued, thus exposing the claimant to the normal liability on discontinuance for the defendant's costs. However, the claimant argued that because the defendant had declined to mediate as required by the Professional Indemnity Pre-action Protocol, *Dunnett* meant that he should be given relief from such a costs order. The defendant produced a number of reasons to excuse that refusal. Those rejected by Lightman J were:

- that heavy costs had already been incurred;
- the serious allegations of professional negligence;
- the fact that the defendant believed he had a watertight case;
- the fact that the claimant's case had already been fully refuted.

The test he defined was that if mediation can have no reasonable prospect of success, a party may refuse mediation with impunity. Lightman J found that on the facts of this case the defendant *'quite exceptionally'* was justified in declining mediation, largely because of the almost obsessive approach of the claimant and his determination to extract a large sum of compensation through the mediation process and finding that he 'was unlikely to accept any mediation which did not achieve that result'. He summarised the position by saying that

'by reason of the character and attitude of Mr Hurst, mediation had no real prospect of getting anywhere. That is not a view which is easily sustainable in any case, but on the facts of this case, it is sustained'.

He went on:

'Refusal is a high risk to take. For if the court finds that there was a real prospect [of mediation success] the party refusing to proceed

---

17 [2002] EWHC 1051 (Ch), [2003] 1 Lloyd's Rep 379.

to mediation may, as I have said, be severely penalised. Further, the hurdle in the way of a party refusing to proceed to mediation on this ground is high, for in making this objective assessment of the prospects of mediation, the starting point must surely be the fact that the mediation process itself can and does often bring about a more sensible and conciliatory attitude on the part of parties than might otherwise be expected to prevail before the mediation, and may produce a recognition of the strengths and weaknesses by each party of his own case and of that of his opponent, and a willingness to accept the give and take essential to a successful mediation. What appears to be incapable of mediation before the mediation process begins often proves capable of satisfactory resolution later'.

The language used by Lightman J suggested that the burden lay on the person seeking relief from a costs sanction (the otherwise successful party), a view later rejected by the Court of Appeal in *Halsey*. Indeed, it was actually always the unsuccessful claimant who was seeking relief from the normal rule that costs followed the event. The case comments powerfully on mediation as an intrinsically better way to resolve disputes. Most significantly, Lightman J declined to excuse refusal to mediate where the refusing party (even rightly) thought he had a watertight case. This echoes the positions of Railtrack, the insurers of Jones Motors, and (eventually) Coats Industries plc. This was re-examined by the Court of Appeal in *Halsey*.

But even assuming that the burden truly was laid on Mr Hurst rather than Mr Leeming to secure costs relief, how did the court come to excuse refusal? Did it have more to do with the claimant's myopic intransigence than fault on the defendant's part? There was no evidence of any willingness on the part of the successful defendant to compromise, and no settlement offers were apparently made at any time. The refusal to mediate flew in the face of protocol requirements, and the overriding objective, though not in the face of any judicial recommendation. So how did the defendant escape a sanction? The answer may lie in looking at the conduct of the party seeking relief, namely the unsuccessful Mr Hurst who proposed mediation. It was his obsession that was, in the court's view, likely to lead to impasse at any mediation, to an extent that forgave refusal to engage in that process. Contrast this with how Mrs Dunnett, Mr Neal, Leicester Circuits and Mr Virani might have felt aggrieved at the refusal to mediate. Each of them apparently offered to engage in the mediation process in good faith whereas Lightman J ultimately felt that Mr Hurst deserved no such relief.

So the unsuccessful party seeking relief from costs must deserve such a benefit and not forfeit it in the light of the way they have conducted their litigation. In *Societe Internationale de Telecommunications Aeronautiques SC v Wyatt Co (UK) Ltd, (Maxwell Batley (a firm), Pt 20 defendant)*[18], the judge declined to penalise the third party who had declined mediation offered by the defendant, largely because the way in which the claimant sought to 'browbeat and bully' the third party into the process by 'self-serving invitations (demands would be a more appropriate word) to participate in the mediation' in which, the judge found, the defendant would never have contemplated being persuaded that their case had no merit. He also found that the timing of proposed mediation excused the third party, a perhaps less convincing excuse to experienced mediators. But an almost equitable requirement of seeking costs relief in this area with clean hands seems to emerge, which is consolidated by the leading case of *Halsey v Milton Keynes General NHS Trust*[19].

Costs sanctions for not mediating were refused in several other reported cases between *Dunnett* and *Halsey*, especially where other settlement methods had been attempted. In *Valentine v Allen*[20], the judge dismissed a claim and found that the claimant's failure to mediate, having rejected other offers to settle, was 'of no cause or effect'. In *Corenso v Burnden Group*[21], the claimant accepted a Part 36 offer late, and asked for all costs, opposed by the defendant because the claimant had refused mediation. On the facts, including the intervention of an intermediary, and various unaccepted earlier offers and counter-offers, and the defendant's abandonment of a counter-claim, the claimant had won and was awarded all costs. In *McCook v Lobo*[22] the losing claimant had written one letter proposing mediation, ignored by the defendants. On the facts again, the failure to mediate was excused, but the court warned the defendants, and thus the legal profession, that they should have responded, 'first as a matter of courtesy and second because of the risk in which he may find himself of having to explain to the court why he did not do so and the risk that a *Dunnett*-type order might be made'.

6.6 *Halsey v Milton Keynes General NHS Trust* and inter-party offers to mediate

The appeal in *Halsey v Milton Keynes General NHS Trust* was conjoined with *Steel v Joy and Halliday,* which was a dispute between two insurers over how to apportion liability for the damages caused by successive torts.

---

18 [2002] EWHC 2401 (Ch) (Park J). Mediation actually settled the main dispute between SITA and Watson Wyatt.
19 [2004] EWCA Civ 576, [2004] 4 All ER 920.
20 [2003] EWCA Civ 915.
21 [2003] EWHC 1805 (QB).
22 [2002] EWCA Civ 1760.

The details of *Steel v Joy* will be considered separately after looking at the principles which emerged from the joint judgment. *Halsey* itself involved very different facts. Mrs Halsey alleged negligence against the hospital in which her husband had died. Her solicitor wrote several times before issuing proceedings in forthright terms, firstly seeking £5,000 costs for preparing and attending the inquest, then seeking £7,500 damages and costs, then seeking mediation. The Trust denied the claim. Later the claimant's solicitor wrote to the Department of Health, warning about the high cost of proceedings in the light of the Trust's refusal to mediate as being 'an unnecessary waste of both costs and resources'. The claimant wrote three or four more letters pressing for mediation, with the Trust still saying that 'on such a low quantum claim, we do not consider this to be a cost-effective use of NHS resources', as it might lead to 'a final bill of legal costs payable by the NHS in the region of £100,000' (the costs estimate proved to be prophetic, even conservative, as to quantum but not as to the paying party).

All attempts to persuade the Trust into mediation foundered, and the claim proceeded to trial where it was dismissed. The claimant unsuccessfully sought relief from an adverse costs order, relying in particular on *Dunnett* and *Hurst v Leeming*, and then appealed against the order for costs. Having heard the witnesses, the trial judge found that the claimant would not have walked away from a mediation without a monetary settlement.

So far the case is all on fours with *Hurst v Leeming* and *SITA v Watson Wyatt,* with a claimant found to be intransigent in demands and unrealistic in openness to a simple non-monetary outcome, and perhaps the case did not require special consideration of principle. Wherever the burden lay over excusing a refusal to mediate, a court had both evidence and authority upon which to excuse the Trust. But the Court of Appeal wanted to take the opportunity to lay down some general principles about how to handle refusals to mediate, and whether and when costs sanctions for doing so might be imposed.

Having discussed ADR orders[23], the Court of Appeal turned to cases where no specific judicial recommendation had been made to use ADR. In the light of CPR 44.3(4) (now 44.2(4)), it found that the burden on altering the normal expectation that costs would follow the event lay upon the party seeking relief (the losing party). Thus the unsuccessful party who proposed mediation must satisfy the court that the successful party who refused should be penalised, the test being that the successful party acted unreasonably in refusing to agree to ADR[24].

---

23 See the discussion of this aspect of *Halsey* in **Chapter 5**.
24 Para 13 of Dyson LJ's judgment.

The court set out six factors which might be relevant in testing out reasonableness in this context, and which were not seen as exhaustive. Oddly, despite the fact that in *Halsey* the burden was firmly placed on the unsuccessful party to show that the successful party's refusal to mediate justified departure from the normal costs order, the six relevant factors identified are framed as a non-exhaustive list of good reasons for *not* sanctioning the *successful party*, rather than as what the unsuccessful party must prove. So, expressing them in accordance with the burden of proof placed by the Court of Appeal on the loser, the *losing party* must establish (presumably on the balance of probabilities – the usual civil burden) that:

- the dispute *was* suitable for ADR;

- the winner's pre-trial *belief that his case was watertight was unreasonable*, perhaps by showing (as will be true for the vast majority of cases) that there were arguable risks facing the winner on one or more significant aspects of the case; or (if this was the case) by observing that the winner did not seek, or, if sought, did not obtain summary judgment under CPR 24, which is surely what someone with a 'watertight' case might be expected to do. Anything short of this standard might be argued to suggest that the case was not obviously watertight;

- *no previous efforts to settle* had been made by the winner, or alternatively that the loser's attempts to settle had been rejected by the winner (though the court noted that even where settlement discussions have failed, mediation often works, this presumably flagging that it might still sanction a winning party who has engaged in settlement discussions but refused thereafter to mediate, if other signs of unreasonableness were manifested by the winner): however, this factor does not reverse in effect comfortably, as the original import of the factor in *Halsey* was that previous settlement attempts engaged in by the winner justified excusing their refusal to mediate;

- mediation would *not have been disproportionately costly*. From the decisions on the facts of *Halsey* and *Steel*, this presumably means that a cost-benefit analysis showed that mediation was on balance more expensive than its chances of success would have justified;

- *trial would not have been delayed* by a mediation;

- mediation *had a reasonable prospect of success* (ie apparently meaning 'achieving settlement'), or that, if it did not, this was because of the winner's intransigence, and not the loser's intransigence over the dispute.

117

6.7 The *Halsey* factors in detail

So what expectations were created by *Halsey* before other courts started to interpret its effects? Some of those principles were expected to have little significance. For instance, **factor 1** (suitability for mediation) seemed unlikely to be deployed often. Very few cases are inherently unsuitable for ADR, as the court in *Halsey* acknowledged. Over 90% of civil cases are said to settle, and any case that is capable of settlement is capable of being mediated successfully. If it is honestly admitted that, especially for local and national government departments, there exists an attitude of mind which means that no one feels able to take a settlement decision and would rather hide behind the skirts of a judicial gown, then there will be cases which are apparently incapable of settlement and therefore not amenable to successful mediation. Public servants do not always have the same approach, or indeed the same freedom from answerability, which might otherwise permit them to take a commercial view on settling. It is also often said that where the parties require a precedent, mediation (and settlement) has no place. This is only true if all parties to the litigation are entirely unconcerned about which way the court decides the precedent, a very rare state of affairs. If either party has a serious legal or commercial interest in ensuring that the decision goes one way but not the other, then there is emphatically something to negotiate about, and a price to consider paying to buy up the risk of any adverse ruling by the court. These factors reduce very considerably the cadre of cases which are inherently unsuitable for mediation.

Indeed, the courts have even positively recommended mediation for certain types of claim. *Burchell v Bullard*[25] and *Rolf v De Guerin*[26] actually propound the concept that mediation is highly suitable for small building claims, while *Vahidi v Fairstead House School*[27] suggested that workplace stress cases should normally be mediated, as the principles for assessing liability in such cases are now well established by decisions of the Court of Appeal and the House of Lords.

Another factor felt in advance to have little likely impact was **factor 4**, relating to avoiding delay to a trial date. A mediation can be set up within days, even hours if necessary. There is no report of a case where refusal to mediate late in the day was excused because otherwise the trial might have had to be postponed. The closest instance is the pre-*Halsey* case of *SITA v Watson Wyatt and Maxwell Batley*, discussed above[28].

---

25 [2005] EWCA Civ 358.
26 [2011] EWCA Civ 78.
27 [2005] EWCA Civ 765.
28 Declining a late offer of mediation (20 working days before trial) was also excused in *ADS Aerospace v EMS Global Tracking* [2012] EWHC 2904 (TCC).

What of the other factors enunciated in *Halsey*? **Factor 3** (previous settlement discussions) never seemed likely to be a strong influence on a costs decision. This factor is really about establishing that the winner might escape a sanction by showing engagement in other settlement attempts (by making a Part 36 offer or participating in discussion). However, *Halsey* rightly recognises that mediation often succeeds where previous attempts have failed. With the burden on the losing party, the loser would have to show that the winner had not (adequately) made attempts at settlement. In fact few mediations take place without some prior, albeit desultory, attempts to settle. Many mediations take place after failed without prejudice discussions.

The most likely factors falling for consideration always seemed to be factor 2 (reasonable belief in a watertight case), factor 6 (prospects of a successful mediation) and factor 5 (the cost-benefit of mediation). Looking at **factor 2** first, it seems inherently unlikely that a loser will be able to show that the winner had an unreasonable belief in having a watertight case so as to excuse a sanction if the winner behaves reasonably throughout the litigation *and* wins on all points at trial or appeal, as the loser will be unable to challenge the reasonableness of the winner's case as vindicated by the court's decision. This is, in effect, why the losing parties failed to get costs relief in the two *Halsey* appeals. But it is also arguably what happened in *Dunnett,* in which the loser did get relief. So the question remains as to whether the loser might still be justified in complaining that it was unreasonable behaviour for the winner simply to refuse to mediate, despite what turned out to be the winner's reasonable belief in litigation success. The *Halsey* judgment suggests that such a mediation would have been a waste of money, which might also bring in **factor 5** as to cost benefit.

But there are three important points to be made about this. First, it is not impossible that at a low-cost mediation, one party will persuade the other to settle by complete withdrawal, either by paying in full or by discontinuing, perhaps coupled with some non-monetary outcome. A classic instance of this kind occurred in the NHS Mediation Pilot supervised and written up by Professor Linda Mulcahy in the late 1990s[29] where one claimant withdrew her claim when she learned for the first time where her foetus had been buried. Like other claimants against the NHS, she discovered that this was all she wanted to achieve. That report underlined the significance of apology, explanation and reassurance of change often sought and found to be satisfying in such cases. Or each party might review its litigation risks and settle very close to one or other party's best case, with

---

29 *Mediating medical negligence claims: an option for the future?* (TSO, 2000), paras 3.12 and 3.13.

a small discount allowed off their best case to buy up the ever-present hazards of litigation.

Second, on occasions, mere engagement in the mediation process – giving parties a chance to speak their mind, to tell their tale to the right listener, and to hear from the right speaker – is sufficient satisfaction. It cannot necessarily be the case that, even where litigation has been embarked upon, such a dispute is only capable of supplying satisfaction through a judicial decision or settlement made in the light of an anticipated judicial decision. A court-room, especially one which placed emphasis on party evidence-in-chief being given in writing, is not necessarily the best place for a party with a sense of grievance to tell their story unfettered by the rules of evidence.

A third related point is that the winner's refusal might also be arguably unreasonable, despite even a reasonable belief by the winner in having a watertight case, in that rejecting mediation also rejects the extra-judicial possibilities which mediations can encompass. Even if Mrs Halsey had little or no chance of winning her claim (and being unable to displace the reasonable belief held by Milton Keynes NHS Trust and the NHS Litigation Authority that the Trust's case was watertight), a mediation would still have served a useful purpose if set up economically and early. Mrs Halsey presumably still remained a potential patient of that NHS Trust (and of the NHS generally) and she had certainly lost faith in it because of her husband's death. A mediation at which the Trust was represented inexpensively by its own claims manager and gave the Trust a chance to have a discussion with Mrs Halsey about what had happened and how it might offer care to her in the future with restored confidence would have been a vitally useful occasion in the ordinary course of events. No admission of liability or payment needed to be made. The Trust would have flagged its denial of compensation in advance (though indicating that it remained open to persuasion and genuinely being so, just in case a new argument emerged at the mediation) and left it to Mrs Halsey to decide whether she would attend on that basis. Mr Halsey's counsel is even reported to have said that the claimant might have been persuaded in the course of the mediation to drop her claim: all she really wanted was an explanation of how her husband had died in hospital.

Similarly, Mrs Dunnett remained a neighbour of Railtrack with a gate in the fence between her paddock and its express train tracks. A mediation at little cost could have attended to non-legal issues between those adjoining landowners without any need to concede liability.

The point is that mediation is not just about delivery of legal remedies: it is about relationships which have been fractured and where legal remedies may not be adequate or even deliverable by the litigation process. An acceptable outcome to a mediation can be achieved even where no damages change hands. As Sir Henry Brooke said in *Dunnett v Railtrack:*

'A mediator [perhaps better expressed as 'Mediation'] may be able to provide solutions which are beyond the power of the court to provide'.

Finally on **factor 2**, what is 'water-tightness' when it comes to pre-trial reasonable belief in success? Is it to the level of the conventional litigation risk of 90%? Or is it the same as the standard required for summary judgment to be sought by claimant or defendant under CPR Part 24, namely that the other party 'has no reasonable prospect of success in pursuing or defending' the claim in question? What mediation does is to encourage the parties to consider whether they want to go to trial and seek their best possible outcome, or alternatively whether they would prefer to buy up any risks of failing wholly or in part by negotiating an acceptable risk-discounted settlement. Presumably success on liability amounts to 'establishing that all claimed heads of damage were fully payable plus interest and full legal costs. Such a paragon of success is rare indeed, and surely a reasonable belief in such water-tightness would generate an application for summary judgment. Even a near certainty of a claim is normally discounted by 10% for litigation risks when any experienced litigation lawyer advises, in case perhaps a party or a key witness dies. So there is hardly any such a thing as a water-tight case. Once risk exists to weaken the prospect of 100% success, even to a small degree, risk-averse clients voyaging on the unfamiliar and frightening seas of litigation with little chart-reading ability may prefer to negotiate a safe haven rather than continue the perils of the voyage, even with a competent skipper.

The more that factor 2 and factor 6 are analysed, the closer they seem to interrelate, and not entirely harmoniously. A litigant's opinion, properly advised, as to their case being water-tight (factor 2) will influence views on whether mediation will settle the case, or whether the mediation has a 'reasonable prospect of success' (factor 6), success here connoting settlement. On the face of it, belief in the water-tightness of one's case, whether reasonable or unreasonable, inevitably threatens deadlock on anything other than terms reflecting that party's certainty of view and thus the consequent 'failure' of the mediation. So can a mediation 'succeed' in these circumstances?

This question then begs another, namely what is 'success' at a mediation? While settlement is unsurprisingly the broad aim of any mediation, is success only to be measured by settlement on the mediation day? It must certainly include settlement later, something which often happens. Might it anyway be that testing out a case so that the parties discover after due reflection that it *is* genuinely worth submitting to trial is a useful exercise?

Furthermore, rejecting the use of mediation on the basis that a party thinks they have a watertight case and that mediation is unlikely to succeed for that reason assumes that parties and their advisers genuinely hold the views they assert. It would be very surprising if any party were to admit on the record, let alone to a judge who was considering whether to make an ADR Order, or even to impose a retrospective costs sanction, that any part of their pleaded case was other than almost certain to prevail. Things change dramatically as soon as the veil of confidentiality descends at a mediation, especially when the mediator is meeting privately with one party under a deeper seal of confidentiality. Provisional concessions are made, strengths and weaknesses prioritised, and parties move time and again towards seeking and reaching a compromise. But they do so with available legal advice and subject always to their right to walk away and revert to litigation if acceptable terms do not emerge. So mere assertions to a judge that a party has a watertight case and therefore that mediation has no reasonable prospect of success are not persuasive to experienced mediators who have so often seen many changes of heart during confidential mediation discussions.

In *Halsey.* the court discussed the hypothetical question of the intransigent party. They said that if a party who *offered* mediation was unreasonably obdurate in attitude, so as to make settlement in that mediation unlikely, the offer might safely be rejected without sanction. This is what happened in *Hurst v Leeming.* However, if an unreasonably obdurate party refuses another (reasonable) party's offer of mediation, saying that there was no reasonable prospect of a successful mediation, this might well merit a sanction, as an obdurate party cannot rely on his own obduracy to show that a mediation will fail. So the court would have had no problem in sanctioning Mr Hurst if it had been he who declined an offer to mediate made by Mr Leeming.

But this formulation becomes more difficult if the parties are also identified as winner and loser. A litigant with an unreasonable belief in the watertightness of his case will often turn out to be the loser in the litigation, and one whose reasonable belief in having a water-tight case will normally have won. Mr Leeming, as the winner at trial, might arguably have been determinedly (though as it proved, rightly) intransigent about the strength of his position, with his 'intransigence' vindicated at trial. It was his firm (intransigent?) view of his likely success in litigation, coupled with his view that Mr Hurst was highly unlikely to compromise, let alone concede, that led him to refuse to mediate. But Railtrack was equally winner of its litigation and yet was penalised for refusing to mediate. So an intransigent loser who offers mediation but gets his prospects of success wrong may be sanctioned for intransigence (despite offering to engage in a process which at least offers the prospect of debate about compromise without prejudice); and an intransigent loser who declines mediation faces indemnity costs (as happened in *Virani v Manuel Revert*). But does it, or should it, always follow that a winner who declines mediation, as Mr Leeming or Railtrack did respectively to Mr Hurst and Mrs Dunnett (maybe even obdurately or intransigently, though perhaps reasonably), should escape any sanction for refusing mediation? This could either be because he is found to have had a reasonable belief in having a watertight case (factor 2); or on the basis that both the strength of his case and the obduracy of his opponent would mean that the mediation would be a waste of time and money (perhaps thus involving factor 5 relating to cost-benefit) and have no reasonable prospect of success (factor 6)?

Although the court in *Halsey* never says so specifically, it seems that they might have found against Mrs Dunnett, had the same set of facts been presented to that panel rather the *Dunnett* panel of judges. For *Dunnett* certainly seems to decide that a winner who has been **unreasonably** intransigent in refusing mediation, so as to damage the theoretical prospects of success at mediation if held, but thereby losing the non-judicial non-monetary benefits offered by the mediation process, can rightly be penalised for that intransigence. *Rolf v De Guerin* takes the same view, where Mrs Rolf, a not at all successful party (awarded £2,500 instead of the £70,000 she claimed, though she won on another issue of principle) persuaded the Court of Appeal to vary the normal costs order because Mr. de Guerin unreasonably refused mediation until too late. Perhaps the wisest remark on all this comes from Dyson LJ in *Halsey* when he said 'it may be difficult for a court to decide whether the mediation had a reasonable prospect of success'.

Furthermore, the overriding test established by *Halsey* is the one that CEDR suggested in its submission to the Court of Appeal (sadly not acknowledged by them) namely that 'did the successful party in all the circumstances unreasonably refuse to engage in ADR'. The above discussion of the factors perhaps suggests either that they have to some degree confused that simple issue or that it has not been as germane to that outcome in practice as first thought.

Concluding this discussion with **factor 5**, which deals with cost-benefit, the mediation community has always recognised that this is a legitimate concern. While there is little objective evidence as to the precise extent that mediation saves money, common sense and pragmatism suggest that mediation would not have established itself in the commercial world if parties did not feel that it was value for money. Furthermore, litigation itself scarcely possesses a good track record for economy. While the vast majority of cases settle, the question remains 'when and how' in order to ensure economical disposal of disputes. Mediation can bring the possibility of discussing settlement much earlier than litigation, even to the pre-issue stage as suggested by the Pre-action Protocols and their Practice Direction, thus reducing the investment in litigation, particularly if the parties are prepared to take a broad brush approach to settlement.

With a well-established market now for mediators to keep costs down, and a number of time- and cost-limited mediation schemes available, mediators' fees should be a relatively insignificant element in the cost of the process, unless parties or their advisers seek to splash out on the most expensive mediators, who are often barristers or ex-barristers. The largest costs in relation to mediations are incurred when parties attend a mediation heavily lawyered. Then aggregate hourly legal costs rates can make it a very expensive exercise even when those costs are borne by each party, and even more so if one party eventually pays both sides' costs. So everything depends on the type of mediation organised. They can be time-limited by agreement and at discounted rates for the mediator, and the level of representation arranged with an eye to proportionality on each side. Since *Halsey,* it is usual for mediation agreements to provide that the costs and fees associated with the mediation be treated as costs in the case, whether the mediation settles the case or not. This means that the ordinary costs principles of reasonableness and proportionality can and should be factored into arguments on costs. If a potential paying party warns a potential receiving party not to exceed a certain level of representation, this can cap costs to a reasonable level.

In the event, Mrs Halsey lost her appeal and was ordered to pay the very considerable costs of trial and appeal, as she did not have the benefit of Legal Aid costs protection. It is salutary to recall, in relation to the way civil justice impacts on innocent participants, that the appeal had nothing whatsoever to do with finding out about why her husband died. It discussed esoteric issues relating to costs and mediation in which she had no personal interest. It is to be hoped that the solicitors who encouraged and advised her to articulate the robust line taken in her behalf, which attracted such criticism from the Court of Appeal, eventually took steps to protect her from the consequences of the advice they gave her.

6.8   *Steel v Joy and Halliday:* a first case study on applying the *Halsey* factors

Despite its markedly different facts, the appeal in *Steel v Joy* was conjoined with the appeal in *Halsey* and bears the same neutral citation. Mr Steel was injured in separate accidents in 1996 and 1999, involving different defendants and insurers, D1 and D2, both of whom admitted liability to the claimant. The claims brought against each were consolidated, as the issue related to the relative contribution made by each defendant to the exacerbation of a previous condition. D1's negligence accelerated his condition by 7–10 years, as would have D2's negligence on its own, but taken with the first accident, it only caused 3–6 months of extra disability. D1 argued that D1 and D2 should share the whole claim, whereas D2 only accepted liability for the 3–6 month exacerbation. D1 proposed mediation to C and D2 two months before trial, but D2 asserted that this was a point of law requiring a judge's decision and declined. When warned of possible costs consequences they replied 'We are not prepared to compromise on the point of law and therefore mediation would be pointless'. They did win their point of law, and D1 sought not to have to pay their costs as they had refused mediation. The judge took the view that mediation so late in the day could probably have achieved little on this topic. The Court of Appeal agreed, and applying their six core points, found:

1   that D2 wanted the point of law decided by the court, and they were entitled to do so without fearing penalty;

2   that D2 reasonably (and rightly) believed that their case was watertight and that D1's case had no merit;

3   there was no suggestion that previous settlement negotiations were relevant; there were none;

4   mediation would have created disproportionate cost, set against a two-hour trial of the issue;

5   it was late in the day and substantial costs had already been incurred, though there was no suggestion that mediation would have delayed the trial;

6   D1 had not shown that mediation had a reasonable prospect of success.

Overall, the Court of Appeal found that D1 had not proved that D2 had acted unreasonably in refusing to mediate, and confirmed the judge's costs order.

It has always been a perfectly cogent reason for litigating rather than mediating that a point of law needs decision. Precedent is what courts are there to provide, and mediation cannot possibly give rise to a legally binding precedent. Nor, incidentally, can arbitration. This is not to say that cases built around liability issues cannot be mediated; quite the reverse. If the party seeking a precedent is content to live with the outcome, win or lose, there is no risk factor at stake. However, if that party would welcome a favourable precedent but might dislike or be disadvantaged by an unfavourable one, risk abounds and settlement may be wise. Mediations have often settled where parties decide on reflection to buy up their risk of an adverse precedent, even where the law is entirely novel[30]. So points of law do not of themselves make mediation unlikely to succeed or inappropriate. In *Steel,* D2 was actually arguing that the law was settled and that D1 was seeking to overturn good clear law, a view which the Court of Appeal shared in rejecting D1's arguments.

It is easy enough for a party who has won to say that this ground justified their refusal to mediate. The challenge is to predict the legal outcome correctly before trial and decline to mediate on that basis, and it was for getting that right that D2, perhaps understandably, escaped sanction in *Steel.* The penalty for getting it wrong is substantial. To chance losing the point of law **and** to face possible indemnity costs, as happened in *Virani v Manuel Revert* (where the Court of Appeal sanctioned a party who refused to mediate because it thought it would win a point of law) is risky indeed.

What of the other reasons in *Steel?* Counsel for D2 mentioned a likely figure of £20,000, sensibly characterised by Dyson LJ as 'surprisingly high'. The cost of a mediation largely depends on the aggregate hourly rate of the lawyers who attend it, plus the (comparatively modest) mediator's fee. As suggested in relation to *Halsey* above, D2 could have attended at a mediation for perhaps two hours with a senior claims manager (many of whom are well qualified to handle their party's case in the informal and without prejudice surroundings of a mediation) and without legal representation; or perhaps D2's panel solicitor would not have charged D2 too much for attending. The level and thus the cost of representation at mediation is within the unfettered choice of each party. There is usually no need to bring two solicitors, plus leading and junior counsel, to a mediation. Fees for mediator and provider (if any) would have been split unless otherwise agreed, either on a fixed fee or an hourly rate basis. Parties need stay no longer than they wish at a voluntary process. So a mediation need cost each party no more than its share of the hourly rate of the mediator and the representation it chooses to arrange, if any.

Mediation shortly before trial is a very different matter from having to consider vacating a trial date, something which never arose in *Steel v Joy.* Mediating late in a case's life can still save enormous costs, especially in a large case, when the parties can enjoy the expensive luxury of having all the evidence in place. It will certainly be cheaper than court-door settlement, which is a hugely wasteful exercise. Any case which settles there or very shortly before trial should have been mediated successfully at least

---

30 The retained organs litigation again comes to mind.

two or three months earlier. As the Deputy High Court judge in *PGF II v OFMS*[31] pointed out, it is difficult to argue that mediation would not have worked if a case actually settles before trial.

It is almost always because preparation has not been done in good enough time that settlement occurs so late, and only rarely because entirely new material has suddenly emerged at the last minute to change the risk perspective.

Why did the court find that D1 had failed to show that mediation had a reasonable prospect of success? They relied in effect on the fact that D2 felt there was no room for compromise in the law, and that to engage in mediation when D2 was simply unwilling to shift would be a waste of time and money, because there would have been no settlement.

Chapter 7 examines the way *Halsey* has been interpreted and applied in terms of the imposition or not of costs sanctions for refusal to mediate.

---

31 [2012] EWHC 83 (TCC).

Chapter 7

Costs sanctions for refusing to mediate 2: the impact of *Halsey*

Decisions since *Halsey v Milton Keynes General NHS Trust*[1] and its con-joined appeal *Steel v Joy and Halliday,* in which unsuccessful parties have tried to persuade the court to sanction a winner who declined to mediate, naturally fall into two clear camps:

– those where a costs sanction was sought but not imposed, and
– those where the court did reduce an unsuccessful party's costs burden to some extent because the winner declined to mediate (sanction cases).

This chapter looks at these two groups of decisions, some in outline and others in more detail, seeking to extract as much guidance from these as possible and trying to discern trends.

Certainly there is some indication that some judges now understand more clearly what mediation involves and can achieve, having perhaps been less well-informed in the mid-2000s. Fewer judges nowadays would now state publicly the rather bleak view expressed in a 2006 judgment: 'I suppose that the main task of a mediator is commonly to lower the expectations of the parties to a point where agreement is possible'. Mediators would claim that their function has a much more positive purpose and effect than that. Experience too will have added to the sum of judicial knowledge. In another 2006 case, *Askey v Wood*[2], the Court of Appeal declined to sanction a successful party who refused to mediate under the Court of Appeal scheme despite the single judge's recommendation, on the basis that it was a liability only case and it would be sterile to debate changes in per-centage liability when no valuation had been placed on the claim. In fact, appeal mediations on percentage liability have now taken place a number of times, even where quantum was unclear.

This chapter now examines the impact of *Halsey* on subsequent decisions about costs sanctions for failing or refusing to mediate.

---

1 [2004] EWCA Civ 576, [2004] 4 All ER 920.
2 [2005] EWCA Civ 574.

7.1 Cases where a sanction was *not* imposed for refusing to mediate

It is striking that the only *Halsey* factors which have received much judicial attention are, as predicted in **Chapter 6**, factor 2 (the successful refusing party's reasonable belief in the strength of their case); factor 6 (mediation had no reasonable prospect of success); and factor 5 (adverse cost-bene-fit). The other four factors have hardly featured in argument or judgment in cases since *Halsey*. In fact even factors 2 and 6 have featured in rather unexpected places and ways.

In terms of prospects of success (factor 2) the clearest discussion took place in *Daniels v Metropolitan Police Comr*[3], a case which was not actu-ally about mediation, but during which the authority of *Halsey* was applied to a situation where the Commissioner had refused to negotiate at all in a claim brought by a mounted officer over a fall from a horse. The claim was defeated at trial, but the Commissioner was roundly criticised by the claimant's counsel for ignoring a modest claimant's Part 36 offer. The court gladly placed the burden on the losing claimant to justify relief from liability for the defendant's costs (the court probably well knowing that the claim was union-funded) and firmly rejected the claimant's arguments. This was a close parallel to *Halsey* itself, where the court was suspicious that the requests for mediation were a ploy to extract a settlement (and substantial costs) out of a very weak case. The defendant police force in *Daniels* also deployed the 'floodgates' argument, knowing both that the claimant herself had other employment claims in the pipeline, and also that other mounted officers were likely to bring claims similar to hers. They had no wish to be seen to be paying out on a weak case, even if it meant that disproportionate costs were run up by both sides in litigating it.

It is interesting to note that, far from placing any reliance on *Halsey* factor 5, to the effect that mediation would have been too costly, the argument is almost always put on the basis that refusing mediation is (or is not) vindi-cated *despite* the fact that the litigation was run at hugely disproportionate cost. Ward LJ has repeatedly bemoaned disproportionate litigation costs in an honourable track record of exhorting use of mediation that spans *McMillen Williams (a firm) v Range*[4], *Burchell v Bullard*[5], *Daniels v Met-ropolitan Police Comr*[6], *Egan v Motor Services (Bath) Ltd*[7], *S v Chapman*[8],

---

3 [2005] 44 LS Gaz R 30.
4 [2004] EWCA Civ 294, [2004] 1 WLR 1858.
5 [2005] EWCA Civ 358.
6 [2005] EWCA Civ 1312.
7 [2007] EWCA Civ 1002.
8 [2008] EWCA Civ 800.

Dibble v Pfluger[9], *Wright v Michael Wright Supplies Ltd*[10]. Other judges have expressed similar concerns[11]. But even Ward LJ acknowledges that on occasions parties must be allowed to litigate without mediating if they have a proper motive in declining, coupled with a sound judgment as to the strength of their case which the outcome of the case justifies. As will emerge below, a party who does not negotiate or mediate and gets his risk assessment wrong before losing has been readily sanctioned on costs orders both before and after *Halsey.*

In *Hickman v Blake Lapthorn*[12], in which D2 (a barrister) declined to mediate when D1 (solicitors) wanted to do so with the claimant C, the court refused to fix liability on D2 for the additional costs of defending proceedings. As it turned out, a pre-trial settlement proposal would have given the claimant £20,000 more than the judge awarded, but the costs incurred in securing that reduction were over £200,000. The judge in *Hickman* looked at the *Halsey* tests. It is not clear whether he was really finding that D2 had a watertight case (clearly he did not). In effect he found that a mediation as between D1 and D2 and C could have succeeded, were it not for D2's intransigence. He seems to have asked the overarching question 'was D2 reasonable in declining to mediate?' (rather than 'has D1 shown that D2 acted unreasonably?') and answered yes.

Losing the sympathy of the court through lying or exaggerating actually seems one of the most potent underlying reasons for courts to decline to allow a loser to escape normal costs consequences, even where the winner refused to mediate or negotiate. Ms Daniels was disbelieved in several material respects and the court was disinclined to favour her on costs. In *Qualifying Insurers Subscribing to the Assigned Risks Pool v Ross and Co (a firm)*[13], decided shortly after *Halsey,* a solicitor in person who lost and tried to escape costs consequences by using alleged refusal to mediate failed to win that point because he was regarded as responsible for the breakdown of mediation which had in fact been set up, but which he then refused to participate in unless a condition precedent was met. This case has echoes of Lightman J's pre-*Halsey* decision in *Hurst v Leeming*[14], involving an apparently similarly intransigent solicitor in person. The Court of Appeal in *Halsey* disagreed with Lightman J's proposed test in *Hurst* that, 'viewed objectively, did the mediation stand any reasonable prospect of success?'

---

9   [2010] EWCA Civ 1005.
10 [2013] EWCA Civ 234.
11 See also Mummery LJ in *Pennock v Hodgson* [2010] EWCA Civ 873 and *Bradford v James* [2008] EWCA Civ 837 on the wisdom of mediating boundary disputes; and Jacob LJ in *IDA Ltd v University of Southampton* [2006] EWCA Civ 145 as to patent entitlement disputes.
12 [2006] EWHC 12 (QB).
13 [2004] EWHC 1181 (Ch).
14 [2003] Lloyd's Rep 309.

a question which Lightman J answered negatively in *Hurst*, thus relieving Leeming of any sanction. In *Halsey*, the court proposed a wider test which encompassed consideration of 'the parties' willingness to compromise and the reasonableness of their attitudes'.

A loser's proposal to mediate must be unequivocal to have any impact. In *Re Midland Linen Services*[15] the judge found the loser's attitude to mediation was 'inconsistent and uncertain', finding that this might well have inhibited success for a mediation, and that the loser had failed to satisfy the burden of proof placed on him. In *Wethered Estate Ltd v Davis*[16], refusal of a pre-issue mediation was justified because the ultimate loser refused to remove a trespassing vehicle from the winner's property first, an instance of the court supporting a pre-condition because presumably the winner was found to be right about that issue at trial (ie had a reasonable belief that their case was right, perhaps even watertight, on that point). Similarly, in *Vale of Glamorgan Council v Roberts*[17], the loser complained that the winning council failed to respond to offers to settle which amounted to assertions of the merit of his case or offers to buy the land in dispute, something which the council were never bound to do. The loser never proposed mediation in correspondence, and Lewison J declined to penalise the successful council for failing to propose mediation. Again, the intransigence of the loser cost him success in altering the normal cost consequence of losing.

Late offers of mediation were discussed in two cases, though in neither was delaying in trial at stake. In *Palfrey v Wilson*[18], a neighbour dispute, the Court of Appeal found for D on the basis of adverse possession, refusing to hear an argument based on title, and ordered C to pay D's indemnity costs. The loser C had proposed mediation late in the litigation but this did not justify altering the judge's costs award. In *Nigel Witham Ltd v Smith*[19], C ended owing D £1,600 at end of a construction claim in the TCC. D's costs were over £120,000. Mediation in the form of a settlement conference was only tried late when the vast majority of costs had been incurred. Settlement was not achieved. Coulson J (who has regularly examined mediation issues in his judgments) held that, as D definitely won and had not refused mediation pre-issue point-blank, but insisted on clarification of the claim first (which was not done until after issue), early mediation was not likely to have succeeded because of C's intransigence, and D was not sanctioned. Here again, as in *Wethered,* the court was prepared to find that a pre-condition to mediation imposed by the refusing party was reasonable.

---

15 [2004] EWHC 3380 (Ch).
16 [2005] EWHC 1903 (Ch).
17 [2008] EWHC 2911 (Ch).
18 [2007] EWCA Civ 94.
19 [2008] EWHC 12 (TCC).

Occasionally the courts apply factor 2 (reasonable belief that a case is 'watertight') and factor 6 (reasonable prospects of success in mediation) in a way which comes as a surprise to mediation practitioners, in that the judicial assessment of whether a case might settle at mediation does not accord with mediator experience. One such case is *Swain Mason v Mills & Reeve (a firm)*[20], in which both those factors arose. The Court of Appeal decided not to sanction the winning defendant who had firmly rejected mediation throughout, the court having been impressed by the sheer size of the gap between the parties as suggesting that mediation had no reasonable prospect of success. The facts were that the Swain family sued their former solicitors Mills & Reeve for failing to advise them of the adverse tax implications of completing a management buyout of their family company in the event that (as sadly happened) Mr Swain died during a relatively risk-free heart procedure scheduled for shortly after completion of the buyout. His death meant that his estate was replete with cash instead of shares exempted from IHT and CGT by business relief. The avoidable tax charge (and the claim against the defendants) was for about £1.3 million.

The litigation history was very tortuous. There were two aborted trial dates; an attempt to amend by the claimants, coupled with an attempt by the defendants to have the claim dismissed under CPR Part 24 (both of which failed), followed by unsuccessful interlocutory cross-appeals which took three days; a seven-day trial in which the claim was dismissed; a costs hearing; and finally another appeal, in which the trial decision was upheld and the claim stood dismissed. The basis for dismissing the substantive claim was that, because of the way the claim was pleaded (late amendment having been refused) the Swains could only succeed if Mills & Reeve had been told formally about Mr Swain's proposed heart procedure and asked to advise more fully on any adverse tax consequences. As the judge found as a fact that they were not, and as no separate overriding duty to advise more fully either arose or was allowed to be argued (because of the disallowed late amendment), the claim failed at trial and on appeal.

Despite 'winning', Mills & Reeve initially received only 50% of their standard basis costs from the trial judge as part of an issue-based award. It was clear that Mills & Reeve did not win every battle, even though they were declared winners of the war. An unspecified portion of this discounted percentage was attributed by the trial judge Arnold J to their steadfast refusal to mediate at any stage, despite invitations to do so from the Swain family, and also despite mediation being recommended by Peter Smith J while he was assigned to the case earlier in its long life. Mills & Reeve appealed the costs order, arguing that they had won far more comfortably than a 50% costs award indicated. They only succeeded to the extent that the Court

---

20 [2012] EWCA Civ 498.

of Appeal disapproved of Arnold J's sanctioning of their refusal to mediate, and the Court of Appeal increased the costs proportion recoverable from the claimants from 50% to 60%. No costs figures are given in any of the judgments, but each party had leading and junior counsel throughout the four main hearings, so that even 10% of Mills & Reeve's costs of the whole protracted litigation must be a very considerable sum.

During the costs appeal, the court looked closely at the analysis of when to sanction for refusal to mediate set out in *Halsey*, and especially at the inter-related factors 2 and 6. Did Mills & Reeve reasonably believe they had a watertight case sufficient to excuse them from mediating, and did media-tion have no reasonable prospect of success, again sufficient to excuse their refusal? Arnold J (as reported in the Court of Appeal judgment, his costs judgment being unreported) took the following line:

> 'There was a real possibility that, had there been a mediation, both parties would have gained a better understanding of the weak-nesses in their own case, and that it was "not unrealistic" to sup-pose that mediation might have produced a settlement',

although he concluded that 'it was more likely than not that it would have been unsuccessful,' but not so unrealistic as to justify 'the defendant's intransigent refusal at every stage even to contemplate the possibility of mediation'. He therefore decided to reflect in his costs order his view that the defendant's approach that 'the claim was utterly hopeless' was an unreasonable position to take.

To a mediator this judgment of the trial judge reads very sensibly. At the outset of the trial the final outcome was far from clear, and the result of the trial was frankly close. There was certainly sufficient doubt about the qual-ity of Mills & Reeve's win for the trial judge to deprive them of half their costs. There was some evidence which might have persuaded a judge that Mills & Reeve had sufficient knowledge of Mr Swain's operation to be fixed with a wider responsibility, and the wider case, which the Swains were not allowed to argue for introducing it so late, was only finally excluded at the substantive trial itself, after several attempts to get it included as an argu-ment which might have given the Swain family a better chance of success. So on the face of it there were sufficient risks for both sides to consider within the scope of confidential assisted negotiation at a mediation, espe-cially if it had been convened early in the dispute. It would have provided a good opportunity for each side to argue the relative strengths and weak-nesses of each other's cases in a way that would have rendered discussion of a risk-discounted settlement useful, and yet leaving each party free to revert to litigation if they so chose.

However, this view was not taken by the Court of Appeal's judgment on this aspect of the case (delivered by Davis LJ and simply agreed to by Lord Neuberger MR and Richards LJ) which reads:

'At all stages the parties were in reality a hundred miles apart. The claimants had sought £750,000 and costs by a Part 36 offer served shortly before the first trial. The defendants' best offer had never been more than a "drop hands" approach (before proceedings). Its assessment of the strength – or rather weakness – of the claimant's pleaded case on breach of duty never altered'.

He went on: 'it is difficult to see, given the circumstances, how a mediation could have had reasonable prospects of success' and he felt unable to attach the label of 'intransigence' to the attitude of the defendants, noting that:

'nothing changed in this particular case (unlike many cases) to necessitate a re-evaluation on the question of liability. A reasonable refusal to mediate does not become unreasonable simply by being steadfastly, and for cause, maintained'.

It would surely be naïve to expect that any winning party against whom a sanction is sought for not mediating is ever going to admit that there was the slightest possibility of compromise through mediation, when their entire prospects of success in justifying their refusal to mediate lay in asserting that their case was effectively water-tight and compromise thus not worth even discussing. Moreover, even a losing party will not confess to any weakness in their claim in trying to discharge the burden placed on them by *Halsey* to shift the normal costs liability for this reason, as the weaker they admit their case to be, the more this would justify the winner's refusal to consider compromise. Contrary to the Court of Appeal's diagnosis in *Swain*, experienced mediators might well feel that it would have been possible to help these parties to a consensual solution, that mediation was certainly worth a try, and that for a party to decline point blank to mediate might well amount to an unreasonable refusal which might properly risk a costs sanction.

What is the mischief when courts are generous to those who refuse to mediate, especially where mediation was recommended by a judge, of itself alone sufficient to justify a costs sanction according to the Court of Appeal in *Halsey*? The answer is that in a court system where, despite being authorised to do so by the Court of Appeal (again in *Halsey*), ADR orders are still rarely made outside the Commercial Court, post-trial costs sanctions are the only deterrent to unreasonable refusal. This still ignores the fact that a judge actually *did* recommend mediation to the parties in

135

Swain, advice rejected by the defendants. As a result, in the absence of ready discipline over lawyers and clients who do not mediate when it could work to the benefit of their clients, the overall losers are all other litigants who are not advised about the benefits of mediation, with its scope for conjuring settlements from the most unpromising of opening stances. Ultimately the courts also lose out in having to try cases which could and perhaps should have been settled, even on terms strongly favouring one party against another, while yet another case clogs the court system and obstructs another from being tried.

It should be borne in mind that it was never suggested that the Swain family's request for mediation was a mere ploy. If they genuinely wanted to sit down with their opponents and discuss their strengths and weaknesses, why should a refusal of such a request not be penalised? If judges actually thought more widely that mediation has the capacity to close big gaps, they might make ADR 'orders' (ie 'robust recommendations') more often, and be more ready to penalise failure to observe existing duties to use ADR, such as those set out in the Pre-action Protocols and the Pre-action Conduct Practice Direction. As it is, at the conclusion of his judgment Davis LJ remarked:

> 'The trial and its outcome will have been disastrous for the four daughters of Mr Swain: not only in costs terms but also (it is not difficult to apprehend) in terms of anxiety, pressure and emotional upset. The trial judge himself indicated at the end of his own judgment concerns at their likely feelings at the outcome'.

Such an approach hardly matches the Court of Appeal's decision to relieve Mills & Reeve from sanction when, in effect, they were found to have rejected their former clients' apparently genuine wish to sit down with them in a risk-free confidential mediation environment to discuss whether their dispute was capable of settlement, particularly as everyone had been advised by a judge to do so.

Finally on this topic, in *ADS Aerospace Ltd v EMS Global Tracking Ltd*[21], ADS issued a claim for over $16 million for breach of contract and repudiation relating to the delivery of satellite tracking devices. Funding was by CFA with ATE cover. Before trial, ADS offered to settle for £4.2 million inclusive of costs, and AMS offered £100,000 inclusive. At trial, ADS's claim was dismissed entirely: so EMS were the effective winner. EMS abandoned a claim for indemnity basis costs, but ADS sought a 50% reduction in their liability for EMS's costs on the basis that EMS had refused to mediate. Privilege having been waived at the costs hearing, the judge was told

---

21 [2012] EWHC 2904 (TCC).

that in March 2012, EMS raised the possibility of settlement discussions, in response to which ADS said they wanted to await exchange of lay and expert evidence, due respectively in April and the end of May. ADS ignored an offer of £50,000 inclusive made in April and also a further defendant settlement enquiry in mid-May, but on 31 May (having characterised EMS's £50,000 offer as a nuisance offer) ADS proposed a mediation on or after 11 June, less than 20 working days before trial was due. EMS replied that they did not think a mediation was likely to be 'a worthwhile or successful investment of time and costs' and it would deflect from trial preparation. They suggested a 'without prejudice' discussion. ADS commented that with costs said to exceed £1 million, expense was hardly an issue, and argued that mediation would be better than 'without prejudice' discussions, but again EMS rejected formal mediation and re-offered a discussion. Akenhead J declined to deprive the winning defendant of its normal expectation of a favourable costs order. His decision concentrated on ADS's unwillingness to respond to several settlement overtures made by EMS up to very shortly before trial; and ADS's unrealistic expectations, making settlement unlikely.

The judge felt that mediation would have been too late to be worthwhile, and more expensive than a 'without prejudice' discussion, especially bearing in mind that security for costs of £100,000 had been ordered by Ramsey J because of ADS's impecuniosity. He also found that EMS's belief in the strength of its case was not unreasonable, though commenting:

> 'of course, it is easy in the light of a judgment which was strongly in its favour for it to argue that this is the case'.

Later, he said:

> 'It might be said that a good mediator would have been able to "work on" the claimant to accept what would in effect be a nuisance offer, but in the context of this case, with the sensible solicitors and counsel (who the claimant did engage in this case), I have no doubt that without prejudice discussions would probably have achieved the same result or at least got to the same stage'.

He thought it highly unlikely that anyone would have persuaded the highly committed claimant's director to accept that a nuisance value payment was adequate.

7.2 When neither party tries to mediate

It will be remembered that the shift to court case management effected by the CPR in 1999 was largely driven by Lord Woolf's view that the legal profession could not itself be entirely trusted to progress cases efficiently. Hence he recommended the reforms embodied in the CPR which transferred case management responsibilities to the courts, and also innovatively extended the court's remit over unreasonable litigation conduct to the pre-action period. It can be expected that the resolve of procedural judges to manage litigation tightly and rigorously will have been greatly strengthened by the Jackson reforms and the 2013 amendments to the CPR (see **Chapter 13** for a discussion of these).

Occasions will arise when there was no effective winner in a trial, or one party's win was marginal. In retrospect the courts may be asked to consider whether a refusal to mediate or engage in settlement discussions might tip the balance[22]. Such a situation arose in *Brown v MCASSO Music Productions Ltd*[23]. The claimant sought copyright over lyrics to a rap number. Shortly after issue, the defendant offered £500 inclusive of costs but no copyright, and proposed use of the Musicians Union Dispute Resolution scheme. The claimant declined, indicating reservations about the MU scheme's independence in the light of past experience, but indicated willingness to discuss disposal if liability were admitted. The defendants declined, and made no better offer before the three-day trial two years later, at which the court awarded 10% copyright to the claimant plus £180 damages and ordered him to pay the defendant's costs. On an appeal against the costs order, the Court of Appeal found that neither party had won (the defendants had fought copyright and lost a proportion, while the claimant had been awarded far less than sought and only a modest proportion of the copyright) and that there should be no order as to costs of either the trial or the appeal.

In *Longstaff International Ltd v Evans*[24], the problem was that there had been a mediation but a further dispute broke out over implementing the settlement by convening a second mediation. C Ltd and D1/D2 were deadlocked after a trial over R Ltd, a joint venture company. Disputes were settled after a long mediation, with shares in R Ltd being transferred to C with a 12-month warranty as to financial stability of R Ltd in the mediated settlement agreement. Any dispute from the settlement had to be mediated first. Certain debts were owed to R Ltd, and a dispute arose as to whether they were repayable on demand or on sale of properties on which they were secured. A mediation notice was served as the expiry of the 12-month warranty period approached. C Ltd issued proceedings against D but later discontinued them. C argued that D1/D2 should neverthe-

---

22 In *Asiansky v Bayer-Rosin* [2003] EWCA Civ 1405 the Court of Appeal restored a claim struck out by the Master because one party had failed to mediate, but was not told that they had indeed proposed mediation as well.
23 [2005] EWCA Civ 1546.
24 [2005] EWHC 4 (Ch).

less pay C's costs. The Master made no order as to costs, and the Court of Appeal agreed, as all parties had conducted the litigation aggressively.

McMillen Williams (a firm) v Range[25] was a case decided just before *Halsey* in which the Court of Appeal lost sympathy with *both* parties because of the way they ran their cases and declined to negotiate, even though there was technically a winner. The defendant was a family solicitor employed by the claimant firm on a contract of employment which paid her by results, but receiving payments on account of what she was expected to earn. She left having been overpaid by £18,000 and the firm sued her. She counter-claimed for misrepresentation and also alleged that this agreement was regulated under the Consumer Credit Act 1974, and won at trial. The firm appealed. Both sides ignored the single judge's recommendation to try ADR and refused to negotiate. The employer firm won on appeal, but the court made no order as to costs in view of *both* parties' intransigence, with Ward LJ boldly declaring 'a plague on both your houses'. These two cases are important when it comes to whether a court should contemplate penalising both parties if there is a mutual, or perhaps even a collusive, failure to mediate, a step that Jackson LJ was reluctant to endorse in his final report (see **Chapter 13**).

An interesting decision on this topic comes from South Africa in the case of *Brownlee v Brownlee*[26], a family dispute in which the judge felt that both lawyers had failed to consider mediation, running up hugely disproportionate costs. He cited *Egan v Motor Services (Bath) Ltd*[27], made no order as to costs between the parties and imposed a cap on what the lawyers could recover as costs from their clients.

Occasionally too cases arise which show that the possibility of a retrospective costs sanction comes far too late in a case, and that an earlier ADR order was what the litigants really needed, as they seemed unable to help themselves to find a way towards settlement. One such was *Newman v Framewood Manor Management Co Ltd*[28]. The claimant, C, and her husband were long leaseholders of a flat in a superior residential development, managed by the defendant company whose directors were some of the flat owners. The development offered residents a swimming pool, a gym and a jacuzzi. C's flat was near the doorway to the pool, but damaging condensation in the stairwell through that doorway led the defendants to decide to block it up. They also replaced the jacuzzi with a sauna at a cost of over 320,000. Claims were also made for tree roots damage and failure to replace gym equipment. The appeal revolved around whether the court

---

25 [2004] EWCA Civ 294.
26 South Gauteng High Court (Johannesburg) 25 August 2009.
27 [2007] EWCA Civ 1002.
28 [2012] EWCA Civ 159 and [2012] EWCA Civ 1727.

could or should award damages and/or specific performance of the lease covenants over replacement of the jacuzzi with a sauna. In the event, the Court of Appeal awarded damages refused below but declined to order restoration of the jacuzzi, awarding £2,500 for future loss of use, and £500 for delayed supply of gym equipment (which was eventually installed). The defendants found a solution to the damp problem between judgment and order at the trial and undertook on terms acceptable to the claimant to restore the doorway in two months.

If ever there was a set of circumstances that cried out for mediation it was these. The parties were inextricably entwined with each other for years to come, as lessee and management company of the claimant's home. The claimant's husband had even at one time been a director of the defendant company. The trial judge was found by the Court of Appeal to have got the main plank of the claimant's case wrong, requiring large-scale reversal on the merits. The total damages awarded were just under £6,500, of which £1,250 was unchallenged on appeal. Lord Justice Etherton starts the costs judgment with the words:

> 'This is a very sad and unfortunate case, in which the costs of successful litigation far, far exceed the amounts recovered by the claimant. Sadly, it is a situation, particularly where people are living in close quarters with others, that we see too frequently in these courts'.

Surely a mediator could have helped the parties to agree exactly the same outcome months if not years before, thus avoiding the enormous expenditure of court time and legal cost that followed. Yet there is absolutely no sign from the recital of facts that either side seriously pursued settlement discussions or mediation, or any pre-action duty to contemplate settlement or mediation. No reference is made to any Part 36 offer, albeit that non-monetary as well as monetary remedies were sought, though not of a kind that necessarily prevented use of Part 36. No reference is made to any direction by the court for the parties to consider mediation. The losing defendants tried to escape some of the costs consequences by complaining that the claimant had failed to engage in settlement discussions or mediation. In rejecting a sanction for this, the Court of Appeal pointed to meetings proposed on both sides, which were rejected by each other. It seems that no substantive without prejudice discussion ever took place. Some without prejudice correspondence was adduced (presumably after waiver of privilege) to suggest that the claimant had been unreasonable in setting pre-conditions for discussions, but the court took no account of this.

In this case there was a winner of sorts, who received extremely modest damages earned at hugely disproportionate cost. The claimant was awarded 95% of her costs, which were ordered not to be recoverable by the defendants from the service charges to the flats. The court said that this case was not a 'near miss' in terms of settlement. How this can be so with a maximum value (ignoring costs) of £6,000 when consensual structural arrangements were negotiated soon after trial is incomprehensible. In common sense terms, these parties were never far apart, and their proximate contractual relationship drove them unavoidably closer, even if legal principles and costs at stake drove them apart in the litigation[29].

The challenge for the courts in such cases is that if procedural decisions are left to each party to seek on an adversarial basis, where both parties or their lawyers might be inclined to agree to ignore the possibility of mediating, it has to be left to the courts to raise the issue of their own motion. In cases like *McMillen* and *Newman,* procedural judges possessing new-found zeal as a result of the Jackson reforms may have to decide whether to make ADR orders to protect parties from their own inability or refusal to see that litigation is highly unlikely to be worthwhile in terms of costs recovery, especially if there is merely a narrow or unmeritorious win.

7.3   Cases where a sanction *was* imposed (or a non-standard costs order was made)

The first case in time after *Halsey* in which a costs sanction was imposed for not mediating (though without its being cited in the judgment) was *Yorkshire Bank v RDM Asset Management*[30], a first instance decision on costs. C claimed to have been the successful party and sought costs, subject to losing part of their claim on an issues-lost basis, but also arguing up the fact that D (asserted to be the loser) had declined to mediate. Neither side offered much by way of settlement before trial. Taking the now well-established view that it was best to award costs to the ascertained winner and then discount that successful party's costs to reflect any partial lack of success on discrete issues, rather than making cross-orders in favour of each party, the judge found that D's new solicitors instructed during the case had acted 'somewhat intransigently' and that declining to mediate was unreasonable. Mediation had had a good prospect of success, based interestingly on his assessment of the witnesses on both sides which suggested that they were likely to have reached a settlement at a mediation. Instead of giving C a 50% costs recovery by C, the judge increased D's costs liability by awarding 65% to C.

---

29 See also Rix LJ in *Brewer v Mann* [2012] EWCA Civ 246, ordering a retrial over the sale of a Bentley car and expressing disappointment that a mutually satisfactory solution had not been found 'to avoid much trouble, distress and risk' (and costs at stake before the retrial probably in excess of £500,000).
30 (30 June 2004, unreported), Mercantile Ct.

One of the first decisions to discuss the *Halsey* factors fully in imposing a sanction was the costs judgment in *P4 Ltd v Unite Integrated Solutions plc*[31] delivered by Ramsey J, an oft-reported judge in this area. C had claimed £70,000 for goods allegedly converted by D, and was awarded £387, which did not beat a Part 36 offer by D of £6,000. On the face of it D was the successful party, and the normal costs order would have been for D to bear C's costs up to D's Part 36 offer, and for C to bear D's costs as from the Part 36 offer. However, C argued that D had failed to provide relevant information early enough to influence C's approach to the dispute and to the Part 36 offer, and also had refused to mediate, thus justifying a variation on the norm, suggesting no order as to costs throughout. D argued that C should pay all the costs of the action both before and after their Part 36 offer. The failure to provide information was properly criticised and the judge went on to apply the *Halsey* factors. Indeed, C offered mediation before issue, then after nine months of silence issued proceedings and then offered mediation again. D's solicitors accused C of 'a cynical attempt' 'to belatedly seek protection' [*sic*] from the costs sanctions outlined in *Halsey*'. C reacted fiercely that they had offered mediation before proceedings. In response, D rejected mediation on the basis that:

– D had 'a very strong case' and it was an 'all-or-nothing' case;

– other settlement attempts had been made which C had rejected;

– mediation would be disproportionately expensive;

– mediation had no reasonable prospect of success: the parties were a long way apart on issues of both fact and law; and C's Part 36 offers had actually escalated during the dispute, demonstrating unwillingness to compromise.

The final position before trial (after the judge had rejected D's application for summary judgment on their defence) left C seeking a further increased settlement figure of £73,000 plus costs, and D offering to accept a £20,000 costs contribution if C discontinued. The gap therefore persisted, and although he did not analyse the situation quite in this way, judgment for C for £387 rather suggested that neither side had won. After carefully recording each side's submissions on all the *Halsey* propositions except delay to trial, Ramsey J found as follows:

– that the case was 'a classic example of a case which lent itself to ADR' before issue, with disputed facts and no special need for resolution of a point of law;

---

31 [2006] EWHC 2640 (TCC).

-   that D could not reasonably have thought it had a watertight case when it declined mediation, as even later clarification of the strength of D's case would have enabled issues to be narrowed;

-   as mediation often succeeds when other settlement methods have failed, the previous offers made by each side did not excuse refusal: interestingly, he particularly noted that letters from solicitors making offers are not a proper substitute for an ADR process which both involves the clients themselves and also engagement with a neutral. If this reasoning is right, there will be very few occasions when this proposition will justify refusal to mediate;

-   in declining to apply the disproportionate costs proposition, Ramsey J pointed out not only the huge costs to trial, but also the relevance of lost opportunity costs for parties and their witnesses;

-   on prospects of success for mediation, Ramsey J took as his starting-point the fact that 'the vast majority of cases are capable of settlement and are in fact settled'. In this case, D tried to use C's increasingly unrealistic assessment of its prospects of success, evidenced by C's increasing its Part 36 offers several times, yet only securing £387 damages, as justification for applying Dyson LJ's intransigence rule in *Halsey.* Ramsey J acknowledged a challenge here but found that C was not in his view intransigent, and that any such intransigent would have moderated at a mediation, again reading the demeanour of the witnesses he heard. In the event, Ramsey J ordered costs on the usual basis, giving C costs up to the Part 36 offer (justifying this in part by D's refusal to mediate) and ordering C to pay D's costs thereafter.

In *A-G for Zambia (for and on behalf of the Republic of Zambia) v Meer Care & Desai (a firm)*[32], Peter Smith J sanctioned the claimant for refusing to mediate with certain parties, despite there being fraud allegations, He said that if he had been asked to make an ADR order he would have done so, and imposed a sanction even though he thought the mediation would probably have failed, despite which he thought that there was 'a prospect of a successful mediation ... lost in my view by what was an unreasonable stance'. He therefore made a 5% reduction from costs otherwise awarded against one defendant.

In *Vector Investments v JD Williams*[33], D employed C, a developer, to create a call centre from an existing building. C issued proceedings in May 2006,

---

32 [2007] EWHC 1540 (Ch).
33 [2009] EWHC 3601 (TCC).

claiming just over £6 million for the work carried out, and sought summary judgment but this was rejected. D made a 'without prejudice offer save as to costs' (though not specifically under CPR Part 36, so as to avoid the normal costs consequences of acceptance) of £400,000 in August 2007, which was in effect ignored by C. In December 2008, C and D settled the dispute by D's agreeing to pay £750,000 plus VAT to C, but leaving costs liabilities to be determined by the court. In a costs trial, C claimed to have been the successful party, because the settlement was more favourable than the offer of £400,000. D claimed to be the winner, having reduced a claim of over £6 million to £750,000, at least justifying no order as to costs.

D argued that C had ignored its £400,000 offer, justifying a sanction for unreasonable conduct in not negotiating. Separately they argued that C had caused them unnecessary time and trouble over a badly organised piece of disclosure. Ramsey J, following *Multiplex Constructions (UK) Ltd v Cleveland Bridge UK Ltd)*[34], held that in commercial litigation, the winner will normally be the net payee of damages. Thus C, as recipients of £750,000 plus VAT from the settlement, was the 'winner'. But C had failed to negotiate after receiving D's £400,000 offer, as a result of which a further £3.5 million in costs had been run up to secure an increase of a mere additional £350,000 for C above the £400,000 offer to settle. Such a failure to negotiate after receipt of an admissible offer (whether or not formally made under CPR Part 36) justified reducing C's costs by 50% from 21 days after the offer. The judge also disallowed £20,000 off C's costs for obstructive disclosure. As to the costs of the costs trial (a concept very much a feature of post-CPR litigation life) he awarded C 70% of its costs on the costs trial, having 'won' but had several issues decided against it.

The *Halsey* propositions have also been considered in two inheritance cases. In *Jarrom v Sellars*[35], the claimants CC were executors who brought proceedings to remove a caveat served by the defendant D who eventually consented to removal before a full trial of the issues. Though D still contemplated a new estoppel claim based on a promise of inheritance given by the deceased, she was unquestionably the loser in the caveat proceedings. At the costs hearing following the consent order, D sought to resist an order for costs against her on the basis that the executors had refused to meet or mediate before proceedings were issued. The judge agreed that it was unfortunate that no meeting took place, and refused to penalise D by awarding CC's costs against her: so no order as to costs was made when an adverse order might have been expected, leaving the estate to bear the executors' costs.

---

34 [2008] EWHC 2280 (TCC).
35 [2007] EWHC 1366 (Ch).

In *Gill v RSPCA*[36], G's parents, F and M, owned a 287-acre farm worth probably over £2 million in North Yorkshire. G, a university lecturer, was their only child and limited her university work so as to help her parents on their farm, harbouring an expectation of inheriting it on the deaths of her parents. However, F and M made 'mirror' wills in 1993 leaving everything to the survivor and then to the RSPCA, asserting that they had made adequate provision for G in their lifetimes. F died in 1999 and M in 2006. Neither had been members of the RSPCA and indeed M had expressed disapproval of their opposition to hunting. After M's death, G claimed to set aside her mother's will for:

1 **want of knowledge and approval** of the will by M when she signed it;

2 **undue influence** by F on M not to provide properly for G; and

3 **proprietary estoppel**, in that G had relied and acted upon to her detriment on assurances from M as to her expectations over inheriting the family farming business.

G relied on claims 1 and 3 from the issue of proceedings, and only added claim 2 six months later, at which point she also particularised the detailed basis of her estoppel claim. C lost on claim 1 but won on claims 2 and 3, and sought her costs from the RSPCA on the standard basis up to a date just before the litigation was issued, and thereafter on the indemnity basis. The RSPCA claimed its costs from the estate up to the date of trial and opposed the orders sought by G. In relation to claim 1, the judge regarded the RSPCA as the winner, having successfully defended G's claim under that head, and ordered that it should have its costs of defending this issue from the estate on the standard basis, leaving G to bear her own costs attributable to pursuing that part of the claim unsuccessfully. In relation to 2 and 3, however, he regarded G as the winner. G sought a sanction against the RSPCA for alleged intransigence throughout the litigation. A substantial bundle of correspondence marked 'without prejudice save as to costs' was produced to the judge. This showed that each had made offers to the other before issue. G had actually had to obtain an injunction to prevent sale of the farm pending resolution of her claim, and the consent order for which incorporated a requirement to consider whether the claim could be resolved by ADR. However, the RSPCA made it clear that it would not mediate and would seek a swift trial, making a cash offer of £650,000 plus standard basis costs but would only mediate on the basis of that offer being accepted, and rejected a further suggestion of mediation during the start-stop trial which spread over several months.

---

36 (2009, unreported), Ch D.

The judge remarked that

> 'despite the claimant's repeated attempts to resolve her dispute with the RSPCA by mediation or some other form of ADR, they remained resolute in its opposition thereto, which opposition continued after the commencement of the trial. Further they clearly displayed a lack of enthusiasm in relation to the resolution of the dispute by a negotiated settlement'.

He added that the RSPCA's attitude was

> 'inconsistent with the Court's expectation of a willingness to participate in a well-established procedure which is proven to result in improved *quality* of settlements and an increased *incidence* of settlements' [author's emphasis].

He noted that the claimant had made several offers, which, if accepted by the RSPCA, would have resulted in lesser benefit to her than she was awarded at trial. He therefore ordered that the RSPCA should bear G's costs of claim 3 throughout on the indemnity basis; and that G and the RSPCA should bear their own costs of claim 2 down to six months after the issue of proceedings, but that thereafter the RSPCA should bear C's costs of claim 2 on the indemnity basis, plus the costs of the application for the injunction to restrain them from selling the farm pending resolution of the claimant's claim. The costs of the executors, who had taken a neutral stance in the proceedings, were ordered to be borne by the estate on the indemnity basis. The judge's approach was largely supported on appeal by the RSPCA.

Both these inheritance cases illustrate the risks that parties take in declining to mediate or discuss settlement. In *Jarrom,* the loser avoided an anticipated costs burden and in *Gill,* the broad winner won a better outcome by obtaining indemnity instead of standard basis costs orders. The penalties for intransigence for the RSPCA in particular were very heavy. But in neither of these cases was there a specific recognition by the judge in his decision that he was applying the *Halsey* factors in accordance with the *Halsey* burden of proof[37].

In *Rolf v De Guerin*[38], the Court of Appeal alleviated a costs order in part because the defendant had refused to mediate until just before trial, when

---

37 See also *Lilleyman v Lilleyman* [2012] EWHC 1056 (Ch) where the claimant failed to beat a Part 36 offer but because of his 'no holds barred' conduct of the litigation the defendants were only awarded 80% of their costs.
38 [2011] EWCA Civ 78.

it was too late to save the substantial costs incurred. The appeal mainly turned on the trial judge's inexplicable decision to order the claimant to pay the defendant's costs from the date of her own Part 36 offer to settle, albeit at a much higher figure than the damages she was ultimately awarded. But once that error had been corrected, the defendant's intransigence over mediation in a case where neither party was a clear winner was sufficient to justify no order as to costs throughout the litigation, saving the claimant from being responsible for the defendant's trial costs.

Finally the case of *PGF II v OFMS Co*[39] illustrates that judges with experience of mediation themselves may well bring new insights into what a mediation might well have been expected to achieve. C brought a dilapidations claim for just over £1 million against D. The day before trial, C accepted a Part 36 offer of £700,000 made by D nine months earlier. C sought an order under CPR 36.10(4)(b) for D to pay their costs from their Part 36 offer until settlement, challenging their normal liability to pay D's costs after late acceptance under CPR 36.10(5)(b). They lost on two substantive points. However, C had proposed mediation twice, ignored by D. The deputy judge applied the *Halsey* tests and burden of proof, and found that these amounted to unreasonable refusals, giving rise to grounds for varying the normal costs order. Mediation had had reasonable prospects of success (never easy to challenge when a case actually settled just before trial). C's offer to mediate was genuine and, although not repeatedly followed up, there was no evidence of simply going through the motions of offering mediation. An adverse order against D should not merely be made from the hypothetical mediation date, finding that the basis for the sanction is the unreasonable conduct, which in this case coincided with the Part 36 offers made in April 2011. No order as to costs was made as from then, each party bearing their own. Furthermore, there had been a previous mediation between the parties in 2010 over another aspect of the service charge. The implication sought to be raised by D was that C had adopted an unreasonable stance within the confidentiality of the mediation and that this was a legitimate factor in deciding whether a later mediation would have been successful. The judge declined to receive evidence of the previous mediation because PGF declined to waive privilege. He also refused to draw any adverse inference from C's refusal to waive that privilege, for, as he commented:

'to do so would be to undermine the very protection given to the parties in relation to their conduct in a mediation'.

The judge also said:

---

39 [2012] EWHC 83 TCC.

'The court should be wary of arguments only raised in retrospect as to why a party refused to mediate or as to why it cannot be demonstrated that a mediation would have had a reasonable prospect of success. First, such assertions are easy to put forward and difficult to prove or disprove but in this case are unsupported by evidence. Secondly, and in any event, it is clear that the courts wish to encourage mediation and whilst there may be legitimate difficulties in mediating or successfully mediating, these can only be overcome if those difficulties are addressed at the time. It would seem to me consistent with the policy which encourages mediation by depriving a successful party of its costs in appropriate cases that it should also deprive such a party of costs where there are real obstacles to mediation which might reasonably be overcome but are not addressed because that party does not raise them at the time'.

He also commented:

'Experience suggests that many disputes, even more complex disputes than the present, are resolved before all material necessary for a trial is available. Either parties know or are prepared to assume that certain facts will be established or, during the course of a mediation, such information is made available, often on a without prejudice basis. The rationale behind the Halsey decision is the saving of costs, and this is achieved (or at least attempted) by the parties being prepared to compromise without necessarily having as complete a picture of the other parties' case as would be available at trial'.

7.4 Other post-*Halsey* cases on costs sanctions for failure to mediate

Although not strictly giving rise to consideration of *Halsey,* there have been several other cases in which failure to mediate has had an impact on the ultimate costs order. In *Roundstone Nurseries Ltd v Stephenson Holdings Ltd*[40], D had contracted to build a concrete floor slab for C, but it failed. There was a dispute as to whether D were liable for its failure or a sub-contractor for BB, who was not sued as such by C. Stays for mediation were sought from the court and granted, but mediation never proceeded because D refused to come unless BB were there. C without warning entered judgment in default of defence. Coulson J held that the costs of preparing for the abandoned pre-issue mediation to be held in accordance with the Construction and Engineering pre-action protocol were recover-

---

40 [2009] EWHC 1431 (TCC).

able as costs in the action, payable on the standard basis by D, who should not have cancelled the mediation on short notice, in a decision reminiscent of the pre-*Dunnett* decision of *Leicester Circuits v Coates Brothers*.

In *Rowallan Group v Edgehill*[41], the claimant was penalised for inappropriate behaviour during a mediation. D obtained summary judgment in C's claim, and sought indemnity costs against C. C had issued proceedings in the middle of a mediation day without warning, so as to get in first. He asked the mediator to see if D's solicitors would accept service at the end of the mediation. C also failed to beat D's Part 36 offer. Lightman J found that an indemnity costs order was amply justified.

One thing that *Halsey* did not do was to make any impact on the law of privilege and without prejudice communications. It was argued that *Halsey* had quietly reversed the effect of *Walker v Wilsher*[42], but this was rejected by the Court of Appeal in *Reed Executive v Reed Business Information*[43]. C and D had engaged in several actions over use of the name 'Reed'. At trial, D had to pay damages. C appealed for a higher award and broadly lost. On costs, C asked that the order should consider: (1) 'without prejudice' negotiations; and (2) D's refusal to mediate. The Court of Appeal held that *Walker v Wilsher* had not been overruled by *Halsey,* so as to enable a court to admit evidence of 'without prejudice' negotiations on costs issues unless specifically rendered 'without prejudice save as to costs' as in *Calderbank v Calderbank*[44], a formula which had not been used by C and D in this case. On the open facts laid before the court, no sanction against D was justified.

Although *Halsey* has been considered and cited in several other cases dealing with the extent of privilege and confidentiality arising in relation to mediations, this was never its real concern, and such complex topics are for consideration in **Chapter 9**.

7.5 A summary on costs sanctions

The following propositions can be derived from the decisions on this topic:

- – any party, successful or not, who ignores a court recommendation to mediate or an ADR 'order' risks a worse costs outcome than they might otherwise have hoped to achieve, for that reason alone;

---

41 [2007] EWHC 32 (Ch).
42 [1889] 23 QBD 335, which prevented without prejudice material from being admitted to decide costs liabilities.
43 [2004] EWCA Civ 887.
44 [1976] Fam 93, CA.

- where an *unsuccessful* or only partly successful party ignores another party's proposal to negotiate or mediate, they may face an additional costs penalty, such as indemnity costs, for their refusal;

- costs sanctions may be imposed on a *successful* party who declines to use mediation at the behest of an opponent in mediation, though it is for the unsuccessful party to show that they should be imposed. The court will weigh such issues as are set out in *Halsey* (and any other relevant matters) to determine whether to do so;

- where *both* parties decline or fail to mediate in circumstances where the court thinks they should have done, they may face costs sanctions.

But as always with costs decisions, they are very fact-dependent and fall well within the discretion of trial judges, and thus will only rarely penetrate to the Court of Appeal for more authoritative guidance. To each of the above propositions there have been contrary decisions, hence the detailed accounts of how they came to be decided, so as to illustrate how such decisions are reached. There have not really been any clearly discernible trends in recent years, though some recent cases like *Swain* and *Framewood* have generated surprise because of the court's unwillingness to penalise failure by either one party or, in the latter case both, for failing to mediate.

Chapter 8

Contracting in advance to use ADR

Mediation has in the main been seen as the domain of litigation lawyers, who conduct the dispute to be litigated and decide the best way in which it is to be resolved. The role of transactional lawyers, both in-house and external, is considered less often. Yet in many ways, mediation as a process is actually very much suited to transactional lawyers, they being used (unlike most litigation lawyers) to the cut and thrust of negotiation with their client at their side in order to achieve acceptable deals. They also have a significant role during the negotiation of the original transactions themselves as to how they might provide for dispute resolution in case a deal breaks down. They may well also be needed to work out the implications of a re-negotiated deal which emerges from a mediation, where complex tax issues, property transfers, issues relating to competition, share options and pensions frequently emerge and are by no means necessarily within the comfort zone of litigators.

This chapter looks at the law relating to the options available to contracting parties in a commercial contract in providing in advance that mediation and other ADR processes are to be used as the primary means of resolving any disputes which may arise in the future in the terms and conditions in the contract. This is an area which is not free from legal controversy, and the experience of other common law jurisdictions more advanced in ADR than the UK suggests that the law may well develop and change in the future. Because there is still only limited definitive Court of Appeal authority on the effectiveness of ADR contract clauses, the current position is set out fully.

8.1 What is an 'ADR contract clause'?

An ADR contract clause is a clause in a commercial agreement of any kind by which the contracting parties agree to attempt to resolve any disputes between them by the use of one or more ADR processes. It may be a very simple, short clause, or alternatively set out a lengthy and complex process, escalating from one stage to another while disputes remain. It may specify a particular ADR procedure, such as mediation, or leave the parties to agree on one as and when a particular dispute arises. Where it contemplates the use of a *non-binding* ADR procedure, such as mediation, executive tribunal, or early neutral evaluation, it can clearly only require the parties to *attempt* resolution. A clause requiring use of a *binding* ADR procedure, such as expert determination or adjudication, can oblige the parties to abide by any award which results from it. Arbitration clauses, which are not considered in their pure form here, were the earliest form of clause of this type, and these in effect sought to exclude or at least delay the involvement of the courts in determining a dispute. These have been upheld as effectively doing so for many years.

It will therefore be seen that 'ADR contract clause' is not a particularly accurate (though convenient) label: they could equally be called 'dispute resolution clauses'.

8.2   What do ADR clauses aim to achieve?

The whole thrust of ADR tends towards a non-binding, 'without prejudice' approach, designed to provide an opportunity for the dispute to be discussed, and resolution explored, in a relatively risk-free and confidential environment. The use of a contract clause to *compel* parties to take part in, for example, mediation might therefore be regarded as contrary to the essential philosophy of ADR. After all, if the parties are only attending a mediation because they are contractually obliged to do so, it may be difficult to achieve settlement. Mediation presupposes some degree of willingness on the part of both or all parties at least to explore the various settlement options and to listen to the other side's arguments, whatever view is eventually taken. This may be absent among parties compelled to attempt mediation. Similar arguments arise in the debate over whether the courts should compel disputing parties into mediation by order.

However, the primary value of an ADR clause lies not in its element of compulsion, but in the fact that it puts (usually) mediation on the agenda. It is a reminder to the parties that, when they signed the agreement, an alternative process was viewed as a sensible step to take in the event of a dispute arising. It may even helpfully remind them that there was a time when relations between them were better. Most importantly, it overcomes any reluctance to suggest mediation when a dispute arises, for fear that such a suggestion may be viewed as an indication of weakness. Mediation can be discussed and attempted merely because it is in the contract. It is difficult to overstate the importance of such clauses in enabling parties to set up an informal procedure. There has been a widespread assumption that the suggestion by one party of a willingness to use mediation will be perceived by the other(s) as a sign of weakness. Whatever the truth of this since the CPR were introduced, such a fear acts as a significant barrier to many disputes reaching mediation (or other ADR processes). ADR contract clauses constitute by far the most effective way of circumventing this fear. The existence of the clause provides ample justification for mediation to be suggested, discussed and entered into freely and voluntarily and on an equal basis without any assumptions about the relative strength of each party's position. If mediation is not felt to be suitable after all, the parties can always agree to waive the requirement. Indeed, since some ADR clauses may not be enforceable as a matter of law (see **8.4** below), either party may even be able to avoid the obligation unilaterally.

In fact, the inclusion of ADR clauses in contracts is a vital element of good dispute systems design and management. It is an attempt to pre-empt future disputes by putting in place the appropriate resolution structure while the parties are still on good terms. At the very least, it provides yet another argument to deploy before the court in inviting the judge to refer a case to ADR, because the resistant party already signed up to its use before the dispute began. However, there are increasingly strong indications that courts will require parties to comply with the machinery set out in ADR contract clauses and deny access to the courts until this has been done, as has been the case with arbitration clauses for some time now.

Proper consideration of ADR therefore should begin at the contractual, non-contentious stage. Those involved in drafting and preparing contract documentation need to be as informed and aware of the various ADR possibilities as those who will eventually handle the resulting disputes. Creative design and mobilisation of contractual dispute systems ought to be considered the responsibility of non-contentious lawyers and contracts managers.

8.3 Enforceability of ADR clauses

While the primary value of an ADR clause does not necessarily lie in its enforceability as a matter of law, but rather in its role as a pretext for discussion of possible ADR solutions, it is clearly important to know whether or not the courts are likely to enforce such a clause by staying proceedings or granting a non-suit injunction. If ever a remedy were to amount to a potential breach of Article 6 of the European Convention on Human Rights by barring access to a public trial by compelling prior use of mediation, it is a non-suit injunction.

Before addressing the legal position on the enforceability of such clauses, there is considerable debate on whether it is appropriate or even desirable for ADR clauses to be enforceable and enforced. The arguments were neatly summarised by Giles J in the Australian case of *Hooper Baillie Associated Ltd v Natcon Group Pty Ltd*[1]:

---

1 (12 April 1992, unreported) at pp 24–25.

'Conciliation or mediation is essentially consensual, and the opponents of enforceability contend that it is futile to seek to enforce something which requires the consent of a party when co-operation and consent cannot be enforced; equally they say that there can be no loss to the other party if for want of co-operation and consent the consensual process would have led to no result. The proponents of enforceability contend that this misconceives the objectives of alternative dispute resolution, saying that the most fundamental resistance to compromise can wane and turn to co-operation and consent if the dispute is removed from the adversarial procedures of the Courts and exposed to procedures designed to promote compromise, in particular where a skilled conciliator or mediator is interposed between the parties. What is enforced is not co-operation or consent, but participation in a process from which co-operation and consent might come'.

8.4   The position under English law

A series of decisions at first instance have now considered the enforceability of ADR clauses in English law: first, Judge Hegarty QC sitting as a High Court judge in Liverpool District Registry in *Cott (UK) Ltd v FE Barber Ltd*[2]; then McKinnon J in *Halifax Financial Services Ltd v Intuitive Systems Ltd*[3], Colman J in *Cable & Wireless v IBM*[4], and Ramsey J in *Holloway v Chancery Mead Ltd*[5]. It was only in 2012 that the Court of Appeal has had the opportunity to rule on the requirements for an enforceable obligation to use mediation before access to a court is granted[6]. Until then, no higher court had directly ruled on such clauses apart from the House of Lords in *Channel Tunnel Group Ltd v Balfour Beatty*[7], dealing with a very narrow type of expert determination clause. Before looking at those later cases, it may help to review the legal position from first principles.

An agreement to negotiate is unenforceable

Until the decision of the House of Lords in *Walford v Miles*[8], there was still some doubt about this proposition, stemming from the dictum of Lord Wright in *Hillas & Co v Arcos Ltd*[9]. However, the position following *Walford*

---

2 [1997] 3 All ER 540.
3 [1999] 1 All ER Comm 303.
4 [2002] EWHC 2059 (Comm).
5 [2007] EWHC 2490 (TCC).
6 In *Sulamerica ia Nacional de Seguros v Enesa Engenharia* [2012] EWCA Civ 638.
7 [1993] 1 All ER 664.
8 [1992] 1 All ER 453.
9 (1932) 38 Corn Cases 23.

v Miles is clear, namely that an agreement to negotiate is not enforceable in law. This case followed and endorsed the decision of the Court of Appeal in *Courtney & Fairbairn Ltd v Tolaini Brothers (Hotels) Ltd*[10]. It is worth looking at *Walford v Miles* in some detail, as it has been cited in the recent cases discussing the principles behind enforcing agreements to mediate.

The case concerned the sale of a photographic processing business, and the central issues were the enforceability of a contract to negotiate and the terms of a 'lock-out' agreement (ie an agreement not to negotiate with any other parties whilst negotiations were continuing with one party). In 1986 the vendors decided to sell the business and received an offer of £1.9 million from a third party. In the meantime new purchasers (the later claimant in this case) had entered into negotiations with the vendors and in March 1987 the vendors agreed in principle to sell the business and premises for £2 million. It was also further agreed in a telephone conversation that if the purchasers provided a comfort letter confirming that their bank had offered them loan facilities, the vendors would 'terminate negotiations with any third party or consideration of any alternative with a view to concluding agreements' with the purchasers, and that even if the vendors received a satisfactory proposal from any third party before that time they would 'not deal with that third party and would not give further consideration to any alternative'.

Subsequently the vendors withdrew from negotiations and decided to sell to a third party. The proposed purchasers brought an action against the vendors for breach of the lock-out agreement under which the proposed purchasers had been given an exclusive opportunity to try to come to terms with the vendors and which was collateral to the 'subject to contract' negotiations which were proceeding for the purchase of the business and the premises. The proposed purchasers alleged that it was a term of the collateral agreement, necessarily to be implied to give business efficacy to it, that so long as the vendors continued to desire to sell the business and the premises, the vendors would continue to negotiate in good faith with the proposed purchasers. It was contended that the consideration for the collateral contract was the proposed purchasers' agreement to continue negotiations.

On appeal, the Court of Appeal held that the alleged collateral agreement was no more than an agreement to negotiate and was therefore unenforceable. On further appeal, the House of Lords held that a lock-out agreement, whereby one party for good consideration agreed for a limited specified time not to negotiate with anyone except the other party in relation to the sale of his property, could constitute an enforceable agreement. This was

---

10 [1975] 1 All ER 716.

confirmed by the Court of Appeal in *Pitt v PHH Asset Management*[11], where Sir Thomas Bingham MR's lead judgment found that a lock-out agreement for a period of two weeks relating to the sale of land was enforceable. However, an agreement to negotiate in good faith for an unspecified period was not enforceable, nor could a term to that effect be implied in a lock-out agreement for an unspecified period, since a vendor was not obliged under such an agreement to conclude a contract with a purchaser and he would not know when he was entitled to withdraw from the negotiations. Furthermore, the court could not be expected to decide whether, subjectively, a proper reason existed for the termination of the negotiations. It followed that the alleged collateral agreement was unenforceable.

Lord Ackner gave the lead judgment in *Walford v Miles*. In it he said (at 459):

> 'Mr Naughton accepted that as the law now stands and has stood for approaching 20 years an agreement to negotiate is not recognised as an enforceable contract. This was first decided in terms in *Courtney & Fairbairn Limited v Tolaini Brothers* where Lord Denning MR said:
>
>> "If the law does not recognise a contract to enter into a contract (when there is a fundamental term yet to be agreed) it seems to me it cannot recognise a contract to negotiate. The reason is because it is too uncertain to have any binding force ... It seems to me that a contract to negotiate, like a contract to enter into a contract, is not a contract known to the law ... I think we must apply the general principle that when there is a fundamental matter left undecided and to the subject of negotiation, there is no contract"'.

In the *Courtney* case Lord Denning had rejected the dictum of Lord Wright in *Hillas & Co v Arcos Ltd* as not well founded, saying:

> 'There is no bargain except to negotiate, and negotiation may be fruitless and end without any contract ensuing: yet even then, in strict theory, there is a contract (if there is good consideration) to negotiate, though in the event of repudiation by one party the damages may be nominal, unless a jury thinks that the opportunity to negotiate was one of some appreciable value to the injured party'.

Having considered a proposition put forward by Bingham LJ in the Court of Appeal in *Walford v Miles* that there was an obligation upon the vendors

---

11 [1993] 4 All ER 961.

not to deal with other parties which should continue to bind them 'for such time as is reasonable', Lord Ackner concluded:

> 'However, as Bingham LJ recognised, such a duty, if it existed, would indirectly impose upon the respondents a duty to negotiate in good faith. Such a duty, for the reasons which I have given above, cannot be imposed. That it should have been thought necessary to assert such a duty helps to explain the reason behind the amendments to paragraph 5 and the insistence of Mr Naughton that without the implied term the agreement, as originally pleaded, was unworkable – unworkable because there was no way of determining for how long the respondents were locked out from negotiating with any third party. Thus, even if, despite the way in which the *Walford* case was pleaded and argued, the severance favoured by Bingham LJ was permissible, the resultant agreement suffered from the same defect (although for different reasons) as the agreement contended for in the amended Statement of Claim, namely that it too lacked the necessary certainty and was thus unenforceable'.

In essence, then, *Walford v Miles* confirmed that a contract to negotiate is unenforceable, since a court cannot say with sufficient certainty what the obligations are that it is being asked to enforce, and in any meaningful way monitor or assess compliance.

A court can require compliance with certain procedures as a condition precedent to the commencement of litigation or arbitration proceedings

This general principle was established in the case of *Scott v Avery*[12]. Whilst the eventual jurisdiction of the court cannot be ousted, it can nevertheless be validly delayed or stayed, in that the parties can properly impose on themselves, by way of agreement, a series of intervening steps which have to be completed as a condition precedent to either party commencing litigation or arbitration.

This principle translates easily into the mediation arena. Many short form ADR clauses simply require parties to attempt resolution by an ADR process. However, it is equally possible (indeed, increasingly common) for the clause to express compliance with, and exhaustion of, the ADR phase as a condition precedent to the issue of any proceedings, usually with a specifically timed moratorium. Such a clause at least has the effect of introducing a slightly clearer, and therefore more certain, set of steps into the

---

12 (1865) 5 HL Cas 811, 10 ER 1121.

process, which arguably a court might find easier to enforce. However, as to the clause used in *Halifax Financial Services v Intuitive Systems*[13], as will be seen, the court did not find that the steps specified were clear enough, or even whether they had been implemented or breached. Thus, unless drafted with great care, the uncertainty problems raised in *Walford* persist, since the court still has to determine whether compliance with that condition precedent has been achieved, so that proceedings could be validly issued. For example, would a party who attended a mediation but terminated it by leaving after an hour be said to have 'attempted to mediate'?

Whilst it may be difficult to produce a set of criteria or rules by which compliance can be judged in every situation, it is in practice often very clear to the parties whether they have attempted to settle a case through ADR or not. It is, of course, even clearer to the mediator, who is not in a position to confirm or deny compliance after the event, partly because of the contractual commitment to confidentiality and partly because his role during the mediation would be fatally compromised if the parties felt that the mediator could eventually pass judgment on their conduct.

The problem is, of course, exacerbated by a lack of comprehension of what mediation actually involves. Thus, the uncertainty argument is strengthened because it is assumed that mediation procedures are inherently either too unclear or too flexible to be able to require compliance. As use of mediation has grown, however, this argument has lost some of its impact, since there is greater familiarity with mediation practice and the processes themselves have become more regularised. Indeed, although mediation is a very flexible and adaptable process, it is already possible to say with some consistency what constitutes, in procedural terms, a 'typical' mediation. It must also follow that the more detailed the process spelt out in an ADR clause, the greater the likelihood of its being enforceable. Thus a simple commitment to attempt an ADR process leaves too many procedural issues unresolved (not least as to which ADR process will be used). Conversely an agreement to use mediation, under the auspices of a particular provider organisation, or using a certain individual mediator, where the procedural requirements for the process (eg a timetable for submitting case summaries and holding the mediation, who will attend the mediation, etc) are spelled out in detail, must inherently be more capable of enforcement.

It is worth noting, however, that such detail may in fact be counter-productive. Mediation (of all the ADR processes) has a unique flexibility to respond to the very particular exigencies of a given situation. The greater

---

13 [1999] 1 All ER Comm 303.

the emphasis on a pre-arranged structure, the less the opportunity to adopt a particular approach and format of mediation which the situation demands. There is therefore some measure of balance to be achieved in the drafting of such a clause.

It is also important to distinguish between various kinds of ADR process. Some, such as early neutral evaluation, contain no element of negotiation about them. There, the parties simply make oral and/or written submissions to an agreed neutral, who makes a non-binding evaluation, which the parties can then use to inform their negotiations. There is no reason in principle why the uncertainty objections raised in the *Walford* case should apply to such a process. Indeed, since the process is not inherently one of negotiation at all, the *Walford* case is not relevant to any assessment of it.

Finally, the uncertainty objections in *Walford* can be very largely minimised by the use of specific time periods, or 'lock-out' agreements. For example, rather than requiring the parties to mediate prior to issuing proceedings, an ADR clause may simply impose a time period between the dispute arising and proceedings being commenced during which proceedings may not be issued. Provided it follows the *Scott v Avery* form, there is no objection to such a clause. During the intervening time period, the clause can either impose an obligation to use ADR, or simply offer it as an option, subject to the parties' consent at the time (specimen ADR contract clauses are available on the CEDR website (www.cedr.com)). As a matter of law, this changes little. An obligation to use ADR would still be vulnerable to the uncertainty arguments and an option to use ADR is in fact no more than the parties already have in any event, even without such wording.

In practice, however, the position is very different. A specific breathing space is created, during which the parties are unable to issue proceedings. ADR is on the agenda during that period, whether by obligation or option, and there can therefore be little concern about raising it with the other side. Many parties, faced with an intervening period during which they may either negotiate and/or use ADR, or do nothing, will sense the value in trying to use all available means to resolve the dispute. If the breathing space were not imposed on them, it is likely that some of them would be tempted to miss out the ADR, and even the negotiation, phase, and a valuable settlement opportunity might be lost.

Finally, where there is a concern that the imposition of a breathing space may prejudice a party's position in the event that, for example, immediate injunctive relief is required, express provision for that can easily be made in a clause giving rights to bypass the ADR or negotiation phases in such circumstances.

159

Is mediation equivalent to negotiation, such that the law regarding agreements to negotiate applies equally to mediation?

So far in this section, it has been assumed broadly that mediation is a form of negotiation, and thus that the law regarding the enforceability of agreements to negotiate applies equally to agreements to use mediation. However, a clear distinction has been drawn between ADR processes which involve a large element of negotiation (eg mediation, mini-trial, and so on) and those which do not (eg judicial appraisal, early neutral evaluation and expert determination). Clearly, the latter category is exempt from any of the problems relating to agreements to negotiate. The remainder of this section therefore applies to the former category of non-adjudicative processes, and mediation in particular.

On the face of it, those processes are extremely similar to negotiation. Indeed, their aims and objectives are almost indistinguishable from those of direct negotiations. Both seek a consensual result, with no ability to mandate any concession or change of position from the other side. Both can be abandoned by either party at any time. Neither requires or permits the imposition on the parties of any form of binding judgment. The outcome of both types of process is either a mutually acceptable agreement (which the parties can agree should have binding or non-binding status) or no agreement at all. Following this rationale, the law applicable to negotiation should also apply to mediation.

However, whilst mediation and negotiation may share the same aims and objectives, there are fundamental differences of process. Anyone familiar with both will immediately appreciate this. The introduction of a third party (a neutral and independent mediator) fundamentally changes the terms and conditions of the negotiating process. The parties submit themselves to management by a third party in a process with an independent dynamic and momentum of its own, to a far greater degree than they do in direct negotiations. Indeed, the mere fact that the process has such a momentum and a structure beyond that generated by the parties themselves, distinguishes it very significantly from direct negotiations. The process elements of a mediation are to a large extent governed by the mediator's own input and perceptions of what will prove effective, even allowing for the fact that the parties must at least consent to any such process decisions.

It is therefore possible to say, at least to some extent, that mediation as a process exists as a structure which is independent of the parties themselves. The implication of this is highly significant. If it is possible to identify such processes or structures with sufficient clarity, the uncertainty objections raised in the *Walford* case begin to fall away. By agreeing to use mediation, the argument runs, the parties are not agreeing to negotiate, but rather to submit themselves to a series of objectively definable processes, the effect of which is likely to be greater on them than if they merely entered the direct negotiation process. To quote again from Giles J in the *Hooper Baillie* case:

'What is enforced is not co-operation and consent, but participation in a process from which co-operation and consent might come'.

If that rationale is adopted, it becomes much easier to countenance enforcement of an mediation clause.

To use an analogy, assume that a husband and wife have a particular problem in their marriage. They may agree between themselves to attempt to resolve it by discussion. Clearly they cannot be compelled to resolve the problem. Realistically, neither can they be compelled to 'discuss it' since that is too vague an obligation to define effectively. How productive do discussions have to be in order to constitute compliance? If they set aside an hour to do so, and simply sit in silence, or scream at each other, have they complied? And for how long do the discussions need to continue? On the other hand, they might agree to attempt to resolve the matter by seeking the assistance of a counsellor. Even more expressly, they might commit to having 10 weekly sessions with the counsellor. This is an easy obligation to monitor. It contains no assumptions that they will succeed in reaching resolution but merely a commitment to submit themselves to a particular and definable process. Implicit in it is an assumption that the counselling process constitutes something independent of the parties, a pre-existing structure into which the parties will submit their differences.

Necessarily, the counselling process itself is not easy to define in advance, in terms of the detail of how a particular session will progress. But that does not mean that it does not have enough of a structure of its own to enable the parties to know in advance what obligations they will take on when they agree to use it. Exactly the same is true of, for example, the mediation process. Indeed, the only difference between the two (in terms of ensuring compliance) is that counselling is currently better known and more widely used than ADR and thus more easily permits an immediate and objective recognition of what is involved.

In summary then, the mediation process is appreciably more formal than direct negotiation, in a way which tends to distinguish the two processes and therefore the law applicable to each. This suggests that an ADR clause requiring mediation ought to be enforceable if it is clear enough.

The practicality of enforcement

Is it practicable to enforce an ADR clause then, by stay or non-suit? Subject to the arguments set out above, there happens to be one statutory

161

provision which specifically provides for such a step to be taken, albeit by a side-wind. The Arbitration Act 1996 made sweeping changes to the framework for arbitration. Section 9 of the Act provides:

> '(1) A party to an arbitration agreement against whom legal proceedings are brought (whether by way of claim or counterclaim) in respect of a matter which under the agreement is to be referred to arbitration may (upon notice to the other party to the proceedings) apply to the court in which the proceedings have been brought to stay the proceedings so far as they concern that matter.
>
> (2) An application may be made notwithstanding that the matter is to be referred to arbitration *only after the exhaustion of other dispute resolution procedures* [author's emphasis].
>
> (3) An application may not be made by a person before taking the appropriate procedural step (if any) to acknowledge the legal proceedings against him or after he has taken any step in those proceedings to answer the substantive claim.
>
> (4) On an application under this section the court shall grant a stay unless satisfied that the arbitration agreement is null and void, inoperative, or incapable of being performed.
>
> (5) If the court refuses to stay the legal proceedings, any provision that an award is a condition precedent to the bringing of proceedings in respect of any matter is of no effect in relation to those proceedings'.

This provision was inserted to reflect the effect of the House of Lords decision in *Channel Tunnel Group v Balfour Beatty*[14]. In theory, therefore, if a contract contains a stepped clause which provides for, say, mediation to be followed by arbitration, and one party issues proceedings without using either mediation or arbitration, a court would be bound to order a stay under s 9(4).

Enthusiasm about this provision was tempered by the decision of McKinnon J in *Halifax Financial Services v Intuitive Systems Ltd*[15], in which he held that the stepped ADR/arbitration procedure devised for a contract between the claimant and a software designer did not make compliance with its procedures mandatory. More importantly, he held that it was doubtful whether such clauses were enforceable. He drew a distinction between determinative procedures such as arbitration or binding expert

---

14 [1993] 1 All ER 664.
15 [1999] 1 All ER Comm 303.

determination as against non-determinative procedures such as negotiation, mediation, expert appraisal and non-binding evaluations. This contract had a series of non-binding processes coupled with a series of moratoria on issue of proceedings, leading towards permission to issue proceedings unless arbitration was agreed. No mention was made of s 9 of the Arbitration Act 1996 in the judgment, but he distinguished the case before him from *Channel Tunnel Group* Ltd v Balfour Beatty on the grounds that the Channel Tunnel case involved a clause which was 'nearly an immediate effective agreement to arbitrate, albeit not quite'. The *Halifax* clause could not be construed as close to being nearly an immediately effective agreement to arbitrate. He drew comfort from the judgment in *Cott (UK) Ltd v FE Barber Ltd*[16] on the basis that, although the judge had been prepared in principle to order a stay for ADR, the relevant clause required the case to be referred to an expert whose decision was to be final and binding, and was thus going to lead to a determinative rather than non-determinative outcome. H was prepared to allow enforcement of a commitment to a determinative process, but not a non-determinative process like mediation.

In truth, McKinnon J in *Halifax* felt that the stay sought by the defendant under the ADR clause was being used as a device to delay the start of proceedings and keep the claimant unjustifiably out of his claim. If the decision had gone to mere exercise of discretion as to whether to grant a stay or not, he would have found against the defendant, because he felt it was time for the claim to proceed. He found specifically that the claimant 'has not rushed to litigation or refused to consider a negotiated settlement'. If the claimant had rushed to issue, it is clear that the CPR give ample grounds to a court to penalise such an approach.

This underlines what the true incentives and disincentives are for unreasonable parties since the CPR came into effect. A rogue party who issues court proceedings too early, especially in the face of a pre-agreed commitment to ADR, is going to face a serious risk of costs sanctions under CPR 44.5, for ignoring the letter (where applicable) or the spirit of the pre-action protocols and the overriding objective in CPR Part 1, extending as they do to unreasonable conduct pre-issue. Even where the aggressor 'wins', the party aggrieved simply needs to point out to the court that there was no good reason for failing to try ADR first, and a court should be prepared to be sympathetic over the costs order to be made.

The issue next came before Colman J in the Commercial Court in *Cable & Wireless v IBM*[17]. He was being invited by the claimant to make a declara-

---

16 [1997] 3 All ER 540.
17 [2002] EWHC 2059 (Comm).

tory judgment about a contractual provision in a Global Framework Agreement for the provision of worldwide information technology, whereas the defendant wanted him to stay proceedings under an 'escalator' clause for dispute resolution which required the parties to enter stepped negotiation and then, if unsuccessful, 'to attempt in good faith to resolve the dispute or claim through an alternative dispute resolution procedure as recommended to the parties by CEDR', though this was not to preclude proceedings from being issued. *Halifax* seems not to have been cited, for it is not mentioned in the judgment. Colman J reviewed *Courtney & Fairbairn v Tolani Brothers* and *Paul Smith Ltd v H&S International Holdings Inc Holdings Ltd* as supporting the concept that an agreement to negotiate is not enforceable. But he observed that CEDR's procedure, as set out in its then published Model Mediation Procedure and Agreement, coupled with the freedom to withdraw from the process if unproductive, provided sufficient certainty for a judge to decide whether a party had complied with the terms of this clause for it to be enforceable. He said that courts should not be astute to accentuate uncertainty and therefore unenforceability in relation to references to ADR in contracts, and commented:

> 'For the courts now to decline to enforce contractual references to ADR on the grounds of intrinsic uncertainty would be to fly in the face of public policy as expressed in the CPR and as reflected in the judgment of the Court of Appeal in *Dunnett v Railtrack*'.

Of course one can point out that the clause in question did not itself incorporate CEDR's then published Model Mediation Procedure. CEDR could have chosen to recommend early neutral evaluation or mediation in any form of design, which hardly amounts to certainty of chosen process. A clause which merely delegates responsibility to advise to an apparently well-reputed service provider might be regarded as a slightly surprising way to satisfy a court that there was more than a mere agreement to negotiate. But this was the first time that a senior and well-respected judge had taken this view. Perhaps the fact that by then costs sanctions awaited any unreasonable pre-issue refusal to mediate, whether or not such an ADR clause exists, had tempered the need for such debate.

Two more cases have clarified and established the approach of the English courts[18]. In *Holloway v Chancery Mead Ltd,* a construction dispute about a development covered by the National House Builders Council contract which specified a form of dispute resolution to be used before arbitration, Ramsey J discerned three essential requirements for an available procedure to exclude a party from an adjudicative process:

---

18 And see also *Harper v Interchange Group* [2007] EWHC 1834 (Comm).

- there must be a clear binding undertaking to engage in the alternative process;
- there must be clear provisions over the selection of the neutral; and
- there must be a clearly-defined process to be followed.

Augmenting and explaining the effect of these requirements, he said that there should be no matters requiring additional agreement before the alternative procedure could be started.

On the facts as found in relation to the NHBC contract he held that the house purchaser had not contracted to be bound, but that if he had, the contractual provisions would have satisfied the tests in question.

Finally, the Court of Appeal in *Sulamerica CIA Nacional de Seguros v Enesa*[19] supported the decisions of Colman J in *Cable & Wireless* and Ramsey J in *Holloway*. In the *Sulamerica* case, insurance policies covering oil installations in Brazil contained a clause providing that the parties would seek to have disputes resolved 'amicably by mediation'. In that process, all rights would be reserved, with confidentiality and privilege applying to exchanges within the process which would be terminable by notice. After hearing argument based on *Walford v Miles* and subsequent authorities discussed above, the Court of Appeal were prepared to allow an adequate clause to exclude arbitration or litigation, but in this case, they held that the clause did not satisfy the requirements for certainty outlined by Ramsey J in *Holloway* and immediate arbitration was ordered.

8.5   Types of ADR clause

There is a wide variety of types of ADR clause, examples of which are readily available from providers such as CEDR. Although the precise wording of the clause may seem to matter less if it is unenforceable, the clause should nevertheless be the subject of considerable thought. If the parties do choose to implement it when the dispute arises, it will need to meet the demands of any situation effectively. The nature of the agreement in which the clause appears may well have a bearing on the choice and drafting of the clause. For example, a partnership agreement would suggest the use of a very flexible, facilitative process such as mediation, whereas a highly technical engineering contract might call for an expert determination, adjudication, or early neutral evaluation.

---

19 [2012] EWCA Civ 638.

8.6   Considerations as to ADR clauses

There are a number of considerations to bear in mind. These include:

Length and detail

Essentially, the clause merely needs to stipulate that in the event of a dispute arising, the parties will attempt to resolve it by ADR. A very short form of clause can accomplish that with ease[20]. However, such a clause may beg as many questions as it answers, such as which ADR process will be used; who will the neutral be, and how chosen; is the ADR process a condition precedent to litigation or arbitration; and what (if any) should the timetable be for carrying out the ADR process, and so on. As has been seen, such a clause is unlikely to be enforced by the courts.

However, a brief clause may still be of benefit. It leaves the details of the process open for the parties to decide at the time the dispute arises. The most appropriate type of ADR process might only become clear at that time, and the parties would not want to be restricted by reference to an earlier stipulation. Furthermore, some contracting parties might find it distasteful to draft too detailed a disputes clause at a time when no dispute exists between them. On the other hand, leaving the parties with a choice when the dispute arises can also present problems. If they are unable, when a dispute does arise, to agree the requisite details, the whole value of the clause may be lost. Furthermore, parties wanting some objective justification for not complying with a clause will find it easy to disagree on the details and hence prevent any progress.

The drafting of each clause should therefore be approached afresh each time, with thought given to the context in which disputes will arise, each party's likely attitude, the results which the clause is intended to achieve, and so on. In fact, the principle that contracting parties should discuss the resolution of any disputes *at the time of contracting* is a sound one, and is more likely to increase rather than diminish the trust between the parties, since the otherwise taboo subject will be brought out into the open. That discussion will serve as a much more solid base for the parties to refer to when the dispute does arise. Ideally, the drafting of ADR clauses should be much more than the reproduction of a standard form ADR clause, and in particular the parties themselves, and not just their advisers, should be drawn into discussion about the optimum dispute resolution structures.

Drafting should also be approached with imagination. There is no reason why each contractual context should not have its own custom-designed dispute resolution process. Parties will become increasingly aware of the

---

20 Specimen ADR contract clauses are available at www.cedr.com.

approaches that prove most effective for them through a process of trial and experience.

Content

In terms of the detailed contents to be included in an ADR clause, the following points at least should be considered:

- Will the clause refer to an ADR process to be agreed, or stipulate a particular one (eg mediation)?
- Is there to be a timetable for compliance with the clause or with procedural stages within the clause (eg appointment of a mediator, exchange of case summaries etc)?
- Is the ADR process intended to be a condition precedent to the commencement of litigation or arbitration proceedings, or not?
- Is the identity or discipline of the neutral or mediator to be spelled out in advance? If not, what provision should there be for appointment?
- Is an ADR organisation to be used to nominate or appoint a mediator and administer and supervise the process?
- How will any costs of the process be apportioned?
- Is a tiered process to be used, eg direct negotiations, followed (if necessary) by mediation, followed (if necessary) by adjudication, arbitration or litigation?

Tiered or stepped clauses

ADR clauses present an opportunity for the use of a 'tiered' structure within the clause, that is, a series of steps in the overall dispute resolution process, each designed to handle the dispute if it has not been resolved by the previous step. These can be particularly effective. Indeed, this approach has already been widely used, for example in the introduction of a negotiating phase as a prerequisite to the commencement of litigation or arbitration, and the 'engineer's decision' in some construction contracts. ADR techniques allow for this principle to be developed and used in greater detail.

The principal strengths of a tiered structure are:

- the dispute resolution mechanism in use at any particular stage of a dispute will be the one most likely to resolve it. For example, it may be that the issue of proceedings too early in a dispute will drive out certain settlement possibilities which have not been

167

achievable through initial direct negotiations. The introduction of a mediation phase between the negotiation and litigation phases may well provide a process more capable of teasing out a settlement in that particular environment;

– the resolution processes can increase in formality and structure as it becomes clear that the dispute itself requires that. All the benefits of the litigation or arbitration processes remain available to the parties, but the formality and rigidity they bring is delayed until it is considered indispensable.

Some detailed examples of tiered ADR clauses are available on the CEDR website (www.cedr.com). In terms of drafting, the guiding principle should again be an attempt imaginatively to anticipate likely dispute scenarios, and to match them with relevant methods of resolution.

It is also worth noting that the choice of dispute clause can constitute a powerful form of policy statement to those with whom one deals. The tiered ADR clauses all anticipate mediation being attempted before litigation or arbitration has been commenced, but not thereafter. This reflects the policy approach not to commence litigation until other avenues have been exhausted, but equally not to use any ADR processes once proceedings have been commenced. Those advising government departments or their contractors clearly need to be aware of this approach.

8.7 Areas of relevance

ADR clauses of different types are being used in a wide variety of contexts. Examples of these include general commercial contracts, partnership agreements, terms and conditions of business, construction contracts, development contracts, and so on. In each new application, thought should be given to the type of ADR process most likely to generate resolution.

It is also important to remember the value of ADR clauses in corporate policy statements. Thus many large American companies have adopted a public corporate pledge, to use ADR processes in appropriate situations. Although not legally committing the company to the use of ADR in any particular dispute, this pledge has been used to send a powerful message to those with whom this company deals, and promote the company's public image. This is similar in concept to accords, by which parties, insurers, lawyers, even governments, and others engaged in a particular area of dispute state their intention to use ADR when problems arise[21].

---

21 See, for instance, the UK Goverment's Dispute Resolution Commitment of March 2011 (replacing the Government Pledge of March 2001).

Chapter 9

Mediation privilege and confidentiality

Probably the most fundamental aspect of the mediation process is its offer of an apparently secure and confidential environment in which parties are free to explore the possibility of settlement of their dispute without risking damage to their 'on-the-record' case if settlement does not emerge. Without the assurance that when concessions and offers are made during a mediation behind the veil of confidentiality, such indications of flexibility cannot be misused by an opponent later in litigation, parties will remain cautious and not want to risk exposing any weakness by making proposals. Parties will also want to know for certain what the consequences could be if they or the opposing party choose to adopt what the court might later regard as an unreasonable attitude during a mediation. There is also the question of how much a judge who has decided substantive issues in a case can have access to privileged material when deciding what costs order to make. So the proper circumstances and extent to which a judge can later penetrate behind the veil of confidentiality is of crucial importance.

As the law in England and Wales has developed, it is necessary to look at this question through two related principles – evidential privilege and contractual confidentiality – and to contrast the way these two concepts arise in mediations and in other types of dispute resolution process. The starting-point is to examine the nature of the privilege which automatically attaches to exclude evidence being given about what transpires in all settlement discussions and processes, and the limits of this privilege.

9.1 Evidential privilege for all settlement discussions

The House of Lords made it clear in *Rush & Tomkins v GLC*[1] that all genuine negotiations, whether oral or written, which are undertaken in an attempt to settle a dispute are protected from subsequent disclosure in proceedings, whether or not the label 'without prejudice' has been applied to them. Their Lordships quoted Oliver LJ's rationale for this from his

---

1 [1988] 3 All ER 737.

judgment in *Cutts v Head*[2], a judgment delivered long before ADR and the CPR began to aspire to the same aims:

> '... Parties should be encouraged so far as possible to settle their disputes without resort to litigation and should not be discouraged by the knowledge that anything that is said in the course of such negotiations (and that includes, of course, as much the failure to reply to an offer as an actual reply) may be used to their prejudice in the course of their proceedings'.

Thus if discussions take place before a mediation agreement is signed, or a mediation takes place without a mediation agreement being signed, the 'without prejudice' rule will protect exchanges between the parties themselves as part of the process and preparation for it from subsequent disclosure, subject to the exceptions of, and limitations to, the rule. Clearly such protection applies also to communications through solicitors and counsel for each party. But there is no authority on whether similar protection would be afforded to admissions and offers made or reported to or passed through an independent intermediary such as a mediator, by extension, in the absence of a further protection such as a specific agreement not to call a mediator as a witness (a common clause discussed in **7.4**). But it seems highly likely that this protection would be afforded on public policy grounds.

'Without prejudice' protection does not simply limit later disclosure as between those between whom the privileged communication initially passed. In cases involving parties who were not privy to the privileged communications or settlement discussions or the mediation, there cannot be any express or implied contract: restrictions can only be founded on public policy considerations. In the *Rush & Tomkins* case, having confirmed the privileged attached to communications between direct disputants, Lord Griffiths went on:

> 'But it would surely be equally discouraging if the main contractor knew that if he achieved a settlement those admissions could then be used against him *by any other* sub-contractor with whom he might also be in dispute. The main contractor might well be prepared to make certain concessions to settle some modest claim which he would never make in the face of another far larger claim' [emphasis supplied].

This passage was quoted with approval in *Instance Bros v Denny*[3], in which Lloyd J had to decide whether privileged communications in without prej-

---

2 [1984] Ch 290.
3 (2000) Times, 28 February.

udice correspondence, settlement meetings and at a mediation conducted on CEDR's standard terms should be kept from subsequent litigation about wider disputes in the USA between the same or related parties. He granted injunctions to restrain disclosure of all three classes of communication from use in the US proceedings.

9.2 The current legal status of 'settlement meetings' generally

First, it is important to appreciate what protection is automatically afforded to settlement attempts of all kinds, in order to test out the value of mediation protection, analysing the legal status of *any* without prejudice settlement process. For this purpose it is assumed that there is no difference between a course of 'without prejudice' correspondence; a bilateral negotiation meeting between lawyers without clients; a round-table meeting with lawyers and parties present but no neutral; and a mediation, using the generic title of 'settlement meetings' for convenience for all such occasions. This basic protection will cover every mediation as well as the other types of settlement meeting instanced above, but there are ways in which mediation protection is deliberately made much wider. Where 'without prejudice' privilege applies to what could otherwise be admissible evidence, one party cannot introduce such material if the other party objects. For a judge to hear such evidence, all those to whom the privilege belongs would have to waive it, unless a party can establish one of the exceptions to the rule, discussed below. Parties do frequently waive the privilege, often when seeking to make points about what the proper costs order should be at the conclusion of a substantive trial.

The rationale of 'without prejudice' privilege

Mediation can be viewed – indeed, has been judicially viewed[4] – simply as 'assisted "without prejudice" negotiation', with the 'assistance' being given by the mediator as a neutral third party. This plain view is not accepted without question by the mediation or even the judicial and legal community. Mediations are set up far more formally than (say) round-table meetings, in that a mediation agreement is signed at its outset by both the parties and the mediator, which is intended to import and define several significant legal obligations. The nature and effectiveness of the mediation agreement in doing so is discussed in **Chapter 2**. So what then is the current express or implied status in law and the extent of participant protection shared by all such settlement meetings, including mediations?

---

4 See Stuart Isaacs QC in *Brown v Rice* [2007] EWHC 625 (Ch) and May LJ *Aird v Prime Meridian* [2006] EWCA Civ 1886.

Mediation privilege and confidentiality

As noted above, it is trite law that settlement meetings are assumed to be conducted with the benefit of 'without prejudice' privilege. As Sir David Foskett puts it[5]:

> 'The net effect of negotiations being "without prejudice" is that, subject to certain exceptions, a privilege attached to the content of those negotiations rendering their content inadmissible at the trial of the action to the settlement of which they were directed'.

The authorities make it clear that the origins of the principle derive both from:

- **public policy** in encouraging the settlement of disputes by excluding admissions against interest as admissible evidence; and
- **an implied agreement**[6] between the parties arising out of their offering or agreeing to negotiate in this way.

In any given case, either or both of these justifications may apply. For instance, the fact that 'without prejudice' material may not be admitted to explore how costs liabilities should be determined without waiver or consent by both parties has nothing to do with public policy in excluding admissions, but is a conventional concept based on an implied agreement[7].

It is not necessary for the 'without prejudice' label to be applied specifically to settlement efforts for the privilege to attach, although it often is used to head correspondence, or muttered at the start of a telephone conversation about settlement. It arises automatically: and it has been said that for it not to attach to what appear to be settlement proposals, a very clear statement that the proposals in question are 'open' (in the sense of being reportable to a judge later without need to waive privilege) and not 'without prejudice' must be made to make them available for judicial scrutiny. The privilege attaches to both written and oral communications. So discussions during a settlement meeting will be assumed not to give rise to admissible evidence. The parties may formally record in preparatory correspondence that a settlement meeting is to be 'without prejudice', but there is probably no legal need to do so for the privilege to arise.

---

5 *The Law and Practice of Compromise* (7th edn).
6 Note that such an agreement is not merely implied in relation to a mediation but is (usually) expressly articulated in the mediation agreement. Does this make any difference? This is discussed below.
7 See *Cutts v Head* [1984] 1 All ER 697, CA.

A usual form of provision in mediation agreements is that:

'all information (whether in oral, written electronic or any other form) created for the purpose of, or at, or arising out of or in connection with, the mediation will be without prejudice to and privileged from disclosure and inadmissible as evidence in, any existing or future litigation in relation to the dispute or any other proceedings whatsoever, except where such information would in any event have been disclosable in any such proceedings'.

This probably adds nothing to the general law, even as regards proceedings outside the dispute settled at mediation[8], unless the reasonableness of a compromise reached in a mediation is put in issue in later proceedings by someone with a legitimate interest in those settlement terms[9].

It means that the written case summaries prepared for the purposes of the mediation are also privileged. But it does not mean that documents which are disclosable in the ordinary course but which emerge for the first time at a mediation can have any privilege conferred upon them for that reason alone[10]. It also appears to mean that early communications between parties and the mediator before a mediation agreement is signed will become protected by the later signing of the mediation agreement, as well as being automatically covered by 'without prejudice' privilege. As Lloyd J said in *Instance v Denny Bros Printing Ltd*[11]:

'Mediation is defined as the attempt to settle the dispute by mediation. The process of getting to entry into the mediation agreement is itself, albeit at a preliminary stage, an attempt to settle the dispute by mediation'.

Such matters were considered in *Aird v Prime Meridian*[12]. In a construction dispute, mediation was agreed and an order made for the experts to meet and produce a joint statement. The claimant's expert thought it was agreed that the joint statement would be covered by mediation privilege,

---

8 See *Rush & Tomkins v GLC* [1988] 3 All ER 737.
9 See *Standard Telephones & Cables v Tomlin* [1969] 3 All ER 210 and *Muller v Linsley & Mortimer* [1996] PNLR 74, CA.
10 See the Australian case of *AWA Ltd v Daniels* (24 February 1992), per Rogers CJ Commercial Division of Supreme Court of New South Wales, where disclosure was ordered of a document released expressly 'without prejudice' during a mediation which did not settle.
11 At p 33 of the unreported judgment transcript: see EDR Law on the CEDR website at www.cedr.co.uk.
12 [2006] EWHC 2338 (TCC), (HHJ Coulson QC); appeal decision at [2006] EWCA Civ 1866.

but the order did not make this clear. When he appeared to change his mind over matters in the joint statement after the mediation did not settle the claim, the defendants argued that the joint statement should be made available to the judge under CPR 35.12(3). The trial judge found that it was intended to be privileged, following the view expressed in *Smith Industries v Weiss*[13] that 'without prejudice' protection should only be held to be waived in 'clear and unambiguous circumstances'. However, the Court of Appeal reversed this decision, construing the order and CPR 35.12(3) objectively. In doing so, May LJ commented that mediation confidentiality:

> 'would not apply to documents obviously produced for other purposes which were needed for and produced at the mediation; for example their building contract or the antecedent pleadings in the proceedings'.

This is an unsurprising statement of what anyone in a mediation is likely to expect to be the case. It should make no difference to the fundamentals of mediation confidentiality.

When does 'without prejudice' protection first arise in relation to a mediation? Is it only when a mediation agreement has been signed and the process properly started, or does privilege extend back far enough to prevent the court from hearing evidence about who refused to mediate and why? There are inconsistent decisions on this point. In *SITA v Watson Wyatt and Maxwell Batley*[14], Park J received in evidence a good deal of material which was ordinarily protected as exchanged on a 'without prejudice' occasion when considering whether a successful party who declined mediation should be penalised. In *Leicester Circuits v Coates Industries*[15], a party who pulled out of a mediation very shortly before the due date was penalised in costs, and there was no question raised that the court could not receive evidence of what happened to decide this point. But in *Reed Executive v Reed Business Solutions*[16], the court declined to see correspondence specifically marked 'without prejudice' in which the parties debated whether to mediate. In *ARP Capita London Market Services Ltd v Ross & Co*[17], the successful party who had refused to mediate tried unsuccessfully to argue that 'without prejudice' protection applied to antecedent negotiations over whether to mediate. Courts seem ready to admit evidence of failure to mediate and not to treat the pre-mediation period as privileged, unless

---

13 (23 March 2002, unreported), Mr R Kaye QC sitting in the Chancery Division.
14 [2002] EWHC 2401 (Ch).
15 [2003] EWCA Civ 333.
16 [2004] EWCA Civ 887.
17 [2004] EWHC 1181 (Ch): Sir Andrew Longmore VC.

specifically made 'without prejudice'[18]. The court could, of course, admit evidence if the pre-mediation transactions were marked 'without prejudice save as to costs'[19].

The confidential status of dealings between the mediator and the parties prior to the mediation has just been touched on in the previous section. *Instance v Denny Bros Printing Ltd* makes it clear that a confidentiality clause in a subsequently signed mediation agreement will apply in full to antecedent negotiations. The CEDR agreement in that case provided that 'every person involved in the mediation will keep confidential and not use for any collateral or ulterior purpose all information (whether given orally in writing or otherwise) produced for or arising in relation to the mediation.' Lloyd J specifically said that:

> 'it seems to me right to regard communications preceding the mediation agreement and during the discussions which led to it as being within the scope of the confidentiality clause. I would regard the use of such material for the United States proceedings as being a collateral or ulterior purpose and therefore in breach of the clause'.

A contractual provision which confirms confidentiality for what happens at the mediation is not merely an evidential rule preventing disclosure of admissions and offers at a subsequent trial. Such a term imposes a positive contractual obligation on all signatories to the mediation agreement (including the mediator and the mediation provider) which is enforceable by positive action for an injunction[20] and/or damages.

Several cases abroad have upheld the confidentiality of what passed within a mediation. In *X v Y*[21], a decision of the Tribunal de Commerce in Brussels in 1999, the confidentiality clause in a CEDR mediation agreement was held to prevent a party from including mention of a mediation in subsequent proceedings. The Tribunal ordered the reference to be struck out and imposed stiff penalties for breach.

As might be expected perhaps, two decisions of the US courts illustrate their determination to penalise breach of mediation confidentiality. In

---

18 See also *Framlington Group and AXA Framlington v Barnetson* [2007] EWCA Civ 502, where the Court of Appeal held that where parties might reasonably have contemplated litigation when making without prejudice proposals, privilege will attach. Also see the discussion in *Bradford & Bingley plc v Rashid* [2006] 1 WLR 2066, HL.

19 See *Reed Executive v Reed Business Solutions* above.

20 Such an injunction was granted against a party seeking to disclose what transpired at a mediation in both *Instance v Denny Bros Printing Ltd* and *Venture Investment Placement v Hall* [2005] EWHC 1227 (Ch).

21 (Unreported).

Parazino v Barnett Bank[22], a 1997 Florida appeal case, the claimant who revealed to a newspaper that the bank had made an offer at a mediation which she had refused, hinting that this showed a degree of acceptance of her case, had her entire claim for $100,000 struck out 'with prejudice'. In *Bernard v Calen Group*[23], a New York appeal case, claimant's counsel, who had always opposed a court-directed mediation which failed, applied to the judge to end the mediation, quoting what had happened at the mediation (as he saw it) as evidence of the defendants' having not engaged seriously in the process. The defendant moved for sanctions, and the court imposed a $2,500 fine (payable personally) on the lawyer.

The importance of this attaches to whether a judge can hear evidence of 'admissions against interest', in other words oral or written statements which if allowed as evidence would amount to a concession of a significant fact or position, or even overall liability or causation, to the prejudice of the party making the admission. Normally any relevant statement, whether or not an admission, may be admissible as evidence, especially with the relaxing of the rule against hearsay. But the 'without prejudice' rule protects admissions against interest from being admitted as evidence. On the record, both claimant and defendant may well articulate in their statements of case and their witness statements unqualified and apparently inflexible assertions of the rightness of their respective case. A settlement meeting at which they simply reiterate such positions is unlikely to lead to resolution. So there comes a time when a party may wish to send a concessionary signal that he perceives risks attaching to part of his case and might be prepared to consider settlement on a basis moderated as to that party's perception of risk. He will not readily send that concessionary signal if it might be used against him if settlement does not emerge. Indeed, he may fear that the very sending of that signal will encourage his opponent to take comfort or advantage from that expression of possible weakness, and either be less likely to settle at all or promptly suggest disadvantageous settlement terms by a Part 36 offer. Especially in the current atmosphere of our civil justice system of 'cards on the table' openness and costs penalties for unreasonable litigation conduct, there may arise a fear on the part of a recipient of a concession that disclosure to the judge of any failure to respond to it reasonably or at all may open him to criticism. The bilateral need for solid protection from subsequent disclosure, in order to make settlement meetings both secure and effective, is therefore very plain.

---

22 (Unreported).
23 (Unreported).

Exceptions to non-admissibility of 'without prejudice' communication

The existence of exceptions to protection from subsequent admissibility as evidence of the content of settlement meetings is inevitably de-stabilising. What party will feel safe enough to confide a potential weakness to an opponent within the assumed safety of privilege from disclosure, if their opponent might in certain circumstances be able unilaterally to persuade a judge to receive it in evidence, contrary to the wishes of the party who admitted that weakness?

The circumstances in which a judge can hear 'without prejudice' material in evidence at the instance of one party and in the face of opposition from the other party who shares ownership of the privilege are:

- **Where there is no extant dispute**, and a communication is a mere 'opening shot' (though opening shots which have represented wholly or in part a willingness to negotiate have still been protected[24]): this is unlikely to arise in a formal settlement meeting, which will rarely occur before a dispute has crystallised. A startling finding was made to similar effect in *BNP Paribas v Mezzotero*[25], where a meeting was held to discuss a grievance over sexual discrimination, described by the employee's managers as 'without prejudice', at which the possibility of severance was introduced. The Employment Appeal Tribunal admitted evidence of the meeting, as there was at that stage no dispute, or it amounted to unambiguous impropriety as discussed below.

- **Acts or statements amounting to unambiguous impropriety** made by a party when without prejudice privilege would otherwise prevent admissibility: particularly the making of threats designed to induce settlement. Cases in which 'without prejudice' has been held not to prevent admission of evidence have included cases where an admission of an act of bankruptcy[26], threats to expose the illegitimacy of an opponent's children[27], or to produce perjured evidence to win a claim[28], to harass a neighbour and ruin his family life[29], or an admission recorded covertly at a 'without prejudice' meeting that proceedings had

---

24 See for instance *South Shropshire District Council v Amos* [1987] 1 All ER 340, CA.
25 [2004] IRLR 508.
26 *Re Daintrey, ex p Holt* [1893] 2 QB 116. See the useful discussion of this topic in Foskett, *The Law and Practice of Compromise* (6th edn).
27 *Underwood v Cox* (1912) 4 DLR 66 (Ontario Div Ct).
28 *Greenwood v Fitts* (1961) 29 DLR 260.
29 *Finch v Wilson* (8 May 1987, unreported).

only been brought to produce a better settlement. Even in *Re D*[30], Sir Thomas Bingham noted in passing that a further exception might be where a party had no *bona fide* intention to negotiate. If this last exception were established at the level of ordinary interpretation of those words, it would mean that a party to a settlement discussion could use this as the basis of revealing mere unreasonableness in attitude as a means of removing the veil from a wide range of 'without prejudice' discussions. But all these cases were decided before 1990, and the establishment of a new co-operative approach to litigation. The more recent tendency has been for a restrictive approach to be taken to finding 'unambiguous impropriety'[31]. The application of economic duress was regarded as potentially amounting to this in *Farm Assist v DEFRA (No 1)*[32], though the facts were never finally litigated, as proceedings were discontinued before trial. A reasonably justifiable threat to enforce a patent right in litigation was declared protected in *Unilever v Proctor & Gamble*[33], during which Robert Walker LJ usefully reviewed what might happen at a typical settlement meeting:

'I have no doubt that busy practitioners are acting prudently in making the general working assumption that the ["without prejudice"] rule, if not "sacred"... has a wide and compelling effect. This is particularly true where the "without prejudice" communications in question consist not of letters or other written documents but of wide-ranging unscripted discussions during a meeting which may have lasted several hours. At a meeting of that sort the discussions between the parties' representatives may contain a mixture of admissions and half-admissions against a party's interest, more or less confident assertions of a party's case, offers, counter-offers and statements (which might be characterised as threats or as thinking aloud) about future plans and possibilities'.

As to covert tape-recording (which happened in several cases dealing with this issue), the court have expressly frowned upon

---

30 [1993] 2 All ER 693.
31 For instance it was used to justify admission of alleged threats in *Hall v Pertemps* [2005] EWHC 3110 (Ch), although the evidence was admitted because the judge found that there had been mutual waiver of privilege over what happened at the mediation
32 [2008] EWHC 3079 (TCC).
33 [2001] 1 All ER 783.

it as a means of acquiring evidence[34], although it is not in any sense banned from use in ordinary settlement meetings. All good mediation agreements have a clause which outlaws use of mechanical recording, but few other types of settlement meeting are similarly protected by contract, and are certainly not by law.

One question that does arise is whether the unambiguous impropriety exception will extend not merely to duress but also to material fraudulent, innocent or negligent misrepresentations which induce a settlement agreement, or to issues of illegality? It clearly cannot apply to most questions of vitiation by mistake, so the ordinary law of contract may well apply as further reasons for vitiating a settlement contract which is made during 'without prejudice' negotiations, giving rise to the need to admit evidence of what was said during the settlement meeting[35]. Certainly in *Farm Assist v DEFRA (No 1)*, Ramsey J was willing to accept that evidence of economic duress inflicted during a mediation could, if admissible, vitiate a settlement.

– **As proof merely that such statements were made**, and where they fall short of being an admission against interest. Lord Walker's remarks quoted above in *Unilever v Proctor & Gamble* seem now to represent the accepted judicial approach to without prejudice protection, in a fairly broad way. However, for some time a more purist approach was taken, particularly by Hoffmann LJ in *Muller v Linsley & Mortimer*[36], where he was ready to limit without prejudice protection solely to admissions against interest, and was prepared to admit 'without prejudice' material to assist a later litigant to ascertain how a previous claim had been settled, as that evidence, in his view, was not strictly an admission against interest but simply proof of what had happened or been said. Lord Hoffmann again asserted this narrow interpretation of without prejudice privilege in *Bradford & Bingley BS v Rashid*[37], though accepting that *Unilever v*

---

34 Simon Brown LJ in *Fazil-Alizadeh v Nikbin* (1993) Times, 19 March, CA.
35 See *SIB v Fincken* [2004] 1 WLR 667, CA, for an attempt to admit an admission off the record to contradict a misrepresentation off the record and prove it to be fraudulent. *Held* not admissible, as privilege had not been abused.
36 [1996] PNLR 74, CA; *Muller v Linsley & Mortimer* was followed by Master Bragge in *Cattley v Pollard* [2007] Ch 353, in which a third party was allowed access to mediation documents to ascertain whether there had been double counting in a claim settled by claimants against her in a mediation with her husband's professional indemnity insurers. These issues are helpfully discussed by Wlilliam Wood QC (who appeared in *Cattley*) in *When girls go wild: the debate over mediation privilege* The Mediator, Sept 2008 (the article's risqué title belies the seriousness and usefulness of his views).
37 [2006] 1 WLR 2066.

179

Proctor & Gamble was correctly decided. That dispute between Lords Hoffmann and Walker about the extent of without prejudice privilege in this respect has been resolved by the House of Lords decision of *Ofulue v Bossaert*[38] in favour of the broader interpretation given by Walker LJ in *Unilever.* As a result courts will be slow to find exceptions to without prejudice privilege and are likely to afford broad protection to statements made in circumstances which attract without prejudice privilege.

This exception may still come into play where one party seeks to prove whether or not settlement was reached and on what terms, or to justify otherwise unexplained delay: such an enquiry as to whether a contract was reached during 'without prejudice' negotiations will almost inevitably expose large areas of what happened at a mediation which mediators might well have assured parties would remain secret[39].

- **Facts identified during negotiations leading to settlement** which may help to construe the true meaning of the negotiated settlement: see *Oceanbulk Shipping v TMT Asia Ltd*[40]. Some caution over this exception arises from the decisions in *Chartbrook v Persimmon Homes*[41] and *Mason v Walton-on-Thames Charity*[42], both cases in which pre-contractual negotiations were not admitted in evidence to assist the construction of a contract.

- **Estoppel** from asserting privilege, by which a party who relies on a 'without prejudice' statement and acts to his detriment may be able to call evidence to establish this and enforce his right to what he relied upon.

- **Waiver** of privilege, which can be express or implied by conduct, but requires waiver by both parties to be effective.

If mediation were merely 'assisted "without prejudice" negotiation', any apparently good faith allegation by one party that any of these exceptions to the 'without prejudice' rule applied would licence a judge to make a full public enquiry into what happened at a mediation, despite the assurances which the mediator may have given that what transpires at the mediation is safe from judicial gaze. It would not require *both* parties to waive privilege for such an enquiry to happen. *Brown v Rice*[43] involved a judge's

---

38 [2009] UKHL 16.
39 As *Brown v Rice* illustrates.
40 [2010] UKSC 44.
41 [2011] UKHL 38.
42 [2010] EWHC 1688 (Ch) and [2011] EWCA Civ 1732.
43 [2007] EWHC 625 (Ch).

investigation which was triggered by a unilateral set of assertions by the claimant that a binding deal had been made. Both the effective defendant and the mediation provider (on behalf of the mediator) submitted that the judge should not go behind the veil of privilege to explore this question, but neither succeeded in dissuading him from his investigation. This is an important touchstone case which raises in practical terms a number of the main issues relating to the limits of privilege and confidentiality.

To whom does 'without prejudice' privilege belong?

It is normally regarded as the law that the privilege of protection of 'without prejudice' material from disclosure belongs to the parties jointly. Both or all parties to it must either consent to disclosure or waive or be estopped from relying on the privilege, unless one of the other exceptions applies. On this interpretation of the law, anyone present at a settlement meeting is compellable as a witness once the privilege has been waived by the parties. Thus if simple 'without prejudice' privilege were the only protection for mediations, it also means that, absent another contractual term preventing it, a mediator too would not in any way own that privilege[44] and could not prevent the parties agreeing to disclose to a judge what the mediator said (which may be a matter of personal embarrassment to the mediator, casting doubt – at least in one party's mind – on that mediator's neutrality)[45]. Nor could a mediation provider successfully intervene to prevent disclosure of what it might regard as damaging to the mediation process as a matter of public policy, were it to be disclosed[46].

There are somewhat divergent views as to the privilege which attaches when A and B settle on terms which emerge at a settlement meeting behind the cloak of privilege, and A thereafter sues C for a shortfall in the settlement. C may be a sub-contractor not involved in the original litigation or perhaps an antecedent adviser whom A blames for reducing the value of his claim as settled. C may well want to discover what happened at the settlement meeting to justify the settlement terms complained of. 'Without prejudice' privilege has been held both to exclude later investigation, and

---

44 This was accepted by the court as being so in both *Brown v Rice* and *Farm Assist v DEFRA (No 2)*.
45 See *SITA v Watson Wyatt: Maxwell Batley Pt 20 deft* for an occasion when this happened.
46 See *Brown v Rice and Patel* where intervention did not really work, and *Malmesbury v Strutt & Parker* and *Chantrey Vellacott v Convergence Group* where there was no provider intervention but the judge was given details of offers and counter-offers made at the mediation with the parties' consent, wisely or not.

also not to do so[47]. Where there is such a doubt, clarity is needed in defining the limits of 'mediation privilege', even if not the privilege attaching to less formal settlement meetings.

Settlement meetings and confidentiality

Is there some general implied right of confidentiality, separate from 'without prejudice' privilege, which attaches to settlement meetings? The answer seems to be No, unless some kind of stand-alone confidentiality clause is negotiated and agreed in advance or as part of the settlement terms, supported by valuable consideration. Legal texts and journals such as *Current Law, Kemp and Kemp* and *Clinical Risk* quite frequently publish reports of settlements reached in personal injury and clinical negligence claims. These are presumably not in breach of any confidentiality clause embodied in those settlement discussions, nor in breach of any implied duty of confidentiality. Reports of the content of discussions leading to settlement are rarer, but probably because 'without prejudice' privilege is expected to apply.

The law of confidence, as a stand-alone duty separate from any contractual commitment, emerged from the equity jurisdiction. An injunction will be available to restrain a breach of a duty of confidence which will arise where a person receives information he knows or should know is confidential[48]. By making it a contractual right in a mediation agreement, the need to rely on this principle is obviated in relation to formal mediations. However, a mediator might well be regarded as someone who had received information in circumstances clearly making it confidential, and discussions by Toulson and Phipps, in the leading textbook on confidentiality, suggest that insofar as mediation is concerned, similar considerations apply regardless of whether mediation confidentiality is based on contract or equity[49]. This might be more likely to arise where a mediator misused commercially sensitive information to make a personal profit akin to insider trading. There seems to be no general concept of confidentiality which attaches to settlement meetings wider than 'without prejudice' privilege. Toulson and Phipps suggest simply that without prejudice privilege means that parties agree to a kind of private law duty of confidentiality over what is protected by that privilege. Thus if a party seeks to misuse

---

47 See *Rush & Tomkins v GLC* [1988] 3 All ER 737, HL; *Instance v Denny Bros Printing Ltd* and *Prudential Insurance v Prudential Assurance* on one side: and *Muller v Linsley & Mortimer* and *Cattley v Pollard* on the other. More recently in *Cumbria Waste Management v Baines Wilson* [2008] EWHC 786 (QB), it was held by the judge that both contractual confidentiality and 'without prejudice' privilege prevented disclosure to C where B opposed it.
48 See Hanbury and Martin *The Modern Law of Equity* (17th edn), 25-069.
49 *Toulson & Phipps on Confidentiality* (2nd edn).

allegedly 'without prejudice' material, whether simply correspondence marked or treated as such or subject to a mediation agreement containing the usual clauses as to confidentiality and privilege, an injunction can restrain such misuse if established[50].

9.3 The special characteristics of mediation

Having looked at the legal status of all settlement meetings, including mediations with all other forms, this chapter turns to whether mediations have a special legal status and should be differently regarded. There are a number of key differences in terms both of status and process, of which the most important are:

- the recognition of its special status by the Pre-action Protocols, the CPR, a number of Court of Appeal judgments, and the EU Mediation Directive itself;

- the formality of a mediation agreement signed by all parties and the mediator and any provider, which imports several significant legal requirements into such settlement meetings[51], and includes expressing good faith intentions as to settlement, authority to settle reposing in each party at the mediation, the need for a written signed settlement agreement for its terms to be binding, mediator immunity from the witness-box, and contractual confidentiality as to the content of the mediation discussions and as to the fact and terms of settlement (unless otherwise agreed). These are discussed in greater detail in **Chapters 2** and **3**;

- the presence of a (presumably) trained and skilled neutral to manage the process subject to both the terms of a mediation agreement and a published code of conduct, who has the responsibility of testing out each party's position and helping them make an informed choice for themselves as to whether any settlement terms which emerge or continued litigation is the better route for them.

9.4 Does a unique 'mediation privilege' exist?

Chapter 3 briefly discussed whether some kind of special implied privileged status protecting from disclosure in evidence the information

---

50 As in *Instance v Denny Bros Printing Ltd* (2000) Times, 28 February.
51 In US state and federal jurisdictions with a much fuller statutory framework within which mediation operates, mediation agreements are often not necessary. The attractiveness of a clear legal status for all mediations to that level of detail is considerable.

exchange which goes on behind the veil of mediation. If this has arisen, or if it were created by statute, as has happened in various US jurisdictions, there would be a degree of objective certainty which does not seem to exist currently, and there would be no need to depend on contractual provisions in the mediation agreement as interpreted by private law. Sir Thomas Bingham MR in *Re D (minors)*[52] canvassed the existence of automatic protection for statements made to a conciliator, even if they demonstrated intransigence. He talked of the law as 'recognising the general inviolability of the privilege protecting statements made in the course of conciliation', except where such a statement might prove past or future serious harm to a child. Conciliation in family cases is obviously a different world from commercial mediation, where disclosure of likely serious physical harm is rarely a concern. There is an interesting parallel in this thinking to the provisions of the EU Mediation Directive, discussed fully in **Chapter 10**, which proposed that one of the exceptions to mediator compellability as a witness might be 'overriding considerations of public policy....in particular when required to ensure the protection of the best interests of children or to prevent harm to the physical or psychological integrity of a person'. In *Brown v Rice*[53], the judge was invited to engage in debate about the existence of a separate mediation privilege. He concluded:

> 'It may be in the future that the existence of a distinct mediation privilege will require to be considered by either the legislature or the courts but that is not something which arises for decision now'.

No one has persuaded a court since then to identify the existence of a stand-alone mediation privilege over and above automatic 'without prejudice' privilege, with its exceptions. So the question arises as to whether the existing private law features of mediation which distinguish it from other types of settlement meetings and ADR processes generally are adequate or not. As has already been seen, mediations have chosen to establish themselves formally on the basis of written mediation agreements, essentially to set out key constitutional provisions to govern the process and its outcomes.

---

52 *Re D (minors) (conciliation; disclosure of information)* [1993] Fam 231, [1993] 2 All ER 693, CA.
53 [2007] EWHC 625, paras 19–20.

9.5 Confidentiality created by the mediation agreement

Every well-drawn mediation agreement creates a mutual obligation on the parties to it and the mediator to keep what transpires during a mediation confidential. The CEDR Model Agreement[54] provides as follows:

'4 Every person involved in the Mediation:

4.1 will keep confidential all information arising out of or in connection with the Mediation, including the fact and terms of any
settlement, but not including the fact that the Mediation is to
take place or has taken place or where disclosure is required
by law to implement or to enforce terms of settlement or to
notify their insurers, insurance brokers and/or accountants;
and

4.2 acknowledges that all such information passing between the
Parties, the Mediator and/or CEDR Solve, however communicated, is agreed to be without prejudice to any Party's legal
position and may not be produced as evidence or disclosed to
any judge, arbitrator or other decision-maker in any legal or
other formal process, except where otherwise disclosable in
law.

5 Where a Party privately discloses to the Mediator any information in confidence before, during or after the Mediation, the Mediator will not disclose that information to any other Party or person
without the consent of the Party disclosing it, unless required by
law to make disclosure'.

So clause 4.2 reminds the parties (probably superfluously, as this arises by operation of law) of the application of the 'without prejudice' rule, acknowledging that this privilege is subject to exceptions established by law. Clause 4.1 establishes an overall duty on parties and mediator to keep information arising at the mediation and the fact and terms of settlement confidential.

Clause 5 deals with the deeper level of confidentiality which applies when a mediator sees either party privately, and undertakes not to disclose the content of any such private conversation to the other party without express permission. This is a provision of a different order from Clause 4, as it amounts to a separate contractual obligation undertaken by the mediator to each party. Each party can thus safely debate with the mediator whether

---

54 (13th edn). See the appendix and the generally available model agreement and procedure at www.cedr.com/about_us/modeldocuments.

or not to disclose facts, arguments or proposals to another without fearing that the mediator will make any unauthorised disclosure to another party when meeting privately or in a later joint meeting. The significant trust and responsibility undertaken by the mediator translates into a contractual duty and tortious duty of care not to breach confidentiality.

This is an important aspect of mediation in the UK, where the norm is for mediators to have private meetings with each party as well as chairing joint meetings between each party's team or a sub-group of each team. Its significance was highlighted in two articles by Sir Michael Briggs about how to balance the need for disclosure of what happens at a mediation in later litigation against the need for enforcing confidentiality to protect the value of the mediation process[55]. He argues for privilege to attach to private meeting confidentiality of the kind envisaged by Clause 5 above, so that one party could never compel disclosure of what passed between a party and a mediator in a private meeting, without affording the same protection to what was said in joint meetings. This might work, but even this approach could undermine the sense of security that is essential to underpin party confidence in participating in mediation discussions, which depends on general process confidentiality as well as private meeting confidentiality.

It is trite law that the courts will protect one party from breach of confidence threatened by another, by injunction if it is not too late, or by awarding damages. This is not the place to discuss the law fully, nor to consider the effect of the Human Rights Act 1998. The question here is whether and to what extent the contractual confidentiality provisions in mediation agreements are likely to be enforced. Do these contractual provisions create a right that is wider than without prejudice privilege, which might, for instance, keep such material from a judge at the trial of a case which did not settle at mediation? Also, is this right to confidentiality one which the mediator is entitled to enforce independent of the wishes of the parties, in view of the fact that mediators sign up to and are on the face of it entitled to its benefits as well as being bound by its responsibilities? Obviously a mediator who reports to the world what happened during a mediation must be in breach of their duty of confidentiality as well as their self-imposed and usually contractual duty to observe their code of conduct. Can a mediator or indeed a mediation provider (which is also usually a signatory to any mediation agreement signed under the auspices of their service provision) enforce confidentiality against any other party if they believed it to be in the interests of the mediation process to do so? Or can they use confidentiality to resist an attempt made by another party or an external investigator, whether judge at trial or another body with statutory

---

55 'Mediation Privilege?' (2009) NLJ, 3 10 April.

investigative powers to disclose what happened during a mediation? As has been seen above, mediators possess no property in 'without prejudice' privilege nor any control over its waiver[56].

So do the terms of a mediation agreement as to confidentiality create a right binding all its signatories which might be enforceable by injunction or damages by a signatory who is adversely affected? The starting-point is that judges are currently not barred from hearing information even if agreed by litigants to be confidential, unless one of the well-recognised exceptions applies in terms of legal professional privilege or litigation privilege, as well as 'without prejudice' privilege. As Brown and Marriott[57] make clear:

> 'The mere fact that information may be regarded as confidential by reason of a contractual, professional or moral obligation does not of itself create a right or privilege to withhold it in legal proceedings'.

Toulson and Phipps[58] also state the following principle:

> 'In litigation, a duty of confidence to another is generally no bar to disclosure, although the court will only compel the production of otherwise confidential documents if it considers it necessary to do so. Nor is a duty of confidence to another a ground for refusal by a witness to answer questions or produce documents if ordered to do so by a court of competent jurisdiction, although again a court will require a witness to disclose otherwise confidential information only if disclosure is necessary for the attainment of justice in the particular case'.

The familiar cases involving journalists, doctors, the NSPCC and others are cited as authority for that proposition. They argue that some established form of privilege is necessary to keep material from a judge, so that a party seeking absolute protection from disclosure of material must establish one of:

–   some specific statutory authority, as in some financial services regulations;

---

56 See *Brown v Rice* [2007] EWHC 625 (Ch) and *Farm Assist v DEFRA (No 2)* [2009] EWHC 1102 (TCC).

57 In *ADR Principles and Practice* (2nd edn), para 22-043, citing *Santa Fe International Corp v Napier Shipping SA* (1985) LT 430.

58 *Confidentiality* (2nd edn), Ch 3.

- legal professional privilege (in the form either of lawyer-client advice privilege or litigation privilege);
- 'without prejudice' privilege; or
- public interest immunity.

If either version of legal professional privilege exists in relation to a piece of evidence, then a court cannot admit such evidence if the privileged party unilaterally declines its admission. This principle appears to have been reinforced by Ramsay J in *Farm Assist (in liquidation) v DEFRA (No 1)*[59], in which a liquidator asserted that the claimant company had been coerced into a settlement of an agricultural dispute at a mediation by economic duress inflicted by DEFRA, the Government Department with which it dealt. DEFRA sought disclosure of all advice tendered to Farm Assist by its lawyers and other experts to attack the probability of the alleged duress. The court held that legal professional privilege is not waived in these circumstances and still applies to prevent disclosure of such normally privileged material. Waiver of legal professional privilege will only readily be implied where a client sues his lawyer[60]. But neither of these privileges seems to attach to exchanges between parties or between one party and a mediator during a mediation, though of course they do between a party and his own lawyer at any time when the relationship of lawyer and client exists, including during a mediation. So apart from the very special situation identified in *Re D*, even a mediator who is a lawyer does not act as such with parties at a mediation. They are not his clients in that sense, and lawyer and non-lawyer mediators are in exactly the same position.

It has been argued that the confidentiality created by the mediation agreement itself operates to keep mediation material from a judge, either independently or in tandem with the (usually express) 'without prejudice' clause which both usually contain. Both concepts were considered side by side in *Instance v Denny Bros Printing Ltd*[61]. Confidentiality as contracted for in a mediation agreement was not relied upon as excluding judicial investigation of a mediation in *Brown v Rice*, a case decided purely on 'without prejudice' privilege. The first decision to suggest that confidentiality created by a mediation agreement could exclude material from subsequent litigation was *Cumbria Waste Management v Baines Wilson*[62], a decision of Kirkham J sitting as a High Court Judge. The defendants had acted for the claimants on an agreement with DEFRA arising out of

---

59 [2008] EWHC 3079 (TCC).
60 See *Lillicrap v Nalder* [1993] 1 WLR 94 and *Paragon Finance v Freshfields* [1999] 1 WLR 1183.
61 (1999) TLR, 28 Feb 2000.
62 [2008] EWHC 786 (QB).

the widespread foot-and-mouth disease epidemic in cattle. This had led to a mediation between the claimants and DEFRA which had settled disadvantageously for the claimants, and they sought to recover alleged losses which they had been unable to persuade DEFRA to pay during the mediation, alleging professional negligence in the advice given over the original agreement. The defendant solicitors sought access to what had happened at the mediation, presumably to buttress an argument that the claimants had under-settled or failed to mitigate their losses. The judge declined to allow the defendants to have access to that mediation evidence. The judge's ruling was based primarily on 'without prejudice' privilege and the absence of any exception to that privilege. But she also found that the confidentiality clause bit to prevent disclosure, finding that the facts constituted 'an exception to the general rule that confidentiality is not a bar to disclosure'.

She went on:

> 'In any event I am persuaded that for the reasons identified in 17-016 above, documents within a mediation should be protected from disclosure'.

Her authority is paragraph 17-016 from *Toulson and Phipps on Confidentiality*, which reads:

> 'Mediation and other forms of alternative dispute resolution have assumed unprecedented importance within the court system since the Woolf reforms of civil procedure. Formal mediations are generally preceded by written mediation agreements that set out expressly the confidential and "without prejudice" nature of the process. However, even in the absence of such an express agreement, the process will be protected by the "without prejudice" rule set out above.'

This does not really explain whether there is any distinction between confidentiality and 'without prejudice' and whether the 'without prejudice' rule itself constitutes 'an exception to the general rule that confidentiality is not a bar to disclosure, either generally, or only in the context of a formally constituted mediation'.

The question arose again in *Farm Assist v DEFRA (No 2)*[63]. Having been refused access to Farm Assist's legal advice by Ramsey J in *(No 1)*, DEFRA then tried to bring the mediator (by coincidence the same mediator as had been involved with DEFRA in the *Cumbria Waste Management* case) to

---

63 [2009] EWHC 1102 (TCC).

court by serving a witness summons on her. She applied to set it aside, and Ramsey J decided after argument by the mediator in person and counsel for DEFRA that the witness summons should stand. He found that the mediator did indeed possess a right to mobilise the confidentiality provision in the mediation agreement to prevent herself from being required to disclose information she had received in confidence. Building upon *Re D* and *Cumbria Waste Management v Baines Wilson* (a case in which it would appear that DEFRA were arguing more or less the precise opposite of what they sought to argue in *Farm Assist*) Ramsey J came close to defining a sort of mediation privilege owned by the mediator. Both the parties in *Farm Assist* had indicated willingness for the court to hear from the mediator (perhaps with waning enthusiasm on the part of Farm Assist's liquidator, though its consent was never withdrawn) but their willingness for her to be called did not of itself defeat her objection. However, Ramsey J found that even the mediator's right to confidentiality was capable of being overridden by the court in any given case 'in the interests of justice'. He was persuaded that the allegation was so serious that it was right in the public interest that the mediator's recollection (which she asserted was minimal after many years, and after many subsequent mediations and cases in her private practice) should be placed before the court and tested. There may be differing views as to how the judge chose to exercise his discretion, but he certainly seemed to accept that, short of a public interest overriding it, a mediator's ownership of confidentiality could not be overridden by the parties. Mediator compellability is discussed further in **Chapter 3**.

Without making any judgment as to cause and effect, it is noteworthy that Farm Assist's liquidator discontinued the proceedings very shortly after this judgment, as a result of which the mediator was never called to give evidence in that case. Furthermore, the wording of the confidentiality clause in the Farm Assist mediation agreement is not the same as is found in later editions of standard form mediation agreements. The mediator was not to be called to give evidence about the *dispute*, but Ramsey J decided that she was being called to give evidence about the *mediation* and was thus not protected on the construction of the clause.

Further note of the double protection was noted without further debate in *Mason v Walton-on-Thames Charity*[64]. The claimant attempted to introduce in evidence certain communications made during a mediation. The judge excluded these on the basis of 'without prejudice' privilege, but also said that he had been referred to the mediation agreement;

---

[64] [2010] EWHC 1688 (Ch) and broadly followed when permission to appeal was refused by the Court of Appeal reported at [2011] EWCA Civ 1732.

'from which it was clear that in addition to the general law in relation to without prejudice communications, there was a contractual prohibition which prevented these communications from being referred to subsequently'.

No authority is cited for that statement, made without qualification. But it would appear that, assuming that these authorities (none of which are Court of Appeal decisions) are right, that the current state of English law is that contractual confidentiality as set up in a mediation agreement is enforceable by a mediator as well as by the disputing parties, and it can operate to exclude confidential material from a judge in a subsequent trial of a dispute unsettled by a mediation or a related piece of litigation, unless the judge decides that it is in 'the interests of justice' to admit it. What the interests of justice are remains undiscussed and unclear. Does this allow a judge to admit confidential material if he decides that it makes the task of deciding who is right and wrong easier to admit it? Do the interests of justice include the need for mediations to be able to be conducted confidentially for the benefit of those who participate in them? There are no ready answers to these questions, but they become important in the context of the provisions of the EU Mediation Directive over mediator compellability, discussed in **Chapter 10**.

An interesting but subsidiary question arises as to whom else precisely the right to confidentiality might belong. Take a piece of litigation between an individual whose representation by solicitor and barrister is funded by a legal expenses insurance against a defendant whose defence is funded (both as to legal costs and any damages payable) by an insurer who instructs a panel solicitor and barrister. A mediation ensues to which 'without prejudice' privilege and contractual confidentiality applies. The parties in whose name the litigation is conducted – delighted by the mediation process but not by the prior litigation process – want to tell the world about what happened in both, and they each agree directly with each other to waive privilege and confidentiality. Can they be stopped by either the lawyers or the insurers on the basis that either or both of them own a part of the right to confidentiality and privilege? Does it matter whether the mediation agreement was signed by the parties individually or (as often happens) by their lawyers as their agents? Does the absence of an insurer's signature to the agreement affect the insurer's rights? Can a party to a confidentiality clause take separate advice on confidential material from a second lawyer, or make a report to an insurer, without breaching confidentiality and if so, on what legal basis?

Agreements provide variously as to what is and is not confidential. They normally provide that the fact and terms of settlement are to be confidential, but not the fact that a mediation is to take place or has taken place.

Mediation privilege and confidentiality

Ever since mediation became something encouraged by the court, it seemed right to allow parties to claim (if they so choose) to have chosen to utilise the process. This term can of course be amended by the parties, perhaps particularly in commercial or employment disputes, where even to admit that there is a dispute would be damaging. Equally, there will be disputes of a highly public nature where it would be virtually impossible to keep the outcome of a mediated settlement away from the public gaze, and how and when disclosure of terms of settlement will occur is often agreed as part of the settlement[65].

The above discussion makes it clear that there are a number of doubtful areas which would benefit from clarity. A number of situations are beginning to arise in relation to mediations where the clash between the desirability of a confidential process and other private rights make the need for such clarity all the more pressing. These include:

- whether a lawyer who is later sued for negligence, after a mediation settles a dispute created by his alleged negligence, can have access to mediation material;
- what mediation material is admissible in a claim by a party against his lawyer that he was advised to settle at an undervalue in a mediation, and whether new lawyers representing the lawyer's professional indemnity insurers may have access to it to advise[66];
- where a main contractor and a construction client settle at mediation, and either of them seeks to recover any shortfall in what that settlement achieved from a third party (perhaps a professional or a sub-contractor);
- whether evidence of a material misrepresentation of fact made during a mediation by one party on which the other party relied in settling is admissible;
- whether a lawyer's advice at mediation **not** to settle is open to challenge, when it turns out to have been wrong, leading to a pyrrhic victory or defeat at trial;
- whether a mediator has breached confidentiality in a way which causes either or both parties damage;

---

65 For instance the claims by Samburu tribespeople against the Ministry of Defence in 2002 and the retained organs claims against Alder Hey Hospital in 2004.
66 This point came up in *McCallum v Wilkin Chapman and Marten* (23 September 2008, unreported). New lawyers called upon to advise a solicitor being sued for allegedly advising under-settlement at a mediation felt inhibited from examining mediation material because of the confidentiality clause. Judge Langan QC held that such a clause could not inhibit an investigation into whether negligent advice has been given at a mediation.

192

– where a mediator over-evaluates and gives a negligently or over-assertive false steer which leads to a wrongly based settlement[67].

9.6 Practical considerations for mediation confidentiality

Quite rightly the courts exclude 'admissions' made when parties are trying to explore settlement. Many settlements, both inside and outside mediation, involve agreement by all parties to risk-moderated terms which might be a long way from what a judge, fixed with the task of deciding a winner and loser, would order at trial. The discounts made off a best case are to avoid the risk of being confronted with a worst case outcome in court. So no one should aspire to generate helpful evidence through engaging in a mediation on the basis of not settling.

Before the CPR reforms, there was a degree of worry that an expression of being willing to engage in mediation at all was in itself evidence of weakness, signalling a wish to compromise which would give comfort to opponents and stiffen their resolve to fight on. The combination of the CPR and significant court decisions since then has effectively abolished that fear, as there is a generalised duty to consider ADR without any duty to settle. Similarly, the fear that one party may be engaged in a 'fishing expedition' has largely been neutralised by the current 'cards-on-the-table' evidential regime in England and Wales. There are still common law jurisdictions where it may be negligent for a lawyer not to advise a client to ambush an opponent at trial in certain respects, if permitted in that civil procedure regime. In England and Wales, an ambush is dangerously likely to be met by a successful application for an adjournment with the miscreant party held liable for wasted costs.

What is learned at a mediation cannot be unlearned, even if it cannot be used as evidence. So caution will still be exercised by parties and their representatives over whether they give away every good cross-examination point in advance or hold some points back for surprise use at a subsequent possible trial. There can still be a risk of any settlement meeting (not just a mediation) being used to find out how far a party might go to settle, and then refuse to settle and make a Part 36 offer on the following day of say 10% less than the figure extracted.

Perhaps the main temptation for disclosing what happened at a mediation is where one party attends in good faith to settle but finds the other party intransigent or immobile in view, and feels that they have behaved unrea-

---

67 As arguably occurred in the dramatic Australian case of *Tapoohi v Leuwenberg* [2003] VSC 410.

sonably during the mediation. It is suggested that some parties come to mediation merely in order to escape the risk of any costs sanction for failing to agree to mediation, but once there, refuse to act in good faith and thereby stultify settlement discussions, knowing that their intransigence is protected by privilege from exposure to judicial gaze. This seems to be relatively rare in practice, but is certainly not unheard-of. Mediation does not come without expense in both time and money, and it is very frustrating for one party if the other appears determined to waste that investment. With unreasonable conduct normally attracting judicial ire under the CPR costs regime, there is a strong desire to tell the judge of unreasonable conduct adopted at a mediation and even more frustration at being apparently being barred from doing so.

There have been two cases at least where the judge has been told what was offered by each party at the mediation, but in each of them it seems that both parties waived privilege. In *Earl of Malmesbury v Strutt & Parker*[68], the judge did indeed penalise the claimant for having adopted what he regarded as a seriously unrealistic position over what was offered during the mediation.

One way to approach the problem is by alleging breach of the duty of good faith attendance and attempting to find a settlement at the mediation. But for a judge to investigate this would inevitably require a review of what happened at the mediation in a way and at a depth which risks subverting the privacy of the process and eroding its effectiveness if done in open court. Of course the allegation is that one party conducted themselves in a manner just as likely to subvert the process, but public airing of such allegations will still weaken the process when the allegation is found to be without any basis, and even where it is found to be justified, there would be no control over what might emerge during the hearing.

In general, however, it would seem that senior English judges have no great appetite for peering behind the several veils which comprise mediation confidentiality. In the leading case of *Halsey v Milton Keynes General NHS Trust*[69], Dyson LJ remarked:

> 'We make it clear that it was common ground before us (and we accept) that parties are entitled in an ADR [sic] to adopt whatever position they wish, and if as a result the dispute is not settled, that is not a matter for the court ... if the integrity and confidentiality

---

68 [2008] EWHC (QB) 424: the Earl lost 20% of his costs for refusing to accept less than £9 million at mediation, but only recovered just under £1 million at trial, which was just about what the defendants offered at the mediation. See also *Chantrey Vellacott v Convergence Group* [2007] EWHC 1774 (Ch).
69 [2004] 4 All ER 920.

of the process is to be respected, the court should not know, and therefore should not investigate, why the process did not result in agreement[70].

Ramsey J was a little more inquisitive and thus more controversial in *Farm Assist v DEFRA (No 2)*, a first instance decision. But in *PGF II v OFMS Co*[71], the judge declined to hear evidence taken from the previous mediation because one party refused to waive privilege, and he also refused to draw any adverse inference from that refusal to waive privilege, saying:

'To do so would be to undermine the very protection given to the parties in relation to their conduct in a mediation'.

9.7   Confidentiality and other third party investigations

It will have been noted that the confidentiality provision quoted from the CEDR Agreement above is not actually absolute. The mediator is effectively relieved of liability for breach of confidentiality where information 'is otherwise disclosable at law'. This is discussed at **3.3**, which sets out circumstances when the law or a body with statutory authority might compel a mediator to make external disclosure of what was originally subject to mediation confidentiality. Such enforced disclosure is only ever likely to disadvantage someone who has something illegal to hide.

9.8   Confidentiality, privilege and the Uniform Mediation Act in the US

The Uniform Mediation Act (the UMA) in the United States was drawn up to give US jurisdictions a sound model framework for mediation. Having looked at how it deals with mediator compellability in Chapter 3, this chapter now examines its detailed provisions as to the extent of privilege and confidentiality in mediations. Section 4 of the UMA defines mediation privilege, with different privileges for different participants in the process. Subject to the exceptions set out in section 6, or unless 'waived or precluded' as provided by section 3(c) (prior or subsequent written and signed waiver) or section 5 (see below), mediation communications are privileged and not admissible in evidence on the following basis:

---

70 At para 14. But see *ARP Capita London Market Services Ltd v Ross & Co* [2004] EWHC 1181 (Ch), where Longmore VC was invited to utilise this paragraph of the *Halsey* judgment to prevent investigation into why a successful party had declined to mediate. Eventually Longmore VC decided that the successful party had *not* declined mediation, and ordered the unsuccessful defendant to pay the costs.
71 [2012] EWHC 83 (TCC).

- **a mediation party** may refuse to disclose, and may prevent any other person from disclosing, a mediation communication;

- **a mediator** may refuse to disclose a mediation communication, and may prevent any other person from disclosing a mediation communication *of the mediator*; and

- **a non-party participant** may refuse to disclose, and may prevent any other person from disclosing, a mediation communication *of the non-party participant*.

How do these work? It means that any party to a mediation can veto disclosure of any mediation communication, exactly as applies to 'without prejudice' communications in English law. So neither a mediator nor a non-party participant has a full veto on disclosure. They do, however, have a right to veto disclosure of mediation communications involving them personally. In the light of the definition of 'mediation communication', this covers what a mediator or non-party says in contemplation of or during a mediation. In practical terms, this must mean that a judge will need to assume that such privileges apply unless any owner of the privilege has waived it. Indeed, section 5 of the UMA requires express waiver by the mediator or non-party on the record. Thus in *SITA v Watson Wyatt*[72], where the judge allowed himself to be told what the mediator had said to SITA about involving Maxwell Batley in the mediation, the mediator's alleged remark would not have been admissible under UMA rules without the formal consent of the mediator.

This position chimes with the earlier draft of the EU Mediation Directive before its last extensive amendment, stimulating again the debate about whether more rigorous provisions than required by the Directive should be enacted in England and Wales, perhaps more in line with the UMA.

Finally on section 4, it clarifies what is broadly accepted everywhere, namely that evidence which is otherwise admissible does not become inadmissible solely because it emerges or arises in a mediation[73].

So how does the UMA seek to strike the balance which was identified as necessary in its overall strategy? First, it gives the parties and other participants control over the extent of confidentiality, and second it provides for both prior exclusion of its arising at all and for exceptions which can be claimed after the event in limited circumstances.

---

72 [2002] EWHC 2025 (Ch).
73 Confirming the outcome of the Australian case of *AWA v Daniels* (24 February 1992) NSW Sup Ct (Comm Div), one of the few authorities on this point, and also *Aird v Prime Meridian* [2006] EWCA Civ 1886.

Section 5 of the UMA deals with waiver and preclusion of privilege. As already noted, it requires express waiver by a mediator or non-party. It also visualises express waiver by all parties to the mediation 'in a record[74] or orally during a proceeding[75]'. The essence of waiver is therefore formal and on the record. To deal with the situation where someone acts inconsistently with entitlement to the protection of privilege, it provides that where someone discloses or makes a representation about a mediation communication which prejudices another person *in a proceeding*, they will be precluded from asserting privilege to the extent necessary for the person prejudiced to respond. This in effect releases the person prejudiced from the bonds of privilege for the purpose of response by removing the defence of privilege from anyone who seems to have breached it. UMA waiver is not otherwise capable of being implied by conduct.

A further long-stop precaution is also included which precludes assertion of privilege by anyone who intentionally uses a mediation for the purposes of executing ongoing or future criminal activity.

Section 6 deals with the exceptions to privilege otherwise attaching to any 'mediation communication'. There are four broad classes of situation contemplated.

First, in terms of what might be termed abuse of and within the mediation process, no privilege attaches to a mediation communication which is:

- intended to promote or conceal crime;
- (broadly) germane to child protection;
- a threat of future violence.

Second, and less dramatically, privilege does not attach where a mediation session is open to the public (probably most often encountered in US environmental disputes and rarely encountered in the UK). Nor does it attach to an agreement evidenced by a record signed by all parties to the agreement. This most importantly covers the mediation agreement and any settlement agreement, and excludes oral agreements from privilege. Until *Brown v Rice*, English mediators would have probably have expected this to be the case here. However, the judge in that case canvassed the possibility of there being enforceable oral collateral agreements made at a mediation, evidence as to which would have to be admitted as an exception

---

74 Defined in UMA, § 2 as 'information that is inscribed in a tangible medium or that is stored in an electronic or other medium and is retrievable in perceivable form'.
75 Defined in UMA, § 2 as 'a judicial, administrative, arbitral or other adjudicative process; or a legislative hearing or similar process'.

to the 'without prejudice' rule to determine whether any such agreement had been made. This is one area where certainty would be welcome for all.

The third category of non-privilege relates to evidence as to a complaint or claim based on professional misconduct or malpractice:

- by a mediator, or
- against a mediation party, non-party participant or party representative about conduct within a mediation. However, the UMA specifically prevents a mediator from being called to give evidence in this type of case.

Fourth, and interestingly, an exception to privilege is made where a court, administrative agency or arbitrator finds, *after a hearing in camera*, that in relation to the otherwise privileged evidence sought to be admitted:

- it is not otherwise available; and
- the need to hear it outweighs the interest in protecting confidentiality; and
- the court is hearing a criminal case, *or*
- the proceedings are to decide whether the settlement agreement emerging from the mediation should be vitiated and a remedy for breach given: again the mediator is barred from giving evidence in this type of case.

Relating to all of these four types of case is an overall requirement that only the portion of any mediation communication necessary for the application of the exception from non-disclosure may be admitted. All other mediation communications remain subject to privilege, so that there is no general waiver by one admission of such evidence.

The fourth class of exception meets a number of concerns about how to deal with such matters as misrepresentation, mistake, fraud, duress and illegality being alleged about the formation of a settlement agreement behind the normally closed doors of a mediation, whether it be because the conduct was allegedly criminal, or simply as providing a legitimate basis for a contractual remedy. To determine the initial admissibility of otherwise privileged material behind comparably closed doors seems to be a sensible solution. If it should not be admitted, it is not published in a judgment. If it is admitted, then the hearing proceeds in public. Furthermore, the restriction on any mediator giving evidence in inter-party disputes preserves the integrity of the mediator and prevents the mediator from being called (as the UMA commentary puts it) as a 'tie-breaking witness'.

It should be added that the UMA has provided much of the inspiration for the mediation law reforms in the Republic of Ireland.

9.9 Privilege and confidentiality in Australia

This section deals with the Australian approach to issues of confidentiality and privilege, and to Australian concepts of mediator immunity from suit and competence and compellability as a witness in later proceedings relating to the mediated dispute[76].

With mediation established for a much longer time in Australia than in the UK, as well as having State and Federal jurisdictions giving the opportunity for different approaches within the same common law tradition, it is unsurprising that the legal literature on the topic is rich, and that case law is well developed, though many of these cases parallel the way the law has developed in England. When it comes to the 'principle' of confidentiality of mediation proceedings there seems a greater readiness to regard this as less than absolute. Like the UMA in the USA, there is seen to be a need to strike the right balance between an effective and fair process, and protecting parties from being disadvantaged by opposing parties or a less than competent mediator, both being matters of understandable and important public interest.

'Without prejudice' privilege in Australia seems very similar to that in England and Wales. It was in Australia that the leading case on disclosure of otherwise disclosable documents produced within a mediation was decided, namely *AWA v Daniels*[77]. Following a mediation which did not settle professional indemnity proceedings against auditors, the defendants sought an order in the litigation for the claimants to disclose a deed of indemnity produced at the mediation. Disclosure was ordered and upheld later at trial on the basis that this was in any case a disclosable document, and it should not be possible to prevent a document from being disclosed merely by producing it within a privileged mediation settlement context. Otherwise decisions follow a similar pattern to England and Wales. In *Lukies v Ripley (No 2)*[78], the court specifically extended the concept that privilege is only attracted by genuine attempts at settlement to cover discussions limited to narrowing issues where there was no expectation of overall settlement.

---

76 This exposition owes much to the specific help of Professor Laurence Boulle and the late Miryana Nesic, authors of both the English and Australian versions of *Mediation: Principles, Process, Practice*. Their Australian text is commended as a properly comprehensive source for Australian case law and thinking. Readers are also referred to *Mediation Law and Practice* by Spencer and Brogan (CUP, 2006) for a similarly broad survey.
77 (24 February 1992) NSW Sup Ct (Comm Div).
78 (1994) 35 NSWLR 283.

There has been some debate as to whether disclosure of documents within a mediation otherwise protected by legal professional privilege might constitute a waiver, but the view seems to be that it does not. Australia has not yet accepted a privilege comparable to that enunciated by Sir Thomas Bingham in *Re D (minors)* over disclosures to a conciliator in family proceedings. Communications between married couples are not privileged, although spouses are not compellable witnesses against each other. Nor is any common law privilege for mediation currently recognised in Australia, though the case for developing such a privilege has been argued. Thus mediators are theoretically compellable witnesses, subject only to statutory or contractual protections.

As in England, confidentiality is invoked by contractual means in mediation agreements, and the general view seems to be that courts would enforce this by using contractual remedies where breach and damage could be shown, reinforced by injunction. Boulle and Nesic suggest that information given to a mediator would also be regarded as a situation where disclosure might be regarded as a breach of confidence giving rise to an equitable remedy. Perhaps if a trade or market secret was disclosed to a mediator during a mediation, from which the mediator made a profitable deal, this might (if proven) attract a remedy. The same is probably true in England.

As to statutory protections, unlike in the UK, there are a number of Australian statutory provisions which create protection for mediation confidentiality or, perhaps more strictly, evidential privilege. Federal and State statutes variously make such provision[79], usually following the lines to be found in mediation agreements in the UK, and defining exceptions such as consensual disclosure by parties, fraud, non-concealment of criminal activity, and so on. There are some statutes which create heavy obligations of secrecy, for instance in community justice programmes, where oaths of secrecy are required. Some differences between Australian and English practice are explained by the fact that there is statutory, and indeed quite frequently compulsory, mediation there, such as the Farm Debt mediation legislation in New South Wales[80]. Privacy is also a statutory requirement of mediations under the Native Title Act 1994. Boulle and Nesic summarise the position by saying:

'Given the variations in the statutory regulation of confidentiality, NADRAC [an oversight body] has recommended the pursuit of

---

79 Eg in the Federal Court of Australia Act 1976, Supreme Court Act 1986 (Victoria); Courts Legislation (Mediation and Evaluation) Amendment Act 1994 (NSW); Dispute Resolution Centres Act 1990 (Queensland); Family Law Act 1975 (Co Commonwealth).
80 Under the Farm Debt Mediation Act 1994, under the NSW Rural Assistance Authority.

greater clarity and uniformity among the different systems, but this has yet to materialise in Australia'[81].

They comment favourably on the UMA's provision for in camera determination of issues relating to mediation confidentiality.

Exceptions to the sanctity of the mediation veil identified to date in Australia include:

- where the parties consent, though some legislation even precludes consensual disclosure: otherwise, the consent in question appears to be that of the parties, with the mediator having no voice;
- where agreement at mediation is alleged, either to enforce it or to unravel obscure terms;
- fraud and criminality;
- where mediators had to report to a higher authority under the terms of a scheme;
- (in some cases) on costs issues (though this on the whole is not permissible in England unless the style 'without prejudice save as to costs' is attached to a mediation, which is rarely, if ever, done[82]).

A recent case which gives support to the confidentiality of Australian mediation is *Western Areas Exploration Pty Ltd v Streeter (No 2)*[83]. It also highlights some of the ways in which the substantial statutory structure underpinning mediation operates in Australia. A court-ordered mediation was abandoned, leading to a flurry of affidavits about what happened to inform the decision as to costs in the litigation. The Western Australia Appeal Court decided that the affidavits complaining about what happened at the mediation, which would disclose confidential material, should not even be read by the court. More interestingly, the legislation considered in this case included provisions that a mediator under an ADR Order possesses the same immunities and privileges as a judge, and that a mediation registrar or mediator can only ever disclose what happened at mediation to a court in relation to costs issues, and then only in the form of a formal report as to a party's failure to co-operate[84].

---

81 *Mediation: Principles, Process, Practice*, in Chapter 15 of the Australian edition.
82 See *Reed Executive v Reed Business Systems* [2004] EWCA Civ 887.
83 [2009] WASCA 15.
84 See also Limbery, 'Should mediation be an evidentiary "black hole"?' 35(3) NSWLJ 914.

9.10 Conclusions and problems

The position in England and Wales over mediation confidentiality is far from certain and far from authoritatively established. The cases in which these issues have been discussed are first instance decisions, and it is hard to rely upon the authority of any of them because, for instance, *Brown v Rice* was decided before *Cumbria Waste Management* and *Farm Assist (No 2)*. It is arguable that the decisions in the latter two cases challenge the basic principles of confidentiality law in excluding confidential material from judicial view. It is not known for sure whether there is such thing as 'mediation privilege'. If there is no such thing, should statute invent it, taking lessons from the US and Australia? Bearing in mind, as discussed in **Chapter 10**, that the EU Mediation Directive's provisions set a minimum standard on aspects of confidentiality, allowing member states to implement tougher rules, it is very difficult to know whether English law in this respect is weaker, or equivalent or tougher than the EU minimum. But quite apart from that aspect, it is also very worrying for mediators not to know the precise boundaries of the confidentiality which lies at the heart of the success of the process they deliver.

Chapter 10

The impact of European law on mediation in England and Wales

The use of ADR has grown throughout Europe at a considerable pace, though not at the same pace in every jurisdiction, significantly driven by European institutions seeking to enhance commercial and societal relationships within the European Union. In two important respects, European law has impacted upon the development of mediation in England and Wales: first in relation to the European Convention on Human Rights (the ECHR)[1]; and second in relation to the EU Mediation Directive[2].

10.1 The European Convention on Human Rights

The European Convention on Human Rights (the ECHR) was adopted into English law as from 2 October 2000 as a result of the Human Rights Act 1998 (HRA 1998).

Article 6 of the ECHR is by far the most significant provision in relation to mediation. Article 6(1) of the ECHR provides as follows:

> 'In the determination of his civil rights and obligations ... everyone is entitled to a fair and public hearing within a reasonable time by an independent and impartial tribunal established by law'.

Its significance lies in whether court referral of claims to ADR or, by analogy, the enforceability of ADR clauses, are caught by this provision of the ECHR, by actually or potentially obstructing a citizen's right of access to a prompt fair trial. In making an ADR order, or providing for mandatory mediation, or even in upholding the effect of an ADR contract clause so as to delay access to a public civil remedy, do judges risk attack under Article 6? The answer to this question goes to the heart of the true nature of mediation as a process.

---

1 The Convention for the Protection of Human Rights and Fundamental Freedoms Rome, 4.XI.1950.
2 Directive 2008/52/EC of the European Parliament and of the Council of 21 May 2008 on certain aspects of mediation in civil and commercial matters, OJ L 136, 24.5.2008, pp 3–8.

The point is put into sharp focus by the position of arbitration, which in the US at least is regarded as ADR, though more reluctantly in the UK in view of its adjudicative nature. Arbitration is distinguishable from a non-binding ADR process such as mediation in two ways: first, it is statute-based; and second, it does indeed offer a binding adjudicative process for the 'determination of civil rights and obligations', but in an essentially private hearing before an arbitrator. Parties either contract in advance to go to arbitration or agree to do so when a dispute arises. In doing so, they in effect exclude the jurisdiction of the courts. Bearing in mind that even a statutory provision must yield to the effect of the ECHR if it infringes it, it might be argued that an arbitration could theoretically be impeached for infringing the Article 6(1) requirement for public determination. However, this has never been the approach of European law.

So far as mediation, being non-adjudicative, is concerned, it is difficult to see how this could be regarded as anything approaching a 'determination'. By definition, a decision is *not* made by the neutral in the process; the parties alone decide whether to settle. They remain at all times entirely free to withdraw from the process and return to the path which leads to actual determination of their civil rights and obligations by the independent and impartial tribunal established by law, namely the relevant court (or arbitration). Indeed, mediation agreements often specifically state that:

> 'The referral of the dispute to mediation does not affect any rights that may exist under Article 6 of the European Convention on Human Rights. If the dispute is not settled by the mediation, the Parties' rights to a fair trial remain unaffected'.

It is plain that the European Court of Human Rights (the ECtHR) encourages parties to settle disputes extra-judicially, thus relieving the courts of unnecessary and excessive strains. The fact that submission to arbitration does not infringe Article 6 of the ECHR is just one way in which this encouragement is manifested, and other forms of ADR might be expected to prove to be another. In the case of arbitration, the ECtHR recognises the right of disputants to waive their rights under the ECHR by electing for arbitration. It is, however, clear from authority and commentary that the court might intervene to protect the right to trial in a case where any undue pressure was put upon a party into a non-judicial adjudicative process such as arbitration, or where there was no real opportunity for a party truly to agree (or not) to such a term in a contract.

The leading case on such matters is *Deweer v Belgium*[3], the facts of which, in *Halsey v Milton Keynes General NHS Trust,* provided rather a surprising

---

3 (1980) 2 EHRR para 49.

entry-point into a debate about whether or not mandating mediation is permissible. Deweer's butchery business was found on inspection to be selling pork at more than a prescribed price limit. The inspector threatened provisional closure of Deweer's business, to last until the conclusion of probably lengthy criminal proceedings. However, by paying a 'friendly settlement' of 10,000BF, Deweer could avoid such proceedings and his store could re-open immediately. Unsurprisingly, he chose settlement, but reserved his rights to challenge the proceeding. He then initiated a challenge to the ECtHR, inviting consideration of the effect of Article 6 on whether taking the obvious temptation to pay a generously discounted composition payment fettered his right to a fair public trial, at which he would have had arguable defences. The court expressly approved the concept of waiver of Article 6 rights frequently found 'in civil matters, notably in the shape of arbitration clauses in contracts'. But settlements resulting from 'constraint' which effectively prevents access to the courts are impeachable. The court did not criticise the theory of composition of criminal liability, but concentrated its fire on the fact that unless he paid the composition, his business would have been closed until the end of criminal proceedings, resulting in substantial business losses. On the facts, Deweer was held to have waived his right to go to court only by reason of constraint, which vitiated his consent to paying the friendly settlement.

Much to the surprise of many, the Court of Appeal in *Halsey v Milton Keynes General NHS Trust* launched into a discussion of *Deweer v Belgium*. The surprise emanated from the fact that the conjoined appeals in *Halsey* and *Smith v Joy and Halliday* were both about whether costs sanctions were to be imposed on parties who had declined proposals to mediate by losing opponents, and not about ignoring court-mandated mediation. In neither case had an ADR order been made by a judge, nor did the facts of either case require the court to rule on whether mediation could or should be mandatory. Thus its comments on Article 6 were strictly obiter, though the Court of Appeal quite often seeks to give guidance beyond the strict remit of the cases before it, and its views must be accorded respect.

Dyson LJ set out the argument pithily in para 9 of his judgment in *Halsey:*

'We heard argument on the question whether the court has power to order parties to submit their disputes to mediation against their will. It is one thing to encourage the parties to agree to mediation, even to encourage them in the strongest terms. It is another to order them to do so. It seems to us that to oblige truly unwilling parties to refer their disputes to mediation would be to impose an unacceptable obstruction on their right of access to the court. The court in Strasbourg has said in relation to Article 6 that the right of access to a court may be waived, for example by means of

205

an arbitration agreement, but such waiver should be subjected to "particularly careful review" to ensure that the claimant is not subject to "constraint": see *Deweer v Belgium*. If that is the approach of the ECHR to an *agreement* to arbitrate, it seems to us likely that *compulsion* of ADR would be regarded as an unacceptable constraint on the right of access to the court and, therefore, a violation of Article 6' [emphasis supplied].

As a precedent in the English sense, *Deweer* seemed a strange bed-fellow with *Halsey* or indeed with mediation generally. In *Deweer*, the mischief was for the Belgian authorities to have constrained M. Deweer to avoid both criminal proceedings and concomitant closure of his business by paying a compromise settlement figure. Constraint to settle by feeling compelled to waive Article 6 rights was easy to discern. In mediations, no one is constrained to settle. Once arrived at the mediation, continued participation is entirely voluntary, and even an unreasonable disengagement from the process by one party cannot later be discussed or challenged before a judge because of confidentiality and 'without prejudice' privilege, at least under current English law and procedure[4]. Nor does anyone waive their rights of access to a public court by entering mediation. Nor does anyone ever enter the mediation process on the basis that they **must** settle; or that if they do not, they cannot revert to seeking a remedy in a public court. They never participate in mediation on the basis that a binding outcome will be imposed on them. On the contrary, mediation is symbiotic with litigation: settlements in mediations are often predicated against the risks of failing to achieve the desired outcome through trial. So once mediation is under way, there is arguably no basis for suggesting that such engagement with the process offends Article 6.

The question remains as to whether and at what level of compulsion courts can properly require parties to engage in mediation at all. Even short of being ordered to do so, a party may choose or perhaps feel compelled or (where a mandatory scheme exists) be compelled to mediate first for fear of penalty if they do not. Is this constraining a waiver of Article 6 rights? May a court properly compel parties to try to settle, and spend money on doing so (remembering that many US court-annexed mediation schemes are free), even if they are free not to settle and choose a public trial?

Maybe some subconscious judicial confusion has arisen about the status of mediation from the umbrella title 'Alternative Dispute Resolution'. Superficially it sounds as if ADR and litigation are absolute alternatives; that a disputant must choose between one or the other, forfeiting their rights of access to one if choosing the other, and therefore judges instinctively seek

---

4 Though attempts have been made to do so in the US and Australia.

to protect the pure form of delivery of justice and decline to give support and encouragement to a perceived rival. But as was seen in **Chapter 1**, settlement is indeed the way that the vast majority of civil claims are concluded, and it may be desirable to reduce the call by citizens on the courts, and even to encourage them to make their own decisions as to where their best interests lie to improve social cohesion. To do so is hard to classify as being an infringement of human rights. Indeed, many jurisdictions with extremely strong sensitivities about human and constitutional rights to access to courts mandate mediation and indeed other settlement processes such as conciliation or settlement conferences chaired by judges. Perhaps the more integral that mediation is within the court process, the more acceptable it becomes to mandate it.

What other arguments might be deployed? An order to mediate, particularly if the litigation is stayed pending mediation, might be regarded as hindering a public hearing 'within a reasonable time'. However, in practice a stay is not a necessary component of a court-referred mediation, and even if a stay were granted, it is highly unlikely that the kind of delay that this would create would be regarded in the general scheme of litigation progress as an infringement of such a right. The cases decided by the ECtHR so far deal in much longer delays than is likely to be generated by a referral to mediation, which often takes no more than four weeks from initial referral to outcome.

Are there other instances where the court has approved, delayed or denied access to the courts before a litigant can meet pre-conditions? The ECtHR has held that Article 6 is not infringed by restricting court access to vexatious litigants, bankrupts, mental patients, those required to give security for costs or to pay a previous costs order before being allowed to start fresh proceedings, and those who cannot obtain legal aid on the merits of their case[5]. Requiring parties to mediate is a far less draconian requirement than banning a party altogether from access to the courts, as in some of the above examples. From that perspective, requiring mediation is no more an inherent potential breach of Article 6 than any other aspect of implementation of the overriding objective through active case management as set out in CPR Part 1, or any other compulsory procedural step. The CPR themselves impose a number of procedural requirements on parties before they can appear before a judge for the public trial required by Article 6. Before proceedings can be issued, disputants must comply with the Pre-action Protocols and their Practice Direction (which now require consideration of, but does not compel, ADR). Parties must then pay court fees at several stages, now very substantial. Indeed, in *R v Lord Chancel-*

---

5 *Webb v UK* [1983] 6 EHRR 120; *McVicar v UK* [2002] NLJR 759.

lor, ex p Witham[6], withdrawal of a court fees exemption scheme for those on income support was deemed in breach of Article 6. Parties must also comply with procedural requirements as to directions questionnaires, statements of case, disclosure, and evidence, all buttressed by statements of truth which, if untrue, are punishable as contempt and possible imprisonment. Furthermore, CPR 26.4 already permits a stay of one month at directions stage to explore settlement by ADR or any other means. No one suggests that this provision is in breach of Article 6.

The 2013 amendments to the CPR (discussed further in **Chapter 13**) promise a more rigorous regime of enforcement of obligations under rules, orders and directions, perhaps leading to a renewed willingness to strike out cases and defences for contumely. It might be argued that these CPR requirements operated in such a regime are breaches of Article 6. If they are not breaches, the question arises as to why ordering mediation should be a breach. It is one of the identified tools of active case management, so arguably it stands in no different relationship to Article 6 than any other court rule. On these points, Article 6 is said to require that any restrictions on access to the courts are proportionate, certain, and in pursuit of a legitimate aim: see *Golder v UK*[7]. With ADR given approval in CPR Part 1, a mediation is unlikely to be regarded as breaching such requirements.

Deweer makes it clear that encouraging settlement is a proper activity of any civil justice system and in no way infringes a party's Article 6 rights. Encouragement to settle is one thing, however. The question still arose as to whether it is in breach of Article 6 for a civil justice system to **require** a party to participate in a settlement process before being able to have a day in court.

An answer of sorts has now been given by the European Court's decision in *Alassani v Telecom Italia*[8], the facts of which are set out in **5.6**, and where its significance was discussed. The court decided that the applicants should have used the settlement procedure before issuing proceedings, and that the requirement to do so did not offend Article 6 of the ECHR. Lord Dyson has now publicly accepted[9] that the general European view does not preclude mandatory mediation, at least so long as the mediation ordered is 'merely a preliminary step which the parties are required to go through which, if unsuccessful, would leave them free to litigate'. He still questions whether it is right in practice for a court to force unwilling parties to mediate.

---

6 [1997] 2 All ER 524.
7 1 EHRR 524.
8 C-137/08 18 March 2010, ECJ.
9 In his Chartered Institute of Arbitrators speech in October 2010.

The real issue may lie in the proportionality (a favourite European concept) of the remedy deployed when a breach occurs. If failure to comply with an ADR order meant that an otherwise valid claim would be permanently struck out, or committal to prison for contempt, Article 6 might well come into play[10]. In England and Wales, the remedy for unreasonable conduct in relation to ADR, as any other manifestation, is to impose costs sanctions, even on an otherwise successful litigant. It is submitted that it is unlikely that this will be found to infringe Article 6.

But even as a matter of principle, it is hard to see how such costs sanctions could remotely be classified as breaching Article 6. Judges often impose costs sanctions on what they regard as unreasonable litigation conduct. If to do that is a breach of Article 6, the entire underpinning philosophy of the CPR, which have made such a positive difference to the litigation landscape, would be jeopardised. Parties cannot expect unfettered access to courts on the basis of a financial indemnity against legal costs if they win. This did not happen under the old Rules of the Supreme Court, and even less so now under the CPR. In many jurisdictions without a costs jurisprudence, this does not happen at all. Certainly proportionate orders for security for costs have been upheld as not being in breach of Article 6[11].

Where issues of proportionality may prevail, including allotting to a case 'an appropriate share of the court's resources' and presumably no more, a much more pragmatic regime is possible, where one litigant may be denied excessive access to the courts on the grounds of disproportionate use of court resources. Regulating reasonableness of litigation conduct by costs sanctions is something clearly within the discretion of a given jurisdiction, which can use its own ways of regulation to suit it. No other EU country has quite the same mechanisms of costs controls as the UK, so others may use different models, loosely based around case management in its multifarious forms. The very fact that there is such a range of approaches in how judges are empowered to deal with litigant discipline (whether by costs sanctions or otherwise) emphasises the comparative marginality of such issues to human rights. It is to be hoped that some opportunity will arise to test out some of these areas of uncertainty. As Ward LJ wryly asked in *Wright v Michael Wright Supplies*[12]:

'Was it wrong for us to have been persuaded by the silky eloquence of the *éminence grise* for the ECHR, Lord Lester of Herne

---

10 This is forcefully argued by Shirley Shipman in *Compulsory mediation: the elephant in the room* (2011) 30(2) CJQ 163.
11 Eg *Stevens v SOASS* (2001) Times, 2 February, though excessive court fees were regarded as in breach of Article 6 in *Kreuz v Poland* 11 BHRC 456.
12 [2013] EWCA Civ 234 at para 3.

Hill QC, to place reliance on *Deweer v Belgium* (1980) 2 EHRR 439? See some extra-judicial observations of Sir Anthony Clarke, The Future of Civil Mediations, (2008) 74 Arbitration 4 which suggests that we were wrong. Does CPR 26.4(2)(b) allow the court of its own initiative at any time, not just at the time of allocation, to direct a stay for mediation to be attempted, with the warning of the costs consequences, which *Halsey* did spell out and which should be rigorously applied, for unreasonably refusing to agree to ADR? Is a stay really "an unacceptable obstruction" to the parties right of access to the court if they have to wait a while before being allowed across the court's threshold? Perhaps some bold judge will accede to an invitation to rule on these questions so that the court can have another look at *Halsey* in the light of the past 10 years of developments in this field'.

10.2   The EU Mediation Directive

As part of its commercial harmonisation policies, the European Commission initiated Europe-wide consideration of mediation (only slightly complicated by its use of the term 'mediation' in relation to the entirely different sphere of insurance brokerage). This move emanated from decisions made at the European Council meeting in Tampere in 1999. In 2002 it circulated a Green Paper seeking to canvass the views of member states on ADR in civil and commercial disputes. A summary of responses was published in early 2003, and these led to the drafting of a Directive and a Code of Conduct for neutrals. The draft Directive led to a Directive in final form promulgated in February 2008, which required implementation by May 2011. There were initial fears that the Commission would seek to go down the route of regulation of ADR, but in the event they were persuaded that in a still relatively immature market, its role was to encourage rather than control its use.

The title and scope of both the draft (published in 2004) and the final forms of Directive is worth noting, as the predecessor Green Paper was concerned with ADR in general. The final Directive, however, issued in March 2008, was concerned only with mediation, the prime form of ADR in Europe. Article 1 of the draft Directive stated its intention as being:

'to facilitate access to dispute resolution by promoting the use of mediation' and

'by ensuring a sound relationship between mediation and judicial proceedings'.

The final form of the Directive subtly changed this wording, defining the objective as:

'to facilitate access to alternative dispute resolution and to promote the amicable settlement of disputes by encouraging the use of mediation and by ensuring a balanced relationship between mediation and judicial proceedings'.

It would be painfully protracted to compare and contrast every way in which the draft Directive was amended into the final text of the 2008 Directive, since it is the final form that matters. Where significant differences occur these will be highlighted, but suffice it to say that many changes were wrought to the text of the draft Directive.

The preamble to the Directive spells out the thinking behind these twin themes in greater detail in 30 clauses, which represent a far more formidable statement of intent than the Articles of the Directive themselves deliver, certainly insofar as England and Wales have chosen to implement them. What is impressive is the assumption that the establishment of agreed basic principles over 'extra-judicial procedures for the settlement of disputes in civil and commercial matters so as to simplify and improve access to justice' is an essential step to be taken by Europe as a whole[13]. Other significant points in the preamble are that:

- agreements reached in mediation are more likely to be complied with, making continued commercial relationships more possible;
- the Directive should apply to cases where 'a court refers parties to mediation or in which national law prescribes mediation';
- voluntariness in the mediation context means that the parties are themselves in charge of the process and may organise it as they wish and may terminate it at any time;
- the Directive does not prejudice national legislation making mediation compulsory or subject to incentives or sanctions 'provided that such legislation does not prevent parties from exercising their right of access to the judicial system';
- 'mediation should not be regarded as a poorer alternative to judicial proceedings', hence the need for mediated settlement to be enforceable by courts, except where illegal or unenforceable by national law;

---

13 Clause (3) to the preamble.

- confidentiality of the mediation process is important and procedural rules need to protect this;

- the Directive is not concerned with adjudicatory processes, whether binding or not, nor with judicially chaired settlement conferences;

- framework legislation is necessarily required of Member States to promote mediation and establish a predictable legal framework.

But the Directive's scope is specifically limited to 'cross-border disputes', defined by Article 2 as one where at least one of the parties is domiciled or habitually resident in a member state other than that of any other party. Some member states have ignored this limitation and have either introduced or plan to introduce measures which apply to domestic as well as cross-border disputes, but the UK has limited its procedural changes required by the Directive to cross-border disputes only.

So apart from that restriction, there are interesting statements made in the Directive's preamble which clearly influenced Dyson LJ's change of mind about mandatory mediation as seen in the European context. The voluntary nature of mediation is specifically limited to self-determination of process and continued participation in it, and court mandated mediation is permissible, unless it prevents access to the courts. Whether prevention of access to the courts encompasses undue delay or the expenditure of disproportionate cost in relation to access remains open for debate, and may still require judicial consideration.

Briefly, there are 13 Articles. Article 1 sets out the objectives as noted above; Article 2 defines cross-border disputes; and Article 3 defines 'mediation' and 'mediator', making it clear that neither includes attempts by a judge to settle a dispute within the course of judicial proceedings.

Article 4 encourages member states to ensure effective quality of mediation services and the use of codes of conduct by mediators. Article 5 confirms that courts may invite parties to mediate and hold mediation information sessions. It enacts that national legislation may make mediation compulsory, or subject to incentives or sanctions, so long as access to the courts is not prevented. Certainly the regime in England and Wales permitting ADR 'orders' and the imposition of sanctions for unreasonable refusal to mediate[14] would appear to comply with this Article, and there would even be room for strengthening such approaches if it is accepted that mediation does not in any way 'prevent parties from exercising their

---

14 Discussed in **Chapters 5** and **6** above.

right of access to the judicial system'. This issue is discussed more fully in **10.1** in relation to the European Convention on Human Rights.

Article 6 (discussed more fully below) reflects some of the differences in procedural approach between member states. It provides for parties to be able to request that a mediated settlement can be recorded and confirmed in a formal judgment of a court or public authority, so that it can be enforced as if it were a court judgment, so long as it is not in any way illegal. In England and Wales, mediated outcomes in cases where proceedings have been started will almost always be embodied in a consent order, as otherwise the proceedings will not be brought to an end. But there is no provision for formally recording settlement terms where proceedings have not started, whereas other jurisdictions have such facilities.

Article 7 deals with the admissibility of evidence from mediators but, unlike the draft Directive, not as to the confidentiality of what happened at a mediation. The equivalent Article in the draft Directive[15] suggested that mediators and providers of mediation services should not give evidence of:

- invitations to mediate or a party's unwillingness to mediate;

- offers to settle made in a mediation;

- statements or admissions made by a party during a mediation;

- mediator proposals, or a party's willingness to accept such a proposal (though, oddly, not a party's unwillingness to accept such a proposal);

- any document prepared solely for the purpose of a mediation.

The draft also proposed that a court should not be able to admit any such evidence except to enforce a settlement agreement reached as a direct result of a mediation, or where both the mediator and the parties agree. If implemented, this would have meant that the mediator had a veto on disclosure of mediation evidence, not just the parties. However, major surgery was done on this Article before the final Directive was published. Again this is discussed below in terms of implementation in England and Wales, but in outline, all provisions relating to the exclusion of evidence about what happened at the mediation have been deleted, and the Article merely deals with the compellability of mediators and mediation providers, prefacing the truncated article with the words: 'Given that mediation is intended to take place in a manner which respects confidentiality...'.

---

15 Article 6.

Mediators were not given their proposed veto over disclosure of such evidence, so that if the parties agree a mediator can be required to be a witness. Importantly, Article 7 in the Directive's final form confirms that member states are free to enact stricter measures to protect the confidentiality of mediation.

Article 8 proposes that any relevant limitation period is suspended from when the parties agree to use mediation, or mediation is ordered by a court or a statutory obligation to mediate arises. If the mediation fails to settle the claim, it will resume when one or both parties or the mediator declare it terminated or withdraw from it, though with a minimum of a month's grace from termination. This is the third provision which required implementation in England and Wales and is discussed further below. Articles 9–13 are broadly machinery provisions about implementation and review.

It will be seen, therefore, that the provisions of the Directive are permissive rather than prescriptive. They shy away from harmonising European law and procedure other than over provisions for court enforcement of mediated settlements, limitation and mediator compellability, setting a minimum standard over this and flinching from requiring more extensive protection for the confidentiality of mediation without barring stricter national rules if desired.

10.3 Implementation of the EU Mediation Directive in England and Wales

Implementation of the Directive was required by 31 May 2011, and this was duly done in England and Wales on 20 May 2011 in a thoroughly minimalist way, but one which represented the first statutory and regulatory measures affecting the legal framework of mediation yet made here; until then it had simply been subject to occasional common law decisions of the courts. The provisions introduced only apply to cross-border civil and commercial disputes and do not affect mediations of domestic or non-EU disputes. By contract, Ireland and other EU states have taken the Directive as creating the opportunity to construct a comprehensive legal framework for mediation of all types of dispute.

The machinery for implementation of legislative change was a statutory instrument made under the European Communities Act 1972[16], by which European legislation can be imported without its own separate statute. Such changes as could be made to court rules have been introduced by amendment of the CPR.

---

16 The Cross-Border Mediation (EU Directive) Regulations 2011, SI 2011/1133.

The Ministry of Justice declared itself satisfied that England and Wales are compliant with the Directive in respect of the majority of its requirements, so no proposals were made in respect of Articles:

1 Objective and scope
2 Cross-border disputes
3 Definitions
4 Quality of mediation
5 Recourse to mediation
9 Information for the public

However, Articles 6 (enforceability of settlement agreements), 7 (confidentiality of mediation) and 8 (suspension of limitation) were seen to require changes and additions to English law and procedure to accommodate what the EU Mediation Directive requires for cross-border disputes only. These are now dealt with in turn in some detail.

Article 6: Enforcement of mediated settlements

A new Section III has been inserted in CPR Part 78 (which is entitled 'European procedures') to introduce these provisions. Though using the procedure under CPR Part 23 for a consent order under CPR 40.6 is clearly the right and currently used approach where mediation leads to settlement of issued proceedings, the Civil Procedure Rules Committee rejected its use where proceedings have not yet started, choosing instead to require issue of proceedings under CPR Part 8. If all parties consent to a mediated settlement, the court will make a 'mediation settlement enforcement order' under CPR 78.25, by which immediate access to the court for enforcement will be possible in the event of default. The settlement agreement will have to be attached to the claim form, together with evidence of the parties' consent (which obviously ought to be clear from the face of the settlement agreement). This makes no real change to the current position, except that under Tomlin Order procedure, it was possible to lodge a consent order *without* the schedule of agreed terms attached, simply referring to them as being set out in an identified document (usually the settlement agreement) which did not have to be lodged at court. Previously when proceedings for default in performing a mediated settlement agreement had to be brought, the written agreement had to be produced to the court for the court to be able to enforce it, and that document is not privileged from production by the 'without prejudice' rule. But now the document will have to be produced to the court before there is any question of default, just in case enforcement is required.

CPR Part 5 has been amended to keep the attachments to such an order closed to inspection by a non-party 'without the court's permission'. The amendment does not give guidance over when permission might be forthcoming. There was less need to worry about accidental disclosure of settlement terms when they were not appended to the consent order, but now either a slip-up in the court office or a decision of a judge could expose these terms to non-parties, which is perhaps less than desirable.

Applications for a settlement order will be on paper, with no hearing unless otherwise directed, so normally decided in private without an open court hearing. If a hearing is directed, though, it seems likely in the present climate that it will be in public. Nothing is said about the procedure for actually seeking enforcement in the event of default.

The question arises as to what happens if a cross-border dispute is settled by mediation but has not been registered under CPR 78.25. If a remedy is pursued in England and Wales there should be no problem, as a binding settlement agreement is enforceable as a contract, probably with a good chance of summary judgment under CPR Part 24, so that a party desiring enforcement must sue either on the settlement contract which ended the claim for tort or contract, or on the original breach of the original contract (if not prevented from doing so by the settlement reached). The absence of an order under CPR 78.25 does not seem to make any unregistered settlement unenforceable. It may do in the jurisdictions of other member states. The CPR offer this route 'where the parties, or one of them with the explicit consent of the others, *wish* to apply for a quick route to enforcement'. Lack of such an order just means a slower path to judgment if a party defaults on the settlement terms. As noted, this in practice is a fairly rare event in the absence of the supervening insolvency of the paying party.

These provisions are unexceptionable, though it may well be that they will only rarely be used. They are unnecessary for post-action mediations, as Tomlin Orders achieve the same outcome already, and there may be few cross-border pre-action mediations anyway, and even on those that take place, there may be no wish to use the procedure.

Article 8: suspension of limitation periods

The provisions relating to this Article are contained in the Cross-Border Mediation (EU Directive) Regulations 2011[17], necessarily done by statutory instrument because these represent legislative changes. To the puzzlement and irritation of those with a common law viewpoint, the Directive

---

17 SI 2011/1133.

insists that a limitation period should not be able to expire during a mediation to the prejudice of any party if the mediation does not produce settlement. It requires postponement of any right to rely on the expiry of a limitation period if this would happen after the date on which a mediation starts until the mediation ends and then for a further period of eight weeks thereafter. A further mediation starting within eight weeks of the last one ending further postpones the end of any relevant limitation period. The 2011 Regulations apply to employment disputes as well, for which extensions of time range from two, to four to eight weeks depending on the nature of the potential time-bar.

The start of a mediation is defined as being 'the date of *the agreement to mediate* that is entered into by the parties and the mediator'. This is hardly clear. The italicised words are not defined by the regulations or by the Directive. Could it refer to an exchange of letters between parties and a provider? Ingenuity might conceivably be applied here if the loss of a cause of action is at stake.

The end of a mediation – from which the eight-week period of grace runs – is defined as being the earliest date of the following:

- when the parties reach agreement in resolution of the relevant dispute (though it is hard to see why limitation should continue to be of any importance then); or
- one party notifies all other parties to the relevant dispute that it has withdrawn from mediation; or
- where there are two or more parties, 14 days have expired without response after one has asked the other(s) to confirm whether the mediation is continuing and all have not said yes; or
- 14 days after the parties are told that the mediator's appointment has ended, by death, resignation or otherwise;
- the mediation process expires by effluxion of a pre-agreed period in the mediation agreement.

To the shortest of the above time brackets is added eight weeks (shorter in various types of employment dispute). The time brackets will last as long as parties wish until one 'ends' the mediation by notice. If ever there was a recipe for entering into mediation for an ulterior reason, and a trigger for unwanted satellite litigation, it is these provisions. It is so easy for judges to be wary and dismissive of devices and processes which seem to stimulate satellite litigation, with the risk that they become irritated with the mediation process generally, for interposing itself into the flow of justice in this way at the behest of Europe. The expiry of a relevant limitation period during a mediation, however defined in length, will be a rare eventuality, as no one will be likely to go into a cross-border mediation without adequate legal advice. Such competent advice should have dealt with limitation well before a mediation is contemplated, with international law firms dealing with such cross-border disputes as a matter of regularity. And limitation is a defence which can be waived in English procedure. So who is this provision intended to help? Is it an innocent party who fails to seek advice in time and who foolishly incurs the expense of a mediation without getting advice quickly enough? It surely cannot be intended to get international lawyers off the consequences of inattention to expiry of limitation periods, wherever proceedings might be brought. It is difficult to discern what lies behind these elaborate and wordy provisions, in terms of a problem in English procedural law that warrants such a clumsy response.

Mediation itself derives no benefit from having these time period definitions foisted upon the process as a refuge for a probably negligent lawyer. Limitation is the business of civil justice and not of mediation, which should not be able to be used as a means of avoiding the consequences of a procedural rule which has no relevance to it as a process. A party who discovers perhaps during the mediation day that a limitation period is about to expire is going to be tempted to prolong the mediation until he gets his house in order. How does that dignify the mediation process? A whole new set of concerns is going to arise at and after mediations for lawyers to consider and use tactically, in the highly unlikely event of this provision being relevant in a given dispute.

Currently, where negotiations do not break down entirely with full-scale resumption of litigation, mediations either settle on the day, or, having not settled, discussions go on afterwards to which mediation confidentiality applies. No one necessarily assumes that the mediation is over or not over. They may have to do so now in cross-border disputes, and such thinking may come to be imported into domestic mediation in later years, again to no discernible benefit for the mediation process.

As English procedure had to implement something to comply with the Directive, why a minimalist basis was not used is puzzling, perhaps providing that a cross-border mediation starts when the last required signature has been appended to the written mediation agreement (so there will be no protection for mediations conducted without one), with the end of the mediation by reference to a period of time from that moment, whether it be 24 hours or more. This avoids elaborate notices and notice periods. Mediation activity can then in practical terms continue, but limitation protection would not, except for a brief period of clearly-defined time.

There is perhaps one respect in which the new provisions will be of help, and that is where limitation periods or bars on the issue of process are short. Contract and tort limitations here are lengthy by any standards – three years for personal injury and still subject to discretionary judicial extension; six years for simple contracts and twelve for contracts under seal. But the Mediation Directive's provisions are applied specifically to cases within the ambit of Employment Tribunals by amendments to the Equal Pay Act 1970, the Employment Rights Act 1996 and the Equality Act 2010. These all have very short periods for bringing applications of various kinds, and relief from these in the relatively rare cases involving cross-border disputes might be understandable. At the opposite end of the scale, the Prescription Act 1832 is amended to give relief if the 60-year limitation period for a profit *à prendre* happens to expire while a mediation is still in progress.

Article 7: confidentiality and mediator compellability

This is a topic which has already given some cause for concern in relation to Article 6 of the Directive, now that the court may possibly have access to settlement terms by hearing from the mediator. Article 7 of the Mediation Directive provides as follows:

'1 Given that mediation is intended to take place in a manner which respects confidentiality, Member States shall ensure that, unless the parties agree otherwise, neither mediators nor those involved in the administration of the mediation process shall be compelled to give evidence in civil and commercial judicial proceedings or arbitration regarding information arising out of or in connection with a mediation process, except:

(a) where this is necessary for overriding considerations of public policy of the Member State concerned, in particular when required to ensure the protection of the best interests of children or to prevent harm to the physical or psychological integrity of a person; or

(b) where disclosure of the content of the agreement resulting from mediation is necessary in order to implement or enforce that agreement.

2 Nothing in paragraph 1 shall preclude Member States from enacting stricter measures to protect the confidentiality of mediation'.

The problem is that, as was seen in the previous chapter, it is not clear whether the law in England and Wales on this topic as at present revealed by precedent is more or less strict than that required by the Directive. To enact the provisions of the Directive, even in the limited area of cross-border disputes, without knowing this is hazardous, bearing in mind that confidentiality is the cornerstone of mediation's success. Heedless damage to the concept could profoundly undermine its usefulness.

Again, the precise requirements of the Directive have been enacted in England and Wales, confining the rules to cross-border disputes, importing its definitions and using the same language, often incorporating definitions wholesale. Presumably this has been done in the belief that to enact the Directive's standard either strengthens or at least equates to the standard of English law. If, however, the current English standard – to the extent that it is clear at all – is actually stricter than the Directive's requirements, these provisions represent a watering-down of that stricter law in a way that could prove seriously damaging. The provisions as introduced are far less protective of the mediation process and mediators as witnesses than, for instance, the protection afforded by the Uniform Mediation Act in the USA and other common law jurisdictions where mediation has a maturely-established position in their civil justice systems. Revelation of the common law in this area, as everywhere else, is of course a matter of happenstance, depending on parties having both funds and determination to refer a set of circumstances to a court for ruling. No further reminder of this is needed than *Halsey,* a case about the death of Mr Halsey and never (so far as Mrs Halsey was concerned) about mediation, had it not been for her perhaps misguidedly campaigning lawyer. So knowledge of what the common law is on a particular point depends on a chance set of relevant facts being assembled and litigated. With the English courts very reluctant to litigate on theoretical matters (except where the Court of Appeal chooses to go *obiter* to give general guidance), it may well be a long time before all points relevant to mediation confidentiality could be clarified. In this area at least, the courts have had insufficient opportunity to clarify what the law really is, and what decisions there are have been mainly by courts of first instance.

The substantive changes are contained in Part 2 of the Cross-Border Mediation (EU Directive) Regulations 2011, and changes to procedure are in CPR 78.26 and 78.27. Matching the change of scope between draft and final Directive, nothing at all has been required or enacted about general confidentiality of what passes at a mediation between the parties or between the mediator and each party. The 2011 Regulations deal only with circumstances in which the mediator can be called to give 'mediation evidence' (as defined below) of what happened. Regulations 8 to 10 of the 2011 Regulations deal with this topic and provide as follows:

  – reg 8 defines 'mediation evidence' as 'evidence arising out of or in connection with a mediation process'. This is not actually a definition contained within the Directive, but an echo of the words underlined in the quotation of Article 7 above, with the word 'evidence' substituted for 'information' (whether by oversight or intention). The meaning of this is considered again below;

– reg 9 provides as a starting-point that 'a mediator or mediation administrator has the right to withhold mediation evidence in civil and commercial judicial proceedings and arbitration', but this is expressly 'subject to Regulation 10';

– under reg 10, a court *may* order that a mediator/mediation administrator '**must** give or disclose mediation evidence' where:

  • all parties agree to the giving or disclosing of mediation evidence (all, that is, except the mediator, presumably, even though they are almost always signatories of the mediation agreement and thus technically 'party' to it); or

  • where 'necessary for reasons of overriding public policy', referring to the instances given in Article 7 of child protection or to prevent physical or psychological harm to someone; or

  • the 'giving or disclosure of the mediation settlement is necessary to implement or enforce the mediation settlement agreement'.

How do these provisions compare with the current state of English law? As already noted, there is a dearth of binding Court of Appeal and Supreme Court precedent on this subject. The only source of Court of Appeal comment is in *Halsey v Milton Keynes General NHS Trust*[18], where the assumption was that courts would **not** trespass behind the veil of confidentiality. Dyson LJ said (at para 14):

'We make it clear at the outset that it was common ground before us (and we accept) that parties are entitled in an ADR [sic] to adopt whatever position they wish, and if as a result the dispute is not settled, that is not a matter for the court. As is submitted by the Law Society, if the integrity and confidentiality of the process is to be respected, the court should not know, and therefore should not investigate, why the process did not result in agreement'.

---

18 [2004] 4 All ER 920.

The line of first instance cases which deal with this topic has already been discussed in **Chapter 9**[19]. In *Brown v Rice*, the Deputy High Court judge admitted evidence of what happened at the mediation in order to decide whether a binding agreement had been reached, but did not consider whether contractual confidentiality added to evidential privilege. In *Cumbria Waste*, the Deputy High Court judge held that the mediation evidence could not be released to the defendant solicitors either as an exception to the without prejudice rule, or alternatively on the basis that contractual confidentiality set up by the mediation agreement enabled the other party to the later mediation unilaterally to prevent disclosure to them. In *Farm Assist (No 2)*, the judge held that both parties could waive 'without prejudice privilege', the mediator having no say in this; but that contractual confidentiality agreed in respect of a mediation belonged also to the mediator (and presumably if also a signatory, a mediation provider) who could resist being called to give confidential 'mediation evidence'. However, this was subject to the power of a judge to admit evidence from a mediator 'in the interests of justice', undefined, and allowed to prevail in this instance, though without detailed explanation of his reasons for doing so or the factors he took into account.

The only other cases where what might be categorised as 'mediation evidence' has been heard by an English judge are ones where the parties *both* saw fit to waive privilege and allow that evidence to be admitted (wisely or not) and there was no question of the mediator either being called or being given the opportunity to object on principle. These are *SITA v Watson Wyatt; Maxwell Batley Pt 20 defendant* (Park J)[20], *Chantry Vellacott v The Convergence Group* (Rimer J)[21] and *Earl of Malmesbury v Strutt & Parker* (Coulson J)[22].

There are two more grounds for saying that there is uncertainty about the current position. First, there was unresolved disagreement about the true extent of the 'without prejudice' rule exemplified in the purist position taken by Lord Hoffmann in *Muller v Linsley & Mortimer*[23] and Lord Walker in *Unilever v Proctor and Gamble*[24], at least until resolved in the 2009 decision of *Ofulue v Bossaert*[25], which established a broad interpretation for 'without prejudice' privilege. Second, several of the cases cited above dis-

---

19 *Brown v Rice* [2007] EWHC 625 (Ch); *Cumbria Waste Management v Baines Wilson* [2008] EWHC 786 (QB); *Farm Assist Ltd v DEFRA (No 1)* [2008] EWHC 3079 (TCC); *Farm Assist v DEFRA (No 2)* [2009] EWHC 1102 (TCC).
20 [2002] EWHC 2025 (Ch).
21 [2007] EWHC 1774 (Ch).
22 [2008] EWHC 424 (QB).
23 [1996] 1 PNLR 74, CA.
24 [2000] 1 All ER 201, CA.
25 [2009] UKHL 16.

cuss whether a form of mediation privilege exists as a stand-alone concept, not ruling it out as a concept but without ever quite deciding if this is so.

Given the uncertainty, what makes the current attempt induced by the need to implement the Directive dangerous? First, taking *Farm Assist (No 2)* as the highest point reached by a first instance judge, and assuming that he was right that contractual confidentiality[26] conferred on the mediator a veto on disclosure of confidential information that only a judge could overcome by applying the interests of justice test, it would seem that the judge only felt able to go that far because **both parties** consented to the mediator being called. What cannot be known is whether, if Farm Assist had objected but DEFRA persisted in their application for a witness summons against the mediator, the judge would have felt that he could nevertheless rule that the mediator should be called. If that were to be the case, then the Directive's provision, which requires **both** parties to agree to this would be a strengthening of English law. Contrast *Cumbria Waste,* where the judge found that confidentiality kept 'mediation evidence' even from a later interested party, though calling the mediator as witness was not at issue here. Nor was it in *Brown v Rice,* where the judge did admit 'mediation evidence' despite opposition by the other party and a mediation provider, but the mediator was not to be called to give it.

Second, what are the 'interests of justice' in these circumstances? Article 7 talks of 'overriding considerations of public policy' and not 'the interests of justice', which is a typical English common law procedural concept, which could even justify admission of evidence to make it easier for the judge to reach a decision. Article 7 is specifically concerned about child protection and bodily or mental harm to others. *Farm Assist* was about whether a Government department needed to call a mediator to reveal whether a four year old allegation of duress was credible, having been raised by a liquidator not present at the mediation where it allegedly occurred. No consideration was apparently given to deciding whether the interests of justice were served in that case (and, more importantly, other mediations) in protecting a mediator from the witness box so that disputants in general can have secure conversations within a private process designed to help settle cases and take pressure off the courts. Nor was any consideration given to whether the mediator has little to add to the evidence of the parties who are free (unless legally restrained) to give evidence of what happened at the mediation without needing a neutral mediator to be called as a tie-breaker.

---

26 Subsequent standard form mediation agreements bar mediators from giving evidence absolutely.

Judges are well able to assess the credibility of parties without the help of someone likely to be hampered in so doing because of their duty of neutrality to *both* sides. Perhaps embarrassingly for the judge in *Farm Assist,* the fact that Farm Assist's liquidator discontinued immediately after his decision suggests that he would have had no trouble seeing through the allegation of duress even without the mediator's help. The real point is that when the Court of Appeal look at this whole issue, they may feel that protection for mediators at common law is much higher than that required by the Directive or as found in *Farm Assist (No 2).* They might even discern a form of common law mediator privilege and define it, though this is less likely. Alternatively, after due consultation and debate, Parliament might set a higher standard. Until the true position is known, to adopt the arguably low Directive standard is the thin end of a dangerous wedge, set in ignorance of what it is purporting to replace.

Finally on this, the vagueness of the definition of 'mediation evidence' is striking. The definition used is a formulation (*not* a formal definition) taken from Article 7, with the word 'information' substituted by the word evidence'. In the hands of a subtle judge, encouraged by counsel straining to do the best for a client, might this not lead to an interpretation wholly unintended by the Directive? 'Evidence' is arguably more restricted in meaning than 'information', as it imports the whole law of evidence as to relevance and admissibility. But both are very general in meaning, and it is relevant to recall the practicalities of a mediation to test out the wisdom of this.

Mediators currently reassure parties that confidentiality operates at two different levels. First, 'information' (usually as to risk or intention to settle) which is disclosed and exchanged at mediations between parties, such as offers which demonstrate a provisional willingness to compromise and which are sent as signals between rooms, is confidential and cannot be reported to the judge if no settlement emerges. Second, what a party confides to the mediator in the privacy of that party's room cannot be conveyed to the other party without consent, let alone to the judge. This latter confidential information might well fall within the definition of 'mediation evidence', which could lead to one party compelling the mediator to disclose material in a later trial which that party had no right to hear during the mediation, by virtue of the mediation agreement. So does this wording compel a mediator to disclose not only to a judge but also to the other party what was told to the mediator in confidence, relying on an assurance of confidentiality? If the mediator is forced to give evidence for what a judge decides is 'in the interests of justice', and counsel for one party asks what the mediator was told by the other party in private about a certain topic (short, of course, of an expressed intention to kill or harm someone, as allowed for by Article 7) will the judge order an answer on pain of contempt of court? This wording makes it possible without clearer definition, and leaves enormous discretion in the hands of judges, many of whom have still never attended a mediation. It is extremely worrying. Mediators can really no longer be sure of what they can safely say to parties at mediations to reassure them over confidentiality of what they choose to reveal.

For completeness it should be added that CPR 78 has been amended to add the procedure whereby a party seeks disclosure or inspection of mediation evidence in the control of a mediator or mediation administrator. Where proceedings are afoot it should be done under CPR 23; otherwise (in pre-action applications) under Part 8. The rule specifies exactly the same requirements for such an Order to be made as are set out in reg 10 of the 2011 Regulations (see above).

In this regard there is one rather odd provision which reveals perhaps a misunderstanding by the legislature and the judiciary of what mediators actually do. Regulation 10(c) allows mediation evidence to be given where 'the mediation evidence relates to the mediation settlement and the giving or disclosure of the mediation settlement is necessary to implement or enforce the mediation settlement agreement'. So this cannot be used if the mediation does *not* settle the dispute. Contrast this wording with the provision it seeks to implement in Article 7 of the Directive, which says that evidence is admissible from a mediator or provider 'where disclosure of the content of the agreement resulting from mediation is necessary in order to implement or enforce that agreement'. If this only covers settled mediations, it seems a little odd to need such a provision where a post-action mediation produced a Tomlin consent order which is on the face of the court record, and where a pre-action deal has been recorded in a CPR Part 78 order. In any event, courts are perfectly capable of construing orders and contracts with little help from extrinsic oral evidence. Indeed, if the parol evidence rule is still of importance, they *must* do so without oral evidence.

But there remains the question as to whether a mediator should be considered to be a proper person to give evidence on such issues. Mediators almost never take responsibility for the settlement terms or the enforcement provisions. They leave the drafting to the lawyers for the parties to exercise their professional skill on behalf of their clients to protect their clients from any adverse consequences. Mediators never act as guarantors of the meaning, the fairness, or the enforceability of the settlements that emerge from a mediation. They make it possible for terms to be reached and they may even raise questions and reminders about what needs to be covered. But they never take legal responsibility for such matters. Many of them are not insured to give advice of any kind about anything other than process. So they are highly unlikely to be able to give meaningful evidence about this. This may be another instance of official misunderstanding of what really goes on in mediations, leading to an inappropriate and misdirected provision.

The Ministry of Justice issued a Consultation Paper in 2011 entitled *Solving disputes in the County Courts*[27] which incidentally asked for consultees' views on whether the provisions of the Directive introduced to comply with the minimal requirements of the Directive over cross-border disputes should be extended to domestic mediations and all others conducted in England and Wales which are international but not involving parties from EU member states. The date for consultation passed in June 2011, and nothing has apparently happened since. However, if this is raised again, the issues discussed above certainly need careful consideration and consultation before any wider changes are made. The Irish Law Commission's report produced in response to the Directive is a model for how such changes should be considered and made.

10.4   The EU Code of Conduct for Mediators

Having decided not to embark on a regulatory regime for mediation, the European Commission developed a Code of Conduct to establish levels of expectation for service quality and to provide mediators in every European jurisdiction with a common standard. It is not compulsory, but is available for incorporation by reference into mediation agreements or terms of business. The topics covered by the EU Code are what might be expected. They include a mix of ethical and administrative standards. Its style makes it read as instructions to the mediator rather than as undertakings given by the mediator to the parties. The key provisions are:

- competence and continued training, with the mediator disclosing details of personal background to potential clients, satisfying himself that he is appropriate for a particular dispute;
- independence and neutrality of the mediator, with a duty to disclose any conflict of interest;
- the mediator must ensure that the parties understand the process and the mediation agreement, and also any settlement terms, and must conduct the process fairly, clarifying also the basis of remuneration;
- confidentiality about the process as a whole, including the fact of the mediation, and also as to keeping information given confi-

---

27 March 2011 published for the Ministry of Justice by The Stationery Office.

dentially by one party from any other party, though always subject to any disclosure compelled by law.

By way of comparison, the CEDR Code of Conduct for mediators and other third party neutrals reads as a form of undertaking given by CEDR about neutrals which it nominates. It too covers impartiality and conflict of interest, confidentiality, transparency as to fees and circumstances justifying withdrawal. It also includes an undertaking to take out professional indemnity insurance.

Chapter 11
Mediation and litigation costs

Unlike a number of other common and civil law jurisdictions, litigation in England and Wales involves not only decision-making about what remedies are available to dispose of the substantive issues in any given dispute, but also who should bear the costs of the dispute, whether or not proceedings have been issued. The 'American rule' – that normally each party bears their own costs, win or lose – prevails in the USA, and the so-called 'English rule' means broadly that the winner of litigation in England and Wales receives legal costs in addition to any substantive remedy. The costs at stake can often match or outstrip the sums in dispute. Thus at the end of any hearing, whether a trial or application, the judge will be required to decide what costs order to make in the light of the substantive decision, and there may be lengthy argument on what the appropriate order should be. When settling cases too, whether before issue or before or during a trial, similar regard has to be given to negotiating an acceptable basis for the payment of costs. Thus, almost without exception during a mediation, the issue of where the burden of costs is to lie will arise. This can prove a serious obstacle to settlement, even when substantive matters have been sorted out. Some major areas of dispute have very little by way of costs jurisdiction, such as employment tribunals, and this too has implications both for funding and the way that settlements are crafted at mediations in such cases.

If anything, costs issues have increased in significance in English litigation since the CPR reforms came into effect in 1999. This is partly due to the way the sums at stake have escalated as lawyers' fees have surged ever higher, especially in the commercial field. It is also due to the uncertainties introduced by issue-based costs orders, where judges have a much wider discretion in how they apportion costs liabilities between those who win and lose. It has meant a much greater focus by judges on costs issues at the conclusion of trials. Before the CPR, the costs order would usually be easy to make and would require brief consideration by the judge after pronouncing his decision. The breadth of judicial discretion has now led to frequently lengthy and complex hearings about costs, often some weeks after the conclusion of the substantive trial, preceded by exchange and lodgement of skeleton arguments. The predicted focus of judicial time on costs issues anticipated when the CPR were introduced has certainly come about, and such hearings are probably the single most significant manifestation of satellite litigation generated by the CPR. Indeed, the word 'satellite' is almost inappropriate. With the costs at stake in litigation often dwarfing the damages claimed, in reality a good number of cases are now fought about the disposition of the costs rather than the substantive issues, hardly a matter for pride.

Related to costs considerations are questions of funding. Clearly a party who can afford to litigate has greater power of choice over whether to settle, both within and outside mediations, than a party under financial constraints. Since the huge reduction in scope and availability of state funding of civil litigation through Legal Aid, other means have been developed to enable those who are neither poor nor rich enough to fund their litigation to do so. Use of Conditional Fee Agreements (CFAs), in which a successful party's lawyer can receive a success fee for winning a case as the price for not charging if a case is lost – so-called 'no-win, no-fee' representation – have been permitted in various forms since 1995, and since 2013 significant changes have been made yet again to the permitted funding regimes. The problems that arise from their use are now emerging at mediations, hence the need for some review of their effect and how mediators might help parties to deal with these.

These are complex topics and cannot be covered in full detail, but this chapter outlines the significant ways in which costs can impinge upon mediation practice, particularly for non-lawyer readers of this book, as mediators will find it hard to escape from discussions on costs in English mediations, and need to have some understanding of what is at stake. Funding options and their impact on mediation are considered in outline in **Chapter 12**.

11.1 Costs: some definitions

The legal costs of conducting litigation include:

- the legal costs of the solicitors in conducting the case for their client, both before and after issue of proceedings;
- fees payable to the court on issue of proceedings or applications made during the case, and on filing directions and listing questionnaires;
- any barrister's fees incurred in advising, settling statements of case, and the brief fee and refresher fees for representation at interim hearings and trial, where the barrister is not working under a Conditional Fee Agreement;

- any expert's fees for giving reports on and attending at trial to give evidence;
- other incidental expenses;
- value added tax.

These will be referred to as '*the costs of the claim*', whether incurred by a claimant in making a claim or a defendant or third party in defending a claim, and will include costs incurred both before and after the issue of proceedings. Note that normally the successful claimant may have some expectation of recovering pre-issue costs, but defendants do not have any expectation of costs reimbursement in investigating a claim before issue unless and until proceedings are issued. As will be seen, in damages claims for personal injury or death commenced after 1 April 2013, defendants will have virtually no expectation of recovering costs if they win.

Also relevant are what have been called '*additional liabilities*', more fully considered in **Chapter 12**. These are features of funding litigation which developed since the major reduction in civil Legal Aid as from 1995 onwards. These include *success fees* under Conditional Fee Agreements where a solicitor or barrister take on a claim on the basis that they will make no charge to their client if the case is lost, but will receive a success fee if it is won. They also include premiums paid for insurance policies taken out to protect a claimant against normal costs liabilities if the case is lost, usually called *ATE premiums*. In claims brought between 1995 and 1999, these are recoverable only from the client. Between 1999 and 2013, they have been recoverable from a losing defendant.

A sub-division of the costs of the claim will be those costs and expenses incurred in preparing for and attending at a mediation on behalf of any party. These will be referred to as '*the costs of the mediation*'. A further sub-division, dealt with later in this chapter, are the fees and expenses payable to the mediator either directly or to and through any mediation services provider in respect of the mediator's services in preparing for and conducting a mediation and any agreed follow-up. These will be referred to as '*the mediation fees*'.

The above are definitions developed for the purpose of this book. It is also necessary to define and distinguish several more terms which appear in the CPR, and without which the concepts related to costs of the claim cannot be understood. There are two bases upon which such costs are awarded by a judge or agreed on settlement. The *standard basis* is the norm, and when it is applied, costs are allowable if they are proportionate to the matters in issue, with any doubt over what is sought being decided in favour of the *paying party*. In practical terms, where a party is awarded or agreed to receive standard basis costs, these will rarely cover all the receiving party's liability to its own lawyers for their costs of the claim chargeable to it. That party may still be left with a liability for anything between 20–30% of its costs of the claim, which their solicitor must recover from their client or waive wholly or in part. Conversely, the *indemnity basis* for paying costs is close to 100% of the receiving party's costs of the claim. Proportionality is disregarded on this basis, and any doubt over reasonableness will be resolved in favour of the *receiving party*.

Where agreement proves impossible over how much should be paid as to costs where these have been ordered to be paid by one party to another, the court can be invited to rule on allowable costs of the claim through the elaborate and quite costly procedure of *detailed assessment*, when a costs judge will rule on disputed costs issues between the parties. In cases where the hearing of an application or a trial takes no more than one day, the judge will normally make a *summary assessment* of the costs involved at the conclusion of the hearing.

The Jackson reforms, implemented in 2013, were intended to reinforce the principle of proportionality between costs and the substance of each claim. The addition of the words '*and at proportionate cost*' to the overriding objective makes that point firmly in principle, and additionally it is not sufficient to justify the recovery of costs on the standard basis if they were 'necessarily' incurred but not proportionate[1]. Even if costs are reasonably incurred, they may be disallowed if they are disproportionate to the value and complexity of the case[2].

An increasing number of types of case, involving lower value claims and road traffic accident claims conducted through the RTA Portal procedure set out in Practice Direction 8B of the CPR, now attract fixed costs. As mediators are only very rarely going to be involved in such cases, these are not considered further.

11.2   The basis for litigation costs awards under the CPR

As explained in **Chapters 6** and **7** in relation to costs sanctions for declining ADR, the CPR have encouraged judges to make orders in relation to the costs of the claim in a much more issue-sensitive manner than before. CPR Part 44 provides for such orders to take into account the behaviour of each party both before and after the commencement of proceedings in deciding what order to make. The central provisions of CPR Part 44 are as follows:

---

1 Overturning the effect of *Lownds v Home Office* [2002] 1 WLR 2450.
2 See the definition of proportionality in CPR 44.2(5) as introduced by the Civil Procedure (Amendment) Rules 2013.

'44.2 (1) The court has discretion as to:

(a) whether costs are payable by one party to another;

(b) the amount of those costs; and

(c) when they are to be paid.

(2) If the court decides to make an order about costs:

(a) the general rule is that the unsuccessful party will be ordered to pay the costs of the successful party; but

(b) the court may make a different order ...

(4) In deciding what order (if any) to make about costs, the court must have regard to all the circumstances, including:

(a) the conduct of all the parties;

(b) whether a party has succeeded on part of its case, even if that party has not been wholly successful;

(c) any admissible offer to settle made by a party which is drawn to the court's attention, and which is not an offer to which costs consequences under Part 36 apply.

(5) The conduct of the parties includes:

(a) conduct before, as well as during the proceedings and in particular the extent to which the parties followed the Practice Direction – Pre-Action Conduct or any relevant pre-action protocol;

(b) whether it was reasonable for a party to raise, pursue or contest a particular allegation or issue;

(c) the manner in which a party has pursued or defended its case or a particular allegation or issue; and

(d) whether a claimant who has succeeded in the claim, in whole or in part, exaggerated its claim'[3].

Since the CPR, the courts have in practice frequently made orders departing from the traditional rule that the costs follow the event. The leading case in relation to mediation is *Dunnett v Railtrack*[4], where a successful appellant was refused costs for declining mediation recommended by the court. However, there are many instances of cases which have nothing to

---

3 This provision was renumbered as CPR 44.2 in 2013. Prior to this, it was CPR 44.3, and was referred to as such in many pre-2013 judgments. The pre-April 2013 version of CPR 44.3(4) (c) also made reference to payments into court: these have now been abolished.

4 See **Chapter 6**; and also see the discussion in *Burchell v Bullard* [2005] EWCA Civ 358.

do with mediation where the judge has exercised discretion against parties who had apparently won, yet did not obtain all their costs[5]; or where an offer on Part 36 was not beaten, and yet the defendant did not secure the traditional consequences of victory[6]. Certainty over costs outcomes has been further eroded by the concept of proportionality, which can be used to disallow costs on the standard basis which are found to be disproportionate to the matters in issue. There is however little evidence of widespread disallowance of standard basis costs by costs judges as being disproportionate. While there is little published evidence of costs sanctions being imposed because of unreasonable litigation conduct before issue of proceedings, whether for failure to observe the Pre-action Protocols or otherwise, the Court of Appeal in *Burchell v Bullard*[7] indicates that such powers are there and may be exercised.

The result of this flexibility of approach in making costs orders has been a considerable degree of unpredictability about costs outcomes, something which mediators might test out during the mediation process, where there is a possibility that a party might not recover all their costs as a result of perhaps unreasonable or extravagantly conducted litigation.

11.3 Transferring the potential costs burden in any case: CPR Part 36

As seen in **Chapter 4**, Part 36 of the CPR enlarged the possibilities for parties to encourage settlement of proceedings by imposing significant costs penalties on parties who fail to improve on a formal offer to settle made by their opponent. It has always been clear that a mechanism was needed to enable defendants to settle and avoid adverse costs consequences in cases where they feared that they could not escape liability to pay damages or having to deliver some other remedy. So under the old Rules of the Supreme Court, a defendant could always pay a sum into court offering it in settlement of the claim. Since the CPR, if a *defendant* makes a written offer to settle for a certain sum (no longer having to pay it into court) or on other non-monetary terms, giving the claimant 21 days to accept it, the claimant must decide within that time whether to accept or reject that offer. If accepted, the claim is concluded on the terms set out in the offer, and the claimant is also automatically entitled to costs of the claim on the standard basis up to acceptance. If the claimant rejects the terms of the offer and does better than that offer at trial, he will normally receive at least standard basis costs for the whole claim, or even (if the defendant's conduct of the case is open to criticism) indemnity basis costs. If, however,

---

5 Eg *Mars v Teknowledge* (1999) TLR, 8 July.
6 Eg *Ford v GKR Construction Ltd* [2000] 1 All ER 802.
7 [2005] EWCA Civ 358.

the claimant fails to obtain judgment on terms better than those formally proposed in the defendant's Part 36 offer, he may well only be granted costs up to the date of that offer, and be ordered to pay both (or all other) parties' costs from the date of that offer to the end of the trial. In such a circumstance, whatever lesser sum of damages is awarded will be available to offset the claimant's costs liability to the defendant. If the claimant loses altogether, he will face a judgment for the defendant's costs and be liable to his own legal team for their costs, unless he and his solicitor entered into a funding arrangement under which the solicitor (and often the barrister) agreed not to charge his client any costs unless the claim was won. This is fully discussed in **Chapter 12**. If the defendants fail to pay the offered sum within 14 days of acceptance of the offer, judgment may be entered for the unpaid sum and Part 36 costs protection will be lost[8].

In 1999, CPR Part 36 introduced for the first time the right for *claimants* to make offers to settle. A claimant may serve a written offer to settle on specified terms on the defendant, usually somewhat less than the full amount of the claim, indicating perhaps acceptance of a measure of litigation risk. If the defendant agrees to settle on that basis within 21 days, again the claim is ended on those terms plus standard basis costs payable by defendant to claimant. If the claimant does better than his own Part 36 offer at trial, he may be awarded indemnity costs and interest at a penal rate of up to 10% above base rate on such damages and costs and for such period as the court may order[9].

Part 36 offers can be made by any party either before or after issue of proceedings, normally having exactly the same consequences. So if one party fails to beat a Part 36 offer made by the other before proceedings are issued, the unsuccessful party can in theory have to bear both sides' costs for the whole of the litigation as from the date that the offer should have been accepted. Any Part 36 offer remains open for acceptance so long as it is not formally withdrawn, and can continue to have an influence on a final costs judgment. Additionally, more than one Part 36 offer can be made by the same party, any of which can influence the costs order made at trial. For instance, if a defendant made Part 36 offers of £8,000 one year before trial and £15,000 a month before trial, and the claimant was awarded £20,000 by the judge, all standard basis costs would be payable by the defendant. If however the claimant was awarded £10,000, beating the first but not the second offer, the defendant would have to pay the claimant's costs up to shortly before trial, but the claimant would be liable for the defendant's costs of the trial (often very substantial). If the claimant was awarded merely £5,000, the defendant would be entitled to standard

---

8 See CPR 44th amendment, effective from 6 April 2007.
9 Plus a bonus of 10% if the claimant's Part 36 offer is less than the judgment (see p 237).

basis costs from a year before trial, and only be liable for the claimant's costs up to making the first Part 36 offer.

A trial judge must not be told of the fact or terms of any Part 36 offer until after judgment has been given on the substantive issues at trial, neither may the Court of Appeal be given this information. This is to ensure that when assessing the substantive issues in a trial or appeal, judges are not in any way swayed by the knowledge that a certain award would or would not beat a Part 36 offer and thus have costs consequences.

Part 36 thus creates incentives to settle by allowing proposals to be made without prejudice except as to costs, which, if refused, can shift or increase liability for the costs of the claim. Part 36 procedure allows a claimant or defendant to concede confidentially that they may not win wholly and protect themselves from liability for the cost of unreasonably prolonged litigation.

In *Painting v University of Oxford*[10], the claimant was filmed doing far more than she claimed to medical experts that she was capable of. The defendants successfully sought to reduce their Part 36 offer (in those days also paid into court) from £185,000 to £10,000. The judge (ignorant of both offers when he made his damages assessment) found that the claimant had seriously exaggerated her symptoms and awarded her £23,000 plus costs. On the defendants' appeal, the Court of Appeal found that as the claimant had both been found to have exaggerated and to have refused to negotiate, she should only receive her costs up to the Part 36 offer and should pay both sides' costs thereafter, despite having beaten even the reduced Part 36 offer. This case serves as a reminder of the overall discretionary powers of the court under CPR 44.3 to punish unreasonable conduct and exaggerated claims.

Widlake v BAA acts as a counterweight to *Painting.* Here the claimant reduced her claim from £145,000 to about £35,000 shortly before trial. She was said to have concealed symptoms from medical experts and was filmed behaving normally. The defendants made a Part 36 offer of £4,500 and the claimant was awarded £5,800 plus costs up to the Part 36 offer, but ordered her to pay the defendants costs thereafter. The Court of Appeal said that in a personal injury claim the winner is normally the party who gets money and beats a Part 36 offer, subject to adjustment for a finding of exaggeration. Here the claimant had wisely reduced her claim before trial, unlike Mrs Painting, though she made no counter-offer to the Part 36 offer. Ward LJ commented:

---

10 [2005] EWCA Civ 161.

'Part 36 now also affects a claimant. Whilst not obliged to make a counter-offer, in this day and age of encouraging settlement, claimants who do not do so run the risk that their refusal will impact upon the costs they may otherwise be entitled to recover. Here there was no attempt to negotiate and that counts against the claimant'.

In the much criticised case of *Carver v BAA*[11], the Court of Appeal found that to beat a declined Part 36 offer of £4,250 by £51 should again justify an adverse costs award because the claimant's decision to continue litigation had produced no worthwhile additional benefit, founding that decision on the on-going stress of litigation for little material reward. This decision was specifically reversed by rule amendment on the recommendation of Jackson LJ in CPR 36.14(1), which requires a claimant:

'to obtain a judgment more advantageous than a defendant's Part 36 offer'.

Rule 1(A), inserted in October 2012 to reverse the effect of *Carver,* makes it clear that for these purposes:

'In relation to any money claim or money element of any claim, "more advantageous" means better in money terms by any amount however small'.

A further change has been made to CPR Part 36 by the 2013 amendments to the CPR. A claimant who makes a Part 36 offer which the defendant does not beat is now entitled to receive an additional 10% to the sum awarded to the claimant in any money claim, or (in a non-monetary claim) a 10% uplift on the costs award. The 10% on each of those uplifts is on the first £500,000, reducing to 5% on the next £500,000 with a ceiling of £75,000. There is no corresponding reward for a defendant whose Part 36 offer is not beaten by the claimant.

Defendants are sometimes reluctant to make offers under Part 36, because if they are accepted, there is an automatic entitlement to standard basis costs, plus any success fee and ATE premium which might ride on a 'win' for the claimant if proceedings were brought between 1999 and April 2013, when such recoverability was possible. Courts may still take non-Part 36 offers into account when deciding what costs to award. CPR 44.2(4), as amended in 2013, provides that:

---

11 [2008] EWCA Civ 412.

'in deciding what order (if any) to make about costs, the court must have regard to all the circumstances, including:

(a) the conduct of all the parties;

(b) whether a party has succeeded on part of its case, even if that party has not been wholly successful; and

(c) any admissible offer to settle made by a party which is drawn to the court's attention, and which is not an offer to which costs consequences under Part 36 apply'.

Such offers are made 'without prejudice save as to costs', and were origi-nally approved by the matrimonial case of *Calderbank v Calderbank*[12]. These may seek to limit the costs that a defendant is prepared to bear in the event of acceptance of the offer made on substantive issues. Such offers may even be taken into account where they are withdrawn before trial, if the court decides that they should have been accepted while live[13].

11.4 Qualified one way costs shifting in injury claims

A major change was made in April 2013 to the normal costs consequences of conducting actions in which damages for personal injury, death or dependency following death are claimed, that is personal injury and clini-cal negligence claims (together called 'injury claims' here for ease of ref-erence). Sir Rupert Jackson perceived that in this claims sector, costs were being hugely escalated by the way they were funded on conditional fee agreements (CFAs), permitting recovery from defendants not only the success fee to which solicitor and barrister were entitled under the CFA, but also the insurance premium paid by the claimant for an 'after-the-event' (ATE) insurance policy to protect the claimant against potential liability for the defendant's costs if the claim were lost. This mechanism is explained further in **Chapter 12**. Suffice it to say here that he recom-mended a return to the pre-1999 costs and funding regime, in which any success fees and insurance premiums of this type could only be recovered from the claimant, usually from damages. He offered two benefits by way of compensation to the aggrieved claimant lobby: one, the increase of dam-ages for pain and suffering across the board by 10% and also, two, deprived defendants of the right to claim costs if they defeated a claim, other than in exceptional circumstances. So the general rule is that in injury claims only, a claimant who wins is awarded standard basis costs (subject to the opera-tion of Part 36, which is discussed below), but a defendant who defeats a

---

12 [1976] Fam 93, CA.

13 *Stokes v Western Power* [2005] EWCA Civ 854. For a case where the court refused to apply Part 36 costs consequences by analogy, see *F&C Alternative Investments v Barthelemy* [2012] EWCA Civ 843.

claim is no longer entitled to shift the costs burden back to the claimant. As ATE policies were only needed to protect claimants from liability for the defendant's costs if the claim was lost, such policies would be largely unnecessary if claimants were freed from facing such a liability. So this reform, which **only** applies to injury claims, created what has been called 'one way costs shifting', rather than the norm of two way costs shifting (ie in either direction between litigation parties) which still applies to all other kinds of litigation in this jurisdiction.

Things are never quite that simple, as the name 'qualified one-way costs shifting' (QOCS) suggests. There are exceptions to this concept. The mechanism of doing so is quite interesting and subtle, and needs to be understood by those wanting to appreciate the impact this might have on using and refusing mediation. The way it is done is not by specifically preventing the making of costs orders against claimants in certain circumstances, but by specifying that it is the amount of damages and interest awarded to a claimant which sets the limit as to what costs can ever be recovered from that claimant by a defendant. So if a claimant loses altogether, there are no damages and interest on which a defendant could levy a costs award. If a claimant fails to beat a Part 36 offer made by the defendant, the defendant can only levy a costs award up to the damages and interest actually awarded to the claimant, but cannot deduct costs against the sum representing the claimant's costs up to the Part 36 offer, which are still payable to the claimant for his legal adviser's costs.

This mechanism enables the courts to apply the ordinary principles for costs in any case, whether the case be discontinued by the claimant, or settled under Part 36, or decided at trial. How this works in practice can best be appreciated by looking at a number of examples, in each case assuming that the standard basis applies to any costs award:

- The claimant C discontinues after issue of proceedings on the basis of no damages being payable: in non-injury cases a claimant is automatically liable for the defendant's standard basis costs[14], but under QOCS, as C gets no damages or interest, the defendant D cannot recover costs, to which D would have been entitled before the rule change, in the absence of agreement to the contrary;

- C accepts a Part 36 offer before trial, and thus is entitled to costs under Part 36;

- C goes to trial and wins, beating any defendant Part 36 offer made by D: D (normally) pays damages and C's costs;

---

14 Under CPR Part 38.6, unless a court orders otherwise.

- C goes to trial having made a claimant's Part 36 offer of £100,000, which D refuses: the judge awards £120,000 damages and interest plus £80,000 costs: D must pay that sum plus costs, plus a penalty of £2,000, being 10% of £200,000;

- C goes to trial after D has made a Part 36 offer of £50,000 one year before trial: without finding any exaggeration or unreasonable conduct on C's part, the judge awards C £25,000 damages and interest: C would notionally receive £25,000 plus costs up to the Part 36 offer: D would be (normally) entitled to costs from 21 days after the offer until the end of the trial. D may now deduct any costs awarded to D from C's damages and interest, capped at £25,000, with any balance of damages exceeding D's costs award being paid to C. C receives costs up to the Part 36 offer a year before trial. C's costs for the period after the Part 36 offer are a matter between C and C's solicitor, dependent on the way C's claim was funded. Failing to beat a Part 36 offer on the advice of the solicitor will probably disqualify C's lawyers from receiving any costs for the period after failing to accept the Part 36 offer. If C refused to accept legal advice to accept a Part 36 offer, this should lead to the ending of the funding arrangement and insurance cover at that point;

- C goes to trial and beats D's Part 36 offer by a small amount, having claimed an exaggerated amount and having been found by the judge to have exaggerated. The judge may deprive C of costs (as he did in *Painting v University of Oxford*) despite this theoretical win. D will get costs, but these will be capped at the amount of the damages and interest awarded to C.

There are some defined circumstances when a claimant loses costs protection completely. If a case is **struck out** on the grounds that C has no reasonable grounds for bringing the proceedings, or are found to be an abuse of process; or the conduct of C or C's representative (presumably usually C's lawyer), any costs order can be enforced without permission or limit. Note that the court has to have struck the proceedings out, and the necessary grounds require an actual finding by a judge, not merely a strike-out by operation of law, eg for not paying a required fee. It would seem that a mere finding by the judge that the claimant has exaggerated will not of itself remove the cap if there was no formal strike-out by a judge, unless the defendant persuades the judge to remove the next discretionary ground set out in the following paragraph.

A court **may** give permission for full costs recovery without limit where:

- a claim is found on the balance of probabilities (so less than the usual fraud standard) **fundamentally dishonest** (perhaps this would be used in a *Painting*-type situation); or

– a claim is made or included which is made for the benefit of another (excluding claims for gratuitous care services, recovery of an earnings loaned by an employer or medical expenses (such as under a private health policy) on condition of repayment. Such costs will be ordered if it is just to do so. Also the court is given power to award costs against that kind of litigation beneficiary.

11.5 The impact of Part 36 and QOCS on mediations

Part 36 offers frequently precede mediations and, where a mediated settlement does not emerge, will frequently be made or increased shortly afterwards, based on reappraisal of risks made during the mediation process. Where a Part 36 offer was made but rejected before a mediation, the party who made the offer may argue at the mediation that the party who declined it remains at risk on costs, warning the other party during the mediation that the Part 36 offer remains at a challenging level if settlement is not achieved. Occasionally a mediation leads to settlement on the agreed basis that an earlier Part 36 offer is accepted now out of time, with some compromise agreed on costs since the date of that offer. This has to be done by mutual agreement. A party who does not accept an unwithdrawn Part 36 proposal within the 21 days following the offer can always accept it out of time without needing permission from the court any more, but they will normally be liable for the other party's costs during the intervening period in the absence of agreement to the contrary.

Although the court is never told of Part 36 offers before making the substantive decision about a case, no such secrecy need be used with a mediator, as the mediator makes no judgments. A mediator should always enquire what, if any, Part 36 offers to settle have been made by any party before the mediation. Nothing is likelier to inflame negotiations than a mediator unwittingly conveying a lower offer than that party proposed before the mediation by a Part 36 offer or otherwise.

A mediation of an injury claim to which QOCS means that there will almost never be a dispute as to the defendant's having to bear their own costs and probably the claimant's costs. With CFAs entered into before 1 April 2013, there will still be disputes as to how much the defendant should pay for the claimant's base costs, plus any success fee and ATE premium. It is very unlikely that any exceptions to QOCS will arise (such as fundamentally fraudulent claims: very occasionally defendants choose the mediation to ambush a malingering claimant with film showing lack of disability, but this is very rare). The likeliest scenario for such a possibility is where a mediation leads a claimant to contemplate accepting a figure less than an earlier Part 36 offer, giving rise to a damages fund which the defendant can argue is capable of bearing the defence costs since the offer was made. The parties will be free to negotiate a settlement in the light of the risks that a trial judge will award a worse outcome.

11.6   The status of the 'costs of the mediation' and 'mediation fees'

It will be remembered that 'costs of the mediation' and 'mediation fees' were distinguished as part of the costs of the claim[15]. Having now given an outline of how costs and funding work, this chapter now examines how these fit into the costs regime.

Lawyers can incur appreciable costs in relation to a mediation. Thorough preparation is required, both of the client and in assembling the necessary paperwork and arguments. A case summary is usually needed to set out each party's position or alternatively a jointly drafted summary is circulated for all to agree and use. Counsel may be briefed to attend, and preparation falls only a little short of what is needed for trial, though the informality of the mediation process enables a rather less perfectionist approach to document bundles.

This is rarely wasted work if the mediation does not give rise to final settlement. But attendance at the mediation may involve anything from six hours upwards, and some mediations last for more than 12 hours. Whether the mediation fails or succeeds in engendering settlement, the work done in attending the mediation gives rise to very substantial legal costs. Are these recoverable?

This question needs to be considered before the mediation, as the wording of the mediation agreement is vital to the way costs may be treated later, whether the case settles or not at the mediation. In commercial cases, it has long been the tradition to provide that the mediation fees are shared equally between the parties, and that each party bears their own costs of the mediation, whatever the outcome of the mediation. Often this may be exactly what the parties wish, especially in a commercial dispute where the privacy of the process and its outcome may outweigh other considerations, and where there may be a rough equivalence of negotiating strength. But in claims by individuals against corporations such as insurance companies, banks, and government departments – embracing personal injury, clinical negligence, professional indemnity claims and many other types of claim – a successful claimant will normally expect to recover costs in the event of a favourable settlement. If this is accepted by

---

15 See **11.1** above.

both parties before the mediation, it is prudent to amend the terms of the mediation agreement providing for equal sharing of the mediation fees and each party bearing their own costs of the mediation, by making both heads of outlay 'costs in the claim'. This will mean that liability for these will be regarded as falling on whoever is liable for the costs of the claim generally. Parties are free to debate and agree such matters at the mediation, but in default of agreement to the contrary, the equal share/bearing own costs provisions will bind the parties and no court will have power to go behind that agreement.

This matters, whether the mediation leads to settlement of the claim or not. When the subject of legal costs arises at a mediation, quite often the parties will agree a set figure for costs, or agree a global figure for compensation and costs, leaving client and lawyer to allocate the gross sum between them. If, however, a firm costs figure cannot be agreed, the parties will usually provide in the settlement agreement that one party's costs 'will be paid on the standard basis, subject to detailed assessment if not agreed'. Thereafter the lawyers for each party will try to agree a figure, with the option of commencing detailed assessment proceedings within three months of the agreement or the court order[16]. If agreement cannot be reached, the court will be bound by the default costs provisions in the mediation agreement, and neither the mediation fees nor the costs of the mediation will be regarded as costs in the case disposable by the costs judge. The same considerations apply if the mediation fails to settle the claim. Unless the parties have agreed that the mediation fees and the costs of the mediation are to be regarded as costs in the case, liability for these outlays will not follow the event but be governed by the overriding terms of the mediation agreement.

In *Brawley v Marczinski*[17], a mediation did not settle costs questions in a patent dispute. The judge who tried the issue ordered indemnity costs against the defendant, who appealed. The Court of Appeal held that there was no rule that 'no order as to costs' was the norm where proceedings were compromised. Costs had been properly awarded against the defendants.

These questions were considered by Master Campbell in the Supreme Court Costs Office in *National Westminster Bank plc v Feeney and Feeney*[18], a possession action resolved by a Tomlin Order agreed at mediation. The consent order provided for detailed assessment. The defendants sought

---

16 It would seem that the costs judge will be able to reduce costs on the grounds of reasonableness and/or proportionality: see *Finster v Arriva London and Booth* (11 December 2006, unreported), SCCO.

17 [2002] EWCA Civ 756.

18 [2006] EWHC 90066 (Costs) SCCO.

to argue that the costs of the mediation and the mediation fees were to be included in the costs of the action. The Master held that they were both capable of being treated as such, as being *'work done in connection with negotiations with a view to settlement'*. However, the mediation agreement was not silent about this: it provided that each party should bear their own costs of preparation and attendance at the mediation, and for the mediator's and provider's fees to be shared. The Master held that the parties' agreement over the costs of the mediation was paramount, and the later Tomlin Order did not alter that agreement. However, on reflection he regarded the mediation fees as recoverable as costs of the action, as the parties agreed that they should be borne equally.

11.7   Costs of pre-issue and post-issue mediations

Mediation before issue of proceedings is slowly increasing in popularity and the 2013 amendments to the CPR might well make it more popular. What of the costs of proceedings and the costs of mediation in the absence of mutual agreement in such cases? The normal rule is that defendants cannot recover costs from a claimant who discontinues a claim if it is never issued. Nor does a claimant have an automatic right to pre-issue costs where a claim is settled before issue of proceedings, The claimant must make payment of costs a condition of the terms of settlement in such cases. This question was considered in two cases in the Technology and Construction Court.

In *Lobster Group v (1) Heidelberg Graphic Equipment (2) Close Asset Management*[19] C sued D1 and D2 for losses from alleged defects in a printing machine supplied by D1 and financed by D2. D1 and D2 sought security for costs after a pre-issue mediation, for which each party agreed to bear their own costs and share mediator fees, but which did not generate settlement. The judge held that although security for costs could be ordered for pre-issue costs, security would not be ordered to include the mediation costs, in view of the agreement to bear their own costs.

In *Roundstone Nurseries Ltd v Stephenson Holdings Ltd*[20], D built a concrete floor slab for C. There was a dispute as to whether D was liable for the defects or a sub-contractor E who was not sued as such by C. Delays for mediation were sought and granted, but it never proceeded because D refused to come unless E was there. C without warning entered judgment in default of defence. The judge decided that the costs of preparing for the abandoned pre-issue mediation, to be held in accordance with the Construction and Engineering Pre-action Protocol, were recoverable as costs

---

19 [2008] EWHC 413 (TCC).
20 [2009] EWHC 1431 (TCC).

in the action, payable on the standard basis by D who should not have cancelled the mediation on short notice. It therefore seems that a mediation held because of the obligations to consider settlement before the issue of proceedings will generally be recoverable as costs in the case[21].

11.8 Practical considerations for mediators on costs issues

It is hoped that the above outline will have equipped mediators and others at mediations with a number of ideas as to how the complex issue of costs can arise and might be handled. The following points summarise the key steps to be taken:

1 **Before the mediation:**

- unless it is obvious, the way each party is funding a case needs to be clarified: parties operating under a CFA will not be likely to disclose to an opponent the actual percentage success fee or level of AEI premium, but they are under a duty to disclose to other parties the existence and general nature of a funding arrangement, and may be prepared to disclose details confidentially to the mediator;

- the mediator should be given details of any Part 36 offers made by any party, and any earlier costs orders on interim hearings;

- all parties should bring a reasonably accurate summary of their costs of the claim to date to the mediation, preferably apportioned before and after any material Part 36 offer, and also a projection of costs of the claim from the mediation date to the end of trial;

- parties should decide whether they wish to provide that the costs of the mediation and the mediation fees be shared; borne by each party in any event; or be treated as costs in the case.

2 **At the mediation,** the mediator must ensure that the issue of costs is discussed, and preferably agreed at a precise figure or by inclusion in a global settlement figure. Such matters as reasonableness and proportionality may arise, both as to the base costs and also the success fee and (if any) the level of insurance premium.

---

21 This is also supported by part of the decision in *Chantry Vellacott v The Convergence Group* [2007] EWHC 1774 (Ch) which is hard to reconcile with *Lobster v Heidelberg.*

3 **Failing agreement at the mediation** as to the precise figure for costs, the settlement agreement should probably provide that costs will be paid 'on the standard basis subject to detailed assessment if not agreed'. The receiving party needs advice from their lawyer as to what (if anything) might be deducted from the damages to reflect the difference between standard basis costs and what the solicitor is entitled to charge his client, or (if in receipt of LSC funding) how much might be caught by the statutory charge.

4 **Costs of the mediation:** Another balancing mechanism relates to the way mediation fees and the legal costs of attending the mediation are allocated. Until recently, the usual default position under English mediation agreements was that parties shared the fees of the mediator and provider equally, and bore their own legal costs of preparing and attending the mediation. This could indeed give rise to anger when confronted with a party being unreasonable behind the curtain of privilege, giving rise to irrecoverable expense for the party who mediated in good faith. Cases on whether mediation costs are costs in the case have fallen on both sides of the line[22], so proper balance needs to be established.

To meet this concern against unreasonable exposure to wasted costs, CEDR has made it a standard term in its agreement that at any later stage of the dispute (whether the mediation did or did not settle the dispute) the mediation fees and the associated legal costs of preparation and attendance are to be treated as costs in the case and thus in the gift of the judge in default of agreement. This may mean that there is less need to disclose what happened at the mediation to establish unreasonable conduct, as it is highly unlikely that an unreasonable party will confine their unreasonableness to time of privilege. They may make a ridiculous Part 36 offer immediately after it, which the judge will be able to note and penalise in the ordinary course. The only difficulty will be if the mistreated party settles as a result of the unreasonable pressure brought to bear, as unless a case comes before a judge to award costs, there is no forum to challenge unreasonableness, so a wronged party needs to be brave about continuing to a hearing. This could well be an area for a standard position to be set by law, although always open to the parties to amend it by written variation.

Another less obvious but significant advantage of conferring the status of 'costs in the case' on mediation fees and associated legal costs is to

---

22 See *Natwest Bank v Feeney* and *Lobster Holdings v Heidelberg Graphic Equipment*, as contrasted with Rimer J's decision in which on this point appear irreconcileable, and *Roundstone Nurseries v Stephenson Holdings,* all discussed above in **11.6** and **11.7**.

import the concept of proportionality into such matters. Large legal teams are on the whole an unnecessary luxury at a mediation of all but the very heaviest of cases, and a degree of control over such over-manning might be able to develop so as to ensure that mediation does not itself become over-burdened by expense.

Chapter 12

Litigation funding and mediation

Successful parties in an English lawsuit will want to recover as much of their costs outlay (in other words, their funding commitment to their own lawyers) from the unsuccessful party as they can. This contrasts sharply with many US and other jurisdictions where each party funds their own litigation, win or lose, with little if any risk of being ordered to pay the other side's costs if the case is lost. Even in the UK this arises in some sectors, such as in employment tribunals, which rarely award costs against one or other party. The extent to which funding recovery is possible often relates to the funding mechanism employed. Such mechanisms have changed dramatically in a number of ways over the last 20 years. As the extent to which someone in a mediation can recover their costs will be a considerable concern for them, it is wise for mediators to have some understanding of the mechanics of funding so that they can help parties face the realities of their position and decide whether their wisest course is to choose the certainty of settlement over the hazards and cost of continuing litigation. For them to be able to choose to litigate, they must be able to fund that litigation. Any constraints on their ability to afford to do so will form part of every party's risk assessment over whatever settlement terms emerge at a mediation.

Funding is a complex topic and this chapter seeks to do no more than explain the broad structures and vocabulary in this thorny area, and give an overview of the issues as they may arise for mediators.

12.1   Normal funding

The simplest arrangement is where each client contracts to pay their own solicitor's costs plus other outlays (such as expert's fee, court fees and counsel's fees and all relevant VAT) of the claim, usually on an agreed hourly rate or sometimes a fixed fee. Every solicitor is required by the Solicitors Regulation Authority's Code of Conduct 2011[1] to give 'best advice' to clients and to adopt a new outcomes-based approach which specifies that solicitors must:

---

1 SRA Code of Conduct 2011, Version 7, available at www.sra.org.uk.

'only enter into fee agreements with your clients that are legal, and which you consider are suitable for the client's needs and take account of the client's best interests'.

What are called 'indicative behaviours' aimed at achieving the above outcome include:

- IB(1.3): ensuring that the client is told, in writing, the name and status of the person(s) dealing with the matter and the name and status of the person responsible for its overall supervision;

- IB(1.4): explaining any arrangements, such as fee sharing or referral arrangements, which are relevant to the client's instructions;

- IB(1.5): explaining any limitations or conditions on what you can do for the client, for example, because of the way the client's matter is funded.

The rate or fee may vary for different parts of a piece of litigation and may be the same whether the case is won or lost. There may be an agreed discount from the normal rate if the case is not won. Both sides will normally operate on this basis in commercial claims. At the conclusion of the case, whether ended by trial, acceptance of a Part 36 in due time or settlement, both parties will be liable to pay their lawyer's costs of the claim in full on that agreed basis, but the successful party will hope to recover a large proportion of those costs from the unsuccessful party. If the court orders that costs are recoverable on the standard basis, then the successful party will almost certainly still have to pay a proportion of his own lawyer's costs of the claim. If an indemnity costs order has been secured against the unsuccessful party, then the successful party may well recover virtually their whole costs liability. Where a claim is merely discontinued, the claimant will normally be liable to pay the defendant's costs of the claim on the standard basis. Costs awards may be moderated if a successful or partly successful party is thought by the judge not to deserve the full percentage due to him on the standard basis. If a party lost on one issue which occupied court time, but won overall, the court may only award a percentage of standard basis costs. This is discussed more fully in **Chapter 11**.

One important legal concept that has at times complicated and indeed even frequently defeated the recovery of costs even when awarded is the *indemnity principle*. Put simply, it means that a party who is awarded costs can recover from a losing party no more than he was contractually obliged to pay to his own lawyers for the worst outcome. This was particularly important before the concept of 'no-win, no-fee' became authorised by statute in 1995. It meant that if the terms of the winning party's lawyer's retainer (the contract for services between lawyer and client) provided that if the case were lost the client would not be charged, or were subject to an agreed cap, the losing party could escape having to pay, or only be liable for the capped limit. If the lawyer agreed a special rate with the client which was lower than the generally accepted hourly rates allowable on detailed assessment, then again the loser could limit their costs liability to the lower agreed rate and defeat any claim for costs at the normal local rate.

The rule has been subject both to criticism and to considerable statutory inroads. The first major exception was in Legal Aid cases, where a legally aided party has no obligation to pay their lawyer. Then the development of 'no-win, no-fee' in 1995 led to further statutory exceptions, since by definition in such cases a losing party funded by a conditional fee agreement (CFA) has no obligation to pay their lawyer.

The indemnity principle remains unabolished even after Jackson LJ's report continued the criticism (see **Chapter 13**). So at mediations it is not unheard of for a paying party to ask to see the winning party's letter of retainer to check that there are no terms in it which might modify the paying party's obligations to pay costs. It even remains in place in respect of damages-based costs (contingency fee) funding, adding considerable complication to that funding method.

12.2   Legal Aid funding

Legal Aid, both civil and criminal, has been run since 1 April 2013 by the Legal Aid Agency, an executive branch of the Ministry of Justice, which has subsumed the work of the Legal Services Commission which formerly ran the schemes. Full Legal Aid to conduct or defend proceedings is only available in very limited types of civil claim, and further restrictions on its availability were introduced in April 2013. Formerly it was available generally for clinical negligence claims but now it is virtually restricted to claims on behalf of children in respect of birth damage and high cost cases. The financial limits are set very low, so that relatively few people are financially eligible. Claims brought on behalf of children may well attract Legal Aid funding, as they are normally without means. Some claims will still have Legal Aid granted before 1 April 2013.

Where a claimant (or, rarely, a defendant) has Legal Aid funding for a claim to be brought or defended, that party will normally be protected from any adverse costs order against the opposing party even if he loses or fails to beat a Part 36 offer. When a Part 36 offer is made, however, or evidence emerges which casts doubt on the assisted person's prospects of success, his legal advisers are obliged to report such matters to the Legal

Aid Agency, who may withdraw funding if it seems no longer reasonable to continue it. Occasionally defendants will draw the Agency's attention to such matters themselves by direct correspondence.

Where Legal Aid funding is intact, this costs protection puts an assisted party in a powerful negotiating position at a mediation, since they face no adverse costs consequences if they lose. Defendants may be inclined to propose settlement even if they have a strong defence, as they face having to bear their own costs even if they win. If the Legally Aided party wins, he will usually be entitled to an order for standard basis costs. If his solicitor is entitled to charge the assisted person for work done but cannot recover for that work as standard basis costs (for instance, where the defendant obtained a costs order against the claimant on an interim application), those irrecoverable costs will be deductible from the claimant's damages under what is termed the 'statutory charge'. Legally Aided parties will therefore always seek to recover the maximum for costs at a mediation in order to minimise the impact of the statutory charge on agreed damages.

The statutory charge takes on greater significance if the Legally Aided party loses to any extent. If, for instance, a Legally Aided party is allowed to continue a claim after a Part 36 offer has been made, but fails to beat that offer at trial, such reduced damages as were awarded will first be subject to the deduction of the defendant's costs since the Part 36 offer. They will then have the Legally Aided party's own solicitor's costs incurred since declining the Part 36 offer deducted by virtue of the statutory charge. This can seriously deplete or exhaust the damages fund, and can put pressure on a Legally Aided party to consider a compromise. If the case is lost altogether, with no damages available to reduce costs liability, the court will normally make a costs order 'not to be enforced without the court's permission'. So if the Legally Aided party receives a later financial windfall, the whole costs order might be successfully enforced later.

12.3 Legal expenses insurance ('Before the event' or BTE)

This is now one of the main funding methods for private litigants. Legal expenses insurance may be purchased as a stand-alone policy, or more usually it is offered or purchased as an additional form of cover with a household or motor insurance policy. In effect it indemnifies the policyholder against liability for any legal costs of any claim brought or defended by the insured, whether payable to his own solicitor or to any opposing solicitor, up to a pre-set limit which may be £50,000 or more. If the claim involves defending a claim arising from a motor accident, however, a driver will normally be represented by his motor insurer and his defence funded under the motor policy. The insurer will often require their own panel solicitor to represent the claimant. These policies are also called 'before-the-event' or BTE policies, as the insurer's obligation to provide an indemnity for costs arises before any claim has arisen.

Such an indemnity limit looks very substantial, but, with legal costs as high as they are, this can be rapidly expended on a substantial claim with complex and expensive evidential requirements. It must also be remembered that an opposing party can seek to transfer their costs liability by making a Part 36 offer. Insurers require close monitoring and reporting by the insured's solicitor of any offers to settle which might impinge on the costs liabilities of the parties, so as to ensure that the litigation still has acceptable prospects of success, and they are not at unacceptable risk of paying out costs to or on behalf of their insured.

If a claim funded by legal expenses insurance is lost, the insurer will be liable to pay both the insured's and the opponent's costs up to the indemnity limit under the policy, leaving the insured liable for any additional costs recoverable by the winning party unrecovered from the policy. Solicitors whose clients have to resort to their legal expenses policy to pay for representing the client may have to weigh their risks to their claims reputation or even their panel membership with that legal expenses insurer when considering recovery of their own costs.

Subject to the terms of any such policy, the lawyer acting for the insured will be paid whether the claim is won or lost. There is no element of 'no-win, no-fee' in such a funding arrangement. A defendant will be told that there is a BTE policy in place but will not know (or be entitled to know) the indemnity limit. This may affect a defendant's thinking when weighing the risks of settling or not. They may fear that if costs spiral, recovering costs from the claimant will be difficult even if they win.

12.4 Conditional fee agreements (CFAs) and 'After the event' (ATE) insurance

Conditional Fee Agreements (CFAs) were initially introduced in 1995 to make it possible for a wide range of claimants to seek compensation for road traffic accidents and clinical negligence claims, at a time when government policy was to reduce the cost and availability of Legal Aid for such claims. Their scope has now been widened to most types of claim, most notably commercial claims and defamation, and occasionally the defence of claims. The basic principle behind this type of funding[2] is that a claimant can instruct a solicitor to pursue or defend a claim regardless of means,

---

2 As set out in the Access to Justice Act 1999 but substantially amended by the Legal Aid Sentencing and Punishment of Offenders Act 2012 (known – and hated by many lawyers – as LASPO 2012).

knowing that broadly speaking he will not have to pay his solicitor's costs of the claim if the case is lost. This has given rise to the over-simple tag 'no-win, no-fee' for such arrangements. The solicitor therefore agrees to handle the case based on his risk assessment as to success. If he is wrong, he will carry out the work on the case without charge. But if he is right and his client wins, he becomes entitled to claim a 'success fee' of up to 100%[3]*of his normal base costs* on the case (and *not* a percentage of damages, which will be dealt with in the next section) from the unsuccessful defendant. The riskier the case, the higher will be the percentage mark-up sought. When first introduced, the success fee was borne out of the claimant's own damages, but the Access to Justice Act 1999[4] shifted the burden of success fees across to unsuccessful defendants, only for it to revert to being levied against the claimant's own damages again as from 1 April 2013, as will be seen below. Barristers too have been able to agree to act for clients on a conditional fee basis, so that if a case is lost, the claimant will have no liability for the fees of either his solicitor or his barrister. But there is no question of expert witnesses being able to be paid on a 'no-win, no-fee' basis.

However, if a claimant loses, or fails to beat a Part 36 offer and thus incurring some costs liability to the defendant, the mere existence of a CFA between claimant and his solicitor and barrister provides no protection against the defendant's claim for payment of costs, having defeated the claim. The claimant remains personally liable to pay any adverse costs order. However, it is possible for claimants to insure against potential liability for an opponent's costs in the event of losing the litigation. Such policies have come to be known as 'after the event' policies (ATE). This looks like a misnomer, but while they are of course taken out *after* the accident which led to the claim, they are put in place *before* the real insured event, which is the making of an adverse costs order at the end of the litigation. Premiums for such policies are rated in accordance with the likely costs to be incurred and the risks of failure. Rates can be very high indeed, especially in sectors where claims are hard to bring home successfully, such as clinical negligence.

A party who enters into a CFA must give notice of such a funding arrangement and also of the existence of a litigation protection policy as soon as it is signed or taken out[5]. No details of the percentage uplift or the premium level need be given, as this would disclose to the opposition the view as to risk taken by the claimant and his insurer. Funders of litigation for their members, such as trade unions, are entitled to enter into collective CFAs

---

3 But lower since April 2013 in injury and death claims: see p 256 for details.
4 By amending the Courts and Legal Services Act 1990, s 58(6), in turn replaced by LASPO 2012.
5 See generally CPR 44.3A still in force for pre-April 2013 CFAs.

with their members, and such CCFAs take similar effect to individual CFAs.

Such policies are not compulsory when entering into a CFA, and claims are occasionally run under a CFA without any such protection in place. This happened more before ATE premiums were recoverable from defendants, as premiums can be very substantial, so the temptation to save on that expense may arise again after April 2013. Indeed, the claimant in *Halsey v Milton Keynes General NHS Trust*[6], the leading case on mediation, is said to have had no ATE policy in place. A solicitor who advises a client to do without an ATE policy is seriously hazarding their client's resources. If there is no ATE insurance to protect against an adverse costs judgment, the claimant may risk bankruptcy if he loses, and the successful defendant then has to choose whether to enforce a costs judgment against an often indigent claimant's assets or abandon their costs recovery. So a 'no-win, no-fee' arrangement can lead to serious financial consequences if things go wrong. Another different risk for defendants arises where a claimant has concealed or failed to disclose a material fact to an ATE insurer in taking out the policy, entitling the insurer to void the policy and in effect leave the defendant without a practical costs remedy apart from the claimant. On detailed assessment by the court, a defendant can challenge the success fee percentage mark-up and/or the premium paid as being unreasonable.

The amount of success fees and ATE premiums being recovered by claimants grew enormously, especially in injury and death claims, and Jackson LJ's review of civil litigation costs (see **Chapter 13**) identified this as the prime cause of unacceptable costs escalation. Defendant insurers grumbled at the framework, but doubtless recovered their massively increased outlay from increasing insurance premiums to their general pool of insured policyholders, and motor premiums rocketed. This was of no comfort to the NHS, a major payer of claims in clinical negligence, with no resource other than health budgets to meet escalating claims costs. Jackson LJ took the view that the position should revert to what prevailed between 1995 and 1999, under which success fees and ATE premiums (less common in those days) should, subject to certain limits, be borne by the party who had entered into the CFA and ATE insurance. The reversal of the 1999 provisions was made by the Legal Aid Sentencing and Punishment of Offenders Act 2012 (LASPO 2012) and took effect from 1 April 2013. However, very large numbers of CFAs and ATE policies supporting them were, unsurprisingly, taken out in early 2013 leading up to the change in law, so that a considerable amount of litigation will be conducted under the previous funding rules for some years to come.

---

6 [2004] EWCA Civ 576.

As part of the same review, Jackson LJ also recommended the abolition of referral fees paid by solicitors to insurers and motoring organisations to buy tranches of claims to conduct, and this too was enacted. He regarded as unacceptable the combination of recoverable success fees, ATE premiums, together with claimant solicitors seeking to recover the cost of paying referral fees to buy caseloads from motor insurers, free to receive a substantial income stream from such referral fees, coupled with freedom to increase policy premiums to cover the cost of success fees and ATE premiums, with its consequence (as he saw it) of seriously overheating the costs of accident litigation. The contrary argument deployed was that CFAs afford ready access to justice for all, and that recoverability of success fees and ATE premiums preserved claimants from having unwarranted costs deductions made from their damages, which were calculated to restore them to the position they would have been in had they not suffered a compensable injury. The policy decision was, however, made to implement the approach recommended by Jackson LJ.

Thus for CFA funding arrangements entered into after 1 April 2013, success fees by way of a percentage uplift enhancing a solicitor's base costs cannot be recovered from another party, nor can ATE premiums be recovered. There are few, probably temporary, exceptions: privacy defamation and insolvency claims and claims arising from mesothelioma, and expert fees payable under an ATE policy in clinical negligence claims only remain recoverable from the defendant. Success fees can be charged to the party entering into the CFA, when they will normally come off the damages payable (as by definition the claimant has 'won'). There are limits imposed on success fees in different types of case. In injury and death claims, while the success fee can be up to 100% of base costs, it may not exceed 25% of damages for pain and suffering and past pecuniary losses, after repayment of state benefits. Thus, if a claimant is awarded £15,000 damages for pain and suffering and £25,000 loss of past earnings, of which £5,000 has to be repaid as recoupment of State Benefits, and £100,000 for future losses, the ceiling for success fee will be 25% of £35,000, or £8,750. The claimant's solicitors might well expect to incur £30,000 costs in a case of this size, so the cap will reduce the notional success fee by over £21,000. In all other cases, there is simply a limit of 100% on the success fee, with no percentage cap.

These requirements might well influence lawyers to advise early settlement, as much of the incentive to earn higher costs has gone. There is also potential for apparent, if not actual, conflict between lawyers and their clients during a mediation, even risking a sub-mediation over proffered settlement terms. This will arise equally in relation to funding by the next discussed mechanism and is discussed fully in section **12.5** below.

As QOCS applies to injury and death claims funded by CFA-type funding arrangements made on or after 1 April 2013, no discussion of defendant

256

liability for success fee or ATE premium will arise at mediations of such cases. There may still be a market for ATE insurance to protect claimants from liability for failing to beat Part 36 offers and thus risking the deduction of defendant costs from such damages as they recover. Doubtless such policies will only be issued under very carefully controlled supervision by insurers. But it is too early to discern likely trends, and there are thousands of cases to be settled under the old Rules over coming years.

In large-scale commercial litigation, both claimants and defendants have utilised CFAs with or without ATE insurance, often in the form of discounted CFAs, under which a proportion of costs are paid as normal solicitor and client costs, and a smaller proportion is subject to a success fee.

12.5 Damages-based agreements and contingency fee funding

Though commonplace in the US, contingency fees involving remuneration of the claimant's lawyer by taking a percentage of *damages recovered* (as opposed to a mark-up on *chargeable costs*, as permitted by statute with CFAs) have only just been made generally lawful in civil litigation in England and Wales. They have been allowed outside the civil courts, particularly in employment tribunals, for some time. Strictly, CFAs too are a particular type of contingency fee, the contingency being that the claimant's lawyer is not paid if a case is lost, but is paid on an enhanced basis if the case is won. Both can be characterised by the over-simplified label of 'no-win, no-fee'.

Contingency fees have featured in employment tribunal funding because adverse costs orders are very rarely made. Thus an applicant who is represented has very little prospect of obtaining an award of costs against his employer to pay his own lawyer, even if he wins. If the case is lost, the applicant will rarely be ordered to pay the respondent employer's costs of defending the case. Win or lose, he will remain liable for his own lawyer's costs, unless represented by a trade union through its membership services. The ban on contingency fees in civil claims prior to April 2013, when the law changed, applied to 'contentious business' only, and oddly did not extend to tribunals, which are technically 'non-contentious business'. So a solicitor can agree with a tribunal applicant client that he will not be charged fees if the application is lost, but if he wins, the lawyer will be paid by receiving percentage of the winnings. A similar arrangement is possible in claims for compensation from the Criminal Injuries Compensation Authority – again non-contentious business – where claimants can agree to remunerate their legal representative by a percentage of the compensation recovered. Contingency fee arrangements were even permitted in claims prior to their being issued, as they too were technically 'non-contentious business' until a claim form was filed with the court, at which point they became retrospectively contentious business. Hybrid contingency fee and CFAs were utilised which changed their nature at the point of issue of proceedings.

Under LASPO 2012, what are opaquely styled 'damages-based agreements' (DBAs) are now permitted as a funding mechanism, with detailed provisions contained in the Damages-Based Agreements Regulations 2013[7]. These are understood to be subject to review, and probably amendment, since a new costs war is threatened over the detailed workings of the Regulations. Currently though, there is a cap on all personal injury claims: the sum recoverable as costs and counsel's fees plus VAT of 25% of damages and past losses awarded. In other types of case, the cap is 50% of the damages recovered by the client. In all cases, the lawyer must give credit to the client for all costs received from the opposing party. Furthermore, the indemnity principle applies to recovery of costs from the opposing party, so that the payer cannot be required to pay more than the client was contractually obliged to pay the lawyer.

There are likely to be considerable controversies over these costs. If it proves (as has been suggested by some commentators[8]) that DBAs represent the best deal for clients on the principle of 'best advice', solicitors will, it is suggested, suffer serious limitations on what they can earn.

12.6 Third party funding

The growth of investors interested in funding litigation in return for a stake in the proceeds has begun to grow, especially in relation to commercial litigation. The old offences and torts of maintenance and champerty, which formerly prohibited such funding, have now been abrogated. Such investors render themselves open to adverse costs orders, both under general principles and also as an exception to QOCS costs protection.

12.7 Wasted costs orders

Though hardly to be regarded as a mainstream means of funding litigation, wasted costs orders should be considered here for completeness, as such issues do occasionally arise at mediations. Where a lawyer involved in litigation has acted in a manner which has led to the waste of time and costs, it is open to the court, after hearing representations from the lawyer, to order that he should personally pay the costs wasted by such conduct[9].

---

7 SI 2013/609.
8 Eg Kerry Underwood *'Dead on arrival'* (2013) Sol Jo, May.
9 See the Senior Courts Act 1981, s 51(6) and CPR 48.7.

12.8   Funding problems arising in mediations

Mediations in which claimants have been funded by a conditional fee agreement (on a no-win, no-fee) basis, with an after-the-event insurance, have given rise to much argument in mediations, especially for those signed between 1999 and 2013, when the success fee and the ATE premium have been recoverable from the defendant. The problems may prove even more acute in the post-April 2013 regime, where success fees and (if purchased) premiums on ATE policies are recoverable not from a defendant but from the claimant's damages. There will be an even more direct link between a party's damages and their lawyer's remuneration in DBAs, based on a percentage of damages recovered. Even where a claimant is willing to compromise on a claim on the basis that there are greater risks to success than had been thought, a settlement will almost certainly be a technical 'win' under the terms of the claimant's funding arrangement. In 1999–2013 CFAs, this will entitle the claimant's lawyer(s) to recover a full success fee and ATE premium, even though the agreed damages have been discounted appreciably for risk. Perversely, the riskier the case (and thus the greater likely discount on damages), the higher the success fee and the ATE premium are likely to be, scaled up because of the risk of losing completely. This can give rise to at least apparent conflict between lawyer and client.

Whenever a CFA (or DBA) with ATE was signed, it may well become necessary to involve ATE insurers in decision-making when a claimant wants to compromise a claim during a mediation. If settlement is rejected and the case continues to trial, the ATE insurer has a stake in the risks associated with that, in that if their insured loses at trial, or a Part 36 offer rejected with the insurer's approval is not beaten by the claimant, the insurer faces outlay under the ATE policy. A mediator can sensibly advise claimant lawyers operating under such policies to speak to their ATE insurer before a mediation and be able to consult them by telephone during the mediation in case tricky decisions arise.

In post-2013 CFAs and in DBAs and third party funding cases, there will not be the complication of the defendant's views to accommodate, but there will still be potential for discomfort between party and lawyer over how costs are to be apportioned. This arises especially where defendants insist on making a global offer for all damages and costs, leaving the claimant and lawyer to haggle over division of the sum offered.

However, during mediations of claims funded by 1999–2013 CFAs, many claimant lawyers in practice agree to discount and sometimes even waive their success fee and ATE insurers agree to moderate their premiums, certainly when they are divided into tranches, and the insurer is not yet fully on risk for paying a successful defendant's total costs through to the end of trial.

Another of the problems has been that parties have, in theory, at least not been inhibited in pursuing their case when funded on a no-win, no-fee basis. If they can persuade their lawyer to represent them, or to continue to do so, they incur no liability for costs with their lawyer if the case is lost. This situation arose under CFAs up to 2013, and thereafter will arise under both CFAs and DBAs. Of course such parties remain liable to their opponent for costs in the event of defeat, and so will have to seek ATE insurance and remain liable for the premium on such policies, win or lose. So it may well be the ATE insurer who will moderate the ambition of insured litigants in such cases. Whether this will provide an incentive for them to require use of mediation more frequently by those they insure is another of the unknowns which the Jackson reforms have thrown up.

Chapter 13

The Jackson reforms and the future of mediation

This chapter looks at the impact of the reforms to the civil justice system in England and Wales as engineered following the Jackson Reports on civil costs[1], and their likely impact on the development of mediation, followed by a discussion about whether further reforms or reviews are still needed to enhance the use of mediation.

13.1 Rule changes to require use of mediation

As noted in **Chapter 1**, the amendments to the CPR implemented on 1 April 2013 as a result of the Jackson recommendations for reform have made no changes which might increase direct pressure on parties and their advisers to utilise mediation, whether before or after the issue of proceedings. Sir Rupert Jackson's Final Report made clear his distaste for any judicial compulsion to use mediation (in fact a view shared by many mediators) and the current Civil Procedure Rules Committee clearly share his distaste. Of course his terms of reference were essentially 'to review the rules and principles governing the costs of civil litigation and to make recommendations in order to promote access to justice at proportionate cost', so his review was never going to be a complete re-run of Lord Woolf's review.

If the development in his thinking is traced from his Preliminary Report to the Final Report, however, it is clear that Sir Rupert has moved a long way over ADR in general and mediation in particular. His Preliminary Report made mention of it in its index and had no separate chapter on ADR, although, as often with judicial commentary, he concentrated on mediation when talking about ADR. He opened the paragraphs on this topic in his Preliminary Report by saying:

'it should be said at once that mediation is an excellent method of resolving many forms of civil litigation: indeed, I have undertaken

---

1 Review of Civil Litigation Costs: Final Report (The Stationery Office, 2010); Review of Civil Litigation Costs: Preliminary Report (The Stationery Office, 2010).

some limited mediation training and gained an understanding of its benefits'.

Then he talked of its usefulness in neighbour and family disputes, many ('but no means all') judicial review applications, business disputes which might end up in the Commercial, Mercantile or Technology Courts, but went on to say that 'mediation is not a universal panacea ... although mediation is an invaluable supplement to the process of the civil courts, it is not a substitute for that process'.

Indeed, he actually described ADR as 'by definition the antithesis of the administration of justice by the courts', and quoted with a degree of approval Professor Hazel Genn's criticism of a culture which 'wishes to drive all litigants away from the courts and into mediation, regardless of their wishes and regardless of the circumstances of individual cases'. The tone of his Preliminary Report was cautious, consciously limiting mediation's usefulness, repeating the 'panacea' mantra used by many reluctant commentators (as if any process including litigation trial can be described as a cure-all). It was, perhaps, a little patronising in tone about mediation.

His views seem to have been materially affected by the consultations he received before producing his Final Report, in which ADR had a chapter to itself, and in which he accepted that mediation is highly efficacious in all areas of work, including personal injury and clinical negligence, while still under-appreciated and under-used. His preferred strategy for the development of ADR was one of educating judges and others to encourage its use, which can also be done by structuring the costs regime to provide an incentive to use it, accepting that the use of ADR can itself save costs. A subsequent practical instance of his positive views about mediation's usefulness in delivering what courts often cannot can be found in his judgment in *Faidi v Elliott Corpn*[2]. Judges and the legal profession now have the *ADR Handbook*[3] that Jackson LJ proposed as the main plank of his judicial education process. If this is read by everyone for whom it is intended, knowledge of ADR and mediation will be greatly increased.

So in what practical ways and how effectively will the Jackson reforms be likely to grow the use of ADR and mediation? One innovation which may encourage settlement generally is to add a new reward for claimants who make a Part 36 offer which the defendants fail to beat, giving them a 10% bonus on awards up to £500,000 and a further 5% on the next £500,000. Maybe Part 36 offers by claimants will become a little more common in injury claims.

---

2 [2012] EWCA Civ 287.
3 *The Jackson ADR Handbook* (OUP, 2013).

But the most fundamental structural change introduced as a result of the Jackson report is in terms of costs and funding. There are now be two different regimes in relation to costs shifting within civil litigation, and it will be interesting to see how these develop and co-exist. Each regime – injury claims (with qualified one-way costs shifting) and non-injury claims – will represent a substantial proportion of all issued litigation, and significantly different rules and costs incentives apply to each. Arguably there has never been quite such a dichotomy in civil justice before. Costs and funding remain at the heart of all litigation decision-making because the costs consequences in civil justice in England and Wales can be so dire. A party who loses on the merits, or who behaves unreasonably when winning, or does not win well enough (eg by failing to beat a Part 36 offer) will face considerable expense unless he has insured against such liabilities. The reforms firmly assert control over case and costs management, with tighter tests as to proportionality of costs invested and recoverable from another party, and, it is said, much tougher standards over compliance with case management expected by procedural judges. It is no accident that in CPR Part 1 the overriding objective to deal with cases justly now reads 'justly *and at proportionate cost*' with the added explanation that this includes '*enforcing compliance with rules, practice directions and orders*'.

13.2   The main changes reviewed

The main changes recommended in the Final Report, and implemented, apply to both injury and non-injury litigation, and are as follows:

- – a strengthening of discipline over compliance with court directions; dealing with cases 'justly' as the overriding objective in CPR Part 1 is enlarged to add 'and at proportionate cost'; and adding to CPR Part 3 power for the court to enquire about compliance, and spelling out the relevant material for a court when considering all the circumstances pertaining to an application for relief from a sanction, which include the need for litigation to be conducted efficiently and at proportionate cost and the need 'to enforce compliance';

- – costs budgeting, capping orders for future costs, and costs management by the court, with an expectation that a receiving party under a standard basis costs award will have to explain any departure from their last budget estimate[4];

---

4 Proceedings in the Admiralty and Commercial Court, and designated proceedings in the Chancery Division, the Technology and Construction Court and Mercantile Courts are exempted from costs management and budgeting, presumably on the basis that they are already closely managed.

–   a wider expectation of court intervention through management directions, particularly at what was formerly called 'allocation stage' and is now called 'directions stage';

–   to make it possible to limit or dispense with standard disclosure by agreement or order, to be done by the first case management conference;

–   requiring costs estimates for each expert's evidence;

–   amendment to Part 36 to provide that where a defendant fails to beat a *claimant's* Part 36 offer (but *not* the other way round), an additional penalty may be imposed 10% up to £500,000 and thereafter 5% on any additional amount of the 'sum awarded' (ie on damages (and costs?) in a money claim and on costs in a non-monetary claim;

–   the permissibility of 'damages-based agreements' (ie contingency fees) under which a lawyer may now agree with the client to be remunerated by a percentage of the damages recovered in the event of success, with recoverable costs capped at the level of the DBA;

–   a range of fixed costs for various types of case;

–   tighter provisions as to proportionality of costs: the principle in *Lownds v Home Office*[5] – that costs necessarily incurred are proportionate – is abrogated. Costs are now proportionate:

> 'if they bear a reasonable relationship to:
>
> (a) the sums in issue in the proceedings;
>
> (b) the value of any non-monetary relief in issue in the proceedings;
>
> (c) the complexity of the litigation;
>
> (d) any additional work generated by the conduct of the paying party; and
>
> (e) any wider factors involved in the proceedings, such as reputation or public importance'[6].

As Sir Rupert pithily warns in his Final Report:

> 'If parties wish to pursue claims and defences at disproportionate cost, they must do so, at least in part, at their own expense'.

---

5 [2002] EWCA Civ 365.

6 The new definition of proportionality is set out in CPR Part 44.3(5), as introduced by the 60th amendment to the CPR on 1 April 2013 and the Civil Procedure (Amendment) Rules 2013.

13.3   The continuing place of ADR and mediation in civil justice

Even though there is no specific mention of use of ADR or mediation in the above changes, what must be remembered is what still remains in place in the CPR regardless of the 2013 reforms,, together with the judicial guidance that still exists outside the ambit of the CPR. The basis of costs orders in CPR Part 44 remains exactly the same, with unreasonable litigation conduct, or failure to comply with protocols and court directions or orders, whether before or after issue of proceedings, still providing the basis for costs sanctions. Refusing a reasonable request to mediate before or after proceedings therefore remains a potential basis for sanctions, as it has been since the Court of Appeal decision in *Dunnett v Railtrack*.

'ADR orders' requiring, or perhaps more precisely, 'robustly recommending' parties to try to settle by mediation or some other ADR process also remain in place. Such orders were specifically approved of by the Court of Appeal in *Halsey v Milton Keynes General NHS Trust,* as was the consequence that ignoring such an 'order' could of itself justify a costs sanction against a party who unreasonably declined to act on it. Whether procedural judges will make ADR orders more frequently remains to be seen. The flavour of the Jackson reforms is to create a greater willingness in judges to make demanding directions, coupled with a greater risk of sanctions for parties who ignore court orders.

So nothing structural has been done to alter the effect of the CPR and the decisions interpreting their provisions as they relate to mediation, and all the matters discussed in this book continue to be just as relevant after 1 April 2013 as they were before that date. Much will depend upon whether the judges, fortified perhaps by their reading of the *Jackson ADR Handbook,* take a more active role to promote the use of processes such as mediation by making management orders recommending it.

As to injury claims and the effect of QOCS, under which defendants lose their right to recover costs from a losing claimant except in limited circumstances, in exchange for the abolition of the right of claimants to recover success fees under CFAs and ATE insurance premiums from defendants, there is little room for encouraging mediation in these arrangements. Defendants with no real likelihood recovering their costs even if they win cannot easily be sanctioned for refusing to mediate, because there are no costs for them to forfeit. The opportunity to sanction a defendant can only arise where he has unreasonably refused to mediate in a case where they have made a Part 36 offer which the claimant failed to beat. In such circumstances, there may be a fund of claimant's damages and interest from which they might normally expect to deduct some costs, but which might be restored to the claimant by way of costs sanction for any unreasonable refusal on the defendant's part to mediate. It is unfortunate that QOCS inevitably creates an imbalance of power in this regard, though it is probably a price that claimants will pay for the costs protection they otherwise get. It does rather militate against Jackson LJ's support for growing mediation in the injury sector. A civil justice system that takes the responsibility to consider settlement seriously might well have chosen to treat refusal to mediate or to explore settlement as a further reason for losing costs protection.

13.4 The nature of pre-action obligations to consider mediation

At least three interesting questions remain unanswered. The first is whether judges will be internally encouraged to make ADR orders as a matter of course early in litigation where appropriate, and also to enforce obligations under the Pre-action Protocols to attempt settlement before issue of proceedings more strictly when cases are issued and come before them for directions. Neither has been done, despite their clear legitimacy. With a tougher regime of enforcing obligations one might expect both of these. After all, encouraging and facilitating the use of ADR remains part of active case management under the obligations imposed on judges and parties in CPR Part 1 and the overriding objective. It is believed that revised versions of the protocols are under consideration, and now fall within the ambit of the Civil Procedure Rule Committee. No publication date has been given for these. Indeed the tenor of the newly-amended CPR gives support to what CEDR suggested in its submission to Jackson LJ, about getting judges to take a firmer line with non-compliance over protocol obligations even where both parties are guilty. He rejected these suggestions, but the new rules seem to make those steps more likely.

The second question is whether the forbidding machinery of costs management, budgeting and capping, coupled with the more stringent regime of proportionality will generate so much antipathy and expense to comply with their implications that parties will be driven to settle rather than have to run the gauntlet of those provisions. Clear and effectively binding budgets will have to be filed with the court early on in the life of a claim, making it clear to clients what the cost implications of litigation will be. To invest considerable time and cost in a case and win it, only to find large sums cut from that investment, leaving the lawyer either to forego the cuts or seek to recover them from an unwilling client will be painful indeed. Advance budgeting is extremely difficult and lawyers have a solid track record of under-estimating future costs. Maybe early attempts at settlement will prove to be a better move. Commercial lawyers certainly appear to feel that mediation has much to offer in the new regime introduced by the 2013 amendments.

The third unanswered question is whether the changes in funding – requiring success fees and ATE premiums in CFA cases to be paid by the claimant out of damages, or remunerating the claimant's lawyer by deducting a percentage off the damages under a DBA – will operate as hidden financial incentives to settle earlier. If a lawyer will earn as much under a DBA whether a case is settled early or late, it is hard to escape the conclusion that this might provide an incentive for early settlement, so long as all professional obligations over best advice to the client are fully met.

Thankfully, there should be less dispute over costs at mediations as between the opposing parties, with success fees and ATE premiums no longer recoverable. All experienced mediators have found it possible to get the parties to reach broad agreement about damages, only to find that the costs issues ruin the chances of settlement. The only problem may be that mediators will have to intervene in delicate discussions as between party and lawyer as to the apportionment of damages and costs, with the other party sitting idly by, no longer with a financial interest in such a discussion. Such discussions have always been possible with BTE insurance funding, and as this may overtake ATE insurance funding, maybe different but equally difficult discussions will take place which border on conflict of interest between client and lawyer.

13.5 The overall outcome

Although the new reforms contain no really positive incentives for using mediation, as usual it will be the financial imperatives and pressures that will shape what people do. The price of the greater economy sought by these reforms is greater control, and delivering such control is inevitably more expensive. Judicial control is itself both frightening and irritating to lawyers and their clients. If it costs a lot to be compliant, lawyers may well advise clients to pursue other ways towards dispute resolution.

Supporters of mediation can only hope that the rule-makers will continue to revise their opinions as to the proper place of settlement and settlement providers within this civil justice system. Simply to dismiss mediation as not being a panacea is simplistic. Can it be said that the civil justice is a panacea when it is so complex, expensive and still relatively slow, and when it turns its eyes to the past to determine rights, effectively disabled from attending to the future of the litigants before the court? Horror stories such as the cases of *Burchell v Bullard*[7] and most recently *Newman v Framewood Manor*[8] have demonstrated the largely self-imposed impotence of the courts over not pressing litigants to find a sensible outcome

---

7 [2005] EWCA Civ 358.
8 [2012] EWCA Civ 1727.

if possible, rather than letting them engage in litigation to the ultimate. These decisions make the point powerfully that there is a proper place for firm judicial encouragement of legitimate settlement providers to prevent those practical catastrophes that probably occur daily through a system that declares winners and losers, rather than checking underlying interests, both past and future, in a positive and occasionally creative way.

There are two problems for mediation in the current situation. The first is that mediated settlements usually emerge from a broad mutual agreement over the value of a case in terms of a risk discounted (up or down) evaluation of what will be the outcome at trial. If one party (usually the claimant) cannot afford to go to trial for funding reasons, there is little incentive on a defendant to make a reasonable offer. They can in effect starve their opponent into submission. Second, there must be a temptation for mediators actually to set up shop as a truly alternative dispute resolution service. If civil justice is seen as having priced itself out of contention in the dispute resolution market-place, is there a place for another independent service? This would fly in the face of mediation as a process which operates in the shadow of the law. If settlement does not emerge, there has to be access to justice to decide a dispute in a civil court.

13.6 Some new ways of encouraging settlement

Two changes were introduced in the first half of 2013 which promote settlement to some extent, and, in the first example but not the second, potentially giving some impetus to pre-action mediation. The first is the wording of the new directions questionnaire deployed at what used to be called allocation stage, just after a defence has been filed. As was seen earlier[9], a considerable portion of the first page is devoted to enquiring whether pre-action obligations as to trying to settle a case have been observed by the parties. If parties see failure to observe such requirements as a potential source of sanction, they will ensure that they have either observed them or have a very good reason for not having done so. This will only happen if courts take any opportunity to enforce these obligations in ways that are publicised by local reputation of each procedural judge, or published decision and heavily emphatic practice direction, based perhaps on some automatic or semi-automatic discretionary sanction. While judges can comfort themselves for not doing this by referring to the necessity for keeping mediation voluntary, this will not lead to growth of mediation use. As has been repeatedly said, voluntariness relates to continued participation in mediation and by no means necessarily to initial participation, where pres-

---

9 At **4.5**.

sure to participate even up to mandatory mediation is clearly permissible under current human rights legislation.

The second widening of an existing initiative relates to the vast majority of personal injury litigation in volume terms, namely claims for sums up to £25,000. Doubtless there have been mediations of such cases *pro bono,* and such cases have also been successfully dealt with by telephone mediations. It would be difficult to make a financially viable case for standard mediations based on personal attendance of the parties with a mediator in such cases. The RTA Portal scheme by which undefended pre-issue claims of up to £10,000 in value are conducted on- line with fixed costs according to a set timetable was extended as from 31 July 2013 to such claims of up to £25,000, and also to employer's and public liability claims up to that value. The procedure is set out in two Pre-action Protocols[10], as the portal process applies only to unissued claims. One of the major reforms implemented on Jackson LJ's recommendation was the abolition of referral fees paid by law firms to BTE insurers to purchase the right to act on claims referred to them by insurers and claims management companies. These were often as much as £750–£1,000 per case by the time of the Final Report. In view of the fact that law firms were no longer allowed to buy cases in this way, the drafters of the fixed costs scheme under the extended portal insisted on reducing the fixed fees payable, to reflect the saved expenditure. This was fiercely but unsuccessfully challenged by practitioners. The result is that the scheme is one which claimants are keen to escape, in order to be freer to recover higher levels of costs permitted where proceedings are issued and defended. So if defendants fail to comply with their obligations to respond, they face the sanction that the claimant may issue proceedings and seek fuller costs.

A huge proportion of road traffic cases, as well as employer's and public liability cases, will be covered by these rules. As in other areas, they indirectly encourage pre-issue settlement. An insurer will have to balance the attraction of defending a case against the attraction of keeping claimant costs tied to the fixed costs rates. Apart from raising a seat belt defence or contributory fault (each of which the claimant must accept for the case to stay within the portal scheme) any defence will take a case into the mainstream for court management and potential costs liability.

Unsurprisingly, there is no reference to mediation in the portal rules. Of course in assessing what is at stake in any case, and thus the cost-benefit of mediating, the potential costs need to be aggregated with the

---

10 The Pre-action Protocol for Low Value Personal Injury Claims for Road Traffic Accidents and the Pre-action Protocol for Low Value Personal Injury (Employer's Liability and Public Liability) Claims, as respectively amended and introduced by the 65th amendment to the CPR on 31 July 2013.

sum claimed. But with costs rarely more than £750 in cases where liability is not at issue and quantum is the only outstanding question capped at £25,000, there is little room to afford a conventional mediation. As soon as any such case reverts to the normal procedure either on the fast track or multi-track on a defended basis, the cost-benefit of mediation becomes easier to justify.

13.7 Mandatory mediation?

A book which seeks to discuss the main issues relating to mediation in England and Wales at the current stage of civil justice development cannot avoid devoting at least one section to debating specifically whether mediation should be made mandatory, or at least less voluntary than it is at present. The topic has lurked under the surface of several chapters already, so this need not be an extended discussion. It is predicated on the following points:

–   mandating participation in mediation is not contrary to the principle of voluntariness at the heart of mediation's effectiveness, which relates solely to each party's being free participate confidentially in mediation discussions and to leave a mediation without risk of sanction for unreasonableness or refusal to settle;

–   mandatory mediation does not infringe the rights of a party to a timely public trial by a judge as conferred by Article 6 of the European Convention on Human Rights;

–   a number of other common and civil law jurisdictions have effectively adopted mandatory mediation without any apparent disruption to litigant rights or damage to those legal systems.

So, legally speaking, it is a matter of choice for England and Wales as to whether it is desirable to implement such provisions. Lord Dyson has expressed the view that it is verging on morally wrong to compel parties to mediate. This seems rather extreme, as it assumes that parties and lawyers cannot be fools to themselves when it comes to litigating. The best evidence of judicial frustration with such folly comes from the repeated expressions of regret that parties did not mediate in order to avoid the worst outcomes that can emerge from a court decision. While few mediators enthuse about win/win as a regular outcome to mediations, parties need sometimes to be helped to decide whether win/lose or indeed lose/lose is better than a negotiated outcome within which both parties usually contribute concessions and emerge with a sense of equality of discomfort made bearable by certainty and having positively chosen that outcome. This all depends on whether a mature civil justice system should encour-

270

age settlement and extra-judicial settlement processes more positively than it does. This book argues that it should.

Here are some further pragmatic points that might be considered when assessing the issues which have emerged from the discussion in this book:

- as Sir Rupert Jackson asserted in his Final Report, mediation is under-appreciated and under-used: it is thus presumably worth encouraging positively;

- it is extremely hard to predict in advance whether parties are so far apart that mediation cannot help them bridge the gap between them, and there are really very few indicators that a case is incapable of settlement. Putting it another way, there are very few cases in which there is an absence of litigation risk upon which a price could be put;

- **no** process is a panacea (in the sense of a cure-all) when it comes to resolving disputes. A court decision provides finality and decides a winner and loser, or possibly creates losers all round, on the basis of precedent and evidence-based findings, and often at huge and frequently irrecoverable cost, whereas mediated outcomes can be far more flexible than litigated outcomes: they are not precedent-bound, process-bound or evidence-bound, and can look to the future as well as the past, offering, as they do, the possibility of preserving or restoring useful commercial or neighbourly relationships and incorporating solutions which are not within the gift of a judge;

- it is difficult for judges in the English civil justice system to sustain the position that an unsettled mediation might lead to waste of money in the light of the enormous costs usually invested and not infrequently wasted within the court system, despite the best reforming efforts as to proportionality. In any event the expense in the system comes from what lawyers seek to earn either from their clients or from another party; the courts only deal with what one party can recover from another. This is what makes the South African decision in *Brownlow v Brownlow* so interesting and outside the English experience, where a judge capped what lawyers could recover from their clients because they had mutually failed to advise mediation.

Such assertions are not merely romantic or fanciful. But they do represent a challenge to the judiciary fixed with responsibility for offering a civilised and practical approach to resolving disputes in this society. The Article 6 rights of access to a public trial are a back-stop protection. In many cases a public trial is not what parties either need or want (even if their advisers, who make a living from such activities, quietly do not agree with their clients on that point, and even if judges fear the dilution of their role, or the starvation of the common law), especially in (but not because of) these times of financial restraint in resources.

The consequence of such views is not necessarily for courts to require mediation to have taken place before trial and to sanction those responsible where this does not happen. But judges and civil procedure rules must positively encourage the use of mediation before issue of proceedings, questioning failure to use it or non-compliance with pre-action obligations where this emerges immediately after issue of proceedings and before an action proceeds too far. Where mediation was justifiably inappropriate before issue of proceedings, then positive steps should be taken in drafting directions to order mediation to take place within a defined window, unless a case is clearly unsuitable for mediation.

This begs again the perennial question of which cases are unsuitable for mediation and requires a revisit to the *Halsey* factors. Clearly if a case or a defence is unanswerable, CPR Part 24 offers a swift route to summary judgment. Is success or failure in such an application not the best test as to whether a party has a reasonable belief that its case is water-tight? If summary judgment is not sought, does this not amount to recognition that a case may involve risks of a less than perfect outcome? It must be remembered that mediated outcomes are not only predicated on substantial compromise; one party very often achieves a high proportion of their ambitions, simply because the process has persuaded one party that the other party's case is much stronger than anticipated. It is important to remember that the *Halsey* factor, which excuses from sanction a party who reasonably believed it had a watertight case, only gets discussed when a party who has lost is trying to avoid a costs liability to a winner, who is able to shine the white light of hindsight on its historic appraisal of chances of success. It is easy (as happened in *Swain Mason v Mills & Reeve*[11]) for such a party to say that it rightly felt confident and that the parties were too far apart for mediation to have any prospect of success (thus relying on the other main factor in *Halsey* as well). The successful party there did not succeed in having the claim summarily dismissed under CPR Part 24, and was deprived of an appreciable proportion of its costs even if it won on the facts, so its defence was not risk-free and not therefore un-negotiable. Meanwhile the defendant solicitors had refused to sit down with their former clients who had, on any view, suffered a major loss as a result of what turned out to be non-negligent advice to discuss the implications.

---

11 [2012] EWCA Civ 498.

If the above precept about the unpredictability of outcomes through mediation is right, the other *Halsey* factor relied on in *Swain* – that mediation had no reasonable prospect of success – is hard to establish. Judicial belief expressed in that judgment, that a gap of £750,000 playing a 'drop hands' proposal was a gap too far, is simply not borne out by mediator experience. This is so even if a winning party's assertion that they (and perhaps the other party) were not prepared to move within the confidentiality of a mediation process is credible. The cost of mediating that claim, even if unsuccessful, would have been dwarfed by the cost of the litigation, which undermines any suggestion of reliance on the cost-benefit *Halsey* factor.

So how might the courts define a better test as to sanctioning those who fail to mediate? The following propositions are suggested:

- perhaps the time has come to adopt the suggestion of Lord Phillips, when he was Lord Chief Justice[12], to shift the burden of proof on to a party who refused to mediate to justify that refusal, whether they were the winner or loser at trial. Of course the proposition by Dyson LJ that the burden properly belongs on the party who seeks to alter the normal burden of costs under CPR Part 44 is technically right based on its current wording. But should the wording be altered where a party has declined to mediate and therefore elected to take up court time, in continuing to litigate, denying the opponent the chance to explore settlement? It might take a rule change to achieve, but is this not a right approach? Similarly, it would make sense to make unreasonable refusal to mediate another ground for removing costs protection in injury claims within the new QOCS regime;

- the assumption should not be made that sanctions arise only if one party asks for them: if **both** parties fail to mediate when they should have done, either because of protocol, rule or direction, then both should receive less than they otherwise expected;

- where a judge recommends mediation, and is ignored by one or both of the parties, the norm should be a sanction: this was forgotten, for instance, in *Swain*;

- the factors in *Halsey* really should only be treated as broad and non-exhaustive indicators as to when sanctions might arise: the real question is 'Did this party/these parties unreasonably refuse the other party's invitation to mediate/unreasonably fail to mediate as required by protocol, rule or judicial direction or

---

12 *Alternative Dispute Resolution: an English Viewpoint:* March 2008 delivered to the Supreme Court in India.

recommendation?' It is too easy to be seduced by mechanical arguments that a case was too water-tight, or mediation had no reasonable prospects of success. The key indicator for penalising a refusing winner or refusing to penalise a loser who proposed mediation is unreasonable intransigence in all the circumstances of the case, a proposition borne out by the broad thrust of cases decided both before and after *Halsey*;

– the possibility that mediation can produce good non-judicial and non-monetary outcomes should be viewed as a positive reason for recommending it and as a powerful reason for criticising refusal to mediate;

– the fact that parties are always free to choose to resume litigation without adverse consequence from what they said and did within the confidentiality of the mediation process should always be weighed in assessing if it was unreasonable to decline to mediate;

– sanctions must be consistently and firmly applied and publicised in several cases, so as to send the right message to parties and the judiciary about the importance of getting these matters right.

So reverting to the question of mandatory mediation or not in England and Wales, this book suggests that it is still not necessary as such. However, the existing powers of the courts to order and recommend need to be utilised much more firmly and consistently, operating in the belief that to take such steps is fully within the power and responsibility of judges, in encouraging the use of proper and proven dispute resolution processes, even if they are outside the mainstream civil justice system. It should be a surprise for a trial or appeal judge to find that parties did not mediate before trial. Discovering this should not automatically produce a sanction, but it should automatically give rise to an enquiry during the costs hearing which requires a convincing explanation. In fact, judges should be aiming to encourage mediation by using ADR Orders and recommendations early so as to minimise the need for discussing the possibility of sanction at the end of a trial which in truth is almost certain not going to take place, because so many cases settle. It is the litigants in each case before the courts who may need help and encouragement to use mediation on the instant case to get it settled as quickly, inexpensively and on the best possible self-determined basis, yet free to litigate if acceptable terms do not emerge that make the deployment of ADR orders and directions a much better approach than the threat of a retrospective penalty which will rarely be imposed because of the rarity of trial.

13.8 Reforms to the legal structure underpinning mediation

The supreme irony of the situation in England and Wales is that the legal structure which underpins mediation, a flexible and adaptable process with no precedental or formal component either as to procedure, evidence or outcome, is entirely determined by precedental principles derived and developed through the sometimes erratic vagaries of common law judicial decisions. As has been seen already in Chapter 2, mediation here is a creature of private common law, with virtually no statutory basis. It depends on the interpretation of contract law (sometimes on an admittedly shaky basis when it comes to the enforceability of agreements to mediate) and a number of equitable and quasi-equitable concepts such as breach of confidence and privilege. Few court rules govern its use and none regulate its conduct. The related paradox is that it finds it difficult to publicise its success because of the very confidentiality which makes it work well.

Is this a satisfactory state of affairs? Is there a need for more certainty and safety for the mediation process to reassure both those who use it (parties and lawyers) and those who recommend its use (lawyers and judges)? The areas of importance where there still seems to be unnecessary and unsettling certainty are the following:

- Are there limits on the confidentiality of the process which need clarification to improve the way parties currently feel able to participate? Is there evidence of mediation being hampered by such concerns? Is the current law clear about this?
- In what circumstances and to what extent are mediators immune from suit?
- Are mediators compellable as witnesses of what transpired at a mediation if one or both parties want to call them in later litigation?
- What limits are there on allegations of misrepresentation, undue influence, duress, illegality or other factors potentially vitiating a mediated settlement?
- Is there a true distinction to be drawn between what is said generally and exchanged at a mediation between parties and what one party tells a mediator privately in confidence which impacts on what may and may not be introduced in evidence at a later trial?
- Is there or should there be a fully-defined mediation privilege?
- Should the requirement for a written signed settlement agreement be capable of being outflanked by concepts such as oral

collateral contracts or estoppel, thereby making it possible to receive oral evidence of what happened at a mediation?

– What is the true relationship between 'without prejudice' evidential privilege and contractual confidentiality? Who has a say as to whether either or both can be waived?

As discussions have revealed in this book, these are all legal questions to which there is no authoritative answer, and indeed there are in some cases several inconsistent answers. Fortunately, in the pragmatic atmosphere in which mediation is conducted in England and Wales, there has rarely been the need for such questions to be asked. Mediations are conducted daily in the shadow of such apparently significant ambiguities without there being much, if any, evidence of reluctance to participate among parties, lawyers or mediators. So maybe the motto should be 'leave well alone'.

This would be undeniable, were it not for the fact that cases like *Brown v Rice*[13] and *Farm Assist v DEFRA (No 2)*[14] come along occasionally, almost accidentally impinging on the relatively calm world of mediation in a way that threatens suddenly to unsettle its framework. The law of unintended consequences presents a real danger here, especially where the judiciary does not have personal experience of the process and cannot readily challenge assertions made to push a case.

In the US, the questions raised above were tackled through the process which led to the drafting of the Uniform Mediation Act[15]. In Ireland the discussion was conducted by the Irish Law Commission whose excellent report[16] should represent a model for a progressive common law jurisdiction seeking to take seriously the design of a sound legal framework for mediation. Maybe referral to the Law Commission here would be a good move, even if it would represent a very ponderous process. Leaving this to the Ministry of Justice looks unattractive when considering their approach to implementing the EU Directive, and the thought of Parliament grappling its way through such issues is not pretty. Perhaps an initiative from within the mediation community, sponsored say by the Civil Justice Council, could lead to the production of a consultation and a final report which would command respect so long as those who participate are drawn from a broad constituency of interested parties, such as lawyers, judges, litigation parties, academics and mediators. There is a serious risk that legislation will be required, though, so a strategy for coping with Parliament on such measures would be necessary. Parliamentary time is highly unlikely

---

13 [2007] EWHC 625 (Ch).
14 [2009] EWHC 1102 (TCC).
15 Discussed fully at **9.8**.
16 *Alternative Dispute Resolution: Mediation and Conciliation*: LRC 98-2010.

to be expended anyway on constructing an acceptable Mediation Act, and the chances of Parliament's getting this absolutely right, even with the help of the mediation lobby, are low.

However, it will be no surprise if things gently muddle along as usual, until some crisis is provoked by an assertive party to litigation whose self-interest accidentally hits an awkward spot of principle which drives mediation into an unexpected corner and requires urgent first aid. Such is the centuries-old way of the common law. The possibility of a case with the right facts percolating through to the Court of Appeal are also low. The plea by Sir Alan Ward in *Wright v Michael Wright Supplies Ltd*[17] for another look at *Halsey* on the ECHR Article 6 point is unlikely of itself to generate an appeal sufficiently germane to make this possible. The immediate future depends really on a change of emphasis by procedural judges in building up the place of mediation and other ADR processes as a properly acknowledged and respected part of the civil justice system, for the benefit of the parties to whom it belongs and for whose benefit it exists. One thing that will undoubtedly increase will be the proportion of trial and appeal judges with direct experience in private practice of representing parties at mediations and even of acting as mediators. This will undoubtedly be a driver for change in judicial attitudes to mediation. The relationship between mediation and law and civil procedure is a dynamic one – subject to, and in some respects requiring, change, as this book suggests. Whatever may happen in relation to such change, mediators, parties and their advisers will continue to seek consensually crafted outcomes which are dependent on that other highly significant relationship between mediation and the law, requiring mediating parties to assess what judges will do if settlement is not reached. As has been seen, mediation can assist parties to agree outcomes beyond what judges can award, and participation in the mediation process itself by way of direct encounter and often difficult conversations between those in dispute is also of considerable and underrated value. But all such conversations and possible outcomes are inevitably coloured by the need to weigh carefully what a court is likely to award if agreement is not reached. What are the chances of success? What are the risks that a case will be lost wholly or in part? To what extent is it wise to discount the value of a case (up or down) to allow for such risks? Can terms be found, whether within the power of a judge to order or not, which satisfy both parties and allow them to end the dispute on a mutually acceptable basis, giving both parties more than they would have got if they lost, at the price of accepting less than they would have got if they won? There is nothing unprincipled or inherently unjust about such discussions, especially as any party is free to revert to seeking a judicial decision. Even if a mediated outcome is some distance from what a judge would have ordered on a

---

17 [2013] EWCA Civ 234 at para 3.

win/lose basis – or if it contains components which a judge could never have ordered – what emerges will almost inevitably have been negotiated in the shadow of the law and with due respect for the law. That symbiosis between mediation and the law is fundamental. Mediation cannot do without a strong civil justice system. This book goes so far as to suggest that a sophisticated modern civil justice system cannot do without mediation.

Appendix 1

CEDR Model Mediation Agreement, 13th Edition[1]

THIS AGREEMENT   dated   IS MADE BETWEEN

Party A

    of

Party B

    of

(together referred to as "the Parties")

The Mediator

    of

(a term which includes any agreed Assistant Mediator)

and

CEDR Solve of IDRC, 70 Fleet Street, London EC4Y 1EU

in relation to a mediation to be held

on

at

                                        ("the Mediation")

IT IS AGREED by those signing this Agreement THAT:

---

1 Reproduced with the kind permission of CEDR. For further information please visit www. cedr.com.

The Mediation

1   The Parties agree to attempt in good faith to settle their dispute at the Mediation and to conduct the Mediation in accordance with this Agreement and consistent with the CEDR Solve Model Mediation Procedure and the CEDR Code of Conduct for Mediators current at the date of this Agreement.

Authority and status

2   The person signing this Agreement on behalf of each Party warrants having authority to bind that Party and all other persons present on that Party's behalf at the Mediation to observe the terms of this Agreement, and also having authority to bind that Party to the terms of any settlement.

3 Neither the Mediator nor CEDR Solve shall be liable to the Parties for any act or omission in relation to the Mediation unless the act or omission is proved to have been fraudulent or involved wilful misconduct.

Confidentiality and without prejudice status

4   Every person involved in the Mediation:

4.1   will keep confidential all information arising out of or in connection with the Mediation, including the fact and terms of any settlement, but not including the fact that the Mediation is to take place or has taken place or where disclosure is required by law to implement or to enforce terms of settlement or to notify their insurers, insurance brokers and/or accountants; and

4.2   acknowledges that all such information passing between the Parties, the Mediator and/or CEDR Solve, however communicated, is agreed to be without prejudice to any Party's legal position and may not be produced as evidence or disclosed to any judge, arbitrator or other decision-maker in any legal or other formal process, except where otherwise disclosable in law.

5   Where a Party privately discloses to the Mediator any information in confidence before, during or after the Mediation, the Mediator will not disclose that information to any other Party or person without the consent of the Party disclosing it, unless required by law to make disclosure.

6   The Parties will not call the Mediator or any employee or consultant of CEDR Solve as a witness, nor require them to produce in evidence any records or notes relating to the Mediation, in any litigation, arbitration or other formal process arising from or in connection with their dispute and the Mediation; nor will the Mediator nor any CEDR Solve employee or consultant act or agree to act as a witness, expert, arbitrator or consultant in any such process. If any Party does make such an application, that Party will fully indemnify the Mediator or the employee or consultant of CEDR Solve in respect of any costs any of them incur in resisting and/or responding to such an application, including reimbursement at the Mediator's standard hourly rate for the Mediator's time spent in resisting and/or responding to such application.

Settlement formalities

7 No terms of settlement reached at the Mediation will be legally binding until set out in writing and signed by or on behalf of each of the Parties.

Fees and costs of the Mediation

8 The Parties will be responsible for the fees and expenses of CEDR Solve and the Mediator ("the Mediation Fees") in accordance with CEDR Solve's Terms and Conditions of Business current at the date of this Agreement (including any provision for additional hours if the mediation process extends beyond the allocated hours).

9 Unless otherwise agreed by the Parties and CEDR Solve in writing, each Party agrees to share the Mediation Fees equally and also to bear its own legal and other costs and expenses of preparing for and attending the Mediation ("each Party's Legal Costs") prior to the Mediation. However, each Party further agrees that any court or tribunal may treat both the Mediation Fees and each Party's Legal Costs as costs in the case in relation to any litigation or arbitration where that court or tribunal has power to assess or make orders as to costs, whether or not the Mediation results in settlement of their dispute.

Legal status and effect of the Mediation

10 This Agreement is governed by the law of [England and Wales] and the courts of [England and Wales] shall have exclusive jurisdiction to decide any matters arising out of or in connection with this Agreement and the Mediation.

11 The referral of the dispute to the Mediation does not affect any rights that exist under Article 6 of the European Convention of Human Rights, and if their dispute does not settle through the Mediation, the Parties' right to a fair trial remains unaffected.

Changes to this Agreement

12 All agreed changes to this Agreement and/or the Model Procedure are set out as follows:

Signed

Party A

Party B

Mediator

CEDR Solve

Appendix 2

CEDR Mediation Model Procedure, 12th Edition[1]

1 What is mediation?

Mediation is a flexible process conducted confidentially in which a neutral person actively assists the parties in working towards a negotiated agreement of a dispute or difference, with the parties in ultimate control of the decision to settle and the terms of resolution.

The principal features of mediation are that it:

- involves a neutral third party to facilitate negotiations;
- is quick to set up and is inexpensive, without prejudice and confidential;
- involves party representatives with sufficient authority to settle;
- is flexible, with no set procedure, enabling the process to be designed and managed by the Mediator to suit the parties, in consultation with them;
- enables the parties to devise solutions which are not possible in an adjudicative process such as litigation or arbitration, and which may benefit all the parties, particularly if there is the possibility of a continuing relationship between them; can be used in both domestic and cross-border disputes, two-party and multi-party disputes, and whether or not litigation or arbitration has been commenced.

Many commercial and government contracts now require parties to use mediation in accordance with CEDR's Model Procedure. While mediation is essentially flexible, the Model Procedure set out in this document, taken with the CEDR Solve Mediation Agreement, will give sufficient certainty to enable the process to be set up and used.

---

1 Reproduced with the kind permission of CEDR. For further information please visit www.cedr.com.

Any contemplated or existing litigation or arbitration in relation to the dispute may be started or continued despite the mediation, unless the parties agree or a Court orders otherwise. If settlement terms cannot be agreed at a mediation, the parties are free to revert to litigation or arbitration.

2   Referral to mediation

Referral of a dispute to a mediator or to CEDR Solve for mediation may be as a result of:

- voluntary referral by all parties;
- referral by one party who asks CEDR Solve to secure the involvement of other parties into a mediation;
- responding to a Pre-action Protocol, the Civil Procedure Rules 1998, a Court Order or
- a recommendation by a judge before trial or appeal;
- the provisions of a clause in a commercial or government contract requiring the use of mediation as a step in the parties' agreed dispute resolution process.

3   Choosing the mediator

Parties may choose their own mediator directly, or may ask CEDR Solve to nominate one or more persons to act as the mediator for a dispute in accordance with the wishes of the parties or any relevant Court Order (a copy of which must be supplied to CEDR Solve by the parties as soon as possible after CEDR Solve has been instructed). If the parties require it, more than one mediator can be appointed to work as co-mediators, or the parties can agree on an independent neutral expert to advise the mediator on technical matters.

CEDR Solve will only nominate or appoint a mediator who, in their view, possesses the relevant skills and experience to mediate the dispute for the parties effectively, and who will comply with the CEDR Solve Code of Conduct for Third Party Neutrals ('the Code'). Any nominated mediator will be required to confirm immediately to CEDR Solve if there is any matter which might prevent the nominated mediator from complying with the Code in relation to the mediation of the dispute, such as a conflict of interest. CEDR Solve will then notify the parties of any such matter immediately it is disclosed to them.

If required by either the parties or the Court, or under the published terms of any CEDR Solve dispute resolution scheme, CEDR Solve will appoint a mediator to be used in relation to a dispute, subject always to that mediator not being prevented from complying with the Code in relation to the mediation of that dispute.

The parties may be asked by CEDR Solve to approve the appointment by them of an assistant mediator (who will be a CEDR Accredited Mediator) or an observer to attend a mediation at no cost to the parties, provided that they too comply with the Code in respect of the mediation of that dispute. The identity of any assistant mediator or observer proposed to attend the mediation will be made known in advance of the mediation to the parties, who are free to object to any such nomination or decline any such appointment. The mediator's signature of the mediation agreement binds any assistant mediator or observer to its terms.

4 Preparation for the mediation

Depending on the CEDR Solve service selected by the parties, either CEDR Solve or the mediator when agreed or appointed, will make the necessary arrangements for the mediation as required or agreed by the parties or under the terms of any scheme, including:

- drafting the agreement, submitting it for approval by the parties and preparing the final form for signature, incorporating any agreed amendments;
- facilitating agreement as to the date, venue and start time for the mediation;
- organising exchange of case summaries and document bundles between the parties and the mediator;
- setting up any pre-mediation meetings agreed by the parties and the mediator.

The parties will:

- agree the appointment of the mediator or a process to select or appoint the mediator;
- agree with CEDR Solve the date, venue and start time for the mediation;
- pay CEDR Solve's fees and expenses as agreed under CEDR Solve's Terms and Conditions of business;
- each prepare and exchange a case summary in respect of their approach to the dispute at the mediation and endeavour to agree with all other parties what documents are needed for the mediation;

- send to the mediator (direct or through CEDR Solve) a copy of their case summary and two copies of the document bundles no less than two weeks before the date set for the mediation, making clear whether case summaries have or have not yet been exchanged, whether or not and when CEDR Solve is to effect exchange, and whether all or any part of any case summary or documentation is intended to be confidential for the mediator only;

- notify the mediator direct or through CEDR Solve of the names and roles of all those attending the mediation on their behalf, so that CEDR Solve can inform all Parties and the mediator in advance of the mediation;

- ensure that a lead negotiator with full authority to settle the dispute (or not) attends the mediation to sign the mediation agreement;

- alternatively notify the mediator, CEDR Solve and (unless very good reason exists to the contrary) the other parties of any limitation on authority to settle, for instance lack of legal capacity, or the need for ministerial committee or board ratification, in which case the lead negotiator will need to have power to recommend acceptance of any settlement. Late disclosure of limited authority to settle can call into question that party's good faith involvement in the mediation process, and have detrimental effects on the prospects of success of any mediation.

The mediator will:

- ensure at all times that the Code is complied with in respect of the mediation of the dispute, reporting any conflict of interest or other relevant matter, if any, to CEDR Solve and (subject to any question of confidentiality or privilege) the parties immediately it emerges;

- attend any pre-mediation meetings on terms and agenda agreed by the parties; read each case summary and document bundle submitted in advance of the mediation by the parties;

- make contact with a representative of each of the parties before the mediation to assist in preparation for the mediation.

5   Documentation

Documentation intended to be treated as confidential by the mediator or CEDR Solve (such as a counsel's opinion, an undisclosed expert report, a draft proof of evidence or a confidential briefing for the mediator) must be clearly marked as such, and will not be circulated further without express authority.

One of the advantages of mediation is that its success is not dependent on exhaustive disclosure of documents. Bundles can usually be relatively limited in size, containing only key documents, and case summaries can be quite brief, and can to advantage be prepared jointly by the parties. The parties can ask CEDR Solve to effect simultaneous exchange of case summaries if required.

While documents brought into existence for the purpose of the mediation, such as case summaries, are clearly privileged from later production in those or other proceedings, the fact that a document which is otherwise disclosable in proceedings is produced for the first time during the mediation does not normally confer privileged status on it. The parties must take legal advice on such matters if they arise.

6 The mediation agreement

The agreement to mediate provides the essential legal basis for the mediation. Its signatories (the parties to the dispute, the mediator and CEDR Solve) all agree by signing it that the mediation is to be conducted consistent with both this CEDR Solve Model Procedure and the Code.

A draft mediation agreement will be sent for approval to the parties as part of the preparation process for the mediation, and any proposed amendments can then be discussed and inserted if agreed. The mediation agreement will normally be signed at the beginning of the mediation day on behalf of each of the parties and the mediator, having been pre-signed on behalf of CEDR Solve. In any pre-mediation contact with the parties, CEDR Solve staff and any CEDR mediator once appointed will observe its terms as to confidentiality, even though the agreement has not yet been signed.

7 The mediation

It is normal for each of the parties to have a private room for confidential consultations on their own and with the mediator during the mediation. There should also be a further room large enough for all parties to meet with the mediator jointly.

The mediator will chair and take responsibility for determining the procedure at the mediation, in consultation with the parties.

The likely procedure will comprise:

- preliminary meetings with each of the parties when they arrive at the venue;
- a joint meeting of all attending the mediation, at which each of the parties will normally be invited to make an oral presentation;
- a mix of further private meetings and joint meetings (which may involve all or some of each party's team), as proposed by the mediator and agreed by the parties.

Professional advisers, particularly lawyers, can and usually do attend the mediation. Such advisers play an important role in the exchange of information and opinion on fact, evidence and law; in supporting their clients (particularly individuals) in the negotiations; in advising clients on the implications of settlement; and in drawing up the settlement agreement and any consent order.

No verbatim recording or transcript should be made of the mediation by the parties or the mediator in any form, but participants can make their own private notes which will be undisclosable to anyone else, including in any subsequent litigation or arbitration.

Mediations can last beyond a normal working day and it is important that the key people present for each of the parties remain present or at worst available by telephone for so long as the mediation continues. Any time constraints should be reported to CEDR Solve or the mediator as soon as known, as any unexpected departure can be detrimental to the progress of the mediation and perceived as disrespectful by other parties.

8   Confidentiality in relation to the mediation

The CEDR Solve standard agreement provides that what happens at the mediation is to be treated as confidential by the parties, the mediator and CEDR Solve, including the fact and terms of settlement. However, the fact that the mediation is to take place or has taken place is not normally made confidential, as either or both of the parties may wish to claim credit for agreeing to engage in the process. If it is desired to make the fact that the mediation is taking place confidential also, the agreement can be amended.

Apart from where the parties agree in writing to consent to disclosure of what would normally be confidential, there may be rare circumstances in which the confidentiality of the mediation process cannot be preserved, such as where:

- the mediator or any party or their representative is required by law to make disclosure;

- the mediator reasonably considers that there is a serious risk of significant harm to the life or safety of any person if the information in question is not disclosed; or the mediator reasonably considers that there is a serious risk of being personally subject to criminal proceedings unless the information in question is disclosed.

Such questions might arise in relation to duties under the Proceeds of Crime Act 2002 or related legislation or under any other legislation. Legal representatives (who may themselves be under a comparable duty of disclosure in their own capacity) must take full responsibility for advising their clients of the implications of disclosure in relation to any such matters at a mediation.

9   Conclusion of the mediation

The mediation may end in a number of ways:

- by settlement of the dispute in whole or part, when all agreed matters must be written down and signed by the parties to be binding;

- by one or more parties leaving the mediation before settlement is achieved;

- by an agreed adjournment for such time and on such terms as the parties and the mediator agree;

- by withdrawal of the mediator in accordance with the mandatory and optional circumstances set out in the Code.

The mediator will facilitate the drawing up of any settlement agreement, though the drafting is normally done by the lawyers representing each of the parties. Where proceedings have not been started in respect of the dispute, the settlement agreement will (if so intended and drafted) be a contract enforceable by legal action. Where proceedings have been issued in relation to the dispute, it is normal for a Consent Order to be agreed either at or after the mediation and later lodged to end the proceedings on the terms agreed.

Where the mediation does not end in complete settlement, the Mediator may make contact with the parties thereafter to see whether further progress might be possible. Many disputes which do not settle at the mediation settle later, usually as a result of what occurred or was learned at the mediation.

CEDR Solve endeavours to make contact with all the parties after every mediation to obtain their feedback on both the process itself and, in particular, the mediator. Any feedback obtained regarding the mediator will be given in full to the mediator as part of the mediator's continuing learning and development.

10 Complaints

Any formal complaint about CEDR Solve or any mediator nominated by CEDR Solve should follow the procedure set out on the CEDR website at www.cedr.com.

Appendix 3

CEDR Model Settlement Agreement[1]

Date

Parties

('Party A')

[Address][2]
('Party B')

[Address][3]
[('Party C') etc][4]

(jointly 'the Parties')

[Background][5]

- The Parties have been in a dispute in relation to [......*set out brief details*] ('the Dispute') [which is being litigated/arbitrated [court/arbitration reference] ('the Action')][6]

- The Dispute has been the subject of a CEDR Solve mediation ('the Mediation') conducted under an agreement ('the Mediation Agreement') between the Parties and [ ] ('the Mediator') and CEDR Solve

- The Parties have agreed to settle the Dispute on the terms set out below ('the Settlement Agreement');

[see footnote 4 and set out any key facts or representations]

---

1 Reproduced with the kind permission of CEDR. For further information please visit www.cedr.com.
2 Not strictly necessary.
3 Not strictly necessary.
4 Note that the mediator should not be a party or even a witness to the settlement agreement, even though properly a party to the mediation agreement.
5 While it is not essential for the factual background to be recited, any facts and representations the truth of which form the crucial foundation for the terms of settlement should be set out here to eliminate or at least minimise any later allegations of misrepresentation.
6 Omit this wording and paragraph 4 if there are no court proceedings.

Terms of the Settlement Agreement

It is agreed as follows:

1 [A will deliver......... to B at .... by not later than 4 o'clock on 25 December ...]⁷

2 [B will pay £......... to A by not later than 4 o'clock on 25 December ... by direct bank transfer to ... bank sort code ... account number ......]

3 *[Any other terms]* ....

4a The Action will be stayed and the parties will consent to an order in the terms of the attached Order [*see attached form of Tomlin order*⁸].

OR

4b [A/B] will discontinue the Action on [B/A]'s undertaking not to claim [B/A]'s costs of the Action against [A/B].

OR

4c Judgment will be entered for [A/B] on their [counter]claim with an order that [B/A] pay [A/B]'s costs on the standard/indemnity basis subject to detailed assessment if not agreed.

OR

4d The Action will be dismissed with no order as to costs.

5 This Agreement is in full and final settlement of any causes of action whatsoever which the Parties [and any subsidiaries .... of the Parties] have against each other [it is important that such a clause is only included after a careful check has been made as to whether there are any other possible outstanding causes of action between the Parties which can safely be compromised (or ought not to be compromised) in this way].

6 This agreement supersedes all previous agreements between the parties [in respect of all matters relevant to the Dispute] except for those terms of the Mediation Agreement of continuing effect including the confi-

---

7 Be as specific as possible, for example, how, by when, etc.
8 This is the commonest method of implementing a settlement where proceedings already exist: where there are no proceedings, the settlement agreement stands as an actionable contract where all parties intend that it should be legally enforceable: if a cross-border dispute, and all parties agree, application can be made to the Court for a Mediation Settlement Enforcement Order.

dentiality of the mediation process, the Parties' undertaking not to call the mediator or CEDR Solve to give evidence and the liability of the Mediator and CEDR Solve.[9]

7   If any dispute arises out of this Agreement, the Parties will attempt to settle it by mediation[10] before resorting to any other means of dispute resolution. To initiate any such mediation a party must give notice in writing to the Mediator and to CEDR Solve. Insofar as possible the terms of the Mediation Agreement will apply to any such further mediation. If no legally binding settlement of such a dispute is reached within [28] days from the date of the notice to the Mediator and to CEDR Solve, either party may [institute court proceedings/refer the dispute to arbitration under the rules of ...].

8   The Parties will keep confidential and not use for any collateral or ulterior purpose the terms of this Agreement except insofar as is necessary to implement and enforce any of its terms or as otherwise agreed in writing by the Parties.

9   This Agreement shall be governed by, construed and take effect in accordance with [English] law. The courts of [England] shall have exclusive jurisdiction to decide any claim, dispute or matter of difference which may arise out of, or in connection with this agreement.[11]

Signed

for and on behalf of[12]

for and on behalf of[13]

Note: This Model Agreement (and accompanying consent order) is for guidance only. Any agreement based on it will need to be adapted to the particular circumstances and legal requirements of the settlement to which it relates. Wherever possible any such agreement should be drafted/approved by each party's lawyer. Although the mediator may occasionally be involved in helping the parties to draft acceptable terms, the mediator is not responsible for the drafting of the agreement and should never be a party to it [See also the provisions of the mediation agreement which, if it is based on the CEDR Model Mediation Agreement, will deal with mediator liability, confidentiality

---

9 Only necessary if there have been previous agreements.
10 Alternatively, negotiation at Chief Executive level, followed by mediation if negotiations do not result in settlement within a specified time.
11 Usually not necessary where parties are located in same country and subject matter of agreement relates to one country.
12 Not necessary where the party signing is an individual.
13 Not necessary where the party signing is an individual.

CEDR Model Settlement Agreement

etc. and may not need to be repeated in this agreement, unless the scope of confidentiality is either extended or defined by agreement between the Parties to allow for non-parties with a proper interest in the outcome to be informed, or an agreed Press release to be issued.]

Appendix 4
CEDR Model Tomlin Order[1]

Attachment to Model Settlement Agreement

[This is a Tomlin Order, used in English courts to bring an effective end to proceedings without entering judgment, but enabling agreed obligations to be enforced by court order within the old action if not performed as agreed and avoiding any need to start a fresh action.]

[Action heading]

UPON the Parties to this Action consenting to the terms set out below

BY CONSENT IT IS ORDERED that

1 All further proceedings in this case be stayed upon the terms set out in the Settlement Agreement between the Parties dated ....., an original of which is held by each of the Parties' solicitors [OR CEDR Solve/the Mediator] *OR*

set out in the Schedule to this Order

except for the purpose of enforcing the terms of that Agreement.

2 Either Party/Any of the Parties may apply to the court to enforce the terms of the said Agreement [*or* to claim for breach of it] without the need to commence new proceedings.

3 There be no order as to the costs of this action

OR

[A/B] do pay [B/A]'s costs of this action on the standard/indemnity basis subject to detailed assessment if not agreed][2].

---

1 Reproduced with the kind permission of CEDR. For further information please visit www.cedr.com.

2 A consent order has to contain whatever is agreed as to the costs of the action in the main body of the Order, to provide the basis for detailed assessment of costs if required in the event that the amount cannot be agreed.

CEDR Model Tomlin Order

WE CONSENT to an order in these terms

[Black & White], Claimant's Solicitors

[Red & Green], Defendant's Solicitors

CEDR Solve Code of Conduct for Third Party Neutrals, April 2008[1]

1 Introduction

This Code of Conduct ('the Code') applies to any person who acts as a Mediator or other neutral third party ('the Neutral') in any dispute resolution procedure ('the Process') conducted under the auspices of the Centre for Effective Dispute Resolution ('CEDR Solve') in relation to an attempt to resolve a dispute or difference ('the Dispute') between all the parties ('the Parties') to the Dispute under the terms of a written agreement signed by the Parties the Neutral and CEDR Solve ('the Process Agreement') to seek resolution of the Dispute.

2 Competence and availability

The Neutral assures the Parties that he or she:

    2.1 possesses the necessary competence and knowledge about the Process to deal with the Dispute, based on proper training and updating of education and practice in the necessary skills; and

    2.2 has sufficient time to prepare properly for and conduct the Process expeditiously and efficiently.

3 Fees and expenses

The Neutral undertakes:

    3.1 to make clear either directly to the Parties or through CEDR Solve the basis for charging fees and expenses as between CEDR Solve and the Parties for the conduct of the Process before the Process starts; and

---

1 Reproduced with the kind permission of CEDR. For further information please visit www.cedr.com.

3.2 not to prolong the Process unnecessarily where there is, in the Neutral's opinion, no reasonable likelihood of progress being made towards settlement of the Dispute through the Process.

4 Independence and neutrality

The Neutral:

4.1 will at all times act, and endeavour to be seen to act fairly, independently and with complete impartiality towards the Parties in the Process, without any bias in favour of, or discrimination against, any of the Parties;

4.2 will ensure that the Parties and their representatives all have adequate opportunities to be involved in the Process;

4.3 will disclose to the Parties any matter of which the Neutral is or at any time becomes aware which could be regarded as being or creating a conflict of interest (whether apparent, potential or real) in relation to the Dispute or any of the Parties involved in the Process, and, having done so, will not act or continue to act as Neutral in relation to the Dispute unless the Parties specifically acknowledge such disclosure and agree to the Neutral's continuing to act in the Process: such matters include but are not limited to:

- any personal or business relationship with any of the Parties;

- any financial or other interest in the outcome of the Mediation;

- having acted (either personally or through the Neutral's own firm or business) in any capacity other than as a Neutral in another Process for any of the Parties;

- being in prior possession of any confidential information about any of the Parties or about the subject-matter of the Dispute (but excluding any confidential information given to the Neutral by one of the Parties while acting as Neutral in relation to the Dispute)

- any such matters involving a close member of the Neutral's family.

4.4 will not (nor will any member of the Neutral's own firm or business or close family) act for any of the Parties individually in relation to the Dispute either while acting as Neutral or at any time thereafter, without the written consent of all the Parties.

5 Conduct of the Process

The Neutral will observe all the terms of the Process Agreement (especially as regards confidentiality) and will conduct the Process consistent with any relevant CEDR Model Procedure.

6 Professional Indemnity Insurance

The Neutral will take out professional indemnity insurance in an adequate amount with a responsible insurer against such risks as may arise in the performance of the Neutral's duties in relation to the Dispute before acting as a Neutral.

7 Withdrawing from any Process

7.1 The Neutral will withdraw from the Process and cease to act as such in relation to the Dispute if the Neutral:

- is requested to do so by one of the Parties, except where the Parties have agreed to a procedure involving a binding decision by the Neutral to conclude the Mediation;
- would be in breach of the Code if continuing to act as the Neutral; or
- is required by one or more of the Parties to act or refrain from acting in a way which would be in material breach of the Code or in breach of the law.

7.2 The Neutral may withdraw from the Process at the Neutral's own discretion and after such consultation with the Parties as the Neutral deems necessary and appropriate (and always subject to the Neutral's obligations as to confidentiality) if:

- any of the Parties is acting in material breach of the Process Agreement;
- any of the Parties is acting in an unconscionable or criminal manner;
- the Neutral decides that continuing the Process is unlikely to result in a settlement;
- any of the Parties alleges that the Neutral is in material breach of the Code.

8 Complaints

The Neutral will respond to, and co-operate with, any complaints procedure initiated by a party through CEDR Solve in relation to the Process in which the Neutral acted, including attending (without charging a fee or claiming any expenses for attending) any meeting convened by CEDR Solve as part of that complaints procedure.

Appendix 6
Recommended further reading

Andrews, *English Civil Procedure: Fundamentals of the New Civil Justice System* (Oxford, 2003)

Andrews, *The Modern Civil Process: Judicial and Alternative Forms of Dispute Resolution in England* (Mohr Siebeck, 2008)

Andrews on Civil Processes Volumes 1 and 2 (Intersentia, 2013)

Mackie, Marsh, Miles and Allen, *The ADR Practice Guide: Commercial Dispute Resolution* (3rd edn, Tottel, 2007)

Blake, Browne and Sime, *The Jackson ADR Handbook* (Oxford, 2013)

Boulle and Nesic, *Mediation: Principles, Process, Practice* (LexisNexis, 2001)

Brown and Marriott, *ADR Principles and Practice* (3rd edn, Sweet & Maxwell, 2012)

Foskett, *The Law and Practice of Compromise* (7th edn, Sweet & Maxwell, 2010)

Genn, *Judging Civil Justice (The Hamlyn Lectures)* (Cambridge, 2009)

Macfarlane, *The New Lawyer: How Settlement is Transforming the Practice of Law* (University of British Columbia Press, 2009)

Mackie and Carroll, *International Mediation: The Art of Business Diplomacy* (2nd edn, Bloomsbury Professional, 2006)

Mulcahy, *Mediating Medical Negligence Claims: an Option for the Future?* (The Stationery Office, 2000)

Newmark and Monaghan (eds), *Mediators on Mediation: Leading Mediator Perspectives on the Practice of Commercial Mediation* (Bloomsbury Professional, 2005)

Recommended further reading

Roberts and Palmer, *Dispute Processes - ADR and the Primary Forms of Decision Making* (CUP, 2005)

Spencer and Brogan, *Mediation Law and Practice* (CUP, 2007)

Walker and Smith, *Advising and Representing Clients at Mediation* (Wildy Simmonds and Hill, 2013)

Appendix 7

List of useful websites

For the full suite of CEDR model documents, including international ADR contract clauses in several languages, project mediation protocol and agreement, and other ADR processes, see www.cedr.com/about_us/modeldocs. This should be checked for the latest edition of all CEDR's model documents.

The full judgments of almost all the significant cases cited in this book can be accessed at www.cedr.com/about_us/library/edr_law.

There is a very wide range of articles giving information and opinions about the topics covered in this book at www.cedr.com.

Other websites which contain useful information about mediation, model agreements and documents are maintained by the following organisations, with their website address current as at August 2013 shown:

National oversight bodies

Ministry of Justice: www.justice.gov.uk/courts/mediation

Civil Mediation Council: www.civilmediation.org

Provider websites

ADR Group: www.adrgroup.co.uk

Chartered Institute of Arbitrators: www.ciarb.org

Independent Mediators: www.independentmediators.co.uk

In Place of Strife: www.mediate.co.uk

Academy of Experts: www.academyofexperts.org

LawWorks: www.lawworks.org.uk

Index

307